EASTERN TRADITIONS

World Religions

CANADIAN PERSPECTIVES

World Religions

CANADIAN PERSPECTIVES

Edited by

DORIS R. JAKOBSH
University of Waterloo

Kevin Bond
University of Regina

Mavis L. Fenn
St. Paul's University College

Scott T. Kline
St. Jerome's University

Alison R. Marshall
Brandon University and University of Winnipeg

Anne M. Pearson
McMaster University

Mikal A. Radford
Sheridan College and Wilfrid Laurier University

NELSON EDUCATION

NELSON EDUCATION

World Religions: Canadian Perspectives—Eastern Traditions
Edited by Doris R. Jakobsh

Vice President, Editorial Higher Education:
Anne Williams

Acquisitions Editor:
Maya Castle

Senior Marketing Manager:
Amanda Henry

Developmental Editor:
Jacquelyn Busby

Editorial Intern:
Jeremy Lucyk

Permissions and Photo Researcher:
Lynn McLeod

Senior Content Production Manager:
Natalia Denesiuk Harris

Production Service:
MPS Limited,
a Macmillan Company

Copy Editor:
Gillian Watts

Proofreader:
Jennifer A. McIntyre

Indexer:
David Luljak

Senior Production Coordinator:
Ferial Suleman

Design Director:
Ken Phipps

Managing Designer:
Franca Amore

Interior Design:
Sharon Lucas

Cover Design:
Sharon Lucas

Cover Image:
Courtney Milne

Parchment Image:
© Neosiam/Dreamstime.com

Compositor:
MPS Limited, a Macmillan Company

Printer:
Edwards Brothers

Library and Archives Canada Cataloguing in Publication Data

World religions : Canadian perspectives : eastern traditions / edited by Doris R. Jakobsh ; [contributing authors] Kevin Bond ... [et al.].

At head of title: Eastern traditions.
Includes bibliographical references and index.
ISBN 978-0-17-650117-4

1. Religions. 2. Canada—Religion. I. Jakobsh, Doris R. (Doris Ruth), 1963– II. Bond, Kevin A.

BL80.3.W6473 2012   200
C2011-907681-0

ISBN-13: 978-0-17-650117-4
ISBN-10: 0-17-650117-7

The front cover image is a photography by Courtney Milne. Courtney Milne is a photographer, an artist, author, educator, keynote speaker, and philanthropist. His career has taken him on a global journey that has spanned all seven continents. He has published 12 books of photography, including *The Sacred Earth,* with a foreword by His Holiness, The Dalai Lama. Milne's multi-media shows have attracted audiences worldwide, and his photographs have been shown in more than 200 exhibitions. His limited edition collections are held by more than 25 galleries, museums, and universities. Courtney Milne lives on the Canadian prairie near Saskatoon, Saskatchewan.

CONTENTS

EDITOR'S INTRODUCTION

DORIS JAKOBSH

Welcome to the study of world religions. Contrary to scholarly and media claims in the late twentieth century that "religion is dead" or "religion is no longer relevant," religion is indeed alive and well in the twenty-first century. In an increasingly globalized, multicultural Canada, where every possible form of religious affiliation can be found, it is very likely that you personally will come into direct contact with many peers whose belief systems are different from your own. Your own religious affiliation may not be very important to you; you may not even call yourself religious. However, it is quite possible that despite not "feeling" very religious or perhaps not knowing much about your own religious background, you still have some sort of religious affiliation. I'm reminded of a time when I was in a market in Chiang Mai, Thailand. I stopped to chat with the owner of a little stall and noticed that she had a small shrine set up to Buddha. I asked her about her religion, and she instantly remarked that she wasn't religious! When I asked her about the shrine, the sticks of incense, and the candle that she had lit, she said that was just "tradition." I found her statements remarkable. If a storeowner in Canada were to tend to a religious shrine in the shop while setting up for the day, customers would identify that storeowner as being highly religious.

Often people take part in religious traditions because of parental expectations, or because they might wish to introduce their own children to the traditions of their grandparents. You might not think twice about celebrating Diwali if you are of Hindu, Sikh, or Jain heritage—it is simply what is "done" in your family. Or you might find yourself wanting to have a traditional Christian wedding, and so start discussing being married in a local church or in one to which your family once had connections. If you take some time to look at your development as a child or young adult, it is very likely that religious values have played a role in shaping your life in some way. It is difficult to get away from religion, even if you have grown up in an entirely secular home.

Whether or not you as an individual consider yourself to be religious, the study of religion is important, given that so much of history and culture is steeped in religious traditions. Religious beliefs have had a fundamental role in shaping society, both within families and more broadly at the institutional and political levels. In an increasingly globalized world, most of us are becoming aware of the role played by religion, whether it is in working toward peace or in the stirring up of conflict. A solid understanding of religion is beneficial in negotiating the complexity of worldviews that surround us all, both locally and globally.

Students from the University of Waterloo's 'The Living Traditions of India' visited the city of Hampi in Karnataka, South India. Hampi was the medieval capital of the Vijayanagara empire that was founded in the fourteenth century. Remains of the capital city include an amazing array of religious sites, palaces and public architecture that are spread over a beautiful, hilly landscape along the Tungabhadra River. Today, the ruins are a UNESCO World Heritage Site.

Source: Ketussa Sotheeswaran

In the fall of 2010 I had the privilege of taking a group of twelve students from the University of Waterloo, where I teach in the Department of Religious Studies, for a three-month course in India titled "The Living Traditions of India." The purpose of this full term of study was to allow students an opportunity to experience, in a truly in-depth manner, the religious traditions of India. This included staying at a yoga ashram in the Himalayas, where, upon being awakened at four thirty a.m., we took part in meditation and yoga classes for hours at a time. We were also invited to listen to Sufi musicians, called *qawwali* singers, perform at the Nizammudin Shrine in Old Delhi. Their beautiful, masterful voices soared and fell as they sang about the separation of the lover and the Beloved, Allah.

We had an opportunity to sit at the feet of enlightened women and men across India, individuals who had devoted themselves to the spiritual quest and lives of intense discipline. One of these remarkable individuals was a British-born Tibetan Buddhist nun, Jetsumna Tenzin Palmo, who had spent twelve years of her life in a cave high in the Himalayas, learning the discipline of intense meditation practices. We met Dr. Sadhvi Sadhna, a Jain nun who is the current acharya (leader) of a Jain ashram in northern India. She received us with incredible graciousness and then proceeded to teach us about important principles of Jainism that are applicable to the entire human race, and of the importance of interfaith dialogue in the quest for world peace. Father George, the head of the "Old Seminary," a Syrian Orthodox centre in Kerala, taught us about the long history of Christianity in India, beginning with the travels of Saint Thomas in the early years of the developing Christian movement—making all of us rethink our notions of Christianity as an exclusively Western tradition. We were invited to Dr. Vandana Shiva's biodiversity farm near Dehradun and there were privileged to learn about her vision, her understanding of justice, the ecological movement that she has led for the past twenty years, and how that intersects with her understanding of religion and a deep reverence for Mother Earth. All of these encounters allowed the students to gain a solid experiential knowledge base in the living religions and cultures of India, and, perhaps even more important, to open themselves up to the possibilities and responsibilities of being citizens in an increasingly globalized world.

Our group, which came from diverse religious, ethnic, and cultural backgrounds, was able to discover the variety and depth of religious practices and worldviews other than our own. At times we came face to face with deeply embedded, largely subconscious cultural preconceptions that only our own traditions were normative. Through our interactions with religious leaders and devotees of the varied traditions we were studying, as well as looking at the philosophical, cultural, educational, and political systems that undergird Indian society, all of us were able to come to an understanding that there are alternative worldviews, based on different fundamental premises. It then became our mission to discover how the many religions that we had discovered in India came to be transplanted in Canada, and how those traditions had changed or were still similar to the forms we had encountered in India.

AN INVITATION TO STUDENTS

This textbook is an invitation to study the many and varied religions of humankind, and some of the alternative worldviews that stem from regions far from Canada yet have taken root within Canadian soil. Having taught numerous introductory religion courses, I am excited by the potential for such courses to be engaging and relevant—particularly for Canadian students, and particularly at this time in history. Designed to address both the historical and current impacts and influences of religion, this volume covers areas traditionally considered foundational to the study of religion, but it also adds materials to address contemporary concerns. As the editor of this particular textbook, I had a number of goals and expectations for each chapter as well as for the volume as a whole.

1. It is important that you get a thorough understanding of each particular religion presented in the text, including its history, its central beliefs, and its practices. All of the contributors to this volume are recognized scholars in their fields, and all of them have written extensively on their topics. Perhaps even more important, they have taught introductory courses on their particular areas of expertise. Their rich experience with the subject matter, as well as with teaching, has enabled them to communicate complex concepts in a manner that, without losing depth, is accessible and comprehensible.

2. Each chapter, by and large, includes stories and insights drawn from the writers' experience. Many of the contributors have spent significant amounts of time not only learning about a specific religion from texts or manuscripts but also engaging with it while doing field research and collecting data. Some have immersed themselves within religious communities, both in Canada and internationally. You will find accounts of some of these experiences and insights in the chapters you are about to read, and it is my hope that this more personal approach will contribute to your own interest in the subject matter.

3. The study of religion has traditionally focused on examining and learning about sacred texts. In fact, historically, most scholars of religion were trained almost exclusively in textual studies. While this is changing, often when we teach about religion, we tend to focus on texts. What I have found, however, in speaking and interacting with students, is that many of you seem more interested in the "doing," or performative, aspects of religion than in discussion of sacred texts. As I began to think about how to organize and focus this particular volume, I observed how the history, beliefs, celebrations, and rituals of various religious communities are presented in most introductory textbooks. I found that very often texts do not give sufficient attention to *practical* and *lived* aspects of religious expression. This has often led to students being unable to relate what they are reading to their personal experiences in a particular religion or with people of other faiths.

This textbook has not downplayed the importance of sources within religions, especially the sacred writings and other texts of each specific tradition; contributors were asked to carefully choose material for you to read in each chapter. However, close attention is also paid to "lived" religion. Some authors have addressed this by providing guides to what to expect when visiting a particular worship centre or shrine or participating in various celebrations or rituals. Others have described their own experiences—the sights, smells, and sounds—when they visited a particular religious site. Also, some scholars have explored how religion has implications far beyond specific rituals or notions of "the sacred," including wider social and cultural norms such as family and kinship roles, caste, class,

and race. These, which at first glance appear not to have any connection to religion per se, upon further exploration can often be seen to be rooted in particular religious and ethical worldviews. This approach will allow you to come to a deeper and richer understanding of the many and varied strands of what constitutes religion.

4. A significant and unique feature of each chapter has been a concerted effort to bring a Canadian perspective to each religious tradition covered in this textbook. This includes a substantial history of the religion in the Canadian context, changes that may have taken place within religions as a result of their transplantation to Canada, and also those beliefs, rituals, ethical worldviews, and practices that connect adherents of a particular tradition globally. The volume is primarily directed toward a Canadian student population, and as such it seeks to speak to the religious realities and experiences of you or your peers as you study at a university here in Canada. It is my hope that you will see your own experiences reflected in some way in the discussions to follow. I also trust that some of the issues that are raised will lead to discussion and debate, both within and outside the classroom setting.

This substantial Canadian focus is also significant in terms of specific content. For instance, the history and development of Sikhism in Canada is significantly different from the American experience. In the United States, many of the earliest Sikh settlers married Mexican women and quickly formed family ties that bound them to America. In contrast, the first Sikhs in Canada did not have similar options; therefore, by and large, the early Canadian Sikhs on the West Coast who were largely male and were focused on either returning to their native Punjab in India to join their families or eventually sponsoring them to immigrate to Canada. The significance of this point would be missed in a textbook written for a wider North American audience.

5. The study of women in religion is also an important dimension of this volume. Many of us who teach introductory world religion classes are often dismayed at how little attention is given in textbooks to women's religious realities. This volume has made great strides in moving beyond the general apathy towards and underrepresentation of

women in the study of world religions. While it does not claim an overarching feminist approach, contributors were asked to consider women's roles in the religious traditions of their chapter. This meant going beyond the occasional mention of a remarkable woman in a religion's history. Attempts have been made to address women's roles, rituals, and status, both historically and within the contemporary world. This allows for a richer, more complex and encompassing exploration of "world religions."

6. Scholar Eileen Barker has warned that academics who do not engage in the phenomenon of cyber-religion do so at their own peril (Barker 2005, 81). This warning has been taken to heart in this textbook. Each contributor was asked to move beyond a simple listing of important URLs to address, if only at a rudimentary level, the significance of religion online as it pertains to each religion. Virtually every religion has a presence on the Internet, but scholars have found that the Internet has had a greater impact on some religions than others. For example, the adherents of new religious movements (NRMs) find that the Internet provides an unprecedented presence among the historically established religions. Modern Paganism, for instance, which does not have an established institutional hierarchy and is relatively small numerically, has a significant presence online. This opens up issues of authority: who speaks for modern Pagans, or for any other religious tradition online? This volume will thus be an invaluable resource both for you as students and also for your instructors, to begin examining the ramifications of the Internet for the study of religion generally. The hope is that the issues raised by scholars will be useful to those who may turn to the Web as an initial point of information-gathering about religion.

7. It is also beneficial to learn *how* to study religion. Getting a grasp of the methodologies of the discipline is vital. Sometimes when I am asked what I do for a living, I say that I teach religion. Some people wonder what one could possibly teach, since religion is obviously "about God," and God is something that cannot be proved or disproved. Many comment that religion is a personal, mystical experience, something that is not quantifiable, something that should stay in the realm of faith, not in academia. Some of this perception can be traced to the great scholars of religion, such as Mircea Eliade (1907–86), who wrote that religion is about non-rational experience—something he defined as "the sacred." How can one study the sacred? Rudolf Otto (1869–1937), who is known best for his influential volume *The Idea of the Holy* (1917), believed that "the holy" "is beyond our apprehension and comprehension . . . before which we recoil in a wonder that strikes us chill and numb" (1958: 28).

However, while there are elusive elements in religious experience, there are also many aspects within religions that can be studied empirically. The study of religion in this volume moves beyond a theological and historical approach into the realm of other academic disciplines. Scholars here will look to wider social changes, perhaps economic or political, that may have had an effect on the development of a religion over time. For example, when examining religion in India or in Canada, the impact of colonialism must be taken into consideration.

There are systematic approaches that may be taken in studying a religious tradition, including varied theories of religion and religious knowledge, specific terminologies that are used, methodological considerations, and analytical approaches. These methodologies originate from a wide variety of disciplines, both in the humanities—including the study of history, literature, women's studies, and philosophy—and within the social sciences, for example, in sociology, anthropology, or psychology. You will come to know how the study of religion developed over time, particularly in the first chapter of this volume, which is entirely dedicated to the study of religion.

8. Each author in this volume was asked to carefully choose images that would contribute to your understanding of the tradition being examined. Take the time to look at the images and read their captions. These too will add to your comprehension of the course material.

This is the general format for each chapter:

- Central beliefs
- Sources of the tradition
- History and development

- Spiritual/religious practices
- Authority (or authorities)
- Religious identity
- Religious diversity
- The Canadian context
- Religion and the Internet
- Key terms
- Critical thinking questions
- Recommended reading and viewing
- Useful websites

Adopting these guidelines meant creating a consistency that allows for easy comparisons and a comprehensive understanding of each religion. However, in several chapters the format has been adjusted slightly to allow for a more accurate presentation of the religion in question. Rather than organizing their chapter artificially according to an editorial structure, authors were given the freedom to modify the format when doing so would more genuinely represent the religion.

You will also encounter four types of boxes throughout the textbook that draw attention to texts, rituals, people, places, and other items of particular significance.

- **Perspectives:** In the Perspectives boxes, concepts, symbols, and theories are highlighted to show how their meanings can be understood in different ways and how the significance of objects and principles can depend on the perspective of the observer.
- **Practices:** Each tradition has unique customs or practices that are performed at certain times. Some are still actively carried out while others are no longer practised; some are performed by a select few, others by the masses. The Practices boxes focus on the behaviour associated with each religious tradition.
- **People and Places:** These boxes feature important people and places in each tradition's history: prominent scholars and theorists, temples and churches, innovators, heroes, deities, and much more.
- **Words:** Words, both written and spoken, hold a significant place in the history and culture of the traditions. Hymns, prayers, poems, and stories are featured, as well as excerpts from both sacred and academic texts.

A NOTE TO INSTRUCTORS

You will find Chapter 1, on the study of religion, an excellent resource for students who may be taking a religion course for the first time. The chapter allows students to get a broader understanding of how religion is studied within the different disciplines of academia. The approaches outlined in this chapter, however, were not included in the guidelines for the contributors. Instead, each author was given the freedom to retain his or her own voice and to approach the religion from the perspective of his or her own discipline and research, whether explicitly stated or not. This textbook exemplifies a diverse approach in teaching world religions.

CONCLUSION

As you begin your journey into the study of religions, it is my hope that you will discover the complexities and nuances of the many and varied world religions explored in this textbook. I invite you to move to a greater understanding of the beliefs and practices of your friends and colleagues with whom you share a workplace or a classroom yet whose worldview and belief system may be quite different from your own. Finally, Hindu temples, Jewish synagogues, Christian churches, Muslim mosques, and Sikh gurdwaras, to name just a few, will welcome you warmly should you ask about visiting and even taking part in a religious service. As well, there are rich and varied Native traditions in Canada that are open to inquiry and dialogue. This approach allows for a potentially rich experiential dimension and a deepening of understanding, beyond what you may learn in the classroom. You may even be able to convince your professor to organize a class trip!

Doris R. Jakobsh, Editor
Waterloo, Ontario, Canada

REFERENCES

Barker, Eileen. 2005. "Crossing the Boundary: New Challenges to Religious Authority and Control as a Consequence of Access to the Internet." In *Religion and Cyberspace,* ed. Morten T. Højsgaard and Margit Warburg, 67–85. London: Routledge.

Otto, Rudolf. 1958. *The Idea of the Holy.* Oxford: Oxford University Press.

A NOTE FROM THE PUBLISHER

INSTRUCTOR ANCILLARIES

The **Nelson Education Teaching Advantage (NETA)** program delivers research-based instructor resources that promote student engagement and higher-order thinking to enable the success of Canadian students and educators.

In consultation with the editorial advisory board, made up of dedicated instructors, Nelson Education has completely rethought the structure, approaches, and formats of our key textbook ancillaries. The result is the Nelson Education Teaching Advantage and its key components: *NETA Engagement, NETA Assessment,* and *NETA Presentation.* Each component includes one or more ancillaries prepared according to our best practices, and a document explaining the theory behind the practices.

NETA Engagement presents materials that help instructors deliver engaging content and activities to their classes. Instead of instructor's manuals that regurgitate chapter outlines and key terms from the text, NETA Enriched Instructor's Manuals (EIMs) provide genuine assistance to teachers. The EIMs answer questions such as "What should students learn?"; "Why should students care?"; and "What are some common student misconceptions and stumbling blocks?" EIMs not only identify the topics that cause students the most difficulty but also describe techniques and resources to help students master these concepts. Dr. Roger Fisher's *Instructor's Guide to Classroom Engagement (IGCE)* accompanies every Enriched Instructor's Manual.

Under *NETA Assessment,* Nelson's authors create multiple-choice questions that reflect research-based best practices for constructing effective questions and testing not just recall but also higher-order thinking. Our guidelines were developed by David DiBattista, a 3M National Teaching Fellow whose recent research as a professor of psychology at Brock University has focused on multiple-choice testing. All Test Bank authors receive training at workshops conducted by Prof. DiBattista, as do the copyeditors assigned to each Test Bank. A copy of *Multiple Choice Tests: Getting Beyond Remembering,* Prof. DiBattista's guide to writing effective tests, is included with every Nelson Test Bank/ Computerized Test Bank package.

NETA Presentation has been developed to help instructors make the best use of PowerPoint® in their classrooms. With a clean and uncluttered design developed by Maureen Stone of StoneSoup Consulting, NETA Presentation features slides with improved readability, more multimedia and graphic materials, activities to use in class, and tips for instructors on the Notes page. A copy of *NETA Guidelines for Classroom Presentations* by Maureen Stone is included with each set of PowerPoint slides.

IRCD

Key instructor ancillaries are provided on the *Instructor's Resource CD* (ISBN 978-0-17-664865-7), giving instructors the ultimate tool for customizing lectures and presentations. (Downloadable Web versions are also available at www.WorldReligions.nelson .com.) The IRCD includes:

- **NETA Engagement:** The Enriched Instructor's Manual was written by Scott Wall of the University of Waterloo and is organized according to the textbook chapters and addresses eight key educational concerns, such as typical stumbling blocks student face and how to address them.

- **NETA Assessment:** The Test Bank was written by A. W. Barber of the University of Calgary. It includes multiple-choice questions written according to NETA guidelines for effective construction and development of higher-order questions. Also included are short-answer and essay questions. Test Bank files are provided in Word format for easy editing and in PDF for convenient printing, whatever your system.

   The Computerized Test Bank by ExamView® includes all the questions from the Test Bank. The easy-to-use ExamView software is compatible with Microsoft Windows and Mac OSX. Create tests by selecting questions from the question bank, modifying these questions as desired, and adding new questions you write yourself. You can administer quizzes online and export tests to WebCT, Blackboard, and other formats.

- **NETA Presentation:** Microsoft® PowerPoint® lecture slides for every chapter have been created featuring key figures and photographs from *World Religions: Canadian Perspectives.* NETA principles of clear design and engaging content have been incorporated throughout.
- **Image Library:** This resource consists of digital copies of figures, short tables, and photographs used in the book. Instructors may use these jpegs to create their own PowerPoint presentations.

STUDENT ANCILLARIES

World Religions: Canadian Perspectives also offers an interactive student companion site. This site includes flashcards, crossword puzzles, quizzes, weblinks, and other useful online resources. Go to **www.WorldReligions .nelson.com** to access these engaging materials.

ACKNOWLEDGEMENTS

When I was approached to produce a new world religions textbook that was to have a significant impact on the way Canadian courses in religion are taught, and as the extent of this endeavour took hold, I became increasingly aware that it could not be a one-person job. This two-volume textbook would never have come to fruition without the support, advice, critique, and cajoling efforts of numerous individuals throughout its long process. I am grateful to Bram Sepers, acquisitions editor at Nelson at the time of this text's inception, with whom I had many "visioning" conversations about the necessity and possibility of a new world- and Canadian-focused textbook on religions. Since then I have had the distinct pleasure of working with Heather Parker, Anne-Marie Taylor, Jacquelyn Busby, Maya Castle, and Natalia Denesiuk Harris, among others at Nelson Education, as well as copyeditor Gillian Watts and project manager Jitendra Kumar. Their insistence that this work maintain a high degree of integrity and academic excellence was heartening. I will be forever grateful for their encouragement, humour, patience and overall kindness.

For their thoughtful commentary, I would like to thank the following reviewers:

Martin T. Adam, University of Victoria
A. W. Barber, University of Calgary
Herbert W. Basser, Queen's University
Amila Buturovic, York University
Robert Campbell, University of Toronto
Philippa Carter, McMaster University
Minoo Derayeh, York University
Ellen Goldberg, Queen's University

Aaron W. Hughes, University of Calgary
James Linville, University of Lethbridge
Fadel H. Zabian, Fanshawe College

To each contributor, my thanks for signing on to the mandate and vision of this textbook. You have my sincere admiration for the academically solid, creative, and, perhaps most important, student-focused chapters written. Thank you for every attempt made to accommodate the writing, editing, and production timeline, never an easy task for those of us ensconced in the intensive research, teaching, and service milieu of academia. To the many scholars and teachers I have had along the way, whose love for the study of religion continues to inspire—Harold Coward, Mary Malone, Darrol Bryant, Diana Eck, among others—my deepest gratitude. I am also indebted to my chair and friend, David Seljak, for making time—always a rare commodity—to offer insight, critique, and editing prowess. To Maureen Fraser, thank you for your generous and kind support. To the many students at the University of Waterloo who have also been my teachers, I offer my appreciation.

To my inner circle of friends, who have given far more than they have received for far too long, my enduring gratitude. To my parents, Josef and Sonja Jakobsh, I am truly at a loss to know where one begins to say thank you. To Kaira and Jesse, who seem so easily to embody all that I strive to be, and to Paul Roorda—partner, best friend, beacon, and foundation—all my love.

Doris R. Jakobsh

ABOUT THE CONTRIBUTORS

Scott T. Kline is Associate Professor of Religious Studies at St. Jerome's University in the University of Waterloo. His area of research is religious ethics and politics. He has published in a variety of journals, including *Peace and Change: A Journal of Peace Research*, *International Relations*, and the *Journal of Religion and Popular Culture*, on topics such as interreligious ethics, the role of religion in South Africa's Truth and Reconciliation Commission, Christianity and U.S. politics, and consumer religion. He is the regionally elected coordinator of the Eastern International Region of the American Academy of Religion (AAR) and a former director on the AAR national board. He is currently writing a book titled *Ethical Being*.

Anne M. Pearson teaches courses on Hinduism, South Asian religions, and world religions in the Department of Religious Studies at McMaster University. She lived in India for more than five years. In addition to writing on women, ritual, and Hinduism, she has researched and published on the topic of the reconstruction and transmission of Hinduism in Canada.

Mikal Austin Radford is Professor of Philosophy, Religion, and Culture in the Faculty of Liberal Arts at Sheridan College, Brampton, and at Wilfrid Laurier University, Waterloo, Ontario, where he teaches courses in Asian philosophy and South Asian traditions. His ongoing research specializes in religion, Eastern philosophy, multiculturalism, and transnational identity formation, with a focus on the Jain communities of Canada and the United States. His publications include "Sallekhana, Ahimsa, and the Western Paradox: The Jaina Ritual of Fasting to Death," "Role Models of Jaina Citizenship in the Western World," "Religion as Meaning and the Canadian Context," and "(Re)creating Transnational Religious Identity with the Jaina Community of Toronto."

Doris R. Jakobsh is Associate Professor and the current Director of Women's Studies at the University of Waterloo, where she was nominated for the Distinguished Teacher Award in 2010. She has degrees from the University of Waterloo, Harvard University, and the University of British Columbia. She is the author of *Relocating Gender in Sikh History: Transformation, Meaning and Identity* (Delhi: Oxford University Press, 2003/2005) and *Sikhism*, in the Dimensions of Asian Spirituality series (Hawaii: University of Hawaii Press, 2011), and has edited *Sikhism and Women: History, Texts and Experience* (Delhi: Oxford University Press, 2010) as well as having numerous other publications. Professor Jakobsh is a member of the Steering Committee of the Sikh Consultation of the American Academy of Religion. She also serves on a number of local and international editorial boards and advisory committees associated with the study of religion and Sikh studies.

Mavis Fenn is an Associate Professor in the Department of Religious Studies at St. Paul's University College at the University of Waterloo. She teaches Asian religions with a focus on Buddhism. Her recent research and publications have focused on Buddhism in Canada, Buddhist women, and the work of the International Association of Buddhist Women, Sakyadhita.

Alison R. Marshall is Professor of Religion at Brandon University and Adjunct Professor, women's and gender studies, University of Winnipeg, Manitoba. A China specialist, Marshall works in the areas of Chinese-Canadian history, gender, and religion. Dr. Marshall is author of *The Way of the Bachelor: Early Chinese Settlement in Manitoba* (UBC Press, 2011) and a forthcoming book with UBC Press, *Confucianism and the Making of Chinese-Canadian Identity*.

Kevin Bond, Ph.D., specializes in Japanese religion and East Asian Buddhism. He is an Assistant Professor in the Department of Religious Studies at the University of Regina, where he teaches courses in the history of Buddhism and Shinto. His research focuses on deity cults and the visual and material cultures of early modern Japanese religion.

CHAPTER 1

The Study of Religion

Scott T. Kline

INTRODUCTION

It is an early Sunday morning in mid-February and some 40,000 people have been camped out for weeks awaiting the commencement of this year's three-hour-long procession. For many this is an annual pilgrimage, marked by family reunions, feelings of patriotism, and a sense of community. By noon there will be roughly 200,000 people surrounding the event's site. Many of them will be dressed in brightly coloured jackets and shirts. A few will be wearing hats and clothes to commemorate the tragic death of one of their heroes at a previous gathering. Another forty million people will watch the event unfold on global television. The infield grass is a lush green, which provides contrast to the brightly coloured murals painted around it. Following tradition, the forty-three men who have qualified for this year's event are introduced and ceremonially paraded before the crowd. After the introduction and parade, the master of ceremonies asks everyone in attendance to stand and pray. A prayer leader then asks God to protect the forty-three men in the procession, everyone in attendance, and the country. Immediately following the prayer, a choir sings the national anthem. As the anthem comes to an end, three fighter jets fly low in formation over the grounds, generating a thunderous roar that reverberates off the grandstands and viewing boxes. The mass of people raise their arms in joy and let out a collective scream. As they begin to settle, the master of ceremonies introduces the grand marshal, who takes the microphone and declares, "Gentlemen, start your engines!"

A few months earlier, a larger pilgrimage took place on the other side of the globe. Since at least the seventh century of the **Common Era (C.E.)**, pilgrims have converged on a small tract of land near the Red Sea for a weeklong act of worship. With more than two million people expected to attend, the government has had the city's major sites cleaned and repainted. Security forces have been training for months to deal with the onslaught of visitors. A newly installed air conditioner, one of the world's largest, is set to provide relief to weary travellers as they gather in one of the city's most revered sites. The pilgrims, all dressed in white, follow the same basic itinerary: On the first day they walk counterclockwise seven times around a cube-shaped building. Each time they pass a black stone at the corner of the building, the pilgrims blow kisses and point toward the stone. When they have finished, they make their way to a nearby town, where they will stop to pray and to gather stones. Many will be transported in air-conditioned coaches, while others will choose to make the 15-kilometre walk.

Common Era (C.E.): the term used by scholars instead of A.D. (Anno Domini).

Circumambulation: the act of moving around a sacred object or space.

Hajj: the annual pilgrimage to Mecca, Saudi Arabia, and the fifth pillar, or duty, of Islam. Pilgrims on the hajj are called hajji.

The courtyard of al-Haram Mosque, full of hajji, or hajj pilgrims.
Source: Photos.com

On the second day, the pilgrims arrive at another town not far away to pray and to gather more stones. Later that evening they camp in the open air and pray for much of the night. On day three they journey to another town, where they will spend the next few days praying and waiting for the appointed time to throw their stones at three 26-metre-long walls, an act that represents stoning the devil. After they have hurled their stones, and before leaving town, many make sure to obtain a certificate confirming that an animal has been sacrificed for them; others perform the sacrifice themselves. The final day returns the pilgrims to the city with the cube-shaped building, where they repeat the **circumambulation** ritual from day one. The pilgrimage comes to an end with the pilgrims drinking from a well and offering final prayers.

The two events described here have no obvious connections. The first one is the Daytona 500, the most important car race associated with the National Association for

The Daytona 500. With 200,000 spectators on-site and forty million TV viewers, it is the most important NASCAR race of the season.
Source: Chris Graythen/Getty Images

Stock Car Auto Racing (NASCAR) series. Held every year since 1959 at Daytona International Speedway in Daytona Beach, Florida, the 500-mile (805-kilometre) race is commonly referred to by NASCAR fans as "The Great American Race." It is traditionally the first event in the NASCAR season, which runs from mid-February until early November. The second description is of activities associated with the **hajj**, the pilgrimage to Mecca, which is the fifth pillar, or duty, of Islam. Every able-bodied Muslim has an obligation to make the pilgrimage at least once in his or her lifetime, finances permitting. Many save money for years to attend. Some who cannot personally afford the hajj are supported by their villages, which are often quite poor and may have to save for years to send a single person.

In spite of some obvious differences, the Daytona 500 and the hajj do share certain formal similarities. For instance, they both maintain sets of rituals that are well established and known to those in attendance. Both have defined spaces and structures where the events take place. And both have stories of heroes, saints, and villains that provide complementary narratives for both the NASCAR race and the hajj.

We begin with general descriptions of these events to raise two foundational questions. The first is "What is religion?" This is an important question because it helps us define and limit our field of study. It helps us understand why many religious studies scholars do not treat NASCAR races, any other form of popular culture, or mythical figures such as Santa Claus, the Tooth

Fairy, or the Easter Bunny as objects of study—that is, as religion. It also helps us understand why a number of scholars actually *do* think popular culture, myths, professional sports, and gaming, for example, ought to be studied as religion. And it helps us appreciate the complexities associated with defining *religion*.

The second question is "How do we study religion?" Or, to put it another way, what theoretical and methodological approaches have religious studies scholars employed to analyze and explain the phenomena they consider "religious"? To answer this question, we will need a greater understanding of both the general history of the field, including the scholars who helped shape it, and the scholarly approaches that make up the field of religious studies. We will discover that our approaches often yield different conclusions, even though we are apparently examining the same phenomena. And we will begin to learn and to use the language of religious studies, especially the key terms and concepts that enable us to study religion as an academic pursuit.

In short, our task in this chapter is to introduce you to the study of religion, an expansive field of academic inquiry that draws generously from the humanities (e.g., philosophy, theology, history, literature) and the social sciences (e.g., anthropology, sociology, psychology, linguistics). In this respect, the study of religion is neither a subject nor a discipline with its own distinct methodologies. Rather, as Walter Capps once put it, religious studies is "a *subject field* within which a variety of disciplines are employed and an enormous range of subjects are treated" (1974, 727). If we perform our task well, this chapter should help you understand the field of religious studies, the language we use in the field, and the academic approaches used by religious studies scholars.

WHAT IS RELIGION?

The term *religion* has a long, multi-layered, and obscure history. One of the most plausible etymologies has the term deriving from an early Indo-European root **leig*, which means "to bind." From this root stems the Latin verb *ligare*, which means "to tie" or "to bind"— the English word *ligament* is derived from this verb as well. From *ligare* comes the Latin verb *religare*, which means "to retie" or "to bind fast"; it is a verb that connotes a sense of interconnectedness and permanency.

Catholic: from Latin and Greek words meaning "universal," referring to people and organizations associated with the Catholic Church, the largest Christian communion and, prior to the Protestant Reformation in the sixteenth century, the Christian church of western Europe.

Religious orders: communities and organizations of men or women who seek to lead a life of piety and often to perform some type of service. Members normally commit themselves to poverty, chastity, and obedience to lead a dedicated life.

Historical usage clouds the next etymological stage. The current consensus is that the verb *religare* provided a basis for the Latin noun *religio*, which conveys a sense of reverential awe and respect that one might experience in the presence of a spirit, god, honoured leader, or anyone else held in high esteem. However, *religion* has not always been understood in these terms. In fact, between the fourth and sixteenth centuries C.E., *religion* was thought to derive from the Latin verb *relego*, which means "to reread" or "to be careful." *Relego* was used to denote an action that required conscientious repetition or ritualistic discipline. Vestiges of this understanding of *religion* survive today in the adverb *religiously*, as in "She studies her notes religiously before every class." It is this transformation of the meaning of *religion*—from ritualistic devotion to something that binds—that is crucial to our understanding of religion and the field of religious studies.

Inventing "Religion"

As the historian of religion Jonathan Z. Smith has demonstrated, prior to the sixteenth century, the Latin noun forms *religio, religionis* (religion), the adjective *religiosus* (religious), and the adverb *religiose* (religiously) were terms "referring primarily to the careful performance of ritual obligations" (1998, 270). Western European explorers and **Catholic** missionaries who travelled eastward to China and India and westward to the Indies and Latin America in the fifteenth and sixteenth centuries commonly used *religion* to describe the indigenous peoples' rituals and ceremonial practices. Their frame of reference for *religion* and *religious* was, of course, European Catholicism and those who belonged to Catholic **religious orders**. Members of religious orders,

> **Ritual:** a set of repetitive actions, often coordinated and regulated, that relates to a religion's myths and concept of ultimate meaning.
>
> **Idolatry:** from a Greek term meaning "image worshipper." Nineteenth-century scholars of religion used the term to designate practices that violated Christian religious practices. Contemporary scholars avoid using the term as an academic category because it is a normative category that assumes a Christian standard.
>
> **Virtue:** moral excellence or rightness.
>
> **Piety:** devoutness, usually expressed through spiritual and worldly practices.
>
> **Faith:** trust in the truth or authenticity of a person, idea, or concept. In the nineteenth century, the term became a designation for religion.

referred to as monks and nuns, were characterized by their devotion to the Church, their monastic life, their commitment to prayer, and their disavowal of worldly possessions. As these explorers and Catholic missionaries began to report on the cultures of China, India, the Indies, and Latin America, they used *religion* and *religious* to describe social arrangements, ceremonies, and political structures that resembled those in Spain, Portugal, and much of Western Europe.

Distinctions between *religion*, *custom*, and *superstition* began to define comparative qualities in belief and practice. These comparative qualities were, however, rarely explicitly defined, in part because the Western European Christian frame of reference was taken for granted. In assuming this Western European Christian frame of reference, any perceived differences between Europe and these "foreign" practices were typically filtered through a normative European Christian lens. *Superstition*, for example, generally implied practices that Europeans would associate with irrational belief, magic, and actions that would violate their cultural sensibilities, while *religion* implied **ritual** practices that, at the very least, formally resembled those taking place in churches across Western Europe. This close association between religion and ritual was not, however, without controversy. Back in Europe, theologians and some Church leaders were raising concerns that priests abroad were being too accommodating, if not deceitful, in their attempts to find similarities between

Christian practices and "native rituals." Even when the term *ritual* was used to describe practices that would indicate differences from Christianity—such as cannibalism or "**idolatry**"—the close connection between ritual and religion within Catholicism meant that medieval theologians had to provide arguments for why and how "ritual" could lead to practices that violated Christian doctrine and practice.

By the end of the seventeenth century, the Catholic conception of religion as ritual performance and obligation had begun to give way to an understanding of religion as "**virtue**" and "**piety**." Influenced by Protestant Reformation leaders such as Ulrich Zwingli (1448–1531), John Calvin (1509–64), and to a lesser extent Martin Luther (1483–1546), post-Reformation scholars recast *religion* in more individualistic terms, that is, as a frame of mind oriented toward God that would lead to individual acts of virtue and piety, rather than participation in ritual performances. During this same time, terms such as *service* and *worship* lost much of their ritualistic connotations. Moreover, in line with key tenets of Protestant Christianity, *faith* became increasingly preferable to *religion* because *faith* emphasized the human subject's relationship with God and the subject's capacity to comprehend divine truth apart from the mediating authority of a Catholic priest, bishop, or pope. This Protestant emphasis on the human subject's ability to encounter God and to discover truth apart from the Catholic Church represented a fundamental challenge to medieval church, political, and social power structures. Indeed, the Protestant Reformation forever changed European Christianity. Not only did the Reformation split Western European Christianity into separate Protestant and Catholic traditions, but it also set the stage for various forms of Protestantism to take shape. By the beginning of the eighteenth century, then, Western Europe was no longer simply a geographical region under the authority of a single church—the Catholic Church. Rather, it operated with an ever-increasing variety of Christian traditions, each with different doctrines, rituals, and relationships with political authorities.

Along with the different types of Christianity, there was growing recognition of other "religions," which in the seventeenth and eighteenth centuries were often sorted into four primary species, namely, Christianity, "Mohametanism" (which later became

Islam), Judaism, and what was typically labelled "idolatry" or "**paganism**," which functioned as a miscellaneous category cataloguing cultural practices and social arrangements that fell outside the first three. While recognizing the differences between religions, scholars in the seventeenth and eighteenth centuries remained more interested in their similarities. This preoccupation with finding similarities among the different religions led to a long debate over "**natural religion**"—a debate that would dominate the study of religion for nearly two centuries.

The basic thesis of natural religion was that any human being willing and able to commit to rational questioning and study could discover religious beliefs and practices based on rational understanding. Initially this thesis was the foundation for disputes among Christians, especially between Protestant groups. The idea was that Christians of good faith and will could settle matters through reason. Eventually the thesis was expanded to include non-Christian religions as well. The strong inclination toward harmony in the natural-religion thesis meant that scholars tended to privilege similarities between the religions. The Christian roots of the thesis also meant that scholars often concentrated on a religion's universal claims, its central texts (especially stories of creation), its conception of life after death, its innate impulses to seek truth and the divine, and other topics central to Protestant Christianity. For many eighteenth- and nineteenth-century scholars of natural religion, the issue at stake was not whether another religion was true or not (although it was presumed that Christianity was the truest of them all) but rather the manner in which religion revealed unified truth to different people. There was, in other words, a common universal truth that surfaced in each religion, and it was the scholar's task to observe, classify, and explain "religious phenomena" in their various forms. This process signalled a significant transformation in the understanding of *religion*: it introduced the idea that religion was no longer a theological category but an anthropological category that relied on scholarly observation, classification, and interpretation of data.

By the turn of the nineteenth century there was no shortage of data. Scholars had become fluent in non-European languages. Moreover, colonial officials, travellers, and merchants had begun to learn Hindi, Arabic, Chinese dialects, certain African tribal languages, and other languages that made

Paganism: a broad category used by nineteenth-century scholars to identify groups that were polytheistic.

Natural religion: characterized by the belief that divine truth was manifest in natural phenomena and accessible through human reasons. Natural religion was popular in the seventeenth and eighteenth centuries.

Analects of Confucius: a text written between the fifth and third centuries B.C.E. traditionally believed to contain the sayings and teachings of the Chinese philosopher Confucius (c. 551–c. 479 B.C.E.) and his followers.

Bhagavad-Gita: a Hindu scripture focusing on the story of Lord Krishna; part of the ancient Hindu epic the Mahabharata.

Rig-Veda: a collection of old Indian Sanskrit (Vedic) hymns and one of the four sets of Vedas that comprise Hinduism's authoritative texts.

Pali canon: the collection of scriptures used in Theravada Buddhism.

good political and economic sense. It was an age of expanding empires, increased international mobility, economic globalization, and post-Enlightenment curiosity, and there was growing demand for literature that could explain the social and cultural practices of peoples in faraway places. As a result, translations of "religious" texts began to appear. For example, an English translation of Confucius's **Analects** appeared in the late sixteenth century. Excerpts from the **Bhagavad-Gita** appeared in English in the late eighteenth century. The East India Company financed scholars to write a four-volume translation of the **Rig-Veda** in the middle of the nineteenth century, just before establishment of the British Raj in South Asia. Excerpts from the **Pali canon**, Theravada Buddhism's central texts, began to appear in the late nineteenth century with the assistance of the Pali Society, which was created by three British civil servants posted in Ceylon (now Sri Lanka).

Sweeping studies of foreign cultures and religions were also published and widely read in Europe. For instance, early in the nineteenth century, the twenty-four-volume *Descriptions of Egypt* appeared in France; the scholars had been part of Napoleon's expeditionary forces that invaded Egypt in 1798. This work, which anchored the new field of Egyptology, guided European

Naturalistic religion: a concept developed by anthropologists and scholars of religion in the nineteenth century to categorize the practices of non-supernatural religions, especially those linked with "primitive" peoples (e.g., animism, totemism, fetishism, magic).

Supernatural religion: a concept developed by anthropologists and other scholars of religion in the nineteenth century to categorize beliefs and practices that assumed the presence of a being beyond nature.

Fetishism: a category used by nineteenth- and early-twentieth-century scholars of naturalistic religion to refer to the practice of using objects believed to have supernatural powers. A fetish is the object that is believed to have such powers.

Totemism: a category used by nineteenth- and early-twentieth-century scholars of naturalistic religion to refer to the practice of using an animal or another natural figure to represent a community of people. A totem is the animal (e.g., an eagle or a wolverine) or natural figure.

Shamanism: a category used by nineteenth- and early-twentieth-century scholars of naturalistic religion to refer to groups of people who believe that an intermediary or a messenger (a shaman) can communicate with the spiritual world.

Animism: a category used, especially by nineteenth- and early-twentieth-century scholars of naturalistic religion, to refer to the belief that spirits exist not only in humans but also in other animals, plants, rocks, mountains, rivers, clouds, thunder, and other naturally occurring phenomena.

Magic: a category used, especially by nineteenth- and early-twentieth-century scholars of naturalistic religion, to refer to the belief that human beings can manipulate the natural world through supernatural power or through esoteric knowledge of natural laws.

In this famous painting titled *Napoleon before the Sphinx*, two powerful figures meet face to face: one the face of the first French empire, the other the face of an Egyptian tradition dating back to at least 2500 B.C.E. Nineteenth-century studies of religion were often the result of European empires invading foreign lands.

Source: Apic/Getty Images

thinking on Islam and Coptic Christianity in Egypt for almost a century. Other studies, such as John Bellamy's *The History of All Religions* (1812) and Henri-Benjamin Constant's *Considerations on the Source of Religion: Its Forms and Developments* (in French, *De la religion*, 1824–31), were published to receptive audiences. By the end of the nineteenth century scholars had invented the terms *Hindooism* (1829), *Taouism* (1839), and *Confucianism* (1862). Above all, these scholars created systems of classification (in technical terms, *taxonomies*) that resembled those used by natural scientists to classify and define organisms. The result of this process was that, by the mid-nineteenth century, the study of religion was no longer a theological pursuit or a natural history but a social science.

As Smith has noted, "the most common form of classifying religions, found both in native categories and in scholarly literature, is dualistic and can be reduced, regardless of what differentium is employed, to 'theirs' and 'ours'" (1998, 276). One of the most important distinctions in nineteenth-century research on religion was between **naturalistic** and **supernatural** religions. Naturalistic religions, which were sometimes called "primitive" religions, were often traced to "primitive peoples," or in German *Naturvölker*, which literally translates as "nature peoples." Naturalistic religion was broken down into smaller segments: **fetishism**, **totemism**, **shamanism**, **animism**, and **magic**, as well as tribal, imperial, and ancestor worship, to name just a few. By contrast, supernatural religion placed belief in a divine otherworldly power, being, or beings that would affect worldly affairs from time to time. Influenced by the English naturalist Charles Darwin (1809–82) and Herbert Spencer (1820–1903), who popularized Darwin's theories in the field of sociology, a number of influential scholars, including anthropologists Edward B.

Tylor (1832–1917) and James G. Frazer (1854–1941), thought that these "primitive" religions were in the early stages of evolutionary development, and that with each stage they would begin to look more and more like supernatural religions.

These scholars of naturalistic religion maintained classification categories that privileged religions resembling Protestant and, to an ever-decreasing extent, Catholic Christianity in Europe. The supernatural or spiritual religions, which tended to be synonymous with "high religion," were limited to Christianity, Buddhism, and Mohammedanism (later Islam). In some classifications, Judaism was called a "reformed natural" religion and a "fleshly" religion because it was a "spontaneous" religion and limited to a single "race," as compared to Christianity, for instance, which grew out of Judaism "rationally" and was open to all races. This marked a major shift in the study of religion. The old system of classification, which had the three Abrahamic religions—Judaism, Christianity, and Islam—set against "idolatry" or "paganism," had been replaced by a new model, which classified Buddhism, Mohammedanism, and Christianity as the *supernatural religions* while assigning all other religions, including Judaism, to various classes of *naturalistic religion.*

The invention of "world" or "universal" religions occurred during this wave of interest in non-European religion. The Dutch scholar Cornelius Petrus Tiele (1830–1902) introduced the concept of "the world's religions" in his *Outline of the History of Religion to the Spread of Universal Religion* (1876). He divided the world's religions into two broad classifications: natural (or "naturalistic") religion and ethical religion. Consistent with the nineteenth-century trend to interpret data in evolutionary terms, Tiele thought that naturalistic religion was the lower stage in human development, with animism being the lowest form of religion, totemism being a transitional phase, and **polytheism** being characteristic of the highest form of naturalistic religion.

Tiele divided ethical religion, the higher stage, into two categories. The first was called "national nomistic religious communities." With this category, Tiele attempted to capture religions that were founded on a law or scripture and drew their adherents from a particular nation or ethnic group. These religions included Daoism, Confucianism, "Brahmanism" (later Hinduism), Jainism, primitive Buddhism, and Judaism. The second category of ethical religions was

Polytheism: belief in more than one god.

Proselytization: the practice of converting someone or some group of people to a religion.

called "universalistic religious communities." These religions practised universal **proselytization**, which meant that they accepted followers from all ethnic groups. Tiele included only three "universalistic" or "world" religions: Islam, Buddhism, and Christianity.

The category "world religions" was, from the outset, a controversial designation. In particular, scholars sought to expand the number of world religions by combining Tiele's two categories of ethical religion. Jonathan Smith has captured the profound lack of scientific rigor involved in this process. It was, he wrote, "an odd venture of pluralistic etiquette: if Christianity and Islam count as world religions, then it would be rude to exclude Judaism. . . . Likewise, if Buddhism is included, then Hinduism cannot be ignored. And again, if Buddhism, then Chinese religions and Japanese religions" (Smith 1998, 280).

In many respects, then, "world religions" is a political category, signifying that these religions matter to the academy because they affect global politics. The political foundations of world religions are made even more evident by the scholarly practice of dividing these religions along an East–West geographical line. This East–West orientation is radically political because it assumes a centre of the world: traditionally Europe, the continent that both dominated geopolitics throughout the nineteenth century and the early part of the twentieth century and invented the study of religion. Consequently, the category "Eastern religions" typically meant the religions that originated in the Arabian Peninsula, China, Japan, South Asia, and Southeast Asia. These "Eastern" religions included Islam, Buddhism, Confucianism, Daoism, Hinduism, and Sikhism. It was only in the first half of the twentieth century that Islam became a "Western" religion. Currently the designation "Western religions" means the religions that originated in the Middle East and North Africa but became politically significant in Europe and later in the Americas—Judaism, Christianity, and Islam. Often lost in this "world religions" paradigm are the so-called minor religions, which are commonly designated as spirituality and

> **Substantive definitions of religion:** sometimes known as essentialist definitions, they maintain that religion has an essence that is universal (e.g., the holy, the sacred, or a belief in spiritual beings).
>
> **Sacred:** something or someone that is set apart or holy. It is often used in contrast with *profane*.
>
> **Sui generis:** a Latin phrase meaning "of its own kind." It is used by scholars of religion, especially those from the *Religionswissenschaft* school, who believe that religion is "of its own kind" and must therefore be studied with an appreciation for the irreducible truth that is in religion.

tribal groupings because they demand so little political attention. Based almost solely on political criteria, then, many studies of "the world's religions" exclude the beliefs of indigenous peoples in the Americas and Oceania as well the religions of sub-Saharan Africa.

Defining Religion

So we return to our question "What is religion?" By now it should be clear that defining religion is not an easy task. As we discovered in our brief history of the term *religion*, it has been wrought with theological biases, philosophical and anthropological assumptions about absolute truth, and political agendas. There is, in short, no "pure" or "true" definition of religion. As sociologist Peter Berger wrote in *The Sacred Canopy*, "Definitions cannot, by their very nature, be either 'true' or 'false,' only more useful or less so" ([1967] 1969, 175). So why, then, should we attempt to define religion? The short answer is this: in order to set limits on our field of study, we must establish some boundaries on the phenomena that we wish to study; otherwise, to say that we are "studying religion" means that we are studying everything—which is to say nothing in particular.

Substantive and Functional Definitions

Historically, definitions of religion have fallen into two broad categories: the substantive and the functional. **Substantive definitions** typically provide definitive answers to the question "What is religion?" In general, substantive definitions, which are sometimes called

essentialist definitions, tend to emphasize three features of religion. First, they focus on the "things" of religion, such as gods, belief in higher powers, sacred scripture, the divine, and the holy. A classical substantive definition of religion comes from the anthropologist E. B. Tylor, who defined religion as a "belief in Spiritual Beings" ([1871] 1974, 383).

Second, substantive definitions make claims about the essence of religion. For instance, the German theologian Friedrich Schleiermacher (1768–1834) believed that the essence of religion is to be found in the "feeling of an absolute dependence" ([1830] 1999, 12–18, 26–29). For Schleiermacher, religion is essentially an affective, or emotional, response. Rudolf Otto (1869–1937), also a German theologian and the author of the widely read *The Idea of the Holy* (1917), offered a definition that emphasized a subjective response to an object outside oneself. For Otto, the holy is a non-rational mystery that generates experiences of both fear and fascination. "The truly 'mysterious' object," Otto wrote, "is beyond our apprehension and comprehension, not only because our knowledge has certain irremovable limits, but because in it we come upon something inherently 'wholly other,' whose kind and character are incommensurable with our own, and before which we recoil in a wonder that strikes us chill and numb" (1958, 28).

Similarly to Otto, Mircea Eliade (1907–86), the legendary figure who turned the University of Chicago into a hub for North American religious studies, believed that religion was rooted in a non-rational experience of what he called "the **sacred**." For Eliade, religious phenomena have an essence, "the sacred," that is the cause of religious behaviour and not the effect. Eliade wrote, "A religious phenomenon will only be recognized as such if it is grasped at its own level, that is to say, if it is studied *as* something religious. To try to grasp the essence of such a phenomenon by means of physiology, psychology, sociology, economics, linguistics, art, or any other study is false; it misses the one unique and irreducible element in it—the element of the sacred (1963, xiii). Students who adopt Eliade's definition of religion believe—and we use *believe* deliberately, since there is no way to demonstrate it academically—that religion is essentially *sui generis* (Latin for "of its own kind" or "self-caused"), extraordinary, inscrutable, and common to all humans. (The term Eliade used for people who have this natural inclination to seek the sacred was *Homo religiosus*.)

And third, substantive definitions of religion tend to posit a normative standard that provides moral, spiritual, and psychological guidance for human beings. An excellent example of this normative type of definition comes from William James (1842–1910), the philosopher and psychologist, who stated in his popular book *The Varieties of Religious Experience* (1902) that religion "consists of the belief that there is an unseen order, and that our supreme good lies in harmoniously adjusting ourselves thereto" (1958, 58). Another good example comes from Paul Tillich (1886–1965), one of the most celebrated theologians of the twentieth century, who wrote, "Religion is the state of being grasped by an ultimate concern, a concern which qualifies all other concerns as preliminary and which itself contains the answer to the question of the meaning of our life" (1963, 8).

Substantive definitions create tremendous concern for scholars of religion who work in the social sciences and are accustomed to engaging with phenomena by using empirical frameworks. While these scholars raise a number of objections, there are two that stand out. First, substantive definitions assume realities called the "spiritual" and the "supernatural." The problem with this assumption is that both the spiritual and the supernatural exist outside the realm of academic inquiry. To understand the spiritual and the supernatural as realms of being and existence requires a subjective encounter with "the sacred," "the holy," or any other spiritual being or state. Critics therefore argue that the study of religion in substantive terms eventually becomes an "insiders'" study that may exclude "outsiders" who reject notions of a spiritual or supernatural reality. In the eyes of these critics, substantive claims cannot be proven empirically through scientific means.

Second, critics often argue that substantive definitions are merely parochial theological assertions operating under the guise of universal pretensions. The result, they contend, has been that substantive definitions of religion have yielded studies that have more in common with theological studies than with the social sciences. In more precise terms, the process emanating from substantive definitions of religion assumes certain attributes of liberal Protestant theology: they assert (a) that there is an essence to religion, (b) that this essence is "true," (c) that all human beings either do or may

Homo religiosus: a phrase coined by Mircea Eliade to refer to the human quality of being religious.

Moksha: a Sanskrit term meaning "release," it means the escape from the cycle of birth and rebirth. Nirvana is its equivalent in Buddhism and mukti in Sikhism, although the manner in which humans are liberated from the cycle differs in each religion.

Nirvana: the state of being free from suffering, a central concept in the religions of India.

Functional definitions of religion: favoured by sociologists and others scholars interested in studying what religions "do," they focus on the behaviours of people and how those behaviours are connected to other aspects of the community.

experience this "true" essence in some manner or another, and (d) that this experience leads to a better state of being, whether it is called "salvation," "enlightenment," "**moksha**," "higher consciousness," "**nirvana**," or "oneness with reality."

Functional definitions generally answer the question "What does religion do?" In functionalist terms, religion meets certain human needs, such as providing social cohesion, emotional or psychological support, and intellectual meaning. Functional definitions tend to facilitate studies into the behaviour of religious people rather than their beliefs. Consequently, scholars who use functional definitions are often interested in the sociology, anthropology, and psychology of religion. A classic functional definition of religion is found in the work of the sociologist Émile Durkheim (1858–1917), who wrote, "A religion is a unified system of beliefs and practices relative to sacred things, that is to say, things set apart and forbidden—beliefs and practices which unite into one single moral community called a church, all those who adhere to them" ([1912] 1915, 419). For Durkheim, religion provides social stability, a means to express group identity, and a forum for community gatherings.

Like Durkheim, Karl Marx (1818–83) defined religion in terms of its social function: "Religion is the sigh of the oppressed creature, the heart of a heartless world, just as it is the spirit of a spiritless situation. It is the *opium* of people" (1964, 42). Marx thought that religion only placated the feelings of alienation that the masses were experiencing as they toiled away in their dehumanizing jobs. Religion was an "illusory happiness," a numbing drug that had to be jettisoned in order to discover "real happiness" (1964, 42). Moreover, religion was a bourgeois tool of oppression employed by those who owned the means of production (the bourgeoisie) to control the working class (the proletariat). To achieve authentic happiness, the working class had to rid itself not only of religion but also of capitalism, which in Marx's view meant nothing less than a socio-economic revolution.

Sigmund Freud (1856–1939), one of the founders of psychoanalytic psychology, also believed that religion was an illusion. "Religion," he wrote, "is an attempt to get control over the sensory world, in which we are placed, by means of the wish-world which we have developed inside us as a result of biological and psychological necessities. . . . If one attempts to assign religion its place in [human] evolution, it seems . . . a parallel to the neurosis which the civilized individual must pass through on his way from childhood to maturity" (1918). Daniel Pals, a scholar who specializes in theories of religion, has accurately described the profound reductionism in Freud's thinking. He writes that Freud "does not just say that, *among other things*, religion seems to have certain psychological functions. He asserts that religion arises *only* in response to deep emotional conflicts and weaknesses" (2006, 77).

PERSPECTIVES

The Insider/Outsider Problem

The Canadian scholar of religion Wilfred Cantwell Smith (1916–2000) is widely known for privileging the perspective of the insider in the study of religion. He writes, "no statement about a religion is valid unless it can be acknowledged by that religion's believers" (1959, 42). In effect, Smith is proposing a rule that insiders are the final authority in determining whether or not a scholar's statement about their religion is correct. This rule, however, creates problems for researchers who are interested in studying why insiders act and believe differently. Which insider should be the final arbiter? Or what happens if (or more likely, when) the researcher finds that an insider's claims contradict his or her behaviour? Does the researcher then make a judgment based on criteria outside those of the insiders?

In the 1950s Kenneth Pike, a linguist, coined the terms *emic* and *etic* to help analyze human language. According to Pike, the emic viewpoint studies phenomena from inside a system and relies on insiders to judge the accuracy of a description or, for example, the proper way to say the word *about* in Canada. An etic viewpoint studies phenomena from outside a system and uses criteria derived from extrinsic concepts and categories that are meaningful to the researcher. For Pike, etics are a way of accessing emics; but etic perspectives can claim no priority over emic perspectives. In the 1960s, Marvin Harris, an anthropologist, borrowed Pike's emic/etic concept to study cultural anthropology. Harris disagreed with Pike. For Harris, etics are useful for making relatively objective determinations of fact, which is an essential component of disciplines that purport to be sciences.

Today, insider/outsider debates occur most often when scholars attempt to extrapolate a universal human characteristic from the study of religion while other scholars attempt to refute such universalistic claims as going beyond the scope of academic study. For example, Wendy Doniger and Diana Eck have conducted a number of comparative studies of religion and found that certain shared experiences underlie many myths and rituals, even though they may appear in different forms in various religions. In response, scholars such as Russell McCutcheon, a Canadian academic, maintain that these attempts to locate universal experience are remnants of a liberal humanism that privileges an essentialist understanding of religion over a functionalist one.

Of course, not all functional definitions are as reductionist as those offered by Marx and Freud. For instance, Clifford Geertz (1926–2006), the leading figure in twentieth-century North American anthropology, constructed a definition that is both functional and "realistic" (a term we will discuss below), to the extent that it has enabled scholars to examine the objects of religious experience without reducing them to their fundamental status or nature:

> Religion is (1) a system of symbols which acts to (2) establish powerful, pervasive, and long-lasting moods and motivations in [people] by (3) formulating conceptions of a general order of existence and (4) clothing these conceptions with such an aura of factuality that the moods and motivations seem uniquely realistic. (1979, 79–80)

Geertz's definition of religion maintains wide appeal among scholars in large part because of its flexibility and scope. Other definitions provide even more flexibility and scope. For example, Wilfred Cantwell Smith, the Canadian scholar and former director of the Harvard Center for the Study of the World Religions, recommended using the language of "traditions" to include both religion and secular humanism. Ninian Smart (1927–2001), who helped pioneer secular approaches to the study of religion, suggested using "worldviews" as the common term for nationalism, socialism, and religion.

One common criticism of functional definitions is that they can be too sweeping. While they allow scholars to examine a variety of phenomena that many might associate with religion, such as prayer, ritual performance, and structures of religious authority, functional definitions generally have trouble limiting phenomena. Because functional definitions orient the student to examine structures, forms, and patterns of human activity, it is often difficult to exclude phenomena that appear to bear attributes similar to "religious" phenomena. Examples of this blurring between religion and other, similar forms of human behaviour might include a NASCAR race, the Olympics, the fan culture around a sports team (e.g., "Leafs Nation" or "Habs Nation"), a nationalist political party such as the National Socialist Party in Germany or the Khmer Rouge in Cambodia, a political ideology such as communism, an intentional community committed to living in an ecologically sustainable way, or a virtual online community that gathers regularly to play World of Warcraft. The danger with functional definitions is that the terms *religion* and *religious* grow to be so all-encompassing that they become academically useless categories.

PERSPECTIVES

Functional definitions of religion have allowed scholars to examine contemporary sports as religion. In the United States, football fans cheer for professional teams that have animal mascots—such as the Bears, Colts, Seahawks, Broncos, Dolphins, Cardinals, and Eagles—which are strikingly similar to the clan totems identified in early studies of religion. These totems/mascots provide identifying markers for communities/fans as they gather to support their respective clans/teams. In Canada, Olivier Bauer (2009) has published a book that analyzes the correlations between Montreal Canadiens fans who refer to the Habs jersey as *la sainte flanelle* ("holy

Source: Dave Sanford/Getty Images

Deity: an entity that exists beyond the natural world and is believed to affect the lives of the natural world, often in the form of a god.

Toward a Stipulative Definition of Religion

Students in my introductory courses in religious studies will often ask me this question in some form or another: "If you're searching for a definition of religion, why not just go to the dictionary?" While the question is typically posed with the best of intentions, such as to help alleviate their fellow students' frustration and confusion over why defining religion is so complicated, the problem is that dictionary, or lexical, definitions are limited to ordinary usage. Definitions found in dictionaries such as the *Oxford Dictionary of the English Language* or *Merriam-Webster*'s dictionary state only "the actual way in which some actual word has been used by some actual person" (Baird 1973, 10). A lexical definition of *religion*, then, is simply

PERSPECTIVES

A Note Regarding Dictionaries

Not all dictionaries should be avoided by the student of religion. Technical dictionaries edited, written, and reviewed by scholars in the field can provide students with reliable information. These dictionaries include the *Penguin Dictionary of Religions* (2005), edited by John Hinnells, and the thorough *Harper Collins Dictionary of Religion* (1996), edited by Jonathan Z. Smith. There are also dictionaries that focus on specific religions, including new religious movements, and theoretical approaches to the study of religion. Unlike the general language lexicons, these technical dictionaries often provide historical context and commentaries outlining the usage of the terms. Readers should consult the bibliography at the end of each chapter for help in finding resources.

a cataloguing of the most common ways in which the term has been used. For example, the *Canadian Oxford Dictionary* (2004) contains five separate definitions for *religion*. The first one reads: "the belief in a superhuman controlling power, esp. in a personal God or gods entitled to obedience and worship." For students pursuing an academic study of religion, this definition is unsatisfactory, since not all religions have an absolute **deity** or gods who wield power or demand obedience. For instance, in Theravada Buddhism, which is found in many parts of Southeast Asia as well as India and Sri Lanka, the Buddha (the "Enlightened One") is revered as a sage but not as a god. Because lexical definitions convey popular usage, students of religious studies should avoid them as much as possible.

Another way to define religion is by making empirical statements about religion. This type of definition is called a *real* definition. Such definitions rely on data and some form of proof in their formation. Because these definitions are deductive, which means they arise only at the end of study, scholars who use real definitions tend to rely on their definitions as an integral element in their overall argument. These real definitions are central propositions about the way things are. One good example of a real definition is the following: "Religion consists of very general explanations of existence, including terms of exchange with a god or gods" (Stark and Finke 2000, 91). While real definitions may be phrased in ways that appear to be the same as *substantialist* definitions, they are different. Substantialist definitions assert from the beginning that religion has an essence, while real definitions, which tend to be more functional in orientation, attempt to demonstrate through social scientific methods that religion corresponds to certain objects and phenomena.

Given the nature and objectives of this text, we will adopt a *stipulative* definition of religion. Stipulative definitions are somewhat arbitrary statements designed to limit the range of study for a particular purpose and audience. These are useful working definitions that are subject to revision. Moreover, stipulative definitions can be either substantive or functional. For example, a Christian theologian could, following Paul Tillich, stipulate that religion is "ultimate concern" and then proceed to enquire into the essential nature of higher beings in different religions. Alternatively, a sociologist of religion could, following Durkheim, stipulate that religion consists of "unified systems of beliefs and practices" and then proceed to examine the ways in which religious institutions function to provide social stability.

Since the authors in this text tend to emphasize the social, cultural, historical, and political aspects of religion, let us stipulate the following definition, which we construct with the help of Bruce Lincoln (2003) and Thomas Tweed (2006): *Religions are systems of discourses, practices, communities, and institutions that draw on human and suprahuman powers to provide adherents access to ultimate meaning.*

The Usefulness of Our Definition

Notice that this definition invites us to study the religions in this text as coherent systems that maintain ways of communicating, acting, gathering, and regulating behaviour. It stipulates that religions present humans with special pathways to authentic knowledge and truths. This knowledge and truth could be intellectual (i.e., rational) or experiential (i.e., non-rational). Following Tweed (2006), our definition uses the term **suprahuman** instead of terms such as *God*, *gods*, or *spiritual beings*. With this definition we are suspending our judgment as to whether such suprahuman beings exist, but we are acknowledging that religions do typically include such beings. This choice allows for religions that do not affirm **theism**, such as Theravada Buddhism and certain new religious movements, to be captured by our definition. Furthermore, our definition recognizes that some religions, including Christianity and some forms of Buddhism, believe that suprahuman powers can operate through human beings. We should also note that, because our definition includes references to suprahuman beings and ultimate meaning, we have effectively excluded the study of NASCAR races, fairy tales, most political and social movements, and popular culture as religions.

Our definition is useful because it enables us to study the various expressions of religious phenomena. For instance, through a study of a religion's *discourses*—that is, the formal ways in which people communicate—we can examine two of the primary ways in which religious communities disseminate knowledge about reality, morality, the meaning of life

Suprahuman: an adjective relating to abilities and modes of existence that are greater than human.

Theism: a broad term signifying belief in at least one god.

Myth: in the field of religious studies, a story that communicates a community's norms and values. For scholars of religious studies, a myth is neither true nor false, but important data that enables scholars to understand the various roles that the myth plays in a religion.

Doctrine: the formal teachings of a religion, typically in written form and promoted by authority figures or experts trained in interpreting the teachings.

Before the Common Era (B.C.E.): before the C.E. Used by scholars instead of B.C. (before Christ).

and death, and other core beliefs: **myth** and **doctrine**. The term *myth* comes from the Greek word *mythos*, meaning "word" or "story." Prior to the sixth century B.C.E., the word *mythos* was synonymous with the Greek word *logos*. But as Greek intellectuals such as Plato (429–347 B.C.E.) and Herodotus (c. 484–c. 425 B.C.E.) began to question the stories of the Greek gods, *mythos* came to mean "implausible story" or "irrational story," while *logos* took on the meaning of "reasonable story" or "reason." This Greek legacy remains with us today. Many of us associate myth with fictitious stories such as the classical Greek myth *The Odyssey*, the medieval stories of King Arthur, or the contemporary myth *The Lord of the Rings*. We may also associate myth with a false story or cultural narrative, much as Naomi Wolf did in her book *The Beauty Myth* (1992).

In the academic study of religion, a myth is a narrative that conveys a community's central values and understanding of the world. As scholars of religion, we do not make judgments about whether a myth is literally true or not. Instead, our primary purpose in studying a myth is to help us understand the various roles it plays in a community's network of communication. In this regard, we treat myth as something ordinary. Common myths include stories about creation, heroes, tricksters, salvation/enlightenment, redemption, and the afterlife. We can find them in scripture, oral histories, and collections of teachings by revered leaders, as well as in a religion's art and architecture.

In comparison to myth, which takes the form of stories, doctrine often appears as creeds, confessions of faith, or legal declarations. Doctrine may also appear as theology or a philosophy. In general, doctrine tends to explain the core tenets of a religion by clarifying its myths. Take, for example, the biblical myth about the expulsion of the two original human beings from the Garden of Eden because they disobeyed God (Genesis 3). Christianity interprets this story through its doctrine of original sin, which was developed in the writings of third- and fourth-century C.E. theologians. In effect this doctrine teaches that all human beings are born with the inherited sin of the first man and woman in the Garden of Eden. It explains why people do bad things, why there is human suffering in this world, and why there is a severed relationship between human beings and God. It also points to the Christian doctrine of salvation, which holds that Jesus died as a sacrifice for the sins of not only the first humans but all humankind.

Through a study of a group's *practices*, we can understand the performative aspects of a religion. Religious practices can take many forms, such as singing, dancing, praying, meditating, drawing, painting, writing, dreaming, bathing, walking, running, eating, fasting, having sex, not having sex, dressing in a particular way, working, begging, and so on. Religious practices are rooted in tradition and conducted according to custom. Religious practices can be performed in public or in private. *Ritual* is the name scholars give to a set of practices that is repeated over time, often for the purpose of symbolically retelling or reliving meaningful events in a religion's tradition. In many cases, rituals are carefully choreographed to coincide with a religion's myth, such as in the case of the hajj and the pilgrims who reenact aspects of the prophet Abraham's life.

Two integral aspects of religious practice are time and space. Scholars have long observed that many religious rituals are cyclical. For example, Jewish Passover, Christian Easter celebrations, Islam's month of fasting (Ramadan), and the Hindu Festival of Lights (Diwali) occur according to their respective calendars. Other rituals, such as the obligation to pray five times a day in Islam (*salah*), are daily practices that are linked to the position of the sun or the time of day. A number of religions, including Judaism, Christianity, Islam, and Theravada Buddhism, maintain weekly rest days, which are traditionally set aside for purification and contemplation. Based on observations of religious festivals and rituals, scholars such as Mircea Eliade have developed the concept of "sacred time" in order to distinguish it from ordinary, or profane, time. In sacred time, these scholars argue, religious people move from the routine of profane time into a time that enables them to perform their rituals.

Whether in temples, churches, mosques, prayer rooms, rice fields, tents, or cubicles in an office, religious practices take place in space. In some cases, mythic spaces become focal points for contemporary religious practices, including pilgrimages. For instance, Judaism regards the Temple Mount in the heart of Jerusalem as the holiest site on earth, because it was there, Jews believe, that God's presence dwelled at times in a series of temples that were eventually destroyed. Muslims, too, regard the Temple Mount/Noble Sanctuary as a holy site—it is home to the oldest Islamic building still standing, the Dome of the Rock, which was built in the late seventh century C.E. However, the holiest site in Islam is Mecca, the city where the Prophet Muhammad proclaimed Islam in the seventh century. It is home to the Ka'aba, the cube-shaped building that is the focal point for Muslims at prayer all around the world and the centre of the hajj circumambulation. Although perhaps not directly linked to a religion's myth, a local temple, church, or mosque provides formal spaces where religious practices can take place. Like mythic sites, these places typically have rules that govern the conduct of those who enter. On a smaller scale, there are also informal sites of religious practice that for a period of time become meaningful to religious people. These may be public spaces where someone, for example, stops to pray or meditate (a park, an office building, a shopping mall) or private spaces where someone has created a special place to perform individual rituals (e.g., a shrine or chapel in one's home).

The twofold task of the scholar studying religious practices is (1) to observe the performance, where it takes place, and when, and (2) to raise questions about the meaning it has for the individual and the community. Take, for instance, a young Jewish man living in a suburb of Montreal who decides to grow a beard. Is he letting his beard grow because he is following a Jewish tradition, which is based on a reading of scripture that forbids the shaving of the "corners of the head" (Leviticus 19:27), or is he growing a beard because of aesthetic preference? Unless we understand the context and the traditions, we are prone to misinterpret the practice and its significance.

Through the study of a *community* organized around religious discourses and practices, we can understand the social structures and boundaries for those inside the community. A study of a religious community might involve an examination of its gender roles, its understanding of the family, and its class structure. A study of a religion's social structure could focus on how and why some religions have divided into various **sects** or **denominations**. If we are interested in the politics of the community, we might examine the nature of religious authority within the community and how the community challenges that authority. Or we might ask questions about the role of religion in a country's political and governing structure.

Through a study of a group's *institutions*, we can encounter the ways in which religious discourse and practices take place and cohere around authoritative

Sect: the term has multiple meanings in religious studies and for this reason is often avoided by contemporary scholars. Traditionally it means a group that is opposed to and set apart from a recognized political or religious body. Some sociologists remain interested in the term because it enables them to examine groups that separate from other groups because they claim to be more authentic.

Denomination: a subgroup of a religion.

Gurdwara: a place of worship for Sikhs.

figures, offices, and leaders who are charged with nurturing and defending the community, its practices, and its modes of communication. Scholars sometimes make a distinction between formal institutions (e.g., a temple, a church, a mosque, a **gurdwara**, or a religious school) and informal institutions, which are socially constructed norms and customs that provide social order, even when they appear to contravene a religious doctrine. Studies of informal institutions typically concentrate on gender, family, civil society, informal governance, and emerging challenges to authority.

The Erawan Shrine in Bangkok, Thailand, situated in front of the Erawan Grand Hyatt Hotel in one of the city's busiest shopping districts. Amidst the commotion of a busy city, worshippers, both Thai and foreign, stop to pray at the shrine. The figure in shrine, Phra Phrom, is a Thai representation of the Hindu god Brahma. Despite Thailand's being a predominantly Buddhist country, the shrine remains an important site for many Thai citizens.

Source: © Piti Vedeer/Alamy

An Important Caveat Regarding Data

Now that we have stipulated a definition, we need to add one important caveat: *religion*, as an essence or a unique ethos, does not exist. Jonathan Smith explains:

> While there is a staggering amount of data, of phenomena, of human experiences and expressions that might be characterized in one culture or another, by one criterion or another, as religious, *there is no data for religion.* Religion is solely the creation of the scholar's study. It is created for the scholar's analytic purposes by his [or her] imaginative acts of comparison and generalization. Religion has no independent existence apart from the academy. For this reason, the student of religion . . . must be relentlessly self-conscious. Indeed, this self-consciousness constitutes [the student's] primary expertise, his [or her] foremost object of study (1982, xi).

The issue is not whether the data we study are authentic—people do indeed go to temple, church, and mosque, and some ground their actions in moral codes found in scripture and authoritative teachers. Rather, it is the category we use to classify and define these data that is in question. To put matters simply, *religion* is a category imposed by the religious studies scholar, from the outside, on aspects of a particular culture. The "outsider"—in this case, European explorers and Christian missionaries, colonial bureaucrats and merchants, as well as modern scholars from Europe and North America—is responsible for the term (Smith 1998, 269). *Religion* is therefore not a native category but a category created by the outsider to identify and classify characteristics of phenomena. As students of religion, then, we must recognize that our definitions of religion are always in flux and imperfect.

HOW DO WE STUDY RELIGION?

Religious studies scholars in North America share a common story about studying religion as graduate students. It goes something like this: We are somewhere (usually on an airplane or a bus or at a party) making small talk with someone we have never met, when suddenly our new acquaintance asks, "So, what is it you do?" For those of us who tell the truth and say, "I'm a grad student in religious studies," the conversation typically leads to the question "So, you're studying to be a minister or a priest, are you?" While this story is purely anecdotal, it nevertheless represents a prevalent misconception in North American society that associates religious studies with theological and pastoral training. For many North Americans, *religion* is something personal, it is something we do, so to study religion must inevitably mean that we

are "religious" and likely working toward a religious vocation such as pastor, priest, rabbi, or imam. But the academic study of religion does not mean that we must or even should identify with a particular religion. Nor does it imply that we aspire to be religious leaders. Rather, to engage in the academic study of religion means that we use scholarly methods to examine, classify, analyze, and explain phenomena that we call "religion."

Because religious studies is a subject field and not an academic discipline, there is no science or prescribed methodology directly associated with the study of religion. Instead the academic study of religion relies on methods used in disciplines such as sociology, anthropology, psychology, philosophy, history, and many more sub-disciplines, including archaeology, ethics, linguistics, gender studies, the sociology of knowledge, and ethnomusicology. Consequently, in many North American colleges and universities it is common for a religious studies program to be housed in either the anthropology or philosophy department, and perhaps called the department of anthropology (or philosophy) and religious studies.

In the United States, religious studies departments began to emerge as independent units within the university only in the late 1960s and 1970s. To create stand-alone departments of religious studies in publicly funded universities, scholars from the humanities and social sciences were often granted joint appointments in both their core discipline and the new department. These new departments of religious studies were secular (that is, non-theological) in orientation and consciously organized to teach the major world religions. To emphasize the cross-cultural nature of this new religious studies curriculum, some departments chose to describe their activities as studies in "comparative religion." Amidst the changing social norms of the late 1960s and 1970s, undergraduates flocked to courses on Buddhism, Hinduism, and new religious movements such as the International Society for Krishna Consciousness (ISKCON, or the "Hare Krishnas"), the Jesus movement, and various "hippy" intentional communities.

Unlike the situation in the United States, where the doctrine of **separation of church and state** means that theology was never welcomed in publicly funded universities, in Canada a number of Canadian universities maintain either links to or their own theology faculties and departments. Much like privately funded universities in the United States, such as Harvard, Yale, and Princeton, many Canadian universities owe their existence to previously existing church schools. Moreover, a number of large research universities have agreements with smaller theological colleges to provide training to students seeking a vocation in the church. While courses in theology continue to exist in many of Canada's universities, since the early 1970s the vast majority of the courses offered in religious studies departments are not theologically oriented and do not assume any type of faith commitment on the part of the student.

Whether in the United States or in Canada, students taking religious studies courses will most likely encounter not just one approach to the study but several. Let's highlight a few of the most widely used approaches.

Separation of church and state: a phrase first used by Thomas Jefferson (1743–1826) in 1802 to describe the "freedom of religion" and "non-establishment" clauses in the First Amendment of the U.S. Constitution. The Supreme Court of the United States affirmed this separation in 1878 and in a series of rulings beginning in 1947, leading to it becoming "settled law."

Ontology: the branch of philosophy that studies being, existence, and reality.

Epistemology: a branch of philosophy that is concerned with knowledge and ways of knowing.

Philosophical Approaches

Philosophical approaches to the study of religion use reason to engage with central areas of belief, claims about truth, and the human capacity to construct systems of logic and meaning. Philosophers of religion are typically not interested in social and cultural conceptions of religion. Rather, they attempt to think about questions of meaning and value without resorting to a faith perspective or relying on a faith community. Following the Greek philosopher Plato, many philosophers of religion have, over the years, asked metaphysical questions—that is, questions about non-physical, non-scientific things: Does God exist? How does one speak about God? What is the nature of ultimate meaning? Philosophers of religion often focus on one branch of philosophy called **ontology**, which is the investigation of the nature of being, existence, and reality. Philosophers of religion have also been interested in questions of **epistemology**, which focus on knowledge, how we acquire knowledge, and how we know.

In the Western tradition, philosophy and theology have long worked in conjunction with each other. From the second to the sixteenth century C.E., philosophy and theology were complementary methods of thinking about truth. Jewish, Christian, and Muslim thinkers mounted sophisticated philosophical arguments to uphold the basic tenets of their respective religious beliefs. Toward the end of the Middle Ages, for example, Jewish, Christian, and Muslim thinkers used the Greek philosopher Aristotle's (384–322 B.C.E.) philosophical system to revitalize their respective religious traditions.

Agnosticism: the belief that human beings cannot know whether or not God exists.

Middle Ages: the period in European history between the fifth and fifteenth centuries C.E.

The famous Jewish scholar Maimonides (1138–1204) refashioned Aristotle's philosophical framework to develop arguments on a wide array of topics, from the nature of God's relationship with humanity to the problem of evil. Thomas Aquinas (1225–74) adapted Aristotle's philosophy to develop a comprehensive guide for Christian thought called the *Summa Theologica*. And perhaps the most important Aristotelian thinker of the Middle Ages was the Islamic philosopher Averroes (1126–98; his Arabic name was Ibn Rushd), who is often credited with reintroducing Aristotle into Western philosophy and setting in motion the European Renaissance in the fifteenth century.

By the seventeenth century and the Age of Reason, philosophers had started to distance themselves from theological claims. During this time, two general schools of thought began to emerge: the rationalists and the empiricists. The rationalists argued that, in principle, all knowledge could be gained by the power of human reason alone. In contrast, the empiricists argued that all knowledge had to come through the senses, from experience, which meant a reliance on the physical sciences. The German philosopher Immanuel Kant (1724–1804) attempted to strike a compromise between the rationalists and the empiricists. Kant concluded that using reason without applying it to experience would lead only to illusion, while resorting to experience without first subsuming it to reason would lead only to pure subjectivism. This conclusion could be applied to God's existence as well. In Kant's view, even though we might believe that there is a God, it is impossible to maintain a rational argument for the existence of God. The only viable philosophical position, then, is **agnosticism**; that is to say, we simply do not and cannot know if God actually exists. At the core of Kant's philosophy is the human subject who has thrown off the shackles of "self-incurred tutelage" and begun to think as an autonomous (self-legislating), modern human being. Kant's famous dictum sums up not only his philosophy but also much of philosophy after the

Enlightenment: "*Sapere aude!* Have the courage to make use of your own intellect!" (1991, 54).

Modern analytic philosophy, with its agnostic premises, has tended to focus on the logic and meaning of religious language, including the ways in which religious language generates claims about knowledge and truth. For instance, when someone says, "God loves us," what kind of language is that—a statement of fact or an assertion? For some philosophers, this type of statement cannot be a statement of fact because it is not falsifiable; in other words, it is equally possible to claim that God hates us. While many might believe the statement "God loves us" to be true, from a philosophical perspective the statement is an assertion, rooted perhaps in emotion or illusion. Other philosophers, however, make the argument that such methods of language analysis fail to account for the variety of ways in which knowledge and truth are generated through various discourses. Influenced by European social philosophers such as Michel Foucault (1926–84) and Jürgen Habermas (b. 1929), these philosophers attempt to show that truth is determined by the structures of knowledge and meaning in a particular discourse, whether it is scientific, political, artistic, religious, medical, economic, or moral discourse. This project often takes the form of a genealogy that accounts for the historical forces—many of which were contradictory—that helped generate knowledge and the authoritative discourses that legitimate "truth." While this genealogical approach to the study of religion is philosophical in orientation, many anthropologists, sociologists, historians, and other scholars also engage in this type of historical deconstruction.

Theological Approaches

The term *theology* comes from two Greek words: *theos*, which means "god" or "gods," and *logos*, which means "speech" or "inquiry." Plato used the term *theologia* to describe the rational study of the divine, and contrasted theology with poetic stories about the gods. The early Christian church, under Plato's influence, adapted the term to refer to the biblical account of God's relationship with humanity. Prior to the creation of universities in the eleventh century, theology was closely associated with the activities of Christian monasteries and cathedral schools, which trained young men for the clergy. By the **Middle Ages**, however, *theology* had taken on a narrower meaning. Theology had become a discipline of study in Europe's newly created universities and it competed with the disciplines of law and philosophy for the best students. Between the eleventh and sixteenth centuries, the term *scholasticism* (from a Latin word meaning "that which belongs to the school") was often used to describe the type of theology that was taught in European universities. One classic definition of theology took shape during this period through the work of the Benedictine monk and early "scholastic" Anselm of Canterbury (1033–1109): theology, he argued, is "faith seeking understanding" (in Latin, *fides quaerens intellectum*). Theology continued to be a mainstay of European universities until the late 1960s, when students began to become interested in comparative religion and the social sciences.

The inclusion of theology as a legitimate academic approach to the study of religion has been a topic of intense debate within the field of religious studies since its inception in the 1960s. One objection is that theology presumes that the study of religion is the study of God or gods, which, as we discovered earlier in this chapter, would effectively exclude religions that either have no gods or do not place much importance in deities. Another objection is that many religions, including Judaism and many religions of India, do not conceive of their intellectual heritage in theological terms. Many Jewish scholars, in fact, are quite reluctant to use the term *theology*: it seems to presuppose that human beings can know about the inner life of **G-d**, which according to some Jewish thinkers verges on idolatry. And perhaps the most common objection is that theology is merely a Christian interpretive framework that is ultimately accessible only by "insiders"—that is, by Christians—who must adhere to the tenets of their theological tradition.

In response to the first two objections, many theologians freely admit that the study of theology is not intended to be a framework universally applicable to understanding all religions. But in some instances theological engagement with another religion can provide important insight into both Christianity and the other religion. Gregory Baum, for example, in his book *The Theology of Tariq Ramadan: A Catholic Perspective* (2009), provides an accessible introduction to a contemporary Islamic reform movement led by Tariq Ramadan, which he then compares with modern reform movements within the Catholic Church. This type of scholarship, which seeks to understand a

> **G-d:** the term often used by Jewish writers who believe it is wrong to write the name of their deity.

particular faith in theological dialogue with another religious tradition, is called *comparative theology* and is often associated with *inter-religious dialogue*.

In response to the third objection, defenders of theological approaches point out that there are many different types of theology. Generally these types fall into two broad categories: a sectarian theology that is accessible only to insiders and an academic theology that is open to critical examination by all. *Sectarian theology* is aimed at promoting and transmitting doctrine to like-minded believers. This type presumes that everyone undertaking a study of theology is either already associated with the particular religious group (sometimes termed a *denomination*) or is seeking to become a member. For this reason, sectarian theology is found exclusively in seminaries and church-related colleges in the United States and Canada. By contrast, *academic theology* adheres to the scholarly conventions of the modern university by ensuring that theological examination is open to everyone, that no conclusion can be based on privileged beliefs, and that all conclusions are subject to critical examination.

Sociological Approaches

The sociology of religion considers religion to be a social institution that exists alongside the economy, government, health care, education, and other social institutions. Taken as a whole, these institutions give structure to society and transmit meaning that becomes deeply interwoven with a group's collective identity and self-understanding. The earliest sociologists—Émile Durkheim and Max Weber (1864–1920)—were particularly interested in studying religion because they saw how foundational religion was to the social, political, and economic changes taking place in nineteenth-century Europe.

Durkheim's understanding of history and humanity is based on a theory of social order that brings human beings together through political, moral, and religious activities. According to Durkheim, social behaviour involves people acting as both physical and social beings. Physically, humans act on egoistic (self-interested) needs and desires. Socially, humans construct a social order to govern those egoistic needs and desires. The primary task of the social order, then, is to socialize individuals to conform to the group's norms. A social order provides cohesion when people share the same moral beliefs and worldviews and when these moral beliefs and worldviews are reinforced by collective rituals and symbols. According to Durkheim, religion is the prototypical institution that generates and cultivates the rituals and symbols that continually reaffirm a society's moral beliefs and categories of knowledge. Religion does all of this by separating phenomena into two categories: the sacred and the profane.

In his book *The Elementary Forms of Religious Life* (1912), Durkheim famously argues that the origins of religion are located in totemic religion. Using the Aboriginal people of Australia as his case study, Durkheim observed that the totemic animal functioned as an emblem for the clan, and as the representation of all that was good about the clan, the totemic animal had to be treated as sacred. To harm or to mistreat the totem was therefore often perceived by the clan's leaders as a rejection of social norms, which meant wrongdoers had to undergo some form of rehabilitation or punishment. In more complex societies, Durkheim concludes, religion will likely not be the institution that conveys and nurtures social norms; that role will fall instead to politics, economics, and especially science. In Durkheim's

social theory, the waning of religion in modern societies is cause for neither celebration nor lament, for all societies develop and adapt institutions over time to provide social stability. Any differences between religion and other social institutions are, Durkheim believes, only a matter of degree and not a matter of type. For Durkheim, every institution that provides social cohesion functions in the same basic way, but religion remains an important element in society because it is, foundationally, the institution that unites people, links them to their common history, and strengthens their collective identity.

Max Weber, unlike Durkheim, was not particularly interested in the role of religion in social alienation or in religion's capacity to provide social order and integration. Instead Weber sought to understand and explain the foundations of Western society's regulatory structures by focusing on the situations and decisions facing social actors in specific contexts. For Weber, modern societies had become overregulated, not underregulated, as Durkheim contended. There were, Weber observed, fewer and fewer spaces in society for people to act outside the dominant principles of efficiency, institutional control, and management—that is, the very same principles that fostered industrial and political bureaucracy. In the modern age of bureaucracy, people found it increasingly difficult to act with integrity and

Jacob Zuma, president of South Africa, and his fifth wife, Thobeka Madiba, celebrate their marriage in a traditional Zulu ceremony. According to Émile Durkheim, religious gatherings provide social cohesion and group identity.

Source: AFP/Getty Images

to take responsibility for decisions that directly affected their lives. Modern bureaucracy had, in effect, become a system of external control. On the specific issue of religion in the modern society, Weber argued that if religion were going to survive in modern society, it would have to become bureaucratic and eventually follow the logic of efficiency, performance, and usefulness.

While Weber's work on bureaucracy is an important topic, students of religion are usually better acquainted with his classic study of the relationship between Christianity and capitalism, titled *The Protestant Ethic and the Spirit of Capitalism* (1905). Weber observes that capitalism in northern Europe in the eighteenth century emerged as Protestant Christianity taught people about the virtues of hard work and financial planning. Whereas the Catholic Church taught that only the clergy and those who belonged to religious orders were fulfilling a vocational calling, the Protestant churches told the faithful that work in the secular world was in fact a vocation ordained by God. The values of hard work, coupled with secular jobs that were divinely sanctioned, provided capitalism with a labour force and a cultural spirit that enabled capitalism to flourish. Weber surmised that the religious aspects of capitalism were eventually discarded, but not before Western society had undergone a rationalization process that, with the unwitting help of the Protestant churches, had turned individuals into self-interested maximizers of their utilities and justified the economic structure of modern society.

The work of Durkheim and Weber continues to guide sociologists as they consider contemporary issues such as secularization, civil religion, multiculturalism, religion and nationalism, religious violence, and implicit (or invisible) religion.

Anthropological Approaches

Anthropology is the systematic study of the origins, development, customs, and beliefs associated with human culture. As a social science, anthropology has much in common with sociology. Like Durkheim and Weber, the earliest anthropologists studied religions as human creations and not as divinely inspired or essentially truthful phenomena. One early anthropologist was E. B. Tylor, who hypothesized that humanity had developed the concepts of the soul and the spirit, as well as spiritual beings, to explain non-rational experiences such as dreams, trances, and hallucinations. Influenced by

> **Monotheism:** belief in one god.
>
> **Etic:** analysis of cultural phenomena from the perspective of one who does not participate in the culture being studied.
>
> **Emic:** analysis of cultural phenomena from the perspective of one who participates in the culture being studied.

the evolutionary thought of the late nineteenth century, Tylor theorized that the most basic form of religion was animism, an original form of religion that ascribed spiritual characteristics to natural phenomena such as trees, oceans, and mountains. Tylor further postulated that the basic spiritualism of animism was eventually replaced by polytheism and **monotheism** in higher-order peoples. For Tylor there was a "psychic unity of humankind" that linked primitive peoples to their more highly developed relatives. This perceived unity and his preoccupation with discovering the origins of religion led Tylor to develop a cross-cultural approach to anthropology that was closely shared by another British anthropologist, James Frazer, author of the widely read *The Golden Bough* (1890).

Among contemporary scholars of religion, the most widely read anthropologist is Clifford Geertz, whose essay "Religion as a Cultural System," published in 1966, remains requisite reading in many comparative religion courses in North American and European universities. For Geertz, religion is a complex cultural system that maintains symbols for the purpose of establishing moods and motivations in people, leading to what he called a "worldview." According to Geertz, this cultural system constitutes an inner world of emotions and sentiments that, when bound together through commonly shared symbols and ritual practices, creates the phenomenon "religion." Following Max Weber's method of "understanding" (*Verstehen*), Geertz thinks that the anthropologist's primary task is to understand completely the symbol system of a particular culture in order to gain access to the group's cultural actors. For Geertz this means that anthropologists should provide a "thick description"—that is, an interpretation of the indigenous actors' own perceptions and interpretations of events, based on the scholar's empirical knowledge. Geertz's method marks a change in anthropology from **etic** approaches, which examine culture from the outside and use broader principles, to **emic** approaches,

> **Collective unconscious:** a part of the unconscious mind, it is manifested in similar forms (archetypes) in all humanity because the human psyche organizes experiences in similar ways.
>
> **Archetype:** an innate form of expression generated by the collective unconscious, it is a base or proto-typical idea (e.g., the hero, the trickster, spatial representations such as wheels).

which examine culture from the inside using categories generated from scholarly engagement with the culture.

Geertz's legacy in the subfield of anthropology of religion is open to much debate. Anthropologists such as Talal Asad (b. 1932) have criticized Geertz for presuming that religion maintains an autonomous essence that remains unaffected by political and economic discourses. Others have targeted Geertz for blurring traditional methodological lines in anthropology between ethnography, which entails empirical qualitative research on a particular culture and people through fieldwork and participant observation, and ethnology, which tends to focus on theoretical and historical interpretations.

Psychological Approaches

Psychology is the study of mental functions and their relationship to both individual and social behaviours. As an academic discipline, psychology is relatively new. Many of the pioneers of psychology were philosophers, including William James (1842–1910), the first person to teach a course in psychology in the United States, at Harvard University in 1875. James was particularly interested in religion, and by the time his book *Varieties of Religious Experience* appeared in 1902, he was already a widely respected philosopher of religion. In this first extensive study of religion from a psychological approach, James identified two broad types of religion: institutional and personal. *Institutional religion* refers to a religious group or organization that plays an important role in a society's culture. *Personal religion*, which is characterized by an individual's having a mystical experience, can be experienced regardless of the culture. James was most interested in personal religion because he believed the mystical experience provided the purest access to the structure of the mind. For James, then, the proper object of study was not the social, the cultural, or even the institutional aspects of religion but rather

the "religious genius" (or religious experience) that provided the foundations for social and cultural movements. James subdivided the religious experience into two types: the "healthy-minded" and the "sick-souled." The healthy-minded maintained a generally optimistic outlook on life and excluded the category of evil, while the sick-souled retained evil as a central category. James believed that, while the healthy-minded worked in limited circumstances, the sick-souled was ultimately the experience that would most adequately account for life in the real world, where bad things do happen.

The psychoanalytic theories of Sigmund Freud and Carl Jung (1875–1961) were quite popular in religious studies throughout much of the twentieth century. Freud famously argued that religion is simply a projection of unconscious wants and desires. Moreover, religion sublimates or redirects psychic energy and anxiety into socially acceptable behaviours. It thus acts as a regulatory device that enables individuals to function in a society that is, Freud asserted, itself repressed and largely dysfunctional. At the root of this dysfunction, on both an individual and a social level, was the unwillingness of people to confront their parental relationships. Freud believed that lingering anxieties and guilt stemming from these unexamined relationships were manifested in primitive humans through the creation of gods, which functioned as supernatural parents. Religion continues, Freud theorized, because people need to feel secure and wanted, and religion provides the necessary illusion to alleviate unconscious anxiety and guilt. But, of course, Freud did not believe that religion provided the antidote to fear, anxiety, and guilt. On the contrary, he thought religion was a primary contributor to human pathology. For true liberation, people had to outgrow their infantile reliance on religion and face reality squarely.

Carl Jung, one of Freud's students, criticized Freud for focusing too much on repressed childhood experiences with parents and negative sexual experiences. Instead, Jung postulated that the unconscious mind is a repository of human creativity that was generated from a shared **collective unconscious**. Jung believed that the unconscious contains, among other things, **archetypes** (or recurring patterns) that enable the human ego to find itself in relation to the collective unconscious. There is, Jung thought, a process of discovery that each individual must undergo in order to achieve a sense of self—the *self* being one of the most important archetypes in Jung's theory. Through a three-stage process that corresponds with infancy, adolescence, and adulthood, individuals are eventually able to integrate their psychic weaknesses with their strengths. In Jung's theory, religious symbols play an integral role in achieving a healthy balance because they deflect any totalizing—and thus potentially destructive—tendencies in the unconscious. These symbols, which often take the form of spirits or gods, provide direction and meaning as we work through the anxieties of life and death.

Since the late 1940s, psychoanalytic studies of religion have given way to methods that are more in keeping with the empirical approaches found in contemporary psychology labs and departments. For instance, Gordon Allport (1897–1967) developed the Religious Orientation Scale to determine the various psychological dimensions of religious practice. Allport suggested that there are two types of religion: (1) intrinsic religion, which displays characteristics of deeply held faith and devotion, and (2) extrinsic religion, which displays characteristics of utilitarian manipulation such as attending church or a temple to gain social status. Daniel Batson challenged Allport's binary distinction of intrinsic and extrinsic religion by adding a third orientation, the quest, which allows for acceptance of doubt and critical questioning on the part of the subject. According to Batson, the Quest Scale permits scholars to understand the complexity of religious motivation of subjects because it provides an open-ended, active approach to existential questions and rejects pat answers that may be categorized easily as either intrinsic or extrinsic religion.

Current research in the psychology of religion continues to be predominantly empirical. Major topics include social control, the relationship between emotions and spirituality, and personality traits associated with traditional theological concepts such as virtue, humility, and forgiveness (Emmons and Paloutzian 2003).

Phenomenological Approaches

Phenomenological approaches to the study of religion have their foundations in a nineteenth-century philosophical movement that focused on data (phenomena) that could be presented to and experienced by human consciousness. These phenomenologists were not interested in explaining experiences or phenomena by using sociological, anthropological, or psychological frameworks. Instead they advocated for robust descriptions of data. They thought that scholars had to suspend their personal judgments about matters under consideration and, furthermore, that any attempts to explain the "truth" of data philosophically or theologically had to be bracketed out of the inquiry. This approach to philosophy was aptly named after the Greek word *phainomenon*, which means "that which appears."

While the phenomenology of religion is related to these nineteenth-century philosophers (Flood 1999), contemporary phenomenological approaches to the study of religion are more closely associated with the work of two scholars, Mircea Eliade (1907–86) and Ninian Smart (1927–2001). For Eliade and many other phenomenologists of religion, religion is irreducible: it exists *sui generis*. Because it is *sui generis*, religion is unlike any other social institution or experience. Assessments about the truth or reality of religious claims—such as the existence of God, the emancipation of human suffering in nirvana, or the healing power of a shaman—must be avoided, Eliade argued, since the truth of the truth and reality of these claims is essentially embedded in the

Four mandalas of the Vajravali series, c. 1429–56, central Tibet. According to Jungian scholars of religion, a mandala (from the Sanskrit, meaning "circle" or "sacred circle") is an archetypical symbol of wholeness.

Source: Kimbell Art Museum, Fort Worth, Texas/Art Resource, NY

Religionswissenschaft: from the German meaning "study of religion" or "science of religion." Most often translated into English as "history of religions," it is commonly associated with the work of Mircea Eliade.

phenomenon. As a result, Eliade wanted to study only the public forms or manifestations of religion's essence. This pursuit of studying the essence of religion led to volumes on comparative religion. Eliade focused on stories of birth and rebirth, belief systems that geographically divided space into sacred and profane spheres, and instances where the "holy" broke into the historical world and linked together all of reality.

Eliade's insistence that religion was *sui generis* helped create a school of thought within the field of religious studies called **Religionswissenschaft**, a German term meaning "study of religion," but most often translated as "history of religions." The main methodological characteristic of the "history of religions" school is that scholars must both bracket any preconceived notions about the phenomena being studied and at the same time empathize with their subjects.

Ninian Smart's approach to religious studies is, in comparison to Eliade's, considerably more modest. Although a phenomenologist, Smart was not particularly concerned with establishing a school of thought or even developing a grand theory to situate all religious phenomena. Rather, he often employed basic historical methods, which also relied on rigorous descriptions, to chronicle the characteristics of phenomena commonly called "religion." To help categorize these phenomena, he devised the "dimension theory" of religion, which identified aspects (or family resemblances) among the world's religions. Smart's seven dimensions of religion are

- **Doctrinal and philosophical:** the systematic formulation of religious teachings in a systematic form.
- **Mythical and narrative:** the stories, which are often in the forms of revelation, that communicate meaning and concepts that are integral to the religious community.
- **Ethical and legal:** the moral customs and legal rules that regulate human behaviour in a group and in many cases are regarded as revealed.
- **Ritual:** the forms and orders of religious ceremonies, which may be public or private and in many cases are regarded as revealed.

- **Experiential:** the private emotions of group members, including feelings of awe, guilt, ecstasy, bliss, mystery, love, and liberation.
- **Institutional:** the social frameworks and belief systems practised by a group and often the bases for determining community identity and membership.
- **Material:** ordinary objects or places that have become sacred or supernatural, either symbolically or manifestly.

These seven dimensions connect to each other, Smart argued, to form a multidimensional organism. For Smart the study of religion was a fine balance between objective scientific method and subjective participation. This perspective led him to the conclusion that the study of religion is a "human science" because it involves a careful, rational, and verifiable method that recognizes data derived from both impartial observation of sensory experience (objective phenomena) and impartial observation of psychological experience (subjective phenomena). In other words, Smart believed that the study of religion is not simply a science corresponding to its objects but a science that takes into account the inner feelings and attitudes of religious peoples, for without these subjective experiences, understanding human life and activities is simply impossible.

Phenomenological approaches to religion are among the most widely used in the field of religious studies. This is due in part to the enormous influence that Eliade and Smart had on students for nearly thirty years. In spite of phenomenology's success, however, these approaches have faced serious challenges. For instance, critics who tend to favour empirical methods often charge phenomenology of religion with lacking scholarly rigour. They argue that phenomenology is unscientific because scholars (a) enter into their study with predetermined assumptions about the data they are looking for, and (b) interpret the phenomena based on subjective participation, including intuition. Moreover, many critics, especially those who are concerned with the roles of gender, race, class, and nationality in scholarship, contend that phenomenological approaches do not pay adequate attention to the biases of the scholar and the assumptions built into phenomenological approaches. It is these biases, they charge, that lead many North American phenomenologists to claim that there are universal structures, ways of being, and essences common to all religions.

Some Important Scholars of Religious Studies

Friedrich Schleiermacher (1768–1834)—a German theologian who defined religion essentially as "a feeling of absolute dependence."

Karl Marx (1818–83)—a German social theorist who thought the bourgeoisie used religion to serve their own interests by politically immobilizing the proletariat with the "opium of the masses."

Sigmund Freud (1856–1939)—the founder of psychoanalysis, who believed religion is an illusion we humans create to help us cope with feelings of weakness, anxiety, and unworthiness.

Émile Durkheim (1858–1917)—a founder of modern sociology who thought religion provides cohesion, group identity, and a moral framework for societies.

Max Weber (1864–1920)—a German sociologist who sought to understand the causes of human behaviour by examining how people's beliefs and ideas affect actions.

Rudolf Otto (1869–1937)—a German theologian who defined religion as "the holy," a non-rational mystery that is both terrifying and fascinating.

Paul Tillich (1888–1965)—a theologian who defined religion as "ultimate concern."

Sarvepalli Radhakrishnan (1888–1975)—president of India from 1962 to 1967 and a scholar of religion who attempted to make "Hinduism" intelligible to Western audiences.

Mircea Eliade (1907–86)—founder of the "history of religions" school at the University of Chicago and the most significant scholar of the late twentieth century to argue that religion is *sui generis*, that is, unique.

Wilfred Cantwell Smith (1916–2000)—a Canadian scholar who helped develop the idea of world religious traditions and who understood religion as essentially an inner experience.

Clifford Geertz (1926–2006)—a American anthropologist whose best-known work, "Religion as a Cultural System" (1966), provided the field of religious studies with a definition of religion for more than a generation.

Ninian Smart (1927–2001)—a scholar who popularized a phenomenological approach to the study of religion and who, beginning in the 1960s, helped establish departments of religious studies in the United Kingdom and the United States.

Talal Asad (b. 1932)—a postcolonial anthropologist who is critical of European assumptions built into established approaches to the study of religion.

Jonathan Z. Smith (b. 1938)—an American scholar who has published on a wide range of subjects, including approaches to the study of religion.

Wendy Doniger (b. 1940)—Mircea Eliade Distinguished Service Professor of the History of Religions at the University of Chicago and a scholar specializing in the religions of India, religious myth, and ritual.

Diana Eck (b. 1945)—director of the Pluralism Project at Harvard University and a scholar known for her humanistic approach to religion and interreligious dialogue.

Amina Wadud (b. 1952)—an American-born Islamic scholar and imam who takes a feminist approach to readings of the Qur'an.

Tariq Ramadan (b. 1962)—a Swiss-born public intellectual who advocates for a politically responsible form of Islam that engages in dialogue with the cultures where Muslims reside.

"Other" Approaches

As with most academic fields, historically the field of religious studies has been dominated by white North American and European men of economic means.

While there certainly remains a great deal of male white privilege, since the late 1960s important movements in the academy, and particularly in the field of religious studies, have sought not only to include marginalized voices in course curricula but also to

> **Feminism:** a political, cultural, and economic movement as well as a critical framework aimed at the liberation of women from structures and situations of injustice.
>
> **Postcolonial:** a broad approach to academic study that examines and critiques the lasting effects of colonialism on people who were colonized.
>
> **Orientalist:** an increasingly outdated term for one who studies the cultures and peoples of "the East." *Orientalism* is the term used by Edward Said to describe an inherent bias in Western scholarship that assumes an imperial view of the world.

maintain faculty who have been historically marginalized because of gender, race, class, or nationality. These were the people and perspectives often objectified in scholarship as "the other"—that is, they were either objects of study or simply overlooked. Today, however, these "other" voices are revitalizing religious studies scholarship and playing integral roles in reshaping religious studies programs. For the most part these "other" approaches are not rooted in discrete methodologies such as sociology, anthropology, or psychology. Rather, they are integrated into virtually all aspects of religious studies, and particularly into the areas of philosophy, theology, sociology, anthropology, and psychology.

For example, **feminism**-based approaches to the study of religion attempt to overcome androcentric (male-centred) scholarship by advocating for gender-balanced and gender-inclusive scholarship. Feminist scholars reject the notion that scientific studies of religion emanating from the social sciences were truly objective or neutral, for the simple reason that they normally overlooked the role of women in society and women's experiences. One way to correct the androcentrism is to reexamine both the methodologies and the data in order to recover once-lost women's perspectives. Feminist scholars typically argue that it is possible to have a normative perspective—such as the equality of women—and yet remain relatively objective within a certain methodology. Claims of absolute neutrality and objectivity simply do not hold up to scrutiny, since a scholar always maintains a perspective. For this reason, feminist scholars of religion attempt to adhere to the scholarly protocols of a particular approach while at the same balancing the view that women

should not be underrepresented in research or in the academy. Another way to correct the androcentrism is to mount courses focusing on women in religion. As Rita Gross notes in her book *Feminism and Religion* (1996), one ironic, if not ill-informed, response to courses on women in religion is that they are biased because they include more information about women than men. "But," Gross contends, "these kinds of claims only mask a desire to hear familiar perspectives and emphases, a wish that assumptions that have been taken for granted should not be challenged" (15).

Postcolonial approaches to the study of religion are also raising penetrating questions about who and what has been historically included or excluded in the study of religion. More specifically, postcolonial scholars seek to identify and analyze the social, political, economic, and cultural practices that arise in response to and resistance to colonialism. They argue that, in spite of the widespread political decolonization of Africa, Latin America, the Caribbean, and parts of Southeast Asia in the twentieth century, vestiges of colonialism remain firmly embedded in the logic systems of modern institutions, including the academy and the study of religion. Postcolonial scholars often cite the work of Frantz Fanon (1925–61), who in his book *The Wretched of the Earth* (1961) explored the psychological and social effects of colonization on the people of Algeria. Another important figure in the development of postcolonial theory was Edward Said (1935–2003), who in his book *Orientalism* (1978) highlighted the ways social scientists, specifically **Orientalists** (Western scholars who study Eastern cultures), have disregarded the views of those they actually study. Said wrote:

> To the extent that Western scholars were aware of contemporary Orientals or Oriental movements of thought and culture, these were perceived either as silent shadows to be animated by the Orientalist, brought into reality by them, or as a kind of cultural and international proletariat useful for the Orientalist's grander interpretive activity. (208)

In the broad field of religious studies, Talal Asad is one of the leading figures bringing postcolonial critiques to bear on approaches to the study of religion. As we discovered earlier in this chapter, Asad has raised serious questions about the structural biases and unexamined privileges embedded in the field of religious studies,

Mohandas K. Gandhi (1869–1948) on the Salt March, 1930. Gandhi's leadership in India's overthrowing of British colonial rule inspired anti-colonial struggles in Africa and Southeast Asia, as well as black civil rights struggles in the United States.

Source: Time & Life Pictures/ Getty Images

especially in the subfield of anthropology of religion. A new generation of postcolonial scholars has begun to investigate specific cases of secular modernity in postcolonial societies such as Egypt, Turkey, South Africa, India, and Pakistan. Scholars who study the Aboriginal peoples of the Americas, Australia, and other regions may also identify themselves as postcolonial theorists. On the whole, the postcolonial scholars often focus their attention on issues of gender, class, and the formation of the human subject within a colonial and postcolonial context.

"Other" approaches that have begun to take hold in the field of religious studies also include studies that concentrate on the plight of the poor in a society: lesbian, gay, bisexual, transsexual, and queer (LGBTQ) people, and persons with disabilities. While feminist and postcolonial approaches and those that focus on the economically oppressed, LGBTQ people, and persons with disabilities are not identical, they do share certain critical perspectives in response to the imposition of categories and methods of study that are not only inappropriate but also complicit in the further marginalization of women, the colonized, the poor, lesbians, gays, bisexuals, transsexuals, queers, and persons with disabilities. At a minimum, these scholars share a basic belief that all students of religion, whether senior professors or students in a class on introductory religious studies, should be critically aware of the "other" and their relationship to the "other" as they engage in cultures, societies, and religions that are not their own.

CONCLUSION

At the outset you may have wondered why a text on world religions would begin with a chapter on the study of religion. Would it not be more interesting to jump right into an examination of a specific religion? Indeed, we recognize that you are reading this text because you want to learn something about the world's religions. However, now that you are at the conclusion of this chapter, we hope you understand that learning about the world's religions first requires a basic grasp of the definitions, concepts, and scholarly approaches used in the field.

As a student of religious studies, you are entering into a network of conversations that includes prior scholars, contemporary scholars, and your fellow students. To help you enter that network, this chapter has attempted to identify a number of the primary conversations taking place within the field, the terms used in those conversations, the general approaches or ways of speaking used by scholars, and certain critical challenges to the dominant ways of studying religion.

As you begin to examine specific religions in this text, the tendency will no doubt be to forget about some of the issues raised in this chapter. To help you avoid this, we encourage you to draw on our definition of religion to ask questions about a religion's ways of communicating, its ritual practices, its communal bonds, and its institutional structures. Use the key terms we highlighted in this chapter. Consider

how various scholarly approaches to the study of religion might affect our understanding of the religion we are examining. Raise questions about how issues such as gender, race, class, ethnicity, and other marginalizing factors play out in a religion and in our understanding of that religion. In short, build on the material in this chapter to develop your critical thinking skills.

KEY TERMS

Agnosticism, p. 18
Analects of Confucius, p. 5
Animism, p. 6
Archetype, p. 22
Before the Common Era (B.C.E.), p. 13
Bhagavad-Gita, p. 5
Catholic, p. 3
Common Era (C.E.), p. 1
Circumambulation, p. 2
Collective unconscious, p. 22
Deity, p. 12
Denomination, p. 15
Doctrine, p. 13
Emic, p. 21
Epistemology, p. 17
Etic, p. 21
Faith, p. 4
Feminism, p. 26
Fetishism, p. 6
Functional definitions of religion, p. 9
G-d, p. 19
Gurdwara, p. 15
Hajj, p. 2
Homo religiosus, p. 9
Idolatry, p. 4
Magic, p. 6
Middle Ages, p. 18
Moksha, p. 9

Monotheism, p. 21
Myth, p. 13
Natural religion, p. 5
Naturalistic religion, p. 6
Nirvana, p. 9
Ontology, p. 17
Orientalist, p. 26
Paganism, p. 5
Pali canon, p. 5
Piety, p. 4
Polytheism, p. 7
Postcolonial, p. 26
Proselytization, p. 7
Religionswissenschaft, p. 24
Religious orders, p. 3
Rig-Veda, p. 5
Ritual, p. 4
Sacred, p. 8
Sect, p. 15
Separation of church and state, p. 17
Shamanism, p. 6
Substantive definitions of religion, p. 8
Sui generis, p. 8
Supernatural religion, p. 6
Suprahuman, p. 13
Theism, p. 13
Totemism, p. 6
Virtue, p. 4

CRITICAL THINKING QUESTIONS

1. Do you think it is possible for a scholar to engage in an objective study of religion? Is an objective study even desirable?

2. If you were to stipulate a definition of religion, what would it be? What would be the strengths and weaknesses of this definition?

3. What does it mean when we say that the field of religious studies is interdisciplinary?

4. If you were to invent a religion, what would it include? On what sources would you draw to invent your religion?

5. How have issues such as gender, race, class, and ethnicity affected the study of religion?

RECOMMENDED READING

Braun, Willi, and Russell T. McCutcheon, eds. *Introducing Religion: Essays in Honor of Jonathan Z. Smith*. London: Equinox Press, 2009.

McCutcheon, Russell T., ed. *The Insider/Outsider Problem in the Study of Religion: A Reader*. London: Cassell, 1999.

———. *Studying Religion: An Introduction*. London: Equinox Press, 2007.

Peach, Lucinda. *Women and World Religions*. Upper Saddle River, NJ: Prentice Hall, 2001.

Segal, Robert A. *Blackwell Companion to the Study of Religion*, new ed. London: Wiley-Blackwell, 2008.

Stausberg, Michael, ed. *Theories of Religion: A Critical Companion*. New York: Routledge, 2009.

USEFUL WEBSITES

American Academy of Religion:
An association of more than 10,000 teachers and scholars of religion.

Canadian Society for the Study of Religion:
Dedicated to interdisciplinary and critical research into religion.

The Pluralism Project at Harvard University:
Conducts research into the diverse religions present in
the United States and their impact on American society.

REFERENCES

Baird, Robert D. 1973. *Category Formation and the History
of Religions.* Berlin: Mouton de Gruyter.

Bauer, Olivier. 2009. *La religion du canadien de Montréal.*
Montreal: Fides.

Berger, Peter. (1967) 1969. *The Sacred Canopy: Elements
of a Sociological Theory of Religion.* Garden City, NY:
Doubleday.

Capps, Walter. 1974. "On Religious Studies, in Lieu of an
Overview." *Journal of the American Academy of Religion*
42, no. 4: 727–33.

Durkheim, Émile. (1912) 1915. *Elementary Forms of the
Religious Life*, trans. Joseph Ward Swain. New York:
Macmillan.

Eliade, Mircea. 1963. *Patterns in Comparative Religion*,
trans. Rosemary Sheed. New York: Meridian Books.

Emmons, Robert A., and Raymond F. Paloutzian. 2003.
"The Psychology of Religion." *Annual Review of
Psychology* 54: 377–402.

Flood, Gavin. 1999. *Beyond Phenomenology: Rethinking the
Study of Religion.* London: Cassell.

Freud, Sigmund. 1918. "Civilization and *die
Weltanschauung*." http://www.fordham.edu/halsall/
mod/1918freud-civwelt.html (accessed 24 August 2010).

Geertz, Clifford. 1979. "Religion as a Cultural System."
In *Reader in Comparative Religion: An Anthropological
Approach*, ed. William A. Lessa and Evon Z. Vogt, 1–46.
New York: Harper & Row.

Gross, Rita. 1996. *Feminism and Religion.* Boston: Beacon
Press.

James, William. 1958. *The Varieties of Religious Experience.*
New York: Mentor Books.

Kant, Immanuel. 1991. "What Is Enlightenment?" In *Kant:
Political Writings*, ed. Hans S. Reis, 54–60. Cambridge:
Cambridge University Press.

Lincoln, Bruce. 2003. *Holy Terrors: Thinking about Religion
after September 11.* Chicago: University of Chicago Press.

Marx, Karl. 1964. "Contribution to the Critique of Hegel's
Philosophy of Right." In *Karl Marx and Friedrich Engels
on Religion.* New York: Schocken Books.

Otto, Rudolf. 1958. *The Idea of the Holy.* Oxford: Oxford
University Press.

Pals, Daniel. 2006. *Eight Theories of Religion*, 2nd ed. New
York: Oxford University Press.

Said, Edward. 1978. *Orientalism.* New York: Random House.

Schleiermacher, Fredrich. (1830) 1999. *The Christian Faith.*
New York: T & T Clark.

Smith, Jonathan Z. 1982. *Imagining Religion: From Babylon
to Jonestown.* Chicago: University of Chicago Press.

———. 1998. "Religion, Religions, and Religious." In
Critical Terms for Religious Studies, ed. Mark C. Taylor,
269–84. Chicago: University of Chicago Press.

Smith, Wilfred Cantwell. 1959. "Comparative Religion:
Whither and Why." In *The History of Religions: Essays in
Methodology*, 31–58. Chicago: University of Chicago Press.

Stark, Rodney, and Roger Finke. 2000. *Acts of Faith:
Explaining the Human Side of Religion.* Berkeley:
University of California Press.

Tillich, Paul. 1963. *Christianity and the Encounter of the
World Religions.* New York: Columbia University Press.

Tweed, Thomas A. 2006. *Crossing and Dwelling: A Theory of
Religion.* Cambridge: Harvard University Press.

Tylor, Edward B. (1871) 1974. *Primitive Culture*, vol. 1.
New York: Gordon Press.

Timeline

- **c. 3000–1700 B.C.E.** Indus civilization in Pakistan and north-western India.
- **c. 1500–500 B.C.E.** Sanskrit-based Vedic culture develops in the Gangetic plains; Vedic texts compiled.
- **c. 800–400 B.C.E.** Upanishads composed, plus ancillary texts of the Vedas ("Vedangas").
- **c. 200–100 B.C.E.** *Yoga Sutras* of Patanjali composed.
- **c. 400 B.C.E.–400 C.E.** Sanskrit dharma shastras (including the Manusmriti) composed, as well as the two great epics, the Mahabharata (including the Bhagavad-Gita) and the Ramayana.
- **327–325 B.C.E.** Alexander of Macedonia invades north-western India.
- **c. 100 B.C.E.** Early Mathura sculpture among the first images of gods in temples.
- **c. 50 C.E.** Images of gods with several pairs of arms first documented in India.
- **c. 100–500 C.E.** Hinduism expands in Southeast Asia.
- **c. 300–1300 C.E.** Sanskrit Puranas composed.
- **c. 400–500 C.E.** Vatsyayana's *Kama Sutra* composed.
- **600–1700 C.E.** Bhakti movement spreads slowly from southern India to much of the rest of the country.
- **c. 788–820** One of Hinduism's most famous philosophers, Shankara-Acharya of Kerala.
- **1000–1026** First series of Afghan Muslim incursions into India under Mahmud of Ghazni; looting of Hindu temples.
- **1336–1565** Kingdom of Vijayanagara, last Hindu empire in India (in modern state of Karnataka).
- **1556–1707** Muslim Mughal Empire centred in north-central India (capitals in Agra and Delhi).
- **1400–1500s** North Indian poet-saints Mirabai (Rajasthan), Caitanaya and Kabir (Bengal), and Tulsidas (Uttar Pradesh).
- **1510** Portuguese occupy Goa, holding it until ousted in 1961.
- **1600** British East India Company given first charter.

- **1784** Sir William Jones founds Asiatic Society in Calcutta.
- **1828** Ram Mohan Roy founds Brahma Samaj.
- **1857** British Crown, under Queen Victoria, takes over administration of India from East India Company.
- **1875** Swami Dayananda Sarasvati founds Arya Samaj.
- **1893** Swami Vivekanada makes presentation on Hinduism at first World Parliament of Religions in Chicago.
- **1905** First Hindus settle on West Coast of Canada.
- **1947** India wins independence from British rule; partition into republics of India and Pakistan.
- **1948** Mahatma Gandhi assassinated.
- **1950** Constitution of India formally accepted.
- **1964** Death of Jawaharlal Nehru, Republic of India's first prime minister.
- **1970s** Indians expelled from Uganda, Africa, and migrate to Canada and United States.
- **1975** Shankarrao Thatte opens first school for training women as Hindu priests: Shankar Seva Samiti in Pune, Maharashtra, India.
- **1992** Hindu nationalists attack Babri-Masjid mosque in Ayodhya, intent on reclaiming spot for Hindu temple in honour of Ram.
- **2000** Venkatachalapathi Samuldrala is first Hindu to lead opening prayer at session of U.S. House of Representatives.
- **2002** Communal violence breaks out between Hindus and Muslims in Gujarat.
- **2004** Canada's most expensive Hindu temple, the BAPS Swaminarayan Mandir in Toronto, opens.
- **2010** Kumbh Mela festival in Hardwar, northern India, is largest gathering of Hindu ascetics and pilgrims in the world.
  Uttar Pradesh court issues historic ruling on ownership of India's most disputed religious site, in Ayodhya; land is divided between Hindus and Muslims.
- **2011** Re-creation of Athiratham twelve-day vedic fire sacrifice in Panjal, Kerala, for the first time since 1975.

CHAPTER 2

Hinduism

Anne M. Pearson

INTRODUCTION

Hinduism is one of the oldest living religions in the world. In numbers it ranks third behind Christianity and Islam, with more than 900 million followers, constituting some 14.5 per cent of the world's population. While the vast majority continue to reside in India, the place of this religion's birth, about 1.5 million Hindus have emigrated to North America over the past century. In this chapter you will learn about central Hindu teachings on themes such as the human condition, concepts of karma and rebirth, and unusually vibrant portrayals of the divine, as well as important forms of Hindu religious practice and ritual, within the context of a long history of development and a variety of sacred texts. You will also learn about the history and forms of Hinduism that have been transplanted onto Canadian soil, beginning at the turn of the twentieth century. As Hinduism has developed in this different cultural context, new patterns of community life and new questions about religious identity have emerged, and so we ask, What does it mean to be Hindu in Canada?

Flashing lights; blaring music from loudspeakers; red powder filling the air, your nose, your hair. *What's going on?* That was a question that struck me forcefully when, undergraduate degree in hand and travelling in India, I arrived in the city of Pune in the middle of the annual Ganpati festival. Ganpati Puja is one of the major religious festivals of the state of Maharashtra, propelled by the nineteenth-century Indian nationalist B. G. Tilak into the forefront of Maharashtrian expressions of cultural pride and identity—giving an old god a political twist. The streets were raucous, filled with masses of people, especially young men, chanting, drinking, and throwing red powder at everyone nearby. Large stages had been set up in various streets and alleyways with plaster images of the elephant-headed, pot-bellied Lord Ganesha, or Ganapati, decorated with flickering electric lights and garlands and smeared with the ubiquitous red powder.

The mood was certainly festive, but it was also slightly menacing, especially for a naïve single female. None of my readings of Vedas, Upanishads, and other texts for my courses in Toronto had provided me with an explanatory frame of reference. We had not studied Ganesha Chaturthi (the god's "fourth," a monthly religious observance), let alone the Maharashtrian Ganpati festival. During my subsequent months in the country, I came across a number of such festivals, rituals, and other expressions of Hinduism—living Hinduism, or what has been also termed "popular" traditions of Hinduism—some new, some very old. Something had been missing from my undergraduate education; Hinduism was no longer a monolith based on ancient Sanskrit texts transmitted and interpreted by Brahmin scholars. Now it seemed clear to me that there were actually multiple Hinduisms to understand.

> **Dharma:** religious or moral law, that which upholds the universe, Hinduism being the *sanatana* (eternal or universal) *dharma.*

DEFINING HINDUISM

Even the words *Hindu* and *Hinduism* are not clear-cut. The word *Hindu* derives both from the Sanskrit word *sindhu,* referring to a river that flows from the Himalaya Mountains into the Arabian Sea, and from the Arabic word *hind,* the general name the Arabs gave to the South Asian subcontinent. The country east of the River Indus came to be known as India, its people as Hindus or Indians, and their religion as Hinduism. But the people of the Indian subcontinent themselves may refer to their land as Bharata and to their faith or way of life simply as **dharma** (duty, order) or, today, as Hindu dharma. For centuries, individual Indians were more likely to describe themselves by sect or lineage (for instance, as Shri Vaishnava), by caste group (for instance, as Havik Brahmin or Rajput), or by sect and location (for instance, Kashmiri Shaiva). These and the following factors make defining and even adequately describing the vast web of ideas, beliefs, narratives, rituals, and practices to be found under the rubric *Hinduism* particularly problematic. Nevertheless, there are features of Hinduism that, taken together, tell us what is distinctive about this religion and what is important to Hindus.

One feature of Hinduism is the fact that, unlike many other religions, it has no one historical founder or precise founding date. Nor does it identify with a single holy book, although the earliest group of texts, called the Vedas (books of "knowledge"), have been the most revered. Another feature is that Hinduism is so intimately interlinked with Indian culture—its social structure, aesthetic expressions, food, philosophical views, and so forth—that it is particularly challenging to tease them apart. Like many ancient religions, Hinduism is also marked by extraordinary diversity. One often has to say, *Well, in this part of northern India, among such and such a group, they do this, but in Tamil Nadu (or Gujarat or Trinidad) they do that.* Further, Hinduism has tended to be inclusive, to embrace new ideas and practices, whatever their source. Thus ancient ideas and ritual practices often survive alongside new ideas and practices, and new ideas—such as those deriving from Buddhist or Jain traditions or from reformist movements—have been synthesized with the older views. Hindu funeral ceremonies, still based largely on Vedic texts, are a good example of the longevity of ancient ritual practices on the one hand and the adaptability of the tradition on the other: ideas about honouring one's ancestors continue side by side with beliefs in reincarnation.

Finally, a characteristic feature of Hinduism is its renowned tolerance. Considerable latitude is given to its adherents regarding how to be a Hindu, especially in matters of belief. For example, while most Hindus believe in the law of **karma** (that all actions have moral consequences or effects) and in the round of physical rebirth (**samsara**), not all Hindus do. In other words, Hinduism has no single set of beliefs that all those who describe themselves as Hindu are required to accept. Nor is there a single institutional arbiter of orthodoxy, or correct belief. Thus there has been freedom of choice about which views, which texts, which concepts to accept or reject, and how to interpret them. This tolerance, however, has its limits; family traditions, gurus, or sectarian leaders can exert strong and confining influences. One of Hinduism's twentieth-century philosophers, S. Radhakrishnan, wrote in 1927 that while Hinduism "gives absolute liberty in the world of thought it enjoins a strict code of practice. The theist and the atheist, the sceptic and the agnostic may all be Hindus if they accept the Hindu system of culture and life." What counts is conduct, not belief (Radhakrishnan 1927, 55). This idea of conduct may be the best way to define the word *dharma,* likely the most important term to understand when learning about Hinduism.

One organic metaphor used to describe Hinduism is that of a great banyan tree. Looking down on this tree from above, you would see myriad leaves, branches, flowers, then multiple trunks extending down from the branches. You might wonder where the centre was. How can you clearly describe such a lush, spreading tree? Well, if you start at ground level, the initially confusing picture begins to give way to a coherent shape; you'll find that the "trunk" of Hinduism reveals some key concepts and practices with which most Hindus do identify. We first turn to examining the "soil" and "roots," in order to gain an understanding of the historical origins of Hinduism, before proceeding up the rest of the tree and its branches to learn about this religion's conceptual and practical developments. Readers of this chapter should note, then, that they will find descriptions of Hinduism's central beliefs, sources of the tradition, and religious practices embedded in an account of the history and development of this ancient and complex religion. The information presented in this chapter draws on historical, textual, theological, and anthropological research.

> **Mantra:** a syllable or series of words recited for its effect in meditation; a sacred sound.
>
> **Rishis:** ancient sages and visionaries; hearers and transmitters of divine revelation that became the corpus of texts called the Vedas.

HISTORY: PEOPLE, CULTURE, TEXTS

The soil from which Hinduism evolved would be the Neolithic peoples who farmed, kept domestic animals, and lived and traded in small communities in the Indian subcontinent from about 6500 B.C.E. In this soil we would also place the *adivasis*, or "first inhabitants," who possibly corresponded to groups that today are often referred to in India as "tribal peoples." In this soil grew two particularly large roots: the Indus civilization and Vedic-Aryan culture.

The archeological remains of the Indus civilization, found in more than a thousand sites spread throughout western India and eastern Pakistan, especially along the Indus River and the now dried up Ghaggar-Hakra, were rediscovered only in the late nineteenth century, with systematic excavation beginning after 1917. This civilization, which formed from the integration of several regional cultures, appears to have flourished between 2600 and 1900 B.C.E. One of the world's first great urban civilizations, its remarkable features include fairly uniform, well-planned towns surrounded by fortified walls, with wide streets, raised two-storey houses built of fired bricks and containing private bathrooms, elaborate drainage systems, public wells, and water reservoirs. The people grew wheat and barley, lentils and dates; they wove dyed cotton, kept domesticated animals, used specialized techniques for stone working, ceramics, and metallurgy, and may have been the first peoples to use wheeled transport. They also developed a written script that remains inconclusively deciphered.

Little is known about the people's political or religious life: there are no recognizable centres of government or temples. The people buried their dead in simple wooden coffins along with pottery vessels—perhaps for food in the afterlife. The many stone seals and tablets that have been found show images of plants, trees, and animals such as horned bulls, water buffalo, elephants, rams, and one tiger-like creature with horns. There are also some seals that show human images—famously, one bejewelled figure referred to as a dancing girl; another a bearded male, sometimes described as a priest-king; and another a striking image of a horned man in a yoga-like seated posture, which some Hindus believe may be an early portrait of the god Rudra-Shiva. What does this archeological evidence tell us about the religious worldviews of the Indus civilization? While nothing can be said with any certainty, several aspects of this civilization are notable for their possible influence on later Hinduism: the baths suggest the abiding concern among Hindus with religious bathing, signifying physical and ritual purity; the figurines and seals of feminine figures may suggest later Hinduism's interest in goddess worship; the yogi-like figure may prefigure Hinduism's interest in asceticism and the practice of yoga.

In the centuries following 1900 B.C.E., the Indus civilization declined; its major towns were gradually abandoned, likely because of overpopulation and climatic changes that led to extended droughts. Meanwhile, and somewhat later, another "root" was developing. This second major root of the tree of Hinduism is what might be termed Vedic-Aryan culture. What we know about the ancient religion of the Aryans ("noble ones"), a pastoral people who favoured cows and horses and who gradually settled into the north-central Indian plains of India along the Ganges River, is through ancient Sanskrit texts composed over many centuries between about 1500 and 600 B.C.E.—the Vedas. Interestingly, Sanskrit is linguistically related to the ancient language of the Persians, as well as to Greek and Latin, suggesting a common origin for all these languages, including their modern descendants such as Italian, French, Hindi, Panjabi, and Gujarati. Hence all of these languages are referred to as Indo-European.

Sources of the Tradition

The hymns, prayers, **mantras** (sacred syllables or phrases), and ritual practices recorded in the Vedas are said to have been "heard" by ancient **rishis** (sages or seers) during states of meditation millennia ago.

We do not know anything about who these sages were, or exactly where and when they lived. What is important is that for Hindus the Vedas are considered to contain ancient and sacred knowledge. Four genres or groups of texts are included in the category of Vedas: the Samhitas, the Brahmanas, the Aryanyakas, and the Upanishads. The earliest and perhaps most important genre of the Vedas is the four Samhitas, or "collections." These consist of the Rig-Veda, the oldest collection, which contains some 1,028 hymns addressed to various gods. Next there is the Yajur-Veda, or book of Vedic ceremonies; the Sama-Veda, or metrical hymns intended to be sung; and finally the last book, the Atharva-Veda, a collection of additional hymns, stories, and ritual incantations concerning a broad range of subjects, from the problems of co-wives and gambling to healing illnesses. This originally oral literature was transmitted by families of trained Brahmin priests for hundreds of years before being finally written down. In fact, in the traditional Hindu view, oral communication of the sacred remains the most authentic and potent form. The Vedas are thus the textual substratum of what is now called Hinduism.

For many peoples of India over the centuries, and still today, to be a Hindu was to follow

Words

Hindu Sanskrit Scriptures at a Glance

Shruti ("that which is heard," or revelation): the Veda, the eternal Word (oral scripture); the most sacred and authoritative texts. The **Vedas** ("knowledge") consist of revelations and religious experiences of the rishis, or ancient sages, compiled between approximately 1500 and 600 B.C.E. They consist of

- four **Samhitas** ("compilations"):
  - Rig-Veda: the earliest; 1028 prayers/invocations addressed to various gods (*devas*)
  - Yajur-Veda: book of Vedic ceremonies
  - Sama-Veda: metrical hymns; collection of extracts from Rig-Veda to be sung
  - Atharva-Veda: collection of additional hymns and ritual incantations; considered to be representative of the "popular" religion of Vedic times
- **Brahmanas:** ritual texts describing "how-tos" for Vedic sacrifice
- **Aranyakas** ("forest treatises"): transition from ritual to theology
- **Upanishads** ("secret teachings"): philosophical and mystical texts dealing with quest to understand ultimate reality (800–400 B.C.E.)

Smriti ("that which is remembered"): written scripture based on the Vedas; important but less authoritative than the *shruti* texts. They consist of

- itihasa (history)
  - the epics: the **Mahabharata**, including the **Bhagavad-Gita** (c. first century C.E.), an epic of a great war (perhaps c. 1000 B.C.E.) and popular source of dharma, and the **Ramayana** (c. first to third century C.E.), an epic of King Rama's war against the demonic powers and source of ideal models for dharmic behaviour.
  - the **Puranas**, or "ancient stories" (fourth to fourteenth centuries C.E.): compendia of mythology, theology, and ritual instruction directed to the praise of particular gods.

- sutras and shastras (authoritative treatises), for example,
  - shrauta sutras: texts on public sacrifices and other rituals
  - grihya sutras: texts on domestic rituals
  - dharma shastras: texts on social organization and behaviour (e.g., the Manusmriti)
  - Brahma sutras: texts of philosophical theology (e.g., Vedanta sutras of Badarayana)
  - natya shastra: texts on the art of dance and drama and Indian poetics

the Vedas, referred to as the *shruti*—literally, "that which is heard," or texts of revelation. While these texts are the most revered and authoritative texts of Hinduism, the majority of Hindus over the centuries have not read them, nor have the Vedas been particularly important in the day-to-day ritual lives of Hindus, although verses are still chanted by Brahmin priests on particular occasions. However, other, later texts and traditions have served to guide Hindus. In particular there is a second order of scripture in Hinduism called *smriti*—"that which is remembered." These texts, composed after about 400 B.C.E., are considered authoritative accounts of learned Hindus who faithfully interpreted the teachings of the Vedas and who compiled, organized, and analyzed the traditions of the community, applying the teachings to various contexts. The *smriti* texts included the dharma *shastras*, or treatises on dharma. The well-known text the Bhagavad-Gita and the beloved epics also technically belong to this second category of scripture, although, because of their influence and importance, they are also sometimes referred to as the "fifth Veda."

Vedic–Hindu Religion

Vedic religion was a religion of ritual and sacrifice (**yajna**) to a variety of gods called **devas**, or "shining ones." The devas were often associated with natural forces such as wind, rain, fire, the dawn, or more abstract concepts such as speech or moral order. Humans and gods worked together to maintain the physical and moral order of the cosmos and to keep the forces of chaos (personified as demonic beings called *asuras*) from encroaching. Much of early Vedic literature consists of hymns and prayers to the devas offering praise or asking for help and forgiveness for mistakes or for breaking laws.

At the most basic level, the rituals of sacrifice—which involved animals at first, then usually just plants, herbs, and clarified butter—were carried out daily at home by a husband and wife. They would chant mantras (sacred syllables) and prayers and pour clarified butter into the constantly burning hearth fire that had been ritually established when they married. This was considered an act of feeding the gods. Agni, the god of fire (from whence *ignite*) and lord of the sacrifice, was considered the mouth of the gods; through

Yajna: sacrifice, the key ritual of early Vedic Hinduism (also spelled *yagya*).

Deva: "shining one," the word signifying the gods in Vedic Hinduism.

the smoke he would take the offerings to the other gods who, energized, could do their work of maintaining the sacred order.

In addition, everyone—all sentient beings, including the gods—had ordained duties and responsibilities for keeping order, harmony, and stability to ensure a prosperous life for all. The focus in the Vedas is very much on the here and now, and most of the sacrifices, along with the prayers and supplications that went with them, are for social and material well-being: for rain, good harvests, fecundity, cows, children—especially sons, because sons carry the lineage and are the agents responsible for rituals such as funeral ceremonies of parents and rites for the ancestors. The following verses from a hymn to Agni from the Rig-Veda (1.1.1–4, 7) express these ideas and longings:

I pray to Agni, the household priest who is the god of the sacrifice, the one who chants and invokes and brings most treasure.
Agni earned the prayers of the ancient sages, and of those of the present, too; he will bring the gods here.
Through Agni one may win wealth, and growth from day to day, glorious and most abounding in heroic sons.
Agni, the sacrificial ritual that you encompass on all sides—only that one goes to the gods. …
To you, Agni, who shine upon darkness, we come day after day, bringing our thoughts and homage.

Source: O'Flaherty, W.D., tr. *The Rig Veda, An Anthology.* (New York: Penguin Books, 1983).

The Vedic texts—the hymns and rituals centring on the sacrifice that they describe—reveal a concern, typical of ancient peoples, with fathoming and to a

---

Brahmin: a member of the priestly class or caste.

---

degree controlling the mysterious forces of the spiritual/physical world to which we are all subject, for health, fertility, and well-being are all dependent on these natural forces.

Over the centuries, Vedic religion—the lowest trunk of the tree of Hinduism—continued to develop and to express new interests, as is indicated in Vedic literature composed from about 1000 to 500 B.C.E. In the set of texts called the Brahmanas (the "how-to" texts) we find detailed explanations of how and when to perform the sacrifices, who should perform them (that is, which ritual specialists), under what conditions, and so forth. They exhibit serious concern about making mistakes in the procedures of sacrifice—mistakes that it was thought could produce disastrous consequences for the reciter of the mantras and spoil the entire effect of the sacrifice. Thus it was that the period of proper Vedic study to learn the mantras was extended to a minimum of twelve years for **Brahmins**. Eventually women and Shudras (those of the lowest class) were expressly forbidden to study—and, some later texts say, even to hear—the Vedas, as they were not permitted to spend the time considered necessary to study and memorize the verses.

Eventually it was believed that the sacrifice, properly done, had a creative power generated through the transformative force of heat. This creative power was equal to or could even surpass the creative power of the gods. Thus the sacrifices themselves were capable of regulating and modifying the workings of the universe to the advantage of the sacrificer (that is, the sponsor of the sacrifice). In other words, in later Vedic religion, proper ritual procedure became all-important and increasingly the specialized arena of carefully trained (male) Brahmin priests, while the individual power of the gods started to fade. In fact, the Vedic gods never re-emerged as objects of worship in the Hindu tradition, though their names and mythologies lived on.

The next set or genre of authoritative Sanskrit texts within the Vedic corpus, called the Aranyakas, or "forest treatises," were composed during and just after the final books of the Brahmanas (perhaps around 700 B.C.E.), and they reveal further development in the

understanding of the sacrifice and thus a new development in Hindu religious thought. Essentially, some people came to view the physical rituals of the material sacrifice and all its hymns and mantras and prayers as replaceable by interior meditation and visualization. The elements of particular sacrifices were replaced by symbols that could be imagined and reflected on. The power of conscious thought, of the human ability to imagine, began to receive attention. If humans could imagine the rituals, perhaps it was not necessary to perform elaborate sacrifices in the material realm, and in fact some thinkers came to reject the need for any external rituals. We will see in the next section, following a description of Hindu views of creation and cosmology, how such reflections led to the emergence of the final set of texts that constitute the Vedic corpus, the Upanishads. It is in these texts that one finds articulated for the first time what we may now call the central classical Hindu beliefs.

The most common symbol of Hinduism is the mantra *om*, as presented in the stylized form of devanagari script letters for *a-u-m*. Om is called the "seed mantra," for it is said that out of its sound all other sounds are found; it represents the totality of the universe. The use of mantras in meditation, prayers, and invocations dates back to the earliest Vedas. They are understood to evoke spiritual forces in the universe that one can draw upon during rituals or meditation. When Hindus perform the "waving of the lamp" ritual called the *arati* at the end of worship, at home or in a temple, they often draw the om symbol in the air with the steel plate of flames.

Source: oblong1/Shutterstock

CENTRAL BELIEFS

In the Beginning: Cosmology and Creation

One way in which cultures encapsulate their worldviews is through their myths, for example, in creation stories. Creation stories provide key narratives that explain and interpret the origin of the world or the universe and all therein, as well as the place of human beings in that world. Such narratives serve as a culture's map of the cosmos and of life.

Hinduism has preserved a number of creation myths and cosmologies, some of which became more elaborate over the centuries, so introducing, in typical Hindu fashion, new ideas in the process. Several central ideas about creation and cosmology are common to them all. First, the universe has no absolute beginning and no final end. Second, the world was not created or manifested out of nothing; that is, life emerges from inert matter or some form of potentiality, an uncreated substratum that becomes moulded and ordered. Human beings are not necessarily the object of creation, but are one group of beings among many others. For Hindus, the purpose of creation is the manifestation of order (*rta*, or dharma) in the universe. Third, the universe (and thus our world) undergoes vast cycles of creation, dissolution, and re-creation. Fourth, there is a divine intelligence behind it all.

Perhaps the earliest creation story is based on the interconnection between the terrestrial and celestial realms of existence: the conjugal union of the world parents, Earth (Prithvi) and Heaven (Dyaus, from whence *Zeus*), produces all of creation (Rig-Veda 6.7). Another creation story (Rig-Veda 1.32) is that of Indra, the warrior-king and most prominent god in the Rig-Veda, who kills the great serpent demon Vritra after the demon "enclosed the waters that were requisite for human life." Having released the waters, Indra sets the sun in the sky, and cosmic order is established. This story speaks of the primordial battle between the forces of order/truth/life and the forces of disorder/untruth/non-life, a theme that is prominent in the Vedas and subsequent Indian literature.

The important "Hymn of Man" (Rig-Veda 10.90) describes the creation of the world through sacrificial dismemberment of the body of a primeval being in the shape of a man. From each part of his body comes some aspect of the natural world, including the gods and the four classes of human beings, which are based on their occupations and duties. This sacrifice of the primeval man is the material cause of the universe, underscoring the centrality of sacrifice as the core ritual act in early Hinduism. It is an act so powerful that it creates the universe itself.

Words

The "Hymn of Man"

1. The Man has a thousand heads, a thousand eyes, a thousand feet. He pervaded the earth on all sides and extended beyond it as far as ten fingers.
2. It is the Man who is all this, whatever has been and whatever is to be. He is the ruler of immortality, when he grows beyond everything through food.
3. Such is his greatness, and the Man is yet more than this. All creatures are a quarter of him; three quarters are what is immortal in heaven. . . .
6. When the gods spread the sacrifice with the Man as the offering, spring was the clarified butter, summer the fuel, autumn the oblation.
7. They anointed the Man, the sacrifice born at the beginning, upon the sacred grass. With him the gods, Sadhyas, and sages sacrificed. . . .
9. From that sacrifice in which everything was offered, the verses and chants were born, the metres were born from it, and from it the formulas were born.
10. Horses were born from it, and those other animals that have two rows of teeth; cows were born from it, and from it goats and sheep were born.

11. When they divided the Man, into how many parts did they apportion him? What do they call his mouth, his two arms and thighs and feet?

12. His mouth became the Brahmin; his arms were made into the Warrior, his thighs the People, and from his feet the Servants were born.

13. The moon was born from his mind; from his eye the sun was born. Indra and Agni came from his mouth, and from his vital breath the Wind was born.

Source: O'Flaherty, W.D., tr. *The Rig Veda, An Anthology*. (New York: Penguin Books, 1983).

Brahman: a neuter noun referring to the non-gendered, abstract absolute, the Divine that pervades the universe.

Finally, three Vedic creation hymns from the last book of the Rig-Veda (10.81–2, 10.121, and 10.129) include Hinduism's earliest speculative questions. Here some basic assumptions and older themes are being questioned, not as to their veracity but as to their deeper meanings. Who is this creator, the One, who preceded all the known gods? Even the gods themselves cannot know: he is beyond understanding. Rig-Veda 10.121 speaks of a golden embryo (or womb) that evolved in the beginning and from which have sprung the many creatures on earth. The ending refrain poses a surprising question: "Who is the god whom we should worship with our oblation?"* It is answered in the final verse, which is considered a later addition: "O Prajapati, lord of progeny, no one but you embraces these creatures. Grant us the desires for which we offer you oblation. Let us be lords of riches."* The "Nasadiya Sukta" (Rig-Veda 10.129) is also full of questions and searching for the source of all things: what stirred in the beginning in that watery darkness before existence and non-existence? We will see that such early speculative questions, found occasionally in the Vedic Samhitas,

become of enduring and central concern in the final Vedic texts, the Upanishads.

Later texts, such as the great Sanskrit epic the Mahabharata and the medieval Puranas, offer elaborations of cosmology and cycles of time. Creation begins with emanation of the universe out of a divine, unmanifested, and singular substance and terminates with dissolution and re-absorption back into the "absolute," until, after a period of quiescence, the whole cycle starts again. Within these unfathomable cycles there are sub-cycles—the system of *kalpas* and *yugas*. In this vision of cycles of time, two things are particularly noteworthy: first, that knowledge and practice of religion tends to decline over time until the world collapses, and second, that we are living in the most degenerate of the four sub-cycles, the Kali Yuga, when dharma has waned to its lowest ebb. This is the time when, as the Vishnu Purana (Book 6.1) describes, status is acquired by wealth, not virtue; the "minds of men will be wholly occupied in acquiring wealth; and wealth will be spent solely on selfish gratifications"; people forget their duties; people die young; and life becomes a daily struggle as famine and taxation oppress them. This dark Kali age ends in a great conflagration and flood: the god Vishnu descends as Kalkin to destroy sinful humankind, and the great turning of the world cycles begins again after a period of quiescence.

The Upanishads, the Concept of Brahman, and the Search for Liberation

In the texts of late Vedic religion, the Aryanyaks and the Upanishads, we can see how thinkers were searching for the one in the many—the source of the power of thought and, indeed, ultimate reality. This search lead to **Brahman**. The word *brahman* means "great," and it came to signify the mysterious power of the sacrifice and also to signify truth or ultimate reality. Brahman, then, was no ordinary deva who could be induced by worship to grant wishes. This interest in discerning the truth about the nature of reality and the ultimate power that animates the world is reflected in the Upanishads (also known as the Vedanta, the end or conclusion of the Vedas). The Upanishads are a collection of what have been called "spiritual illuminations," many in the form of dialogues between students and teachers. It is in these texts that one finds a view of

---

PERSPECTIVES

The Four Yugas

In the cycle of time in Hinduism, creation equals one day of the god Brahma; dissolution of the universe is the ensuing night. Together they equal one *kalpa.* Each kalpa consists of 1000 *mahayugas* (world cycles), or 4.32 billion years. Each mahayuga consists of 4.32 million years and is divided into four *yugas*, or world ages, during which dharma declines.

Cycles of Time: The Four Yugas

Krita Yuga

Treta Yuga

Krita Yuga ("perfect" yuga) = 1 728 000 years
Dharma is firmly established on four legs, like a sacred cow. Men and women are born virtuous, devoting their lives to the fulfilment of their dharmic duties.

Treta Yuga ("triad" or "three-legged" yuga) = 1 296 000 years
During this yuga, the cosmos and human society are supported by only three-quarters of its total virtue, and so duties are no longer the spontaneous laws of human action but have to be learned.

Dvapara Yuga

Kali Yuga

Dvapara Yuga ("two-legged" yuga) = 864 000 years
Knowledge of dharma is beginning to be lost. People begin to grow mean and acquisitive. Vows, fasts, and ascetic practices are recommended.

Kali Yuga ("dark age" or "one-legged" yuga) = 432 000 years
Only 25 per cent of dharma is left; the world is unbalanced and at its worst stage of moral decay.

Karma: literally "action"; the law of cause and effect.

Atman: the self, usually referring to the spiritual essence of a person, "soul" or spirit. In Sanskrit, the term is ātman.

Moksha: liberation from the cycle of rebirth and from a state of ignorance about the nature of self and reality; the ultimate goal of Hindus (synonymous with *mukti*).

Guru: a spiritual teacher, who may be non-Brahmin, male or female.

the material world as a place of entrapment. Here one learns about the doctrine of rebirth or reincarnation, the concept of the moral law of **karma** that fuels the rebirth process, the concept of the **atman** ("imperishable Self" or perhaps "soul"), and a new ultimate goal of life—that of **moksha**, or liberation from the cycle of rebirth. One also finds in these texts descriptions of the necessary or most efficacious means to reach the goal of moksha, such as forms of mental and physical training (including meditation and, later, the practice of yoga) and even the renunciation of worldly life, including sex, traditional occupations, material wealth, and family. This salvific knowledge leading to liberation that the Upanishads unveiled was something new, something not previously revealed in the earlier Vedic texts. One famous verse from the Brhadaranyaka Upanishad clearly expresses the longing for this liberating knowledge: "From the unreal lead me to the real! From darkness lead me to light! From death lead me to immortality!"* (Olivelle 1996, 1.3.28).

The Upanishads explore the connections between the rituals of sacrifice, the cosmic realities (gods, heavenly bodies, forces in the universe), and the human person (the body and its vital powers and faculties). One meaning of the term *upanishad* is "hidden or secret teachings," because of the hidden nature of these connections and because these teachings were not for everyone to hear. The role of the wise (knowledgeable) teacher, or **guru**, who could explicate these deeper truths assumes great importance from this point on in Hinduism. The term *upanishad* is also translated as "to sit near," as in to sit near or at the feet of a guru.

It has been said that the philosophers of the Upanishads were the pioneer freethinkers of their age; while stepping beyond the traditional priestly view

of the cosmos, in typical Hindu fashion they did so without dissolving it. These philosophers largely turned their backs on the realm "interpreted in the myths and controlled by the complicated rituals of the sacrifice—because they were discovering something more interesting. They had found the interior world, the inward universe of man himself, and within that the mystery of the Self" (Zimmer 1951, 356).

Human Beings and Their True Essence

As the "one behind the many," the source of the universe, Brahman cannot be fully comprehended by our finite, embodied minds, yet real knowledge about this ultimate reality was held to be possible. The ancient Hindu tradition recognized that such knowledge was obtainable through study of the sacred texts, meditation, and, above all, knowledge of the Self. But what is this Self? Are we identical with our bodily frames? Are we the sum total of our senses and appetites, feelings and emotions, beliefs and practices? Or is our essence something intangible? What *are* we really? The search for the hidden interconnection between all things, for ultimate reality—for Brahman—recorded in the Upanishads led to discovery of the immortal Self, an inner essence so very difficult to find or understand.

In one popular story, it is said that the gods once had a conference to discuss where to put the "secret of life" (that being the quality of divinity within us). First they thought it should be put on top of a mountain, then at the bottom of the ocean or perhaps deep in the jungle. But in all of these places the gods thought humans would find this secret. Then one said, "Let's put the secret inside man—then he'll never find it!" And so they did.

The Upanishads disclose that the essence of each human being is the imperishable Self, or soul, which does not die with the body and which may be identified with Brahman, the cosmic soul. The human soul/self (or atman) is described as intangible, indestructible, unbound (Brihadaranyaka Upanishad, 3.9.26). The difficulty in describing this intangible yet wondrous Self is suggested by these logic-defying statements: "Finer than the finest, larger than the largest, is the self (ātman) that lies here hidden in the heart of a living being. Without desires and free from sorrow, a man perceives by the creator's grace the grandeur of the self" (Katha Upanishad, 2.20). In other places the heart is called the "city of Brahman" that contains everything, but when old age overtakes the body, the atman remains free from evil, age, death, sorrow, hunger and thirst, for its seeks only reality.

A number of descriptive metaphors set within a dialogue became classic analogies for the nature of the Self and its relation to Brahman in Indian philosophy. For example, from the Chandogya Upanishad (Chapter 6) one learns about the sage Uddalaka Aruni and his son/pupil Shvetaketu. The sage tries to teach his son, who has returned from years of traditional Vedic schooling and is puffed up with pride, about the true nature of one's inner Self and its connection to ultimate reality, that is, to Brahman. This knowledge is not what Shvetaketu learned and he has difficulty understanding what his father/teacher is telling him. Aruni uses various metaphors and similes to educate his son, in one instance asking him to pull out a fig seed and then divide it. Shvetaketu tries to find something inside the tiny seed but cannot. And yet, exclaims his teacher, the huge fig tree grows from this seemingly empty and certainly tiny seed. In another instance the sage asks his son to bring him a glass of water and put salt in it. The next day the son is asked to extract the salt from the water, but he cannot, for it has entirely dissolved. After each exercise Aruni tells his son: "The finest essence here—that constitutes the self of this whole world; that is the truth; that is the self (ātman). And that's how you are, Śvetaketu."*

"And that's how you are," or "That thou art," became known as the great formula of Vedantic truth, one that reduced the myriad things of the natural world to a single, hidden, intangible, yet all-pervading essence. Aruni taught Shvetaketu to look beyond the visible principles, names, and forms celebrated in the Vedic hymns.

> The life essence was now to be conceived of as invisible (like the void within the seed of the fig), all suffusing (like the salt in the water), intangible, yet the final substance of all phenomena. It could be ascertained but not grasped, like the dissolved salt—and was extremely subtle, like the presence within the seed. Therefore, one was not to regard oneself as the gross and tangible individual; not even as the subtle personality; but as the principle out of which those had emanated. (Zimmer 1951, 360–61).

Asana: a specific physical posture described in yoga literature.

In the end, *all* manifested things are transformations of Brahman/atman. Individual appearances, forms, and diversity are not, finally, significant at all. In sum, then, our true identity is an immortal inner Self, a soul, but this true identity, this Self, is not easily known. As the Katha Upanishad states (4.1), "The Self-existent One pierced the apertures outward, therefore, one looks out, and not into oneself. A certain wise man in search of immortality, turned his sight inward and saw the self within."*

Yoga

Because truly knowing the Self requires great effort, yoga and practices of asceticism were developed as tools for the control of body and mind. The goal in the philosophy of yoga was to eventually achieve union with God; the term *yoga* comes from a Sanskrit verbal root meaning "to yoke," as in to yoke the self with God. Yoga was systematized as a philosophy and practice in a text called the *Yoga Sutras* (c. 100 B.C.E.–200 C.E.) ascribed to the author Patanjali. This text describes the path of emancipation of the inner self from the bondage of the body, senses, and mind. Along the path one strives to starve the ego-mind to allow the inner spirit (called *purusha* in this text) to shine forth like a luminous jewel at the bottom of a still, clear pond. The second sutra, or aphorism, of this text says: "Yoga is the control of the thought-waves in the mind."

The *Yoga Sutras* describe eight aids to achieving the goal of liberation and perfection (hence this yoga is called *ashtanga*, or "eight-limbed," yoga, as well as Raja, or "sovereign," yoga). The first of these eight limbs is ethical practices, for example, non-violence, truthfulness, chastity, non-acquisitiveness, and compassion. The second limb consists of the "observances," such as purity, contentment, study, austerity, and surrender to God. The third limb consists of what we usually think of as yoga here in the West, that is, a series of physical postures (**asanas**). The next five limbs are breath control and withdrawal of the senses, followed by what the text calls the "internal aids" of fixed or one-pointed

* Patrick Olivelle, tr. *Upanishads*. (New York: Oxford University Press, 1996).

Samsara: the socially constructed world; the wheel of life, death, and rebirth.

attention, meditation, and contemplation—the ultimate mystical experience of unity. The aim of this eight-limbed yoga is to dissociate ourselves from our sensations, thoughts, ideas, and feelings; to learn that these are extraneous associations, foreign to the true nature of Self; to learn, finally, to discriminate between *purusha* (self/spirit or soul) and *prakriti* (nature or primary matter) and so yoke our spirit with God.

Subsequently a number of forms of yoga philosophy and practice developed, such as hatha yoga, which focuses on breath control and the postures, and kundalini yoga, which is associated with the Tantric tradition and focuses on awakening and guiding the life-force "serpent power"—the *kundalini shakti*—along a series of *chakras*, or energy centres along the spine. These forms and new ones have been transplanted all over the world, including, of course, in North America, where students can now experience Bikram, or "hot yoga," and even yoga postures combined with Pilates exercises, called Yogalates—ideas that would seem utterly strange to Patanjali.

Samsara and Karma

It is clear that, from at least the time of the Upanishads, Hindus have accepted belief in the existence of a human soul (or inner self) that is the true (divine) nature of the person and which persists after the death of the body. Another set of key Hindu concepts first enunciated in the Upanishads are samsara, reincarnation, and the law of karma. The majority of Hindus accept the belief that when human beings die, their souls are reborn into another physical body in this world. This doctrine of transmigration affirms not only life after death, in physical rebirth, but also life before death, a pre-existence. The seemingly endless cycle of birth, death, and rebirth to which, in the Hindu view, we are all subject is known as the wheel of **samsara** ("going-through")—the wheel of rebirth.

The doctrine of rebirth as it is now accepted was only hinted at in the Vedas. It was not fully articulated until the Upanishads, when the notion of an imperishable soul was developed simultaneously.

The Bhagavad-Gita compares the rebirth of the soul after death to its continuity through the changing phases of our bodies during our lifetimes: "As the Spirit of our mortal body wanders on in childhood, and youth and old age, the Spirit wanders on to a new body" (2.13).* In another passage it compares the process of rebirth to the putting on of new clothes: "As a man leaves an old garment and puts on one that is new, the Spirit leaves his mortal body and then puts on one that is new" (2.22).*

The wheel of rebirth is both fuelled and directed by the law of karma, or cause and effect, another key Hindu doctrine developed in the Upanishads. The term *karma* means "deed" or "action." In the Vedas the term *karma* is applied principally to sacrifices and sacred actions. It then came to have a moral connotation and tied to the notion of rebirth. The doctrine of the law of karma is encapsulated in this statement from the Brhadaranyaka Upanishad (3.2.13): "Verily, one becomes good through good deeds and evil through evil deeds."† We may think of related ideas encapsulated in such English phrases as "What you give is what you get" or "What goes around, comes around." As Hindus would say, just as causes have effects, actions have consequences and, particularly, moral actions have moral consequences. Thus the Upanishad above states that as a person thinks and acts, so he or she becomes.

Further, the sum total of a person's desires or volitions and deeds in the present life determine his or her predispositions, character, and social status in the next life. Each person, then, is responsible for her own rise or fall in the round of existence. Yet there is always hope, as every response we make to any challenge, every decision we take, every action we do introduces new karmic effects. So past karma is interacting with present karma, and present karma influences future outcomes. In addition, most Hindus would say that there is also a wild card operating: fate, which is unrelated to one's personal karma. Natural disasters may be caused by fate, or simply by chance—one can never be absolutely certain. One can, however, be certain about being born human, and that is the best condition to be born into (rather than, say, a dog, one of the worst conditions), for only as a human can one make ethical choices.

The law of karma came to be seen as an all-sufficient explanation for the different conditions of human beings, such as why some innocents suffer and others are blessed with good fortune. But karma on its own

---

* Mascaro, Juan, tr. *The Bhagavad Gita*. (New York: Penguin Books, 1962).
† Patrick Olivelle, tr. *Upanishads*. (New York: Oxford University Press, 1996).

does not necessarily predetermine an unalterable future. On the one hand, belief in rebirth and the law of karma are a stimulus to action, since by good actions now, one might rise to a better condition in the next life, and conversely, through bad actions one will find oneself in a worse condition, if not in this life, then certainly in the next. On the other hand, the theistic traditions that came to the fore in Hinduism after 100 C.E. allowed for the possibility of God's grace intervening to save a devotee from rebirth. For example, the Bhagavad-Gita (12.6–7) says: "But they for whom I am the End Supreme, who surrender all their works to me, and who with pure love meditate on me and adore me—these I very soon deliver from the ocean of death and life-in-death, because they have set their heart on me."

We turn now to examine Hindu teachings on what it means to live a good life, that is, a life that produces positive karma and is aligned with dharma. We will see that while texts such as the Upanishads may have described the inner essence of all humans as the imperishable self intimately connected with the universal Self that is Brahman, an affirmation of ultimate universal equality does not translate into social equality. Indeed it cannot, for according to the theory of karma and reincarnation, we are each at a different stage of a long road that may eventually lead to salvation from ignorance and liberation from the wheel of rebirth. The attainment of moksha is not considered by most Hindus to be a proximate goal. Instead we must live our lives according to the hand of cards we are dealt, and that means paying attention to such factors as our temperament, age, gender, and class—and to the roles, duties, and responsibilities attendant on such factors.

Dharma: Hindu Social and Ethical Teachings

Hindu teachings concerning how one should live, or human values, goals, and social organization, are found systematically described in the dharma shastras ("treatises on dharma"), texts that are part of the *smriti* tradition. These texts, composed in the period just before and after the turn of the Common Era, tend to be prescriptive in nature. That is, one should not assume that they describe actual practices and beliefs, but rather they interpret and prescribe what the male Brahmin authors understood to be ideals. These texts, then, are legalistic guides for Hindus on how to live righteously

> **Artha:** "goal," referring to one of the four aims or goals of life according to the dharma shastras, that of material prosperity; also relates to statecraft.

for the well-being of the world. Recall that the concept of *dharma* refers to law, duty, and righteousness. The word comes from a Sanskrit verbal root meaning "to sustain" or "uphold," as in to uphold order. Adherence to dharma has the capacity to sustain the world, as is suggested by statements in Hindu texts that describe dharma as the "foundation of the universe," a "means to drive away evil," and "the highest good" (Taittiriya Aranyaka 10.79) or, from the most famous dharma shastra, the Manusmriti (8.15), "When violated, it destroys; when preserved, it preserves."

The scope of dharma extends to three primary areas: the first area concerns the laws governing the spiritual/physical universe; the second area concerns the laws governing society; and the third area concerns the laws governing the individual. The dharma shastras are interested primarily in the latter two areas of application. As these texts were composed at a time when the religions of Buddhism and Jainism were already well established in India, we find that the codifiers of Hindu law were seeking to clarify what it meant to be Hindu rather than what the Brahmins called "heterodox," meaning essentially nonbelievers in the authority of the Vedas. In the process they described four human aspirations (goals or values), four stages in life, and four divisions of human society, as well as spelling out how kings, women, and "outcastes," among others, were to behave.

Human Aspirations and Values

The codifiers of Hindu religious law single out four human aspirations or values around which social and moral duties were grouped. These are called the *purusharthas*, or "goals of man." The first value is dharma itself, here meaning duty and the practice of religion in its individual context, including daily rituals, prayers, and meditation and the practice of virtues such as truthfulness, respect for one's elders, and avoidance of prohibited acts or things such as stealing or lying. The second value is economic or material well-being (**artha**), by which is meant gainful employment, acquisition of material goods, and appropriate disbursement

Kama: aesthetics.

of monies and goods to the family and to the needy. Making money, then, is not viewed as a negative thing in and of itself, as long as it is made under the provisions of dharma and not, for instance, purely self-serving. The third value is pleasure or aesthetics (**kama**), which includes enjoyment and learning of the arts, from music to the art of love. This value is expressed in Hinduism's extraordinary temple architecture and sculpture and in its traditions of classical dance, music, and drama.

The fourth value is moksha itself, which involves the pursuit and achievement of divine knowledge that leads to self-realization and liberation from the wheel of samsara, or rebirth. This last value, moksha, was sometimes viewed as being in tension with the previous three, since many held that the pursuit of moksha could be successfully undertaken only away from society and its focus on the attainment of well-being in this world. To accommodate this aspiration and its other-worldly focus, the Hindu law codifiers assigned its proper place to the fourth and final stage of a person's life.

A story from the epic the Mahabharata (1.41–42) illustrates the nature of this tension and the consequences for those who selfishly choose only the path toward their own salvation. In this story a celibate ascetic named Jaratkaru has spent years practising self-restraint, wandering the earth, living simply, and giving spiritual counsel. He is intent on reaching the supreme goal of moksha. One day he hears pitiful cries emerging from a deep pit. He looks inside and sees a group of people hanging from a clump of grass that is being chewed by a rat. The people spy him and beg him to find their only living descendant who could give them a son to continue their lineage and to tell this lost son about their plight. The rat represents time gnawing away at their last link to their ancestors. Jaratkaru at once admits that he is that very lost son, who has been consumed with his own salvation. He agrees to find a wife and to start a family so that his lineage will be saved. The emphasis in this story is evidently one that emerged from a dharma shastra perspective, for it reaffirms that while the values of asceticism are all very well and good, first one must discharge one's "three debts": to one's ancestors (by having sons), to the gods

(by performing sacrifices), and to society (by living the householder's life).

The Four Stages of Life The dharma shastras articulate an ideal scheme of social organization in which every member of society during every major period in his or her life has certain duties and responsibilities which, if faithfully executed, will lead to personal and societal harmony, order, and righteousness. This is the context-specific nature of dharma. The texts recognize four stages in life. The first is the student stage (the first fifteen to twenty-five years of one's life, depending

A Hindu ascetic encountered on the pilgrimage route to the famous Shiva temple of Kedarnath, in the Himalaya Mountains of Uttarakhand, India. Though meant to occur in the last stage in life, the option of renouncing the world (that is, one's family, possessions, and social position) in order to focus exclusively on spiritual pursuits has been taken up by individuals of any age who feel drawn to this way of life. Becoming an ascetic usually requires one to ritually conduct one's own funeral so that one "dies" to one's former socially constructed identity. Hindu asceticism became highly organized after the ninth century C.E. This ascetic's facial markings and *rudraksha* beads indicates that he is a Shaiva and a member of the Dashanami order.

Source: Anne M. Pearson

on one's caste and sex). The second is the householder stage, comprising the major portion of one's life, when one marries, works at a profession, and raises children (artha and kama are major concerns during this stage, as regulated by dharma). The third stage is that of the recluse (*vanaprastha*—the stage of retirement to the forest). This stage is the period when the children have grown

---

Words

The Manusmriti Dharma Shastra on Caste Duties

But to protect this whole creation, the lustrous one made separate innate activities for those born of his mouth, arms, thighs, and feet. For priests, he ordained teaching and learning, sacrificing for themselves and sacrificing for others, giving and receiving. Protecting his subjects, giving, having sacrifices performed, studying, and remaining unaddicted to the sensory objects are, in summary, for a ruler. Protecting his livestock, giving, having sacrifices performed, studying, tradition, lending money, and farming the land are for a commoner. The Lord assigned only one activity to a servant: serving these (other) classes without resentment. (1.87–91)

Taking into consideration the laws of the castes, districts, guilds, and families, a king who knows justice should establish the particular law of each. (8.41)

Manu has said that nonviolence, truth, not stealing, purification, and the suppression of the sensory powers is the duty of the four classes, in a nutshell. (10.63)

Source: Doniger, Wendy with Brian K. Smith. *The Laws of Manu.* (New York: Penguin Books, 1992).

Sannyasin: a person who has renounced the world in pursuit of spiritual liberation; an ascetic.

---

up and married and one can now simplify one's life and concentrate on explicitly spiritual, moksha-oriented concerns. The final stage in this ideal scheme, *sannyasa*, is that of the ascetic, or "renouncer"—an option taken by relatively few Hindus. It requires one to withdraw entirely from society and to live an ascetic life, perhaps under the tutelage of a guru. It is thought that as a **sannyasin** one is assured moksha at one's bodily death. Women were not encouraged, or in some texts even permitted, to pursue this option, though in reality there are and likely always have been women ascetics as well.

In general, the dharma shastras consider the householder stage to be the most important one, because on this stage depend all the others. As the spirit of our mortal body wanders on further, as we saw, only as a householder can one properly discharge one's "three debts."

Caste and Class In addition to the four stages of life, the dharma law codifiers describe in some detail four major hereditary social divisions called *varna* (from a Sanskrit word literally meaning "colour" but often translated as "caste"). Hinduism has often been distinguished from other religions on the basis of the institution of caste, and Hindus historically distinguished themselves from others on this same basis. The divisions are ascribed scriptural justification through the aforementioned "Hymn of Man" from the Rig-Veda, which depicts the four classes of human beings arising out of the various body parts (mouth, arms, thighs, and feet) of the primordial man sacrificed at the beginning of creation and assigns certain functions to each class.

The four classes, whose interactions with one another the texts seek to strictly control, especially in matters of marriage, food sharing, and ritual functions, are the Brahmins, or priestly class, whose primary function is to perform the ritual sacrifices and to study, preserve, and transmit the Vedas; the Kshatriyas, or governing class; the Vaishyas, or mercantile class, who are to create wealth for the people; and the Shudras, or labourer class, who are expected to serve the other three classes. A fifth category, not mentioned in the Vedas, also emerged. Today this last group, comprising more

> **Jati:** literally "birth," and often translated as "caste" or "sub-caste" when associated with *varna* ("colour"; the four major social classes). Jati is the hereditary social group within which most Hindus seek their marriage partners; each such group typically has an ascribed rank within the social hierarchy.
>
> **Sattva:** the quality of purity, lightness.

than 230 million people, is referred to by the Indian government as "scheduled" or "backward" castes (for the purposes of affirmative action programs). They often refer to themselves as Dalits, or "oppressed ones," to emphasize the fact that they have been subjected by the "higher" classes to extraordinary restrictions of freedom of movement and occupation and treated with disdain for millennia. Other terms that have been used to refer to this class are "untouchables" (referring to the idea that their very touch would ritually pollute the other classes) and Harijans ("children of God"), a term Mahatma Gandhi preferred in order to emphasize the need to treat all human beings with dignity and courtesy.

If we were to assume that the description of the four classes found in the dharma shastra literature was an accurate and adequate description of the elaborate system of graded social division found in Hindu India, either two thousand years ago or today, we would be mistaken. The reality is far more complicated. First, the Vedic concept of *varna* was about delineating functions that had to be performed if cosmic and social harmony were to prevail. Rituals of sacrifice held the key place among these functions; Brahmins were those whose primary duty was to perform the sacrifices and thereby invoke well-being, by cleansing society of anything that threatened disorder.

Second, the concept of *varna* needs to be distinguished from another concept, that of **jati**, a term that is perhaps best translated by the word *caste*. A jati is the group one is born into, identified usually through one's patrilineage and roughly, but not always clearly, related to one of the four *varna* categories. Your jati is a main determinant of whom you can marry and what kinds of food you may share (thus, for example, Brahmins—always a very small minority of the total Hindu population, and themselves divided into jatis—traditionally do not eat the cooked food of "lower"

jatis). There are hundreds of jatis, often relating to occupations, such as oil-pressers, barbers, goldsmiths, or sheep-herders. Women from the barber jati usually performed the function of midwives (a job considered ritually extremely impure), assisting pregnant women of all jatis. But not all those of the barber jati are barbers or midwives by profession, just as not all Brahmins are scholars or priests (nor are all priests Brahmins). In the past, each jati as a group would have particular ritual obligations to the king, who had overall responsibility for the prosperity of the land and people, which was maintained through regular religious rituals.

Third, many Hindus, with the exception of Brahmins, would not readily identify themselves by the names of the *varnas*. Instead they identify with their jatis and are quite aware of the relative status of their jati group vis-à-vis other jatis. Fourth, whole jatis have moved up or down in the hierarchy by, for example, copying the practices of groups perceived as having a higher social status. Such practices might include vegetarianism, or demanding payment of a dowry from the bride's family in a marriage, or changing the family name so it is less associated with a lower-status occupation. The social status of a whole jati may also increase through the acquisition of wealth or political dominance.

Over the centuries there have been a number of attempts to reform, if not abolish altogether, this system of social and ritual division. We may think, for instance, of Basavanna, a twelfth-century mystic and social reformer from the state of Karnataka who rejected birth-based caste divisions and their status ascriptions and called on his followers to do the same. However, not long after his death, his followers ended up being identified as a separate new caste, the Lingayats.

This whole social hierarchy is difficult to dismantle, even today, when it has been contested as never before. The constitution of India bans discrimination based on caste. But, as Gandhi observed, changing laws alone cannot change people's attitudes, especially if people believe their attitudes are supported by the authority of religious texts. Why is the so-called caste system so hard to eliminate? One reason is because it is based on conceptions of inherent (birth-based) differences between people that are linked to past karma. Brahmins are thought to be more filled with **sattva** (spiritual purity), more able thereby to engage in spiritual pursuits and scholarly activities than those in other classes, and

> **Pativrata:** a woman who is vowed to her husband/lord (*pati*); the ideal of the perfect wife.

more able to absorb the temporary impurity associated with their ritual functions. While not as high-status as the Brahmins, the Kshatriya castes too understand themselves to be inherently more pure and fitter to undertake certain types of work and rituals than those "below" them. It should be noted, however, that spiritual power and authority are not the same as temporal power and authority; kings, nobles, and merchants could well wield more power in the political and economic realms.

While scholars continue to debate even how to describe the origins and nature of the "caste system" in India (for example, Quigley 1993; Raheja 1998), some Hindus insist that this institution has nothing to do with genuine Hinduism. Others have used classical Sanskrit sources to argue that Vedic *varna* may be legitimately interpreted to mean recognition of the natural differences between people (as in temperament or talents) and of the variety of tasks that must be accomplished in society. Thus the transmission of "caste" and restricted occupations based solely on patrilineage is a later, misguided interpretation of Hinduism's earliest texts (see, for example, Sharma 1996). While such debates rage on, change in attitudes is in fact occurring, perhaps most rapidly today among the younger, urban, educated population of middle-class Hindus in India and among Hindus living in North America, who are adopting an egalitarian ethos and pragmatic attitude.

Gender and Dharma Returning to the dharma shastra texts, recall that it has been said that dharma is always context-sensitive. We have seen how this plays out in relation to *varna* and stage of life. It also bears on gender. These texts clearly prescribe a special dharma for women, one that locates their primary roles and responsibilities in relationship to men, as daughters, wives, and mothers. The much earlier Vedas also reveal a largely patriarchal social structure in which one of women's important duties was to provide sons for the patrilineage. Nevertheless, the Vedas do not explicitly debar women as priests, and it seems that at least upper-class women did receive some education in the scriptures, and went through the thread-tying ceremony that initiated them into Vedic studies and

allowed women to be engaged in the domestic ritual sacrifices alongside their husbands. The Upanishads indicate that a few women were allowed to pursue their education and become teachers and scholars. The names, activities, and knowledge of several women scholars are mentioned, including Gargi Vacaknavi, who debated with Yajnavalkya, one of the foremost philosophers, and Maitreyi, one of Yajnavalkya's two wives, who is referred to as *brahmavadini*, or "discourser on sacred knowledge."

The dharma shastra texts, however, seem to suggest that scholarly opportunities for women had already been curtailed by the turn of the Common Era. These texts say that Vedic study is not open to women. The initiation ceremony that boys underwent is equated for women with marriage, and the ideal age of marriage for girls is lowered to before puberty, likely out of growing concern for maintaining caste purity. Domestic knowledge, or how to be a good housewife, is deemed the most appropriate training for women in order to fulfil the ideal of the **pativrata**—literally a woman who is "vowed to her husband-lord."

The depiction of women in the dharma shastras (echoes of which may be found in other Hindu literature) reveals the view that when women are under the tutelage and strict surveillance of men—when their chastity is protected—they are worthy of respect. When not well guarded, women are to be avoided by the righteous, for they are morally weak, conniving, and imbued with a host of other negative characteristics. Put another way, women as a whole—the female sex in the abstract—are viewed as naturally lustful and capricious. But assessed in particular roles—as daughters, wives, and mothers vis-à-vis male relatives and values—women are honourable and necessary for the well-being of men and society. Indeed, they are bringers of auspiciousness.

For example, in speaking of women as a whole, the Manusmriti says such things as: "The bed and the seat, jewellery, lust, anger, crookedness, a malicious nature, and bad conduct are what Manu assigned to women" (9.17).* But when discussed in their roles as daughters, wives, and mothers, the negative attributes change. One's daughter is to be regarded as the highest object of tenderness (4.185).* Young unmarried women and pregnant women are to be given special treatment on certain occasions (3.114).* Wives, destined to bear children, are equated with Sri, the goddess of prosperity (9.25).* Thus men who want to ensure

* Doniger, Wendy with Brian K. Smith. *The Laws of Manu.* (New York: Penguin Books, 1992).

Words

A Conversation between Gargi Vacaknavi and Yajnavalkya on the Nature of Brahman

In these excerpts from the Brhadaranyaka Upanishad (8.2–11), the female scholar Gargi Vacaknavi debates with the renowned sage Yajnavalkya:

2. [Gargi] said: "I rise to challenge you, Yajnavalkya, with two questions, much as a fierce warrior of Kasi or Videha, stringing his unstrung bow and taking two deadly arrows in his hand, would rise to challenge an enemy. Give me the answers to them!"
"Ask, Gargi."

3. She said: "The things above the sky, the things below the earth, and the things between the earth and the sky, as well as all those things people here refer to as past, present, and future—on what, Yajnavalkya, are all these woven back and forth?"

4. He replied "…on space, Gargi, are all these woven back and forth."

5. She responded: "All honour to you, Yajnavalkya. You really cleared that up for me! Get ready for the second."
"Ask, Gargi."…
"On what, then, is space woven back and forth?"

8. He replied: "That, Gargi, is the imperishable, and Brahmins refer to it like this—it is neither coarse nor fine; it is neither short nor long; it has neither blood nor fat; it is without shadow or darkness; it is without air or space; it is without contact; it has no taste or smell; it is without sight or hearing; it is without speech or mined; it is without

energy, breath, or mouth; it is beyond measure; it has nothing within it or outside of it. …

9. "This is the imperishable, Gargi, at whose command the sun and the moon stand apart … at whose command seconds and hours, days and nights, fortnights and months, seasons and years stand apart. … This is the imperishable, Gargi, at whose command people flatter donors, and gods are dependent on patrons of sacrifices, and forefathers, on ancestral offerings.

10. "Without knowing this imperishable, Gargi, even if a man were to make offerings, to offer sacrifices, and to perform austerities in this world for many thousands of years, all that would come to naught. Pitiful is the man, Gargi, who departs from this world without knowing this imperishable. But a man who departs from this world after he has come to know this imperishable—he, Gargi, is a Brahmin.

11. "This is the imperishable, Gargi, which sees but can't be seen; which hears but can't be heard; which thinks but can't be thought of; which perceives but can't be perceived. Besides this imperishable, there is no one that sees, no one that hears, no one that thinks, and no one that perceives.
"On this very imperishable, Gargi, space is woven back and forth."

Source: Patrick Olivelle, tr. *Upanishads*. (New York: Oxford University Press, 1996), 44–45 [diacritics omitted].

prosperity in the household must be attentive to their women. In turn, women must never act independently, even within their own house (5.147), or seek to separate themselves from their fathers, husbands, or sons (5.149). A wife must be obedient, always cheerful, clever in the management of her household affairs, and economical in expenditures (5.150–51).* When women fulfil these requirements, praise is heaped upon them—they are noble, pure, wise, good, capable. Those who are held up as supreme ideals for women to follow are those with an unblemished record in their roles as wives, for example, Sita, Savitri, and Parvati. Before turning to the great Sanskrit epics where the role of Sita as dharmic exemplary of wife is illustrated, it is important to note the contemporary scene with respect to religious options for women as Hindus.

In addition to the fact that for centuries some women have challenged traditional gender role expectations to pursue formal asceticism, thence abandoning family and former identities, and others have become renowned for their spiritual accomplishments—for instance, as leaders in the Bhakti movement (see below) and as gurus, like Anandamayi-Ma (d. 1981)—in recent decades women are also being trained as priests. The first school for women priests was the Shankar Seva Samiti, which began in the mid-1970s with a four-month training course. In 1990 another school, Gyan Prabhodini, also in the city of Pune, Maharashtra, opened training programs for women. Both now offer year-long courses so that women may conduct Sanskrit-based rituals for occasions such as life-cycle ceremonies, new business or house openings, and festivals. While there has been opposition among some Hindus to women priests, thousands of women have now been trained, and private priest-training facilities in other states in India are now opening their doors not just to women but also to non-Brahmins.

On the other hand, long-held attitudes that ascribe a greater value to boys are responsible for the fact that the sex ratio in India, as in China, is skewed against females. Modern technology, smaller families, and age-old preferences for boys have meant that the often hidden and somewhat uncommon practice of female infanticide is being replaced by abortion following the now illegal procedure of prenatal sex detection. According to India's 2001 census data, the sex ratio is 933 females to 1,000 males. More recent statistics are not indicating a positive change. The persistence

of dowry-related injuries and deaths of new brides is also indicative of not only materialistic impulses (the demands of husbands' families for more "things" from the bride's family) but also of the relative devaluation of females compared to males.

Dharma and the Great Sanskrit Epics

The great Sanskrit epics, the Mahabharata and the Ramayana, provide models of dharma and over the generations have affirmed key values and normative behaviours. Because of the importance of these epics in the lives of Hindus for the past two millennia, it is crucial for students of Hinduism to know something about them.

The two epics, we have learned, in India are often called the "fifth Veda," a designation that elevates their claims of authority and also speaks to the fact that they have served, in effect, as the "holy books" of the Hindu masses for whom the Vedas were not accessible. In addition to their epic narratives, these texts contain stories of gods, demons, kings, warriors, sages, and ordinary people. They also contain philosophical discourses, morality tales, and genealogies, and record the rise of theism and various religious sects. The epics have served to impart a wide range of knowledge on such subjects as geography, botany, astronomy, political and economic theory, military strategy and weaponry, medical lore, and aesthetics. It is no wonder that the Mahabharata, at 100 000 verses (the longest epic in the world), can say of itself: "Whatever is here may be found elsewhere, but what is absent from here does not exist anywhere" (1.56.33, 18.5.38).

Most Hindus hear stories from the epics from their early childhood, conveyed by grandparents or in the temples by religious scholars or trained storytellers. Indians have watched annual neighbourhood reenactments of key scenes from the Ramayana performed by both folk and specially trained actors, dancers, and musicians. Such enactments last days, even a whole month, as in the grand Ramalila staged annually in Banaras, on the banks of the Ganges River, where the main actors are treated as if they are the very gods they play. In modern times there have also been comic-book, film, and hugely popular made-for-TV versions of the epics. For most Hindus the actual historicity of the events or persons described in the epics has not been an issue as such. Rather, what is important is the enduring attraction of the stories being

* Doniger, Wendy with Brian K. Smith. *The Laws of Manu.* (New York: Penguin Books, 1992).

told, the sense of truth that they convey, and the sense of communal or traditional values and identity being communicated (Flood 1996, 104).

The word *mahabharata* means "great Bharata," in reference to the great history of the Bharata clan (and perhaps its massive size!). The epic is attributed to the Vedic sage Vyasa (whose name means "arranger"). Its stories were initially shaped and carried by wandering bards who sang or recited the stories as ballads in the assemblies of kings or chieftains; it was later set down in Sanskrit and edited by Brahmans between the first and fourth centuries C.E. Both the Mahabharata and the Ramayana deal with intrigues at court that result in a dozen years of exile for the protagonists, culminating in war against those who represent the forces of disorder and unrighteousness. Above all, both epics are about dharma: What is it? How does one know what is right? How does one practise it? The answers offered display some of the most striking differences between the two epics.

The Ramayana has no doubts about its basic morality, including the need to go to war because of the evilness of Ravana, who deserves to be defeated. The Mahabharata, however, is replete with questions, doubts, and uncertainties. It presents such dilemmas as what to do if personal dharma appears to conflict with caste dharma. The character Karna has to decide between loyalty to his adopted kin versus loyalty to his birth family and ancestors (he chooses loyalty to friendship). The warrior Arjuna faces the dilemma of killing his relatives and teachers, whom he knows represent his enemies, or refusing to fight. His older brother Yudhisthira, son of Dharma (and the one who probably most often questions it), asks: Are there times when it is justifiable to tell a lie? If so, then what does being truthful mean?

In brief, the main narrative of the Mahabharata tells the story of the long and bloody quarrel between two groups of cousins, the Pandavas and the Kauravas. This family quarrel over who will rule the kingdom results in banishment to the forest of the five Pandava brothers, along with their co-wife, Draupadi, for thirteen years, and finally ends with a terrible battle in Kuruksetra, where the fate of the world is at stake. On the one hand, everything is done to avoid this great battle, a battle that is viewed with ambivalence by many of the central protagonists. On the other hand, war seems inevitable—fate has decreed it so. Who wins? Apparently the Pandavas, but so many are lost, so much destruction has taken place, there is so much

treachery and intrigue (on both sides) that the epic seems to say, *All are losers.* Krishna's death toward the end of the story marks the beginning of the degenerate age of Kali Yuga, whereas Rama returns to rejoicing in his home city of Ayodhya and inaugurates ten thousand years of ideal rule (Brockington 1998, 25).

The Ramayana has been even more popular than the Mahabharata, in part because it is much shorter than its sister epic, with the narrative focusing on the core story of King Rama, who conquers evil and wins back his bride. Over the centuries King Rama became Lord Rama, a figure transformed from a martial hero into a manifestation of the god Vishnu who descends to earth in human form to restore dharma. Rama and his wife, Sita, continue to be popular figures of adoration among Hindus today. It is also, of course, a compelling story of treachery and bravery, heroism, love, and tragedy.

As a complete written story, the earliest version of the Ramayana is ascribed to the writer-sage Valmiki. Composed around the turn of the Common Era, it is considered the first classic poem of Sanskrit literature. It consists of twenty-four thousand couplets divided into seven books. It should be noted that there have been a number of versions of the Ramayana. Indeed, it is the famous Tulsidas version, composed in Hindi in the sixteenth century and called *Ramcaritmanas* ("Lake of the Acts of Rama"), that is probably best known in northern India today and is treated as a religious text. It has a strongly devotional orientation, emphasizing Rama's role as an incarnation of Vishnu. Today the Tulsidas version is often recited over the course of several days in homes and temples as an act of religious devotion. Another well-known version, and similarly devotional in tone, is that of Kampan, called the *Iramavataram*, composed in Tamil sometime in the tenth or eleventh century.

The story begins with the wise old king named Dasharatha, who is filled with sadness because, despite having three wives, he has no children. On the advice of his Brahmin counsellor he has an elaborate Vedic sacrifice performed. The gods, pleased with this, grant him four sons, destined, it turns out, to help the gods defeat the demon-king Ravana, who was granted the boon of not being conquerable by the gods themselves after he engaged in extraordinary acts of ascetic self-discipline. The god Vishnu gives his blessing in the form of nectar to the three queens, but because Queen Kausalya drinks the major share, her son, Rama, is the one destined to be the "god-protector" and demon-killer. Like Arjuna in the Mahabharata, Rama acquires great mastery over weaponry as he grows up, especially over the bow; he also gains magical weapons from powerful sages.

After winning an archery contest (like Arjuna), Rama also wins the hand of Sita, daughter of King Janaka of Videha. No ordinary woman, she was born magically from a furrow (*sita*) in the earth, and her mother was the goddess Prithvi, or Mother Earth. Now, Rama, as first-born, is supposed to become king, but Bharata's mother, Queen Kaikeyi, makes good on a promised boon from her husband, contriving to have her own son made king and to have Rama banished to the forest for fourteen years. Rama himself insists that his father honour this pledge. He agrees to go to the forest ("my dharma now is the will of my father and mother; I could not bear to live disrespecting their command"); as a dutiful wife, Sita insists on accompanying him, and his younger brother Lakshmana also insists on going.

Rama's father, King Dasharatha, dies from grief. Bharata refuses to become king and tries to persuade his brother to return; when that fails, he puts Rama's sandals on the throne and becomes regent. In the wild forest, Rama and Lakshmana are set upon by a partic-ularly horrible demon, who turns out to be Ravana's sister. Lakshmana cuts off her nose, and in a fury she goes to Ravana to describe what has happened. Ravana is so taken with her description of Sita that he succeeds, through a ruse, in kidnapping her and imprisoning her in his palace in the island-city of Lanka. There Ravana tries in various ways to persuade Sita to become his chief queen, but she refuses. Because he has fallen in love with her, he refrains from forcing himself upon her.

Meanwhile, Rama is beside himself with grief and rage and is single-mindedly determined to rescue Sita. To that end he enlists the support of the king of mon-keys, Sugriva. Eventually the monkey general Hanuman locates Sita in Lanka; on the way over the water from the mainland he encounters fierce opposition, which he overcomes through his magical ability to change size. Secretly Hanuman watches Sita, hears her continuing refusals to accept Ravana's enticements, and at an oppor-tune time is able to quietly tell her that Rama is going to rescue her. He also offers to take her away right there and then, but Sita refuses, as she will not allow anyone other than her husband to touch her. After being cap-tured and then escaping, Hanuman returns to Rama.

A colossal battle eventually takes place between the forces of good—Rama and his allies—and the forces of evil—Ravana and his hordes. Naturally the forces of good prevail. Sita is rescued, but the reunion of husband and wife is not altogether a happy one: Rama verbally abuses her and in effect rejects her as soiled goods. The aggrieved Sita commands a funeral pyre be built and lit, utters a truth vow in which she says, "If I have ever been unchaste in thought, word or deed, may you (Agni) burn me up." Then she throws herself on the fire while Rama looks on silently. The gods intervene: Brahma announces that Rama is really Vishnu, and Agni protects Sita from the flames. Rama takes her back, they all return to Ayodhya in triumph, and Rama is installed as king.

But the story does not end there, especially for Sita. The last book of the Ramayana depicts Rama hearing rumours among the populace about Sita's infidelity while a captive of Ravana. Despite the fire ordeal in which Sita publicly proved her fidelity, Rama decides he must attend first and foremost to his duty, his dharma, as king, and so he banishes the now pregnant queen, even though he knows the rumours to be false. A number of years later, when Rama is in the midst of holding a great Vedic sacrifice, two young singers appear and begin to recite the Ramayana. These two, the twins Kusha and Lava, are in fact the sons of Rama and Sita; they have sheltered with their mother in the ashram of the sage Valmiki, author of the poem. Rama sends for his beloved queen, intending to take her back. However, Sita has had enough: she calls upon her mother, the earth, to receive her. The ground opens and Sita vanishes forever. Consumed by grief, Rama divides the kingdom between his sons and then, fol-lowed by all the inhabitants of Ayodhya, he enters the nearby waters of the Sarayu River and dies. Rama finally returns to heaven as the Lord Vishnu. (Summary adapted from Goldman 1984, 3–17.)

As noted before, the Ramayana, more than any other Hindu text, furnishes models of the ideals of dharma. To review, Rama is the perfect son: he obeys the letter and spirit of his father's wishes and refuses to allow a pledge to be broken (even to his own apparent detriment). He is the perfect king who upholds dharma above all else, sacrificing his own interests for the sake of his subjects and his duties. He is honest and brave. He is even the ideal husband, for he rescues and pro-tects his wife and is a paragon of devoted monogamous love, even if Sita's place in his heart is inferior to that of his male relations and his subjects. Sita, in turn, is the perfect wife. She obeys her husband yet also counsels

> **Jnana:** knowledge; the path of knowledge as a religious discipline; wisdom that brings spiritual liberation.

him. She willingly shares in her husband's misfortunes. She is chaste in thought, word, and deed. She is modest and self-sacrificing (literally) yet strong in the sense of exhibiting fortitude and dignity. She is beautiful and she gives her husband two sons. Note that the epics do not portray women as powerless. However, their power is depicted as derived from self-effacement in a relationship of subservience to the male, a self-effacement occasionally equated in Hindu literature with the spiritual power that ascetics derive from their own self-mortification. Then there is Lakshmana, the ideal younger brother, who defers to the authority of his brother but also offers advice and counsel when appropriate and is his friend and confidante. He puts his brother's well-being before his own and defends his brother's interests. Finally, there is Hanuman, the perfect devotee, who is himself an object of much devotion in north India today. He is dedicated to Rama, self-effacing, but also a great warrior: brave, clever, self-sacrificing, and utterly loyal to his king.

Spiritual Paths and the Teachings of the Bhagavad-Gita

While the dharma shastras are the most explicit and systematic religio-juridical manuals for right conduct and the epics give us models for dharmic behaviour, texts such as the Bhagavad-Gita provide the undergirding philosophical framework for why and how one should live a spiritual life in relationship to God. The Bhagavad-Gita ("Song of the Lord") is one of the most beloved texts in Hinduism. Found in the sixth book of the Mahabharata, it is composed in the form of a dialogue between the great warrior Arjuna and his charioteer, Krishna. The Gita opens with Arjuna, having been asked to blow the conch shell to signal the beginning of the great battle between the rival Pandavas and Kauravas, arriving between the two armies in a chariot guided by Krishna, who, though a prince, has refused to fight in this war. As Arjuna raises the conch to his lips, he sees his brothers and allies on one side and on the other side he sees his cousins, former teachers, friends—not all clearly enemies. He becomes paralyzed

by doubt. Krishna turns to him and at first tries to cajole Arjuna into picking up his great bow, but Arjuna remains despondent. Krishna then proceeds to teach him while Arjuna periodically asks for clarification in the style of the Upanishads.

In the eighteen short chapters of the Gita, three discrete but interrelated paths (called *yoga*s, here meaning "discipline") are laid out that take one toward the goal of spiritual freedom, self-knowledge, liberation from the wheel of rebirth, and union with Brahman, or eternal life with God. One path is the path of action (*karma yoga*). Even God, though unaffected by the law of karma or by the actions of creation, is constantly acting, constantly at work in the world, for if God were not, the universe would fall apart (3.22–24).* All the more, we embodied humans cannot escape action. The text is speaking about karma as "action"—not only ritual action (as in the Vedas), not only the idea of the law of cause and effect, but simply any action. The Gita says that the yoga of action requires that whatever one does, it must be done in a spirit of faith and detachment. Without detachment, action can bind one further to the world. Significantly, the teachings of the Gita reject the idea that one can be freed from the effects of karma by withdrawing from society, nor is renunciation of the world alone able to bring one to perfection (3.4). According to the Gita, the path of action must be informed by pure intentions, sound judgment, and knowledge. Thus, it is rightly informed and pure intention that is karmically significant, not the fruit or results of one's actions. You can control your intentions, but you cannot control either the outcomes or how others react to your actions.

The second path is that of knowledge or wisdom (***jnana** yoga*). Here the focus is on the study of scripture, the practice of meditation, and the acquisition of insight and understanding, "for wisdom is in truth the end of all holy work" (4.33).* "A constant yearning to know the inner Spirit, and a vision of Truth which gives liberation: this is true wisdom.... All against this is ignorance" (13.11).* The third path is that of devotion (*bhakti yoga*). This path involves surrendering oneself to God and allowing God's love to inform and direct one's actions, speech, and thought. This path is considered by the Bhagavad-Gita to be the supreme path: The "greatest of all Yogis is he who with all his soul has faith, and he who with all his soul loves me [Krishna]" (6.47).* The key to each of these paths, to living the

---

* Mascaro, Juan, tr. *The Bhagavad Gita*. (New York: Penguin Books, 1962).

spiritual life, is to cultivate an attitude of detachment or disinterestedness, to act, that is, to perform one's responsibilities out of love of God rather than out of ego or concern for one's own well-being. In short, the goal in this life is to cultivate a positive attachment to the love of God, to dedicate oneself wholly to God while living in the world, and to achieve inner equanimity and peace.

There are several aspects of this important text that are noteworthy. First, the Gita opens the door to self-realization for all people, including women and Shudras. This opening is accomplished in part by allowing very simple forms of worship to be deemed acceptable to God if they are offered with a pure heart. Second, the Gita is a profoundly theistic text; it is one of the first Hindu texts to give such prominence to devotion and self-surrender (**bhakti**) to God. The rise of theism and bhakti in Hinduism gave birth to a whole movement (see below) that began in the south of India and resulted in an outpouring of devotional literature composed in vernacular languages, in the building of temples, and in new rituals of worship—all of which have come to characterize the practice of Hinduism today. Finally, a theology of God, and of Krishna as a manifestation (or incarnation) of God in particular, is articulated in a new way.

Hindu Concepts of the Divine

The names of some Hindu gods have now been mentioned in this chapter, including Krishna, Rama, and Vishnu. Let us look more closely at how Hindus understand the nature of the Divine. At first glance, Hindus appear to believe in many gods. Certainly a visit to a Hindu temple might give this impression, and a cursory read through Hindu literature will acquaint one with a wide variety of names, iconographies, and stories of various deities. Numerous Hindus, however, will affirm that the Divine is ultimately singular, and that the many forms and names of the gods are aspects, emanations, or symbols of the one formless, eternal God.

There are two major views of the nature of the Divine in Hindu religious history, one monistic and one theistic. The monistic view conceives of God, or the Absolute, as an abstract, impersonal principle, the ground or basis for all that is. As we have seen, the most common designation for this genderless reality is Brahman. While the term *Brahman* first appears

Bhakti: the path of fervent, selfless devotion to God as a religious discipline and means of spiritual liberation.

in the Upanishads in the sense of one unchanging reality behind and pervading the changing visible world, even earlier there are hints of the One "who created the many gods" (Rig-Veda 10.121), and "that which is One the sages speak of in various terms" in Vedic hymns. In the Upanishads, Brahman is not generally presented as an object of worship, but rather as an object of knowledge and meditation, best understood through the attributes of being, consciousness, and joy (*sat-cit-ananda*). The most famous exponent of this monistic philosophy, which is called Advaita Vedanta, was the ninth-century philosopher Shankaracarya.

While most of the Upanishads describe a monistic perspective, some reveal a theistic perspective in which God is to be adored as the Lord. The second major view of the Divine, then, is one in which God is both the Supreme Being, responsible for creation, preservation, and dissolution of the universe, and personal and in active relationship with his creation. According to the Svestashvatara Upanishad, for example, God is both the ruler and refuge of the whole world (3.17). In another passage,

> After we have first venerated that adorable God displaying every form, the source of all beings, as residing within one's heart, and then recognized him as the one who bestows righteousness and removes evil, as the Lord of prosperity, as abiding within ourselves (*atman*), as the Immortal residing in all beings—we will find this highest God among gods, the highest master among masters, the God beyond the highest as the adorable Lord of the universe. (6.6–7)

Source: Patrick Olivelle, tr. *Upanishads.* (New York: Oxford University Press, 1996).

Avatara: "descent" of God (often Vishnu) in an earthly form such as Krishna or Rama to restore dharma.

Sampradaya: "sect" (or sub-sect) that usually follows a lineage begun by a founding guru.

The theistic perspective finds one of its most profound expositions in the Bhagavad-Gita, where the entire tenth and eleventh chapters eloquently describe the power, glory, mercy, and fearfulness of God, here identified with Krishna. For example, Krishna is described as the best in each class of things in the following excerpts:

> … of utterances, I am the single syllable aum; of offerings I am the offering of silent meditation…. Of trees I am the tree of life…. Of weapons I am the thunderbolt…. Among creators I am the creator of love…. I am the beginning, the middle and the end of all that is. Of all knowledge I am the knowledge of the Self…. I am death that carries off all things, and I am the source of all things to come…. Know thou that whatever is beautiful and good, whatever has glory and power is only a portion of my own radiance. (10.25–42)

Source: Mascaro, Juan, tr. *The Bhagavad Gita*. (New York: Penguin Books, 1962).

Other texts later on praise Shiva or Vishnu or Devi, the Great Goddess, as the one God who is the supreme creator and ruler and, ultimately, destroyer of the universe. While many Hindus develop a special relationship with one particular deity that has its own characteristics, bodies of myths, prayers, songs, and rites of worship, they readily recognize that other deities may serve the same role as faces of the one God whose true essence is beyond all human comprehension. These, then, are not jealous gods. It should be noted as well that some Hindu theists prefer to worship God without reference to physical iconography or an image, while other theists (probably the majority of Hindus) prefer to conceive of God through certain attributes and to worship the divine in a particular form or image.

The concept of **avatara**, or the "descent" of God in human form, allowed for the possibility of divine intervention in human history, an intervention whose purpose was to restore religious or spiritual order (that is, dharma). Krishna says in the Gita (4.7–8) that whenever there is a decline of dharma and a rise of unrighteousness, then he manifests himself: "For the salvation of those who are good, for the destruction of evil in men, for the fulfilment of the kingdom of righteousness, I come into this world in the ages that pass." Later Hindu texts describe several specific avataras of the god Vishnu, commonly nine in number. These avataras begin with Vishnu rescuing dharma first in the form of a fish, then as a tortoise, the man-boar (Varaha), the man-lion (Narasimha), the dwarf (Vamana), Rama with the axe (Parasurama), Lord Rama, Lord Krishna, and the Buddha; the last in this list is Kalki—the future descent of Vishnu. Scholarship suggests historical origins or perhaps precursors to some of these figures, such as Rama and Krishna, who may have started as independent, then divinized, folk heroes. As for the major Hindu goddesses, what often began as local or regional divine or divinized figures were amalgamated over time into the Sanskritic pan-Hindu pantheon. Even the Buddha is secured under the umbrella of Hinduism, through his placement as a "descent" of Vishnu.

Hindu Gods and Goddesses

Hinduism includes a vast wealth of mythological literature that developed the stories, symbolism, iconographies, modes of worship, and meanings of the divine far beyond what one encounters in the Vedas. Because we are now moving from the trunk of the tree of Hinduism to its major branches, it is important to be aware that, over the centuries, not only did a number of distinct philosophical traditions evolve, but also theological and ritual traditions clustered around particular deities and particular gurus, who became founders of **sampradayas**, or what one might call sub-sects. Examples of such gurus are the Bengali saint Caitanaya (d. 1533), precursor of the International Society for Krishna Consciousness (ISKCON) movement in North America, and the Gujarati swami Narayan (d. 1830). Then there are those sampradayas that arose from the "poet-saints" of the bhakti movement. These sampradayas may be seen as smaller branches emerging from three or four very large branches. These larger branches are Vaishnavism—those who follow Vishnu as the main deity; Shaivism—those who follow Shiva as the main deity; and Shaktism—those who follow the Goddess as the main deity.

Vishnu and Vaishnavism In the Rig-Veda, Vishnu appears in a minor role as a benevolent solar deva. The name *Vishnu* is said to be derived from the root *vish* ("to enter"), so Vishnu is "he who enters or pervades the universe." In one Vedic hymn Vishnu takes three strides, separating the earth from the sky. This image is elaborated centuries later in a myth from the Puranas in which Vishnu, incarnated as Vamana the dwarf, covers the universe in three strides and destroys the power of the demon Bali. In the Puranas and other literature that extols Vishnu as the Supreme Being, Vishnu is the transcendent Lord who dwells in the highest heaven, at the top of the cosmic egg, where, with their Lord's grace, his devotees go upon liberation.

More than any other major deity in Hinduism, Vishnu is associated with kingship and with the protection of dharma. When he comes to be represented iconographically, he is depicted in two major ways. He is shown as a dark blue youth standing upright with a high crown on his head, his four arms holding symbols that represent kingship and his role as protector of dharma, the sustainer of the universe. These symbols are a club or mace (a symbol of kingship), a discus (a weapon, but also a symbol of the cycle of life and death), a lotus (symbol of a throne and of the goddess Lakshmi), and a conch (whose sound is said to ward off evil and whose spiral is symbolic of infinite space). In the second type of depiction, Vishnu is represented as a figure reclining on the coils of the great snake Shesha, floating on the cosmic ocean. In the myths, when Vishnu awakes after a period of quiescence between iterations of the universe, he (re)creates the universe. A lotus emerges from his navel and out of the lotus appears the creator god Brahma, who then manifests the universe, which is maintained by Vishnu and finally destroyed by Shiva.

In images of Vishnu one also often sees the eagle Garuda, who is his **vahana** ("vehicle" or mount). Each major deity in Hinduism came to be associated with a particular animal vehicle, just as each major male deity came to be associated with a particular consort goddess, sometimes described as their **shakti**, or "power." In Vishnu's case his consort is Sri-Lakshmi, who for many centuries, and still today, has been a popular

> **Vahana:** a "vehicle" or mount of the gods, usually a particular animal associated with each deity.
>
> **Shakti:** power or energy associated with the goddess (*devi*).

goddess associated with wealth, prosperity, luck, and well-being. Her primary symbol is the lotus flower.

As we have seen, Vishnu also manifests in the world in the forms of his ten avataras to rescue us from chaos and irreligion; two avataras became especially significant as virtually independent deities, namely Rama and Krishna. Entering a Hindu temple today, one often encounters images of Rama with Sita at his side, as well as Krishna with his consort, Radha. Krishna is especially beloved today in two forms: as the boy-child given to both pranks and miracles as he grew up with his adopted family in the bucolic village setting of Dwaraka, and as the attractive young cowherd (Krishna-Gopala) who plays his flute and draws to him all the village women. His amorous dalliances are likened to God's eliciting feelings of rapturous love from his devotees. One of the wealthiest and busiest temples in India today is the Vishnu temple in Tirupati, Andhra Pradesh, where Vishnu is known as Venkateshvara. Some 100 000 pilgrims visit this temple daily.

Shiva and Shaivism The many sides of Shiva's personality and roles suggests an amalgamation of several originally distinct, as well as ancient, local Hindu deities, for Shiva is full of apparent contradictions. He is both terrifying and gracious, a destroyer and a creator, an ascetic and also a family man, as well as, in iconography, half male and half female in one body. Shiva has been identified with the Vedic deva Rudra, "the Roarer." The three hymns addressed to Rudra as lord of the Maruts (storm gods) in the Rig-Veda (2.33, 1.43, 1.114) depict him as ferocious and destructive. Yet he is also depicted as a healer and cooler of diseases who is praised but also asked not to harm children or kill the horses and cattle. Rudra is called *shiva*, meaning "auspicious," in one place in the Rig-Veda (10.92.9). The "Shatarudriya" ("hundred names of Rudra") is a hymn found in the Taittirya Samhita of the Yajur-Veda that is still sung today, about placating the fearful yet gracious Rudra.

In the Svetasvatara Upanishad (c. fifth century B.C.E.) Rudra is described as the supreme lord of

Hindu Women Making Offerings to the Shiva-linga on Assi Ghat in Banaras. Images of Hindu deities may be in a representational (iconic), abstract (aniconic), or natural form. One of the most commonly worshipped forms of Shiva is his aniconic form as the *linga*, a cylindrical shape usually made of stone, often placed on an image of the *yoni*, representing the feminine creative force, or womb. Thus Shiva and shakti are interlinked in their creative power. The worshippers are offering Shiva *bilva* leaves, which are sacred to him. (Each deity is associated with particular colours, foods, and plants. Vishnu, for instance, is associated with *tulsi*, or basil leaves.) Each major deity is associated with a vahana, or vehicle, and Shiva's is the white bull Nandi, who represents strength, virility, and self-control. In this photo it is perfectly appropriate that the bull, who happened to wander by, should be happily consuming the leaves the worshippers offer to Shiva.

Source: Anne M. Pearson

creation. In this Upanishad the Lord Rudra (i.e., Shiva) is likened to a magician who produces the world through his power and sustains it. The Lord is transcendent, dwelling beyond the cosmos, yet also immanent, dwelling in the hearts of all beings. Some centuries later the Sanskrit Puranas (and other texts, called the Agamas) contain fully developed myths and theologies of Lord Shiva and descriptions of how to worship him, providing the basis for contemporary ritual manuals. Great temples dedicated to Lord Shiva and also to his consort—variously the goddesses Sati, Uma, and Parvati—appeared in the later centuries of the first millennium c.e., especially under the south Indian Tamil Chola dynasty (c. 850–1250 at Tanjore).

Shiva is portrayed in five main forms. (1) He is shown as an ascetic, sitting in a posture of meditation, often with a "third eye" (referring to inner sight) on his forehead, his hair bound up on top of his head like a crown. He wears an antelope skin and a string of beads and holds a trident. (2) He is shown as a benevolent protector and

loving husband, with his consort Uma or Parvati at his side, and with his primary animal vehicle, the bull Nandi. (3) He is portrayed as Nataraja, "Lord of Dance," who dances creation into being and dances the destruction of the world at the end of time. He is depicted holding a small drum, symbolizing the original sound of the universe, the beginning of all things. In another hand he holds a staff, symbolizing authority and punishment; in another he holds a trident, symbolizing power and asceticism, and in another he holds fire, symbolizing destruction and transformation. His hair is a fan of matted locks decorated with snakes, and he is stamping on a dwarf figure that represents ignorance. (4) He is represented by the non-figurative *linga*, a rounded-off cylindrical shape. This phallic form emphasizes his role as creator. (5) Least commonly, he is portrayed in a fierce form as Bhairava, a "terrifying" form similar to the goddess Kali.

Shiva's consort is the goddess Parvati, who is portrayed as a benign wife and mother. She is mother to two sons, Ganesha and Kartikeyya. Ganesha is a particularly beloved god in India. His name is frequently intoned at beginnings, whether reciting a prayer or cutting into the earth to begin construction of a new temple or home, for he is the "remover of obstacles." In the early 1990s, images of Ganesha around the globe were said to miraculously consume spoonfuls of milk that were offered to him by devotees.

The Goddess (*devi*) and Shaktism Hinduism may well have more images of the divine feminine than any other religion in the world. Unlike the male gods, who tend to remain distinct, the Hindu goddesses have often been conflated with one another, and the ubiquitous village goddesses are often identified with some pan-Indian goddess. Any goddess may be referred to simply as "mother goddess." A generic term used for the divine feminine is Mahadevi, or "Great Goddess." It appears in the Puranas and in the texts called *shakta tantra*s, where the goddess is elevated to the position of supreme godhead, the real ultimate power of the universe, while the other great gods are merely her instruments and servants.

Perhaps the most important form of the Great Goddess today is Durga. Note that not all the characteristics associated with and praiseworthy in goddesses are considered praiseworthy in women—especially for such goddesses as Durga and Kali. Both clearly challenge traditional gender roles, for their primary mythological function is to combat demons who threaten the stability of the cosmos. The most prominent myth of Durga is her killing of the buffalo demon Mahisha. The Markandeya Purana (c. fourth century C.E.), for instance, describes how for a hundred years the gods and anti-gods have been fighting against each other. The gods are defeated and Mahisha becomes the lord of heaven. The defeated gods approach Shiva and Vishnu for help, conceding that they are powerless against the great demon. In the end, Durga is created from the combined powers of the male gods, and with her own shakti (power) is able to defeat the forces of evil when they cannot. While Durga's primary mythic associations have been with her role as a warrior queen, protector of the cosmos, and restorer of dharma (a kind of female Vishnu), she is also a mother who protects all beings and a daughter who returns home once a year to visit with her natal family.

Words

Hymn of Praise to the Great Goddess (Mahadevi)

The Sanskrit text called the *Devi Mahatmya*, composed around 500 C.E., developed the philosophical and theological identity and meaning of Durga as the primary deity of the universe. Here is an example of a *stotra*, or hymn of praise, to her that can be found in this text:

"By you this universe is borne, by you this world has been created. By you it is protected and you, O Devi, shall consume it at the end. You are the Great Knowledge and the Great Illusion, you are Great power and Great Memory, Great Delusion, the Great Devi and the Great Asuri. You are Primordial Matter, you are the ground of the three *gunas*, you are the Great Night of the end of the world and you are the Great Darkness of delusion. You are the goddess of good fortune, the ruler, modesty, intelligence with knowledge, bashfulness, nourishment, contentment, tranquillity and forbearance. Armed with the sword, the spear, the club, the discus, the conch, the bow, with arrows, slings and iron mace you are terrible and also more pleasing than everything else and exceedingly beautiful. You are above all, the supreme Mistress. You are the *śakti*, the power of all things, sentient … you are the soul of everything. Who is capable of praising you, who has given form to all of us, to Visnu, Śiva and myself?" asks Brahma.

Source: *Devimahatmya I*, 75 ff. Markendeya Purana, E. Pargiter, trans. (Delhi: Indological Book House, 1969), 81.

Sculpted and painted images show Hindu deities in poses that are meant to reveal their power and attributes. The many arms exemplify the supernatural power of the gods; the implements in their hands are symbols of divine qualities and associations. Traditionally the goddess Durga has eight hands, in which she holds various weapons and symbols of sovereignty: sword, mace, sceptre, trident, snake, conch, discus, and bell. Different forms of the Great Goddess are worshipped during the nine days of Navaratri leading up to Durga Puja, and often temporary outdoor images of the goddess will be constructed for viewing and worship. Many devotees fast fully or partially during this time. It is also a traditional time for newly married women to return to their natal families for extended visits, just as Durga is portrayed as returning home for a respite from the challenges of living with her ascetic god-husband Shiva.

Source: neelsky/Shutterstock

Today Durga is especially honoured during an autumn festival called Navaratri ("nine nights"), which is quite likely related in origin to harvest festivals. Typically nine plants are used in her worship. These plants (as sprouted seeds) are placed in a clay pot with Ganges water; Durga is worshipped as the pot, praised as the source of life. On each night of Navaratri a different form of the great goddess is worshipped, and on the last day the main image of Durga, showing her slaying the buffalo demon, is paraded down the streets and thrown into the nearest body of water (usually a river or pond). This, in fact, is the usual way of disposing of painted clay forms when they have served their function as temporary vessels for the god or goddess during festivals. Rituals of worship for goddesses may include animal sacrifices,

especially of goats and buffalo (the latter representing the demon Mahisha that Durga vanquished). The reason for animal sacrifices, likely stemming from ancient practices, is that their blood is believed to be needed by the goddess to fortify her for her work of protection.

Another significant goddess is Kali. For centuries Kali was on the margins of Hindu devotional practice, but she has experienced a much broader acceptance in Hinduism today. She has even been embraced by some feminists fed up with the androcentrism of Western religions and looking for some other models of the Divine. Kali is not a beautiful, young, beneficent goddess. Rather, she is normally depicted as having a frightening appearance: black in colour, usually naked and gaunt, hair long and dishevelled, and wearing a girdle of severed arms and freshly cut-off heads as a necklace. She has long, sharp fangs dripping with blood, and she laughs loudly, dances madly, and lives in a cremation ground.

Earliest references to Kali date to about 600 C.E. in the Puranas, where she is invoked to vanquish one's enemies. Her most famous appearances in battle contexts are found in the *Devi Mahatmya* (8.49–61), where she is summoned by Durga to help her defeat Raktabija, a demon who can reproduce himself instantly whenever a drop of his blood falls to the ground. Having wounded Raktabija with a variety of weapons, Durga finds that she has worsened the situation, for the demon's blood quickly produces more demons. Kali defeats the demon by sucking the blood from his body and throwing the countless duplicate demons into her gaping mouth. In such episodes, Kali personifies Durga's (or in some cases Parvati's) fury. She represents the goddesses' dark, negative, violent nature, the dangerous dimension of the divine feminine that is released when goddesses become enraged or are summoned to take part in war and killing. Although Kali may be said to serve the realm of dharmic order in her role as slayer of demons, she gets out of control in the battle frenzy, drunk with the blood of her victims, and begins to destroy the world that she is supposed to protect. Thus, is some myths, Shiva places himself beneath the wildly dancing feet of Kali as the only means left to calm the frenzied goddess. The figure of Kali symbolizes those aspects of reality related to destruction, death, and terror. Though called "mother" by her devotees, she is no standard mother goddess: her breasts are shrivelled instead of full; her eyes are flaming and wrathful instead of sweet and compassionate; and instead of giving, she is ever hungry, often demanding blood sacrifice in her worship.

Sarasvati, the goddess of music, learning, and culture, has been likened to the Greek goddess Athena. She is one of the few Vedic goddesses whose stature moved past the Vedic period into classical Hinduism. To this day she is worshipped by schoolchildren, musicians, and scholars as the patron goddess of learning. In iconography she is portrayed wearing white garments, sitting on a lotus playing the vina (a lute-like instrument), and holding a scroll (book) in another hand, often with a swan, her vahana, nearby. For those who supplicate her she removes speech defects and grants charming speech and a musical voice, knowledge, wisdom, and creativity.

The Rise of the Path of Devotion: The Poet-Saints of the Bhakti Movement

The Gita stood at the threshold between the old ritual Brahmanical religion and new forms of Hinduism where the path of God-realization could be open to anyone with sincere faith. These new forms were concurrent with the development of sectarianism and the rise of the bhakti movement. This latter phenomenon was based on a set of ideas exemplified by the lives and poetry of an unlikely group of spiritual leaders. It was first seen in the Tamil south in the sixth century and had slowly swept up to the north by the fifteenth century. Common to the bhakti movement were male and female poet-saints of high or low caste, known by name and surrounded by legendary history, singing songs of devotion to Krishna, Rama, Vishnu, or Shiva in the common language of their area. The religious poetry produced by the mystics of the bhakti movement, composed in such languages as Tamil, Hindi, and Marathi, has been described as "the richest library of devotion in world literature, distinguished not only by its religious intensity but also by the great variety of psychological states and emotional responses it explores" (Lopez 1995, 40).

While the idea of bhakti (love of God) is intimated in some of the Vedas, the word itself does not appear until the Upanishads, and even then very rarely. The *Yoga Sutras* introduce the notion of self-surrender to God, but the concept of love of God as an end in itself is not present. The Bhagavad-Gita makes bhakti one of three principal yogas, or paths to liberation, but with the rise of devotional movements, the way of bhakti became celebrated as the chief means to achieve the goal of union with God. It completely overtakes the place of wisdom or philosophical knowledge—now it is bhakti that destroys all past sins. This bhakti is an outpouring of intense feelings of attachment to the Divine, participating in the joy of God's divine play (*lila*), and expressed in tears, laughter, song, dance, and poetry—in short, "God intoxication."

The *Bhagavata Purana* (c. ninth century C.E.) describes nine kinds of bhakti, including remembering, hearing, and singing the name of God, actual or mental worship of the image of God, and finally annihilation of the self as the crowning phase of devotional life, the ultimate mystical experience of union with God.

Images of how one should regard oneself in relation to God include as a servant to a master, a lover to the beloved, a mother to her child, and a friend to a friend.

The bhakti movement arose initially among two groups of poet-saints from the Tamil south of India. One group, the Alvars, directed their devotion to Vishnu. They included a woman named Antal who sang about her love for Krishna. Their poetry is collected in the *Divya Prabandham*. A larger group of sixty-three called the Nayanars directed their devotion to Shiva. They included court aristocrats, Brahmins, peasants, an untouchable, and a famous woman named Karaikkal Ammaiyar (sixth century C.E.). Their devotional poetry was collected into eleven books, one of which is called the *Tevaram,* which contains the poetry of three of the most renowned Nayanars: Campantar, Appar, and Cunatarar. The *Tevaram* is still much beloved by Tamil Shaivas today, and its poems are often sung at home and in temples. Together the collections of Alvar and Nayanar poetry are referred to as the Tamil Veda.

Another famous Tamil poet-saint was Manikkavacakar (eighth century), who was a minister to the Pandyan court. In his revered text the *Tiruvacakam* he sings to Shiva:

I shall raise my hands in prayer to you; I shall clasp your holy feet and call your name. I shall melt like wax before the flame, incessantly calling out "my Beloved Father." I shall cast off this body and enter the celestial city of Sivapura. I shall behold your effulgent glory. In joyful bliss shall I join the society of true devotees. Then I shall look up to hear you say with your beauteous lips: "Fear Not!" The assurance of your all-embracing love alone can set my soul at ease and peace. (*Tiruvacakam* 25: 8–10, Ratna Navaratnam, trans., in Klostermaier 2007, 274)

Two Poems from Poet-Saints of the Bhakti Movement

Appar (Tamil Nadu, c. 7th century)

Our Lord is not
  the sun of reaching rays
  the moon
  the customs according to the Vedas
  the heavens, the earth, and the three winds
  the fire that destroys
  the water that cleanses;

He comes with graceful compassion
As half Umā of the eyes with red lines,
On His chest a shining garland of snakes.
This Lord is of neither the celestials nor mortals.

Dasimayya (10th century)

If they see
breasts and long hair coming
they call it woman,
if beard and whiskers
they call it man:
but, look, the self that hovers
in between
is neither man nor woman
O Ramanatha.

Sources: (top) K. Pechilis Prentiss. *The Embodiment of Bhakti.* (New York: Oxford University Press, 1999). (bottom) A. K. Ramanujan, tr. *Speaking of Siva.* (New York: Penguin Books, 1973).

From the south, the movement spread northward over several centuries, giving rise to a number of poet-saints, from Tukaram in Maharashtra to the low-caste shoemaker Ravidas in Banaras. They also expressed their love of God in poetry that continues to be sung today among Hindus in homes and temples, in a style called **bhajan**. The poet-saints from south to north displayed a disregard for social conventions, including family life. They questioned and sometimes ridiculed in their poetry the dharma shastra prescriptions for a proper life, various forms of rituals of worship, and expressions of spirituality. Plenty of such examples may be found in the poetry of the Nayanar named Appar, for instance, or in the work of Kabir, the weaver from Banaras claimed today by Muslims, Hindus, and Sikhs. He frequently mocked the superficial spirituality he witnessed around him, as in this verse: "If shaving your head Spelled spiritual success, heaven would be filled with sheep" (Hawley and Jurgensmeyer 2007, 50). Yet this was no Protestant Revolution, for their criticisms were subdued by their emphasis on the unreality of existing social bonds, not their injustice.

Bhajan: devotional song sung in communal context, often accompanied by a harmonium.

Puja: worship; ritual and prayer offered to the deity in the home or temple (another term is *archana*).

Arati: the ritual of circling a flame (*dipa*) in front of the deity, usually at the end of puja.

One very popular North Indian poet-saint was a sixteenth-century woman named Mirabai. She was a Rajput princess whose husband had died soon after their arranged marriage. Mirabai was encouraged to burn herself on her husband's funeral pyre *sati* or at least to behave like a proper widow of her class, but she refused and instead became even more strongly a devotee of Krishna, whom she considered her true husband. The poems ascribed to her tell of how family members tried to poison her, yet she miraculously escaped because of the intervention of Krishna. She became a wandering mendicant, attracting many followers and admirers. She is said to have died by merging with the image of Krishna in a temple she was visiting.

Puja: Worshipping God in Hinduism

The term *puja* means "worship" and is the core ritual of popular theistic Hinduism, largely replacing the older Vedic rituals of sacrifice to the gods, which did not make use of images or temples. Puja is performed every day, sometimes several times a day, by ordinary men and women in their homes and in temples by puja priests (called *purohit* or *pujaris*). Puja is essentially a ritual to honour God (or gods and goddesses) that involves the worshipper receiving and entertaining an image of God, who is treated as a distinguished and beloved guest. The rituals to honour the deity typically consist of symbolic acts accompanied by set prayers or mantras; the worshipper welcomes the deity with a drink of water, makes various offerings to the deity (water, flowers, food, incense), and concludes with **arati**, a ritual circling of a camphor flame in front of the deity (or deities). Elements such as fire and water have multiple symbolic meanings that are evoked in puja. Puja rituals can be very simple, taking only a few minutes, or very elaborate, taking several hours to perform—it depends on the occasion, the place, and the worshipper.

Mirabai (Rajasthan, 16th century)

Words

Life without Hari is no life, friend,
And though my mother-in-law fights,
my sister-in-law teases,
the *rana* [king] is angered,
A guard is stationed on a stool outside,
and a lock is mounted on the door,
How can I abandon the love I have loved
in life after life?
Mira's Lord is the clever Mountain Lifter:
Why would I want anyone else?

Source: *Songs of the Saints of India*, translated by Hawley and Juergensmeyer. (New York: Oxford University Press, 1988).

Practices

The Sixteen Attendances

These practices are used to honour the deity during the ritual of Puja:

1. invocation of the deity (*avahana*)
2. offering a seat to or installation of the deity (*asana*)
3. offering water for washing the feet (*padya*)
4. offering water for washing the hands, head, and body (*arghya*)
5. offering water for rinsing the mouth (*acamaniya*)
6. bathing the deity (*snaniya* or *abhishekha*)
7. dressing the deity or offering a garment (*vastra*)
8. putting on the sacred thread (*yajnopavita*)
9. sprinkling with perfumes (such as *candana*, or sandalwood paste)
10. adorning with flowers (*puspa*)
11. burning incense (*dhupa*)
12. waving an oil lamp (*dipa*)
13. offering cooked food (*naivedya*)
14. paying homage by prostration or solemn greeting (*namaskara*)
15. circumambulation, or "going around" the image (*pradaksina*)
16. dismissal or taking leave of the deity

Today the puja is usually concluded with arati and *dakshina* (giving monetary offerings).

Puja in Temples Worship in public temples is said to be for the benefit of the world because it is addressed to all the deities, who protect the whole population. Hindu temples normally have puja several times a day, beginning just before dawn, conducted by hereditary priests who often live on or near the temple grounds. The priests are usually men, but preparations may be assisted by their spouses or other women. The formal pujas are carried out regardless of whether any devotees are present, but devotees can also request (and pay for) special pujas to be performed on their behalf. Otherwise, devotees come and go throughout the day, announcing their presence to the gods by ringing a bell inside the temple and offering their own prayers to the deities. During festivals or holy days, special pujas are often performed; some of these occasions involve taking portable images of the deities outside the temple and processing them around the temple or the town.

Puja at Home Pujas are performed at home in front of small shrines with pictures or images of the family, clan, and preferred deities, located often in the kitchen or living room; they are primarily for the benefit of family members. In addition to expressing devotion to and affection for the family deities, the worshipper may ask for special blessings or aid for particular problems afflicting the family. Domestic pujas using, for example, incense, candles, and flowers and recitation of hymns of praise may be done by husband and wife together, or by just the husband or just the wife. Children may watch; they gradually participate in the rituals and prayers as they get older.

Structure of Puja Whether at home or in the temple, and no matter what the occasion, all pujas have certain elements in common and the basic structure is similar. Ideally, every puja should be preceded by rituals of self-purification (such as bathing or washing one's hands and face and rinsing the mouth), which makes the worshippers fit to honour the deities. It should be completed with a *homa* (sacred fire ritual), although usually this is now the rite of arati. As scholar of Hinduism C. J. Fuller explains in respect to arati, the identity between worshipper and God is "reinforced when the worshiper cups the hands over the camphor flame, before touching the fingertips to the eyes. By this means, the deity's power and benevolent, protective grace, now in the flame, are transmitted to the worshiper and absorbed through the eyes" (1992, 73).

It should be kept in mind that while puja is designed to please the gods, it is understood that the gods do not require being attended on. The purpose of worship is to honour the deities and show devotion by serving them *as if* they had such needs. As one pujari exclaimed to me one day in Lucknow, as we sat discussing the symbolism of puja, "God dines on our love, not food." The puja "attendances" treat the images of the gods as divine guests. Indeed, hospitality, or the proper treatment of guests, is a regular theme and an important value in Hinduism that dates back to the Vedas.

The Murti Images of the deities have been produced since at least the beginnings of the Gupta dynasty in northern India in the early centuries of the Common Era. The word *murti* means "face," and so an appropriate translation would be "image" rather than "idol." In temples there are stationary images of the presiding deity and also portable festival images used for processions. In the home environment, murtis may include pictures, paintings, lithographs, and small images of stone, clay, metal, or wood. For special occasions, painted clay murtis may be bought in the market, ritually installed and worshipped, then taken outside and immersed in water to be dissolved, the spirit of the deity having been dismissed.

There are three primary types of murtis in Hinduism. The most common is the iconic, in which images are created that "look like" the deities. The design of sculptured images is strictly governed by traditional iconographic rules. The murti is not sacred until it has been consecrated by installing divine power within it through a series of rituals, the final act of which is the painting, or "opening," of the eyes. The second type is the aniconic, where the form is more abstract, for example, the *linga* representing Shiva, or pots filled with water representing the goddess, or rounded rocks—sometimes painted red with large eyes—representing village deities. The third type consists of natural images such as the *shalagrama* (fossils) sacred to Vishnu. Such images are thought to already contain divine power and do not need to be consecrated. In addition, in the Hindu tradition the Divine may dwell in certain places such as mountains, rivers, or holy sites (such as Banaras or other pilgrimage centres); in animals such as cows or monkeys; and in humans such as saints, ascetics, or gurus. Or the Divine may temporally possess and speak through a person while he or she is in a trancelike state.

When a Hindu comes into the presence of a consecrated murti, a sacred place, or a holy person, he or she "takes **darshana**," that is, engages in an exchange of vision. Through this seeing, the devotee may absorb some of the power of the holy person or deity and thereby be blessed with good fortune, grace, and spiritual merit. At the end of puja, especially at the temple, devotees

> **Murti:** image; the embodiment of a deity in the form of an icon used in worship.
>
> **Darshana:** the sacred sight or viewing of a deity or holy person and the reciprocal blessing thus received.
>
> **Prasada:** "favour," referring to food that has been offered to the deity in puja or to a holy person, blessed, and then redistributed to worshippers.
>
> **Vrat:** an optional ritual vow involving fasting, puja, and other rituals, primarily undertaken by Hindu women and usually calendar-based.

are often eager to receive from the hands of the temple priests the **prasada**, what C. J. Fuller has described as "solidified grace." This usually refers to sweets or fruit that have been offered to the deity in the puja and are now being returned to devotees as ritually transformed "leftovers." One thereby shares once more in the blessed power and grace of the deity. The prasada should never be carelessly tossed out; it should be either consumed there in the temple or shared with others later.

Hinduism in the Home

In Hinduism today most religious activities take place in the home. Such activities include daily rites of worship (the pujas mentioned above), observing annual festivals and ritual fasts, singing religious songs or prayers (bhajans) with family members or friends and neighbours, and periodically inviting gurus, pandits, or ritual specialists to come to give talks, conduct recitations of sacred texts, or officiate at life-cycle ceremonies. Further, the home is traditionally the special domain of Hindu women, and while they may not themselves always conduct the rituals, they certainly often initiate and oversee the ritual proceedings.

Vrats: Ritual Fasts Hindu women's own ritual practices tend to express their responsibility for protecting the health and well-being of their families. One of the most common forms of Hindu religious practice is the ritual fast, or **vrat.**

Vrats are optional annual, monthly, or weekly rites that involve fasting and are usually directed toward particular deities. Vrats are an important key to understanding many features of lived Hinduism, for in

> **Samskara:** a rite of passage; a sacramental ritual that marks a life-cycle transition, creating the cultured Hindu person.

addition to fasting, their observance involves worship or prayer, ritual art, devotional singing, storytelling, gift-giving, and sometimes pilgrimage. While Hindu women regularly observe these rites out of a prescribed sense of duty to ensure the well-being of their families, they also use vrats as a form of personal spiritual discipline, a way to actively engage their creativity, and an opportunity to socialize with other women. Priests are not normally involved. The various benefits that women attribute to their observance of vrats help to explain their tenacity and widespread popularity across India, and also their retention in Hindu communities outside of India. One example of a popular North Indian vrat is Karva Chauth ("pitcher's fourth"), which is observed by married women in the month of October for the prosperity, well-being, and longevity of their husbands. On this day women fast until they see the full moon rise in the evening, and then break the fast with a specially cooked meal. There are traditional stories associated with each vrat that explain their significance and efficacy; these have been passed down orally from woman to woman. Today, however, one can find printed booklets that describe the rituals, the stories, the type of fast, and other aspects of a vrat. It is now also possible to consult the Internet and YouTube for direction!

While men also observe vrats, they do so primarily in the context of annual festivals (such as Shivaratri) or in preparation for a pilgrimage; they do not observe vrats for the sake of their wives or children. It is important to note that Hindu girls at marriage traditionally take on their husband's lineage and caste identity and live in his universe. A wife's well-being is dependent to a large extent on the beneficence of her husband and mother-in-law. Widowhood is to be avoided at all costs, as widows are considered inauspicious and were traditionally blamed for their husband's death.

Against this background we may better contextualize the practice of *sati* (also written *suttee*), when a widow burns herself to death on her husband's funeral pyre. This practice was never widespread but it certainly occurred among some communities (Brahmins in Bengal and Rajputs in Rajasthan, for instance) in the centuries leading up to its legal ban in 1829. Because widowhood was considered so shameful, the life of a widow was so restricted, and a measure of heroism was attached to the act of *sati*, a number of women chose (or were coerced) to commit *sati* and thereby redeem themselves and bring great honour to their families.

Women's religious rites, then, often focus on prolonging the lives of their husbands and thereby also avoiding widowhood. Women in general are considered able to promote auspiciousness in a way that men cannot. Women's ability to bear and feed children is seen as evidence of their inherent creative power, or shakti. This is a power of well-being that can be transmitted only by the woman to other members of the family. Vrats are one of the most common ways to do this, and the deity to whom the fast is dedicated is expected to assist the faster in transmitting blessings to her family.

Fasting for special occasions as a spiritual discipline is a common feature of religious life among Hindus. Fasts are often for a twenty-four-hour period and may require total abstention from food and drink, abstention from certain types of food, or eating only certain foods. In fact, a whole host of beliefs concerning the various properties of foods and also beliefs in not injuring other creatures (*ahimsa*) have influenced Indian dietary practices. Ordinary men and women who keep calendrical fasts try to imitate the diet of the ascetic, eating "fruit food," which includes certain fruits and milk, yogurt, and butter—that is, the products of a cow—which are always considered pure. Increasing one's state of purity through diet and abstention from sensual enjoyments is very often an important element of religious practices for Hindus.

Samskaras: Rites of Passage Elaborated in two-thousand-year-old Sanskrit *smriti* texts is a series of what could be called rites of passage: ceremonies marking key transitions in a Hindu's life. These are called **samskaras** and are similar to the Catholic sacraments. There are traditionally sixteen, most of them clustered around prenatal existence and early childhood, such as the "quickening of the embryo" rite, the naming ceremony, first consumption of solid food, first haircut, and the sacred thread ceremony initiating entry into Vedic study. It is mostly high-caste Hindus who would have these rites performed by a Brahmin priest, primarily for male children. Today it is more common to have shortened forms of the samskaras performed, if at all; two exceptions are weddings and funerals, which, while also shortened, continue to be ritually elaborate, as they are the most important of the rites of passage.

Hindu marriages are still normally arranged by the parents of the bride and groom, who look for a suitable spouse with reference to such factors caste/jati, family reputation, level of education, financial stability (for males), and good health. Very often the horoscopes of the prospective bride and groom will be consulted for compatibility. The marriage samskara is meant to create a union of souls that supports the man and woman throughout their married life in the pursuit of dharma. There are significant regional variations in the celebration of the marriage samskara, but common features include worshipping Ganesha; the "giving of the bride," when the bride's parents place the hands of their daughter in the hands of the groom; a fire sacrifice where Agni, the messenger of the gods, is asked to

witness the ceremony; and the "seven steps," in which the bride and groom take seven steps together while exchanging vows, symbolizing the beginning of their journey through life as partners.

Festivals Hindus celebrate an extraordinary number of holy days and festivals throughout the year. Which ones they mark would normally depend on a combination of family, caste, and local traditions, as well as their particular sectarian affiliation or preferred deity. Many festivals mark the birth of a god; for example, Krishna Janmastami celebrates the birth of Krishna. Others, such as Makar Sankranti, celebrate the beginning of the New Year. One of the most popular festivals is the exuberant Holi, also related to the god Krishna, which is celebrated by throwing coloured powders and water on one another. Among the fall festivals, Dusserah and Diwali are the most important. One festival that has become very popular among women in South India in recent decades is the four-day rice-harvest festival of Pongol, which also

---

Practices

A Sampling of Hindu Festivals and Holy Days

A variety of calendars are used in India, and both lunar and solar reckoning, so the dates change from year to year.

Pongol or **Attukal Pongala:** a rice-harvest festival popular in Tamil Nadu and Kerala (January/February).

Maha Shivaratri: a festival dedicated to Shiva, involving an all-night fast and vigil with singing and drumming, followed by a day of fast-breaking and puja (February/March).

Holi: a spring festival featuring a carnival-like celebration with bright colours, bonfires, and pilgrimages, dedicated to Lord Krishna and, to a lesser extent, Kama, the god of pleasure (March).

Ramnavami: marks the birth of Lord Rama. The day may be accompanied by fasting and end with puja and festivities (March).

Sri Krishna Jayanti or **Janamashtami:** celebrates the birth of Lord Krishna (September).

Ganesh Caturthi: a festival in honour of the god Ganesha, remover of obstacles, the god always worshipped first before undertaking any endeavour and often before saying prayers to other deities (September/October).

Dusserah: celebrates the triumph of good over evil, especially the victory of Lord Rama over the demon king Ravana. The festival of **Durga Puja** also occurs around this time (October/November).

Diwali or **Dipavali:** the Festival of Lights, dedicated mainly to the goddess of wealth, Lakshmi (in this context Diwali is the Hindu fiscal New Year). This festival is also associated with the goddess Kali in eastern India; with Rama, marking his triumphant return to his kingdom from defeating Ravana; and with the slaying of the demon Narakasura by Krishna (October/November).

Bindi: the red dot or mark worn on the forehead by Hindu women, traditionally indicating the auspicious state of being married.

marks the auspicious beginning of the sun's journey northward. Hundreds of women may be seen cooking rice on fires outside temples for the Goddess, and celebrations may include drawing elaborate designs in rice powder called *kolam*.

Pilgrimage Pilgrimage is not a religious obligation as such for Hindus, for in one sense the entire country of India is regarded as a holy place. Nevertheless, there are well-established sites and pilgrimage circuits in India, and with the availability of ever cheaper or more convenient modes of transportation, religious tourism is bustling. Perhaps the most important site is Varanasi (Banaras), on the banks of the Ganges River; this is also a good place to die, as dying in this city of Shiva is said to guarantee moksha. One long-standing pilgrimage circuit is to the four *dhams* (abodes) associated with Vishnu and his avatars, which divide India into quarters. At the northern border of the country is Badrinath, on the west side is Dwarka, on the east coast is Puri, and on the southern tip is Rameshwaran.

Hindu Symbols One commonly sees Hindus with a mark on the forehead, which is referred to as a *tilak* ("mark"). One form of a *tilak* is the dot on the forehead of women, called a **bindi**. Now mostly decorative, it traditionally symbolized feminine shakti (energy) and was worn only by married women, just as married women today still apply red powder to the part in their hair. Another forehead mark is the ash or red powder a priest applies to a worshipper as a form of blessing. Finally, ascetics wear lines and dots on their foreheads to indicate their sectarian affiliation. Thus, followers of Vishnu may wear three perpendicular lines or a U shape; followers of Shiva may wear three horizontal lines, with or without a dot above or below, in white ash; and followers of the Goddess may wear a large red dot.

Another symbol, frequently seen in Hindu temples and in homes, is the ancient *swastika* (literally "mark of health or well-being"). In its Indian form (one that the Nazis usurped and inverted), the *swastika* is a symbol of auspiciousness and divine blessing.

RELIGIOUS AUTHORITY AND IDENTITY

It should be clear by now that because Hinduism is highly decentralized and has developed like a wide-spreading, intricate tree with many branches, it is difficult to precisely and adequately describe. A few points may be summarized at this juncture regarding religious authority and identity. To be a Hindu is to acknowledge the authority of the Vedas and to follow Hindu dharma, a way of life that supports order and righteousness. Guidelines as to how one follows Hindu dharma are provided in numerous texts, from the dharma shastras to the epics, as well as from the instructions of particular gurus, Brahmin priests, and family traditions. One source of dharma recognized by the Sanskrit texts is personal conscience; thus room is allocated for individual interpretation and choice.

Brahmin priests have authority over Vedic ritual and other types of Sanskrit-based ritual, but there are many rituals that Hindus, especially women, have long undertaken without needing Brahmin priests or reference to any Vedic text. The Vedic corpus is authoritative but few Hindus have read them; other textual and oral sources have been, in fact, much more influential in the construction of meaning, in understanding what it is to live a spiritual life in accordance with dharma, and elaboration of correct or appropriate practice. In the following sections we will see how issues of Hindu authority and identity have been brought into sharper relief as Hindus are confronted with the forces of colonialism and, for some, with relocation as a minority group into new cultural landscapes.

The Making of Modern Hinduism

The Colonial Encounter

European interest in India began in the sixteenth century and was fuelled by both commercial (trade) interests and, to a lesser extent, crusading interests. This interest was facilitated by urban growth in Europe and its maritime expertise—fleets of ships that could move fast and far. Thus both crusading zeal against the Muslims and commercial zeal against the spice monopolists were the motives that sent Columbus to America in 1492 and Vasco da Gama to Calicut, on the southwest coast of India, in 1498. Da Gama told the first Indians he met on the Malabar Coast that he had come "to seek Christians and spices." These "spices" included sugar, pepper, salt, cinnamon, tea, and saltpetre (used in gunpowder), and later also textiles such as cotton and silk and metals such as silver and gold.

After initial trading forays by England to the coastline of the Indian subcontinent, Queen Elizabeth I, on the last day of 1600, granted a charter to a group called the Governor and Company of Merchants of London Trading into the East Indies, later known as the East India Company. Thus, although Europeans had not come to India intent on conquering it politically, after several centuries that is what in fact happened. By 1857 India (then the whole of the Indian subcontinent) had become Queen Victoria's "jewel in the crown" of the British Empire. The British had a very large impact on India, perhaps more so than the Afghan, Persian, and Turkish Muslims before them, who also entered and conquered large areas of the subcontinent and left a profound and enduring legacy in India's languages, arts, and culture. The British managed over a couple of centuries to impose their system of law and courts, build railroads, redraw boundaries, outlaw certain cultural practices, and make English to this day one of India's major languages.

In the eighteenth century the East India Company tended to discourage European Christian missionaries from coming to India, essentially because they viewed missionary activities as counterproductive to trade. In the early nineteenth century, as Britain began to see itself staying in India not just to trade but to rule, missionaries had a role to play. When the British evangelicals looked to India, they saw a land of idolatry and superstition, with practices such as *sati* crying out for redress. Christian missionaries believed, as one historian put it, that it was "their duty to preach the gospel whose light would dissolve the mists of superstition and cruelty enshrouding the Indian people. ... Their programme was, bring the Christian West to the East, and India will reform herself as a flower turns to the sun" (Spear 1979, 121–22).

Hindu Responses: Reform and Revival Movements

Hindu responses to the presence of the British and of Christian missionaries were varied. Some welcomed the British and their modernizing agenda, while others were offended by European depictions of India and of Hinduism. In the end, both India and Hinduism were propelled into the turbulent currents of political and social change that characterize the modern era. The British planted the seeds of their own colonial demise by, among other things, introducing English and British education. It was their mastery of the English language and law, along with their embrace of nationalism, that enabled a group of Indians to create the movement for independence in the late 1800s.

In response to European Christians' claims that they alone possessed religious truth, Hindus articulated three different positions, all denying the superiority of Christianity. One response was to argue for an equivalence between Christianity and Hinduism, based on the ethical core of each religion and on the way that both religions had become encrusted with superstition, errors in interpretation, and mistaken forms of ritual. The task, then, was not to convert but to reform both religions. For example, Ram Mohan Roy (1772–1833) was a brilliant multilingual Bengali Brahmin, considered the "father of modern India," who founded a reform movement called the Brahmo Samaj ("Society of God"). His attempt to reform Hinduism included working toward abolition of the practice of widow burning, child marriage, and caste prejudices; he also disdained the use of icons in worship. A number of these goals, as well as rejection of the caste system, were championed later by other reformist Hindus.

A second response was to argue that one religion was superior to the others. Those holding this view believed that they could prove the superiority of their religious beliefs "as the normative measure for all religions" (Jones 1989, 213). An example of a proponent of this view is the founder of the Hindu sect Arya Samaj ("Noble Society"), Dayananda Sarasvati (1824–83). Sarasvati was born in Gujarat of a wealthy Brahman family. He rejected his family's practice of puja-oriented Shaivism, was initiated into an ascetic order, and took the name Dayananda. He came to the conclusion that all truth was to be found in the Vedas: the Sanatana dharma, the universal religion whose truths reason and science could establish. He began to travel across India preaching a purified Hinduism that rejected virtually all that had become associated with the religion of his day. He believed that only the Vedas represented the true religion; thus fire sacrifice, not puja with icons, was the right way to worship the one God. The Vedas, not priests, were the proper source for religious knowledge. He adopted a Western (and Christian) organizational form of voluntary religious association with congregational meetings, society officers, missionaries, a creed, and printed literature. After his death, his followers opened Arya Samaj schools that focused on Vedic education and English, including schools for girls, as well as orphanages and famine relief programs. A conversion ritual called *shuddhi* was instituted, partly to compete with Christian missionaries and partly to "purify" and re-admit Hindus who had converted to Islam or Christianity; later, even so-called untouchables could be transformed into members of a "clean" caste. The Arya Samaj remains a strong sect of Hinduism today.

A third response to the challenge presented by Christian missionaries was to declare that all religions lead by different paths to the same ultimate reality. The

Swami Vivekananda Speaks

This is the great ideal before us, and everyone must be ready for it—the conquest of the whole world by India—nothing less than that, and we must all get ready for it, strain every nerve for it. Let foreigners come and flood the land with their armies, never mind. Up, India, and conquer the world with your spirituality! Aye, as has been declared on this soil first, love must conquer hatred, hatred cannot conquer itself. Materialism and all its miseries can never be conquered by materialism.... Spirituality must conquer the West. Slowly they are finding out that what they want is spirituality to preserve them as nations. They are waiting for it, they are eager for it. Where is the supply to come from? Where are the men ready to go out to every country in the world with the messages of the great sages of India?

Source: From the Writings of Swami Vivekananda (1863–1902), lecture in Madras. [Source: cited in S. Hay, ed. *Sources of Indian Tradition,* Vol. Two (2nd ed.), New York: Columbia U. Press, 1988, p. 76.]

renowned mystic and spiritual teacher Ramakrishna (1836–86), the politician Keshub Chandra Sen, and Mahatma Gandhi, for example, each argued that all religions are true, and thus there is no need to convert to another religion; one is justified in remaining in the religion of one's birth.

Swami Vivekananda (1862–1902) was the one of the most noteworthy disciples of Ramakrishna. He was also the first Hindu teacher, or guru, to bring Hinduism (in the form of neo-Vedanta) to America, appearing at the first Parliament of World Religions at the Chicago World's Fair in 1893. Like other Hindu reformers, he viewed the Hinduism of his time as deeply degenerated from its glorious past. He believed that the present state of Hindu decline stemmed from ignorance and Indians' position as a subjugated people who had lost their manliness. To rectify this situation, Indians needed to proudly reclaim their heritage. Not only that, Hindus needed to help the selfish, materialistic West re-spiritualize itself, for while the West had made positive achievements in its treatment of women, its emphasis on work, and its technological and scientific advances, it also suffered serious social problems. He thus positioned Hinduism as the saviour of a spiritually bankrupt Western civilization.

Following his death, the Ramakrishna Mission that Vivekananda initiated spread throughout India. The mission, led by saffron-robed renunciants and often supported by members of the upper-caste, English-educated, urban elite, fused teachings of Vedanta Hinduism with the practice of social service. Today there are numerous Ramakrishna missions with hospitals and schools offering free services, establishing a pattern of salvation through social service (a modern karma yoga) that has been replicated by various other Hindu organizations, such as one led by popular guru Sathya Sai Baba (d. 2011), based in Karnataka, and the Swami Narayana sect, based in Gujarat. In each case, significant financial support derives from Hindus abroad.

Hindu Nationalism and Communalism The British activity of census taking, introduced in 1871 and carried out every five years, required Indians to identify their religion, a practice that served to raise consciousness about differences. Later constitutional reforms (in 1919 and 1935) created separate electorates that linked religion, the census reports, political power, and political patronage. New religio-political organizations emerged that attempted to speak for the interests of specific groups, such as the Muslim League, the Bharat Hindu Mahasabha, and the Sikh Akali Dal. The effects of colonial policies, Christian missionaries, responses from Hindus by way of reform movements, and emergent nationalist parties, then, meant that—in the process of defining and

Throughout India cows are revered, and those Hindus who do eat meat usually avoid eating beef. Cows were honoured for all that they provide: milk, yogurt, and butter (all of which are used in puja), dung for fuel, and labour for plows. Cows were associated early on with non-violence and with Krishna, in his role as the cowherd (Gopala). The cow as a symbol of Hindu India catapulted into the public arena during the independence movement. The cow, like the nation, was glorified as an ever-giving "mother" that should be protected, and stern punishment was meted out to anyone who harmed a cow. An annual festival (Gopashtami) celebrates the cow, where family cows are washed, decorated, and given offerings. Finally, cows have a long association with the myth of the *kamadhenu*, or "wish-fulfilling cow," a magical animal that could give her owner whatever he desired.

Source: © Tatiana Taylor/Alamy

defending Hindu, Muslim, or Sikh identity in the diverse multi-religious culture of South Asia—new boundaries were drawn, new positions were staked out, and the distance between religions grew. Inter-religious tension, called *communalism* in South Asia, continues to plague the subcontinent, even though it reached unprecedented and horrific levels of violence in the months following Partition—the splitting of the subcontinent into two independent countries in 1947.

What is commonly referred to as Hindu nation-alism emerged during the late nineteenth century, when Hindu nationalist leaders such as Aurobindo Ghose strove to heighten patriotic fervour among the masses by fostering pride in the glorious past, when Hindu kings ruled. He and others described India as a "Divine Motherland" in their fiery speeches. Love of country then became an expression of Hindu-ness and love of God. Since then there has been a move-ment (not always unified) that has gained considerable political clout in India, to reclaim India for Hindus and to reconstruct the "essentials" of Hindu belief and practice. It was a Hindu nationalist associated with the Hindu Mahasabha who was Gandhi's assassin. He killed him because he thought Gandhi had betrayed India and Hindus by being too conciliatory toward Muslims, even giving in to Muslim demands for a separate state.

Mahatma Gandhi Mohandas K. Gandhi (1869–1948) is perhaps the best-known Hindu in the world today. He is called the "father of independent India" because of his leadership in the cause of Indian independence, finally won in 1947. He is also known for taking the age-old Indian concept of *ahimsa*, or non-violence, and giving it new applications in the realm of political and social change at the collective level. His idea of *satyagraha* ("truth force"), a concept developed and experimented with during his twenty years as a barrister in South Africa, aimed, among other things, at non-violently redressing wrongs and resolving conflict by transforming relationships between the parties.

Gandhi's effective political and social activism was firmly rooted in his spiritual worldview. He took an avid interest in the teachings of other religions as he sought to deepen his understanding of the Vaishnava Hindu faith of his birth. His voluminous letters and writings articulate several principles that shaped and informed his attitude toward the world's religions and their adherents. One principle was that God is truth, which he later revised to say that truth is God, for it is harder to deny the existence of truth than of God. Another principle was that truth must be weighed by conscience and reason and tested in practice. A third principle was that every world religion has truth in it, but no one religion can legitimately claim to be the exclusive bearer of truth. As early as 1905 Gandhi asserted that "the time had passed when the followers of one religion could stand and say, 'ours is the only true religion and all others are false'" (Nanda 1990, 12), for truth, he believed, is a reality larger than any one religion but one in which all are ultimately grounded.

Further, all religions are imperfect because they are transmitted, interpreted, and practised through imperfect vehicles. Thus error enters into the religious beliefs and practices of all religions. "And if all faiths outlined by men are imperfect, the question of comparative merit does not arise," he concluded (1957, 38). Next, the sincere study of other religions can deepen one's own faith and at the same time lead to equal regard for all faiths and creeds. "I hold that it is the duty of every cultured man or woman to read sympathetically the scriptures of the world," Gandhi wrote in 1926 (*Young India*, Sept. 2). It is through the cultivation of such respectful attitudes and practices,

Gandhi seemed to be saying, that we would be freed to live and work together harmoniously for the well-being of all. "Warring creeds," he warned, "is a blasphemous expression."

It seems probable that Gandhi would have been horrified by the outbreaks of inter-religious violence in India in recent decades, such as those arising around a sixteenth-century mosque built, Hindus claim, on the site of Rama's birth. Though the mosque had not been used for many years, it was illegally demolished in 1991 by militant Hindus. Outrage resulted, and deaths and injuries to hundreds of Indians, both Hindu and Muslim, have continued in subsequent years as the standoff persists. Gandhi said in regard to Rama—in whose name the Hindu militants destroyed the Brabri mosque—that his use of the term *Rama* referred not to "a mere man" whose historical origins are uncertain but rather to God, the "Unborn and Uncreated." He repeatedly appealed for tolerance and respect for different faiths and ways of worship, explaining, "I am myself an iconoclast, but I have equal regard for the so-called idolaters. Those who worship idols also worship the same God who is everywhere, even in a clod of earth" (cited in Engineer 1997, 18–19). Current prominent Hindu leaders such as Swami Agnivesh (past president of the World Council of the Arya Samaj) have spoken boldly and consistently on the need for inter-religious dialogue in India today.

Words

Mahatma Gandhi

Real *swaraj* [self-rule] will come not by acquisition of authority by a few but by the acquisition of the capacity by all to resist authority when it is abused. In other words, *swaraj* is to be attained by educating the masses to a sense of their capacity to regulate and control authority. (26:52).

Source: *Collected Works of Mahatma Gandhi,* vol. 26 (New Delhi: Government of India Publications Division, 1999), 52. [e-book]

My study and experience of non-violence have proved to me that it is the greatest force in the world.

It is the surest method of discovering the truth and it is the quickest because there is no other. It works silently, almost imperceptibly, but none the less surely. It is the one constructive process of Nature in the midst of incessant destruction going on about us. I hold it to be a superstition to believe that it can work only in private life. There is no department of life public or private to which that force cannot be applied. But this nonviolence is impossible without complete self-effacement.

Source: Letter to the Fellowship of Reconciliation in New York, Nov. 14, 1924, in *Collected Works*, vol. 29, 340.

Hinduism Outside India

When in 1888 Mahatma Gandhi decided that he would travel to England to become a barrister-at-law, he was told by his caste elders that leaving India that way would result in loss of his caste status. The reason was an age-old fear that in foreign places, outside the sacred land of Mother India, constant contact with non-Hindus would strip him of his ritual purity, thereby depriving him of "twice-born" status (applicable to those in the three higher castes who had undergone the sacred thread ceremony). He decided to go anyway, after promising his mother to avoid wine, women, and meat.

Despite such rules, Hindus have travelled outside the Indian subcontinent for millennia, principally as merchants and traders, moving across West Asia to Persia, Anatolia, and Greece or eastward to Southeast Asia, where in fact many Hindus settled down. In places such as modern Singapore, Malaysia, Indonesia, and Fiji, Hindus have retained their religious identity while constructing distinctive forms of Hinduism over the centuries. Some places, such as Bali and, of course, Nepal (until 2008 a Hindu kingdom, now a parliamentary democracy), have long sustained a majority Hindu population.

In the eighteenth to nineteenth centuries, the British imported large numbers of Indian labourers to work in their various colonies: East Africa (Kenya, Tanzania, and Uganda), South Africa and the island of Mauritius, and South America and the Caribbean. In particular, Trinidad and Tobago and Guyana (formerly British Guiana) today have large Hindu populations of Indian ancestry. In some of these places Hinduism took on a congregational quality, imitating the Christian and Muslim forms of religious organization and practices around them. Without Sanskrit-educated Brahmin priests, Hinduism was reconstructed from remembered practices, and so in each place it has assumed distinctive forms.

Hinduism Travels West

Before the colonial era, knowledge in Europe and the West about India and its religions was minimal. After 1700, some European colonialists took a keen interest in Indian culture, studied its ancient languages, and began to translate some of its texts into French, German, and English. The new field of European Indology was born, with key figures such as Sir William Jones (1746–94), a father of modern linguistics and founder of the Asiatic Society of Bombay, who marvelled at the connections between Sanskrit, Avestan, Greek, and Latin. Another was Friedrich Max Müller (1876–1904), editor of the "Great Books of the East" series, who himself never managed to get to India but wrote:

> If I were asked under what sky the human mind has most fully developed some of its choicest gifts, has most deeply pondered on the greatest problems of life, and has found solutions of some of them which well deserve the attention even of those who have studied Plato and Kant—I should point to India. (1883, 6)

By the early 1800s translations of texts such as the Bhagavad-Gita had reached Europe and North America, inspiring such thinkers as Americans Henry David Thoreau and Ralph Waldo Emerson and the German philosopher Schopenhauer. Other accounts of Hinduism written by Westerners were less enthusiastic, however. For example, the French missionary Abbé Dubois (1770–1848) was frequently appalled by what he saw of Hinduism, which he described in his influential book *Hindu Manners, Customs and Ceremonies*. Likewise, American journalist Katherine Mayo's popular book *Mother India*—published under the guise of a dispassionate description of the state of "hygiene" in India in 1927 and quickly reprinted twenty-eight times—reproduced typical stereotypes of "ignorant," "helpless" peasant women unknowingly crying out for American intervention and rescue.

We have seen that, by the end of the nineteenth century, the charismatic Hindu religious leader Swami Vivekananda had given a rather different perspective on what Hinduism offered. His legacy in America was the establishment of several Vedanta centres for the promotion and study of Hindu philosophy. After Vivekananda a trickle of other Hindu spiritual leaders travelled abroad to spread their own take on Hindu dharma. One book that became particularly popular in the West is *Autobiography of a Yogi*, on the life of spiritual teacher Paramahamsa Yogananda (1893–1952), which was first published in 1946.

In the late 1960s it became clear that young people in Europe and North America were ready to hear much more about the "spiritual East" and even to convert. When Swami Bhaktivedanta (1896–1977) came from India to New York City, eventually establishing the International Society for Krishna Consciousness (ISKCON), thousands of Americans happily donned

Indian clothes, took Sanskrit names, became vegetarians, and embraced Lord Krishna. His translation of the Bhagavad-Gita, handed out on street corners by devotees, remains one of the most popular English translations of this text. The oldest ISKCON temple in Canada still operates in downtown Toronto, in a large converted church purchased in 1975; most of its present-day attendees are Indian immigrants.

Another successful Hindu teacher in the West was Maharishi Mahesh Yogi (1917–2008), who introduced the philosophy and practice of transcendental meditation, beginning in 1958. He gained the international spotlight when the Beatles and other celebrities became followers, and "TM" took off. Other influential Hindu teachers have included Swami Sivananda (1887–1963), who started the Divine Life Society; Swami Muktananda (1908–82), who brought siddha yoga to the West; and, more notoriously, Osho or Bhagwan Rajneesh (1930–90), who catered explicitly to Western interests, first in his ashram in Pune, India, and then after he moved to Colorado. In his ashram, anyone could become a sannyasi ascetic by wearing orange robes and taking a Sanskrit name. Finally there was Sri Chimnoy (1931–2007), who in 1964 also moved to New York City, establishing centres throughout North America and focusing on promotion of physical as well as spiritual health (for instance, sponsoring marathon runs). In his later years he travelled throughout the world meeting with world leaders to promote peace. All of these gurus, both transplanted Hindus and the occasional Western convert, have succeeded in making Hindu ideas and practices, including Vedanta philosophy, yoga, meditation, devotional music, and ayurvedic medicine, known to a worldwide audience.

THE CANADIAN CONTEXT

"I came to seek blessings for my new car," said a recently minted physician I encountered at the Ganesha temple on Bayview Avenue in Richmond Hill in 2009. A car puja? I asked. "Well, yes, the car's second-hand, but it's new to me and my father suggested we go to temple and have a car puja done, you know, for luck." The ritual for the car involved handing over the keys, a piece of fruit, and a written note showing that the *archana* ritual (that is, puja) had been paid for

to a Sri Lankan Tamil ritual priest, who was wearing a dhoti, his sacred thread clearly visible on his bare torso. He asked the young doctor and her father their *gotra* (family lineage) and proceeded to chant Sanskrit mantras in front of the image of Ganesha—remover of obstacles—for several minutes, then placed the fruit on the figure of the deity. Afterwards he gave the now-blessed fruit back to the client and blessed them further with a mark of ash on the forehead.

Well, anyone who has to drive regularly on Highway 401 may well wish to do a car puja, whether one is Hindu or not. Clearly, for this jeans-wearing, Canadian-born Hindu whose parents had come from South India in the 1970s, this ritual was worth doing, and it had to be done at this temple, one that her parents had been attending for years. In fact, the Sri Lankan Tamil community in Toronto that runs this, the largest South Indian-style temple in the country, is the largest single ethnic group of Hindu immigrants to Canada.

There are some 170 Hindu temples and centres in Canada, many of them clustered in the Toronto area, with new ones being built every year. This thriving temple-building activity attests not just to the growing Hindu population in Canada, which numbers close to 400 000, but also to the interest of Hindu Canadians in successfully transplanting their religion in a new cultural milieu. We have seen that Hinduism is not traditionally a congregational religion and that Hindus are not required to worship in temples; indeed, many Hindus in North America prefer to worship at their home shrines and rarely visit temples. But temples have come to play a much more important role in the lives of Hindus in North America than they do in India, because temples function not just as places of worship but also as cultural, social, and educational centres for the community. Thus, even those who would consider themselves not particularly religious or pious may go to a temple to watch their daughters participate in a Diwali festival dance or to attend a talk by a visiting lecturer or to take a yoga class. Non-Hindu Canadians are also starting to visit Hindu temples to watch music or dance performances, listen to talks, and perhaps enjoy a free vegetarian Indian meal offered at the end of a Sunday afternoon "service." The declaration in 2001 of May as South Asian Heritage Month in Ontario, the popular success of *Slumdog Millionaire* and the films of Indo-Canadian director Deepa Mehta, the achievements of Indo-Canadian writers such as Rohinton Mistry, M. J.

Vassanji, and Anita Rau Badami, and even the popularity of comedians such as Russell Peters and Shaun Majumder are all helping to generate a new appreciation for South Asian culture in Canada.

History of Immigration

South Asians began arriving in Canada in the early 1900s. They heard about opportunities for work in their fellow British dominion from Indian troops who had passed through Canada in 1897 on their way home from Queen Victoria's Diamond Jubilee in London, and also after the coronation of Edward VII in 1902. Most of the several thousand arrivals were single men who came to British Columbia by ship from Hong Kong, looking for work in the lumber and other developing industries. Many expected to return to India when they had saved enough money. Most of these Indian workers were Sikhs and from the Punjab. Because of their greater numbers and the comparatively more important role of the gurdwara, or communal place of worship, the Sikhs were able to set up their first gurdwara in 1908, in Vancouver. The Hindus were content to attend this and other early gurdwaras in Canada, for cultural commonalities outweighed religious differences. Certainly South Asians in general were viewed as all the same by the predominantly white British Columbians, who referred to them as "Hindoos."

South Asian immigrants were not subject to the head tax imposed on Chinese immigrants from 1885 to 1923 (which was followed by the Chinese Exclusion Act), but after the *Komagata Maru* incident in 1914, described in Chapter 4, hostility from the white population of Canada to Indians in particular and Asians in general increased. After the First World War, anti-foreigner sentiment prevailed among the dominant Euro-Canadian citizenry, but even before the end of the war, laws had been passed that effectively stifled immigration from South Asia (and many other parts of the world) to Canada. In fact, between 1909 and 1943 only 878 South Asians were allowed to enter Canada, and many of these were wives and children of men already living here. Those who stayed did not gain full rights for decades. After 1908, Indo-Canadians could not serve on juries, act as school trustees, enter public service jobs, or vote in provincial elections; in 1920 the Dominion Franchise Bill prevented them from voting federally as well. Only

in 1947, with passage of the Canadian Citizenship Act, were Indo-Canadians, among others, granted full citizenship rights, including the right to vote.

In the 1950s a slow trickle of mostly urban professional immigrants from India began to come to Canada. A 1962 reform of the 1952 Immigration Act officially eliminated racial discrimination in Canada's immigration policy, so that any unsponsored person who had the necessary qualifications could be considered for immigration, regardless of skin colour, race, ethnic origin, or religion. In 1967 the "point system" was created so that potential immigrants could be assessed on non-racialized criteria such as education, age, fluency in French or English, and available job opportunities in Canada. The point system was the first major amendment to Canadian immigration legislation that favoured South Asian entrance to Canada. Numbers of South-Asians not seen since the early 1900s began to arrive and settle in disparate parts of the country with their families.

A second important policy that facilitated Asian immigration was the 1976 Immigration Act, which separated potential immigrants into three classes: family (facilitating the sponsoring of immediate family members to Canada), humanitarian (including refugees), and the independent class (those who applied for landed immigrant status from their home countries and were subject to the point system).[1] The relative percentage of immigrants of non-European origin (and non-Christian religious affiliation) grew substantially in the 1970s, and by 1986, 40 per cent of all immigrants came from Asia. Thus the trickle of Hindus entering Canada, mostly from northern India, in the first three-quarters of the twentieth century had changed to a stream by the last quarter and into the twenty-first century. This stream included a substantial number of refugees and others fleeing political instability or persecution in their homeland. Among these were Tamil Hindus from Sri Lanka, arriving in the wake of the civil war that started in 1983; a wave of Ugandan Hindus (and Muslims) accepted into Canada when Idi Amin forced all South Asians out of that country in 1972; and Guyanese Hindus escaping violence and political upheaval in their home country. While Hindu immigrants are now found in all the provinces of Canada, the majority have settled in two, Ontario and British Columbia, with about 73 per cent in Ontario and most of those clustered in the Greater Toronto Area. With second- and third-generation Hindus now growing up here, Hinduism has established firm roots in the Canadian religious landscape. So how was Hinduism reconstructed in this new cultural environment, and what does Canadian Hinduism look like now?

Being Hindu in Canada

Earlier in this chapter we saw that while Hindus share much in common in their religion, they come from a large number of distinct ethnic groups, speak diverse languages, and have distinctive social and cultural practices. Major differences in ways of being Hindu can exist even within the same ethno-linguistic group, depending, for example, on caste or jati traditions. Thus it should not be surprising to encounter a great deal of diversity among Hindus in Canada. Yet the Canadian Hindu picture is also distinctive. It is distinct from that of the United States, for instance: most Hindus in the U.S. emigrated directly from India and have spread throughout that country, whereas Hindus in Canada have come not only from India but also from Sri Lanka, Uganda, Kenya, South Africa, Mauritius, Singapore, Malaysia, Fiji, the United Kingdom, Trinidad, and Guyana, and most have clustered in a handful of major urban centres. Hindus from India had already emigrated once to those countries of origin, in many cases centuries earlier. Thus, emigrating to Canada meant also importing forms of Hindu religiosity that had developed independently of the original homeland.

Further, Canada's multiculturalism policy differs from the American emphasis on integration. When Parliament passed the Canadian Multiculturalism Act in July 1988, Canada became the first country in the world to have a national multiculturalism law, one that not only affirmed multiculturalism as an essential component of Canadian society but also provided a cultural space for its expression. As well, it provided legal impetus for allocation of government funds to support the preservation of ethnic heritages. Heritage language classes were established and a variety of cultural events and heritage preservation initiatives were given funding.

Government officials expected religious groups to define their own identities, especially when it came to incorporation of temples or societies that could receive non-taxable status, or when it came to registration of marriages by religious functionaries (raising questions such as, If there was no Hindu "priest" around

to officiate, could Hindus get married in a Hindu ceremony? Who else could serve this role?). These government expectations required Hindus in Canada to self-consciously determine the basics of their common Hindu identity. Thus it might be asked, for instance, What do English-speaking Guyanese-Canadian Hindus have in common with Fijian-Canadian Hindus or Tamil-speaking Sri Lankan Shaiva Canadian Hindus or Gujarati Swami Narayan Canadian Hindus or ISKCON Canadian convert Hindus?

Furthermore, not all immigrants to Canada who come from a Hindu heritage would consider themselves particularly religious. For some, the appellation *Hindu* may simply be a nominal form of identification (as *Christian* is for many people from a Christian background). They may rarely, even never, visit a temple or perform puja at home, fast, or recite from religious texts. There are, however, at least two factors that make being Hindu in Canada a necessarily more self-conscious attribute than being, say, Christian in Canada.

One factor is the challenge of separating culture from religion. In your homeland, observing caste distinctions, eating vegetarian food or at least avoiding beef, enjoying the traditions associated with annual festivals—any of these practices is a normal part of everyday life. But in Canada, meat (and beef) eating is "normal" and meat is offered, for example, for school lunches, sometimes with no vegetarian options. Hindu children in Canada will then go home and ask their parents, Is this practice a religious obligation? Or, in formulating holiday policies, school boards may ask Hindus, Which are your three most important holy days during which students should be excused from school? Of the dozens of potential holy days and important festivals celebrated among Hindus, which to choose? Suddenly individuals and representative groups must make decisions about these matters.

Another factor that makes being Hindu in Canada a more self-conscious attribute is the simple fact of being identified by the surrounding population as a visible minority of South Asian (what Canadians still sometimes refer to as "East Indian") descent. Many North Americans are not clear about the differences between Jains, Sikhs, and Hindus. They may not be aware that their Canadian neighbours of South Asian heritage may have lived in Canada (or Guyana or Kenya) for generations, or that the largest Muslim population in the world is found among the countries of South Asia. The self-consciousness of being Hindu emerges for Hindu-Canadians most starkly when they are confronted by such ignorance and by stereotypes that are blatantly at odds with their own self-understanding and experience. The attempt to address misconceptions forces Hindus in Canada—as it did educated Hindus in nineteenth-century India confronting negative portrayals of Hinduism by European bureaucrats and missionaries—to identify and articulate what it means to be Hindu as distinct from some other religion, and from Indian cultural practices (including diet, dress, and social customs). Hindus in Canada also encounter a vast diversity of beliefs and practices among their own co-religionists who have emigrated from different regions of India and elsewhere. They encounter, that is, a wide range of local cultures that have imbued and shaped the particular form of Hinduism associated with that region and its history. Often immigrants become aware of the extent of this diversity only when they meet and try to recreate a communal religious life with their fellow Hindus in a diasporic context.

Hindu identity must thus be negotiated on several fronts. One is with the larger—in this case North American secular (yet still strongly Western Judeo-Christian)—culture, including government agencies, which tend to know little about Hinduism. Another is with co-religionists who bring with them a plethora of ways of being Hindu. A third front is the discourses of neo-Hinduism that emerged from India initially in a colonial context, and were then reframed by Hindus and propagated in North America. A fourth is with the second and third generations of Hindu immigrants in Canada and the United States who are deciding for themselves not only what differentiates the Hindu religion from Indian (or Indo-Guyanese or Sri Lankan) cultural practices, but also what constitutes the essentials of Hinduism today. Let us turn now to a review of the history of Hindu organizations and temple building in Canada.

Hindu Organizations

One response to the need to describe and define themselves to governmental institutions, the media, and the larger culture was the formation of Hindu organizations. Initially such organizations were largely local groups who formed associations whose mandate included establishment of a temple, for example, the Prarthana Samaj of Vancouver, which was started in 1967. Later, Canada-wide organizations emerged, such as the

> **Pandit:** a religious scholar or teacher of the oral tradition who transmits the Veda and other religious literature.

Hindu Council of Canada (1983). More recently other organizations have taken advantage of the Internet to advertise their existence and draw members. Examples of these include the Hindu Canadian Network; the United Hindu Congress Canada, whose stated vision is to promote Hindu unity; and the Hindu Federation of Canada, which on its website (www.federationofhindutemples.ca) says the following: "We the Hindus of Canada came from different geographical references, speaking many different languages and being exposed to many different cultural and traditional customs. We have accepted that our religion is Hinduism and our country is Canada and have made great strides in preserving our great heritage in this wonderful country." The website goes on to note that Hindus have been very successful at creating places of worship where they have been able to practise their religion and provide an opportunity for the next generations to develop an appreciation of the Hindu way of life. The site also urges all Hindus to become involved in their communities' welfare "with the conviction that in the eyes of the rest of Canada we are all one (Hindus)," and thus should address issues "as a community working together." There is also concern expressed that Hindus in Canada need to be seen as "progressive and a major contributor to the Canadian Society."

This process of attempting to create a pan-Canadian Hindu voice and identity is particularly evident on the Internet (see below). Yet, by and large, Hinduism in Canada has remained institutionally decentralized, as it is in India. Local organizations have continued to form in order to build temples or propagate the messages of particular gurus, in the latter case to form networks within and outside Canada that focus on the mission and vision of the particular religious leader.

Hindu Temples in Canada

Prior to the mid-1970s, the relatively few Hindus in Canada tended to worship at their home shrines, acting as their own ritual specialists on a day-to-day basis. For marriage, death, and other life-cycle rituals, a learned **pandit** from nearby might be asked to come and officiate. On major Hindu holy days such as Diwali,

Mandir: a Hindu temple.

Pranam: a gesture of respect, often with the hands pressed together in front of the body.

they might rent a hall and organize a cultural show. Children would be encouraged to bring their friends, to show off something of Hindu traditions. As greater numbers of Hindus clustered in urban areas, plans were made to build local temples as some began to feel a need to create a dedicated space outside the home or a rented hall in which to worship and meet.

The early temples established in Canada, such as the Vishnu **Mandir** in Toronto (1981) or the Hindu Samaj temple of Hamilton (1984), were often former schools or churches that had been bought and then renovated. Such renovations and newly constructed buildings were usually the product of compromise; negotiations were necessary among the members of temple committees to satisfy the variety of architectural and ritual norms and expectations of the diverse community they were to serve, as well as the limits imposed by budgets. Questions to be negotiated might include: Which deities should be installed? Should one deity prevail at the centre front or do we give equal space to all? Will the images of the deities be in South Indian style, made of dark granite, or North Indian style, made of white marble? Should the images be placed in a row at the front of the temple or arranged along the sides? Should they be placed inside separate alcoves or built against the walls or separated so that devotees can walk around them? Who should conduct the pujas? Where should the priests come from and what should be their qualifications?

Significantly, to accommodate the busy schedules of devotees and to meet needs beyond merely a dedicated public worship space, many of the early temples in Canada adopted a congregational form of Hinduism in which Sundays took a privileged position in the religious week. This form followed a model similar to what Hindus had established in Guyana, for instance; arriving in the nineteenth century without Brahmin priests, they decided to imitate the Christian and Muslim forms of religious organization around them. A learned member of the community would play a central role, not just as a ritual leader but also as an orator and organizer, performing not just puja to the deities but also sermon-like

talks given from a raised platform, perhaps preceded or followed by devotional music. These talks, in Hindi or English, might be ongoing commentaries on verses from the Bhagavad-Gita or elaborations on traditional religious stories or concepts, given a modern spin. Thus the talks would serve both an instructional and inspirational purpose. Still popular among temples in North America are invitations extended to religious teachers (swamis or gurus) from India to visit their temples, perhaps because they are already on a tour in the area; often these talks attract large audiences.

During the "service," devotees, or "congregants," might come in or leave at any time, as in India, but most sit down on the floor (frequently carpeted) to listen to the proceedings, after first walking up to the deities and offering **pranam** (gestures of respect). Often, but not always, men will sit on one side of the room and women and small children on the other side, but this practice is not enforced. The end of the service is marked by the arati, during which most people line up to wave their hands over the flames of oil lamps on a stainless steel plate that is passed from one person to another, in an act of self-blessing accompanied by congregational singing. After this, at least in North Indian–style temples, they may go to a downstairs room to share in a communal meal—*priti bhoj*—an influence from the Sikh tradition of *langar*, or communal meal. This practice facilitates socializing among community members, much as coffee hour after a Christian church service does. The meal is always vegetarian and is sponsored and prepared by volunteers who sign up well in advance. Anyone is welcome to enjoy these meals or, indeed, to attend the temple services. There is no dress code—one might see anything from the finest Banarsi silk saris to T-shirts and jeans.

In this congregational pattern, the community takes an active part in sponsoring holy days and festivals to be celebrated, setting up classes for children (a kind of "Sunday school"), offering Indian dance or music instruction, and in general caring for one another. This is the pattern typically established at many of the first multi-use Hindu temples set up across Canada. Thus, while puja is conducted for the deities several times a day regardless of who is present to view it, Sundays is the big day for larger gatherings of the community—for participation in group bhajan singing, puja, and meal sharing. On other days there may be regular activities such as,

The BAPS Shri Swaminarayan Mandir, Toronto, is the largest and most expensive ($40 million) Hindu temple in Canada. It was built and funded largely by Gujaratis in Canada under the direction of the central BAPS foundation in India, and is thus similar in form to their equally impressive white marble temples in other parts of the world. Completed in 2007, it consists of two separate buildings, one of which is the temple, with beautiful pillars and statuary carved by artisans in Jaipur. The other building is the haveli, containing a hall, a religious bookstore, a prayer room, and the country's largest Indo-Canadian museum of culture and religion. Like other Hindu temples in North America, anyone is allowed to visit the Hindu temple and watch a "service" taking place. Frequently one can also enjoy a free vegetarian meal after the service.

Source: Anne M. Pearson

for example, yoga and meditation classes, evening pujas to Shiva, or recitals of the *Hanuman Chalisa* (a text in praise of the deity Hanuman). Other activities organized by temple committees include publication of newsletters, religious calendars, and magazines, complete with commentaries on spiritual themes by gurus, excerpts of holy texts, and famous stories from the Hindu tradition, with illustrations. Picnics and youth camps might be organized, and there are often fundraising activities for temple renovations or social service causes in the city or in the "homeland."

New Patterns in Temple Building

Since the 1990s, as the number of Hindus in Canada has grown, especially in the Greater Toronto Area, more temples have been constructed that reflect the particular traditions of the originating homeland—linguistic, ethnic, cultural, and sectarian—and are often specific to particular deities (or forms of pan-Indian/Hindu deities). For example, the Vaishno Devi temple in Oakville (built in 1991), while it does host other deities, is primarily dedicated to the goddess Vaishno Devi (usually identified as a form of Durga), whose famous mother temple, a popular pilgrimage spot, is just north of the city of Jammu, near Pakistan. Many other small temples dedicated to various regional forms of the Great Goddess have also sprung up (for instance, there are several affiliated with the Adi Para Shakti worship linked to Melmarattur in Tamil Nadu, which is led by women dressed in red). Or there might be an English-language focus, such as found in the Vishnu temple in Toronto built by Guyanese Canadians in 1984, rebuilt in 1990 and today drawing some 600 to 700 people to their Sunday services. Even so, some Guyanese-Canadian Hindus have gone on to build other temples that attempt to recapture their own traditional approaches to worship.

Another regional-style temple is the Ganesha temple in Richmond Hill, north of Toronto, first constructed by South Indian Tamils who were seeking to replicate in architecture and ritual the large temple complexes in southern India. Here, rather than adopting a congregational style, this temple focuses on the worship of individual deities (such as Venkateshwara, another name for Vishnu), each of which is housed in its own mini-temple. Several activities are often going on at the same time, involving different worshippers and specialized Brahmin priests attending to the different deities. At the Ganesha temple Sunday is not a special day, though more devotees may come then because they have the day off work. Festivals there typically draw ten to fifteen thousand worshippers (now mostly Sri Lankan Tamils) and may involve a *rath-yatra* procession, where the image of the deity being honoured is a portable one, taken outside for the occasion and paraded around on a large special cart used only for that purpose.

A final example of Hindu temples that follow particularized traditions are the Arya Samaj temples, perhaps the most notable in Canada being the Vedic Cultural Centre in Markham, Ontario, opened in 1996. In Arya Samaj, or Vedic-centred, temples, only the Vedas are used as a source for rituals; no images of any deities are present. The main form of worship is the *agnihotra*, a ritual involving a series of purifications and the chanting of Vedic mantras while making offerings to Agni (who carries all sacrifices to God) at a fire altar. Here, as in most other temples, only well-trained, usually male, priests may officiate.

Thus we now see in Canada a wide array of Hindu places of worship and centres for community gatherings and planned activities, some still serving a generalized Hindu population, others seeking to recreate the forms and traditions of particular ancestral homeland communities. While each has its core supporters and devotees, many Hindus in Canada would feel comfortable dropping in at any one of these temples, recognizing in them their common "Hindu-ness."

Whether old or new, guru-, sectarian- or ethnic-based, most Hindu temples with priests on staff will offer, in addition to regular pujas, particular ceremonies on a fee-for-service basis to mark a special occasion such as a birthday, engagement, memorial day, or rite of passage (samskara). Examples include the Punjabi *mata-ki-chownkis*, which are rituals directed to Durga; an *akhand-Ramayan-path*, which is a non-stop reading of the epic Ramayana; or the *archana* typical of South Indian temples, like the car puja described at the start of this section.

Challenges Faced by Hindus in the Canadian Context

Hindus in Canada have faced specific challenges around the practice of their religion. In India, at the end of a festival such as Durga Puja, the temporary image that houses the spirit of the deity is ceremonially processed to a body of water—a lake or river, for instance—for immersion. This ceremony marks the final leave-taking of the deity's spirit, or "breath," from the clay image. This is also done with images of a more permanent nature that have been damaged after being formally installed in a temple, such as the murtis housed in the Hamilton, Ontario, temple when it was torched by an arsonist following the events of 9/11. However, provincial and municipal guidelines do not always allow such immersions in public water bodies; thus special permission has to be obtained from government authorities.

Another example is death rituals. The first challenge was teaching Canadian funeral directors about the nature and significance of Hindu death rituals, including preparation of the body (in India normally done at home). Clearly, outdoor processions carrying the body on a byre and outdoor cremations are not options, nor is the use of real wood—Canada only uses electric crematoria. Instead of the eldest son (or his alternate) lighting the funeral pyre with a burning ember from a ritual fire, he pulls a switch on the outside of the crematorium. Instead of physical contact with the ritual offerings and the sacred fire—intended to facilitate the release of the soul from the body—there is only recitation of Vedic mantras. While in India the deceased's ashes are normally sprinkled over a body of water (a sacred river such as the Ganges, for instance), laws in Canada prohibit immersion of the ashes of human remains (however, negotiations with various levels of government in Ontario have recently resulted in designation of certain places in Toronto as permissible for sprinkling such ashes). Otherwise,

Hindus continue to place importance on returning the ashes, or a portion thereof, to one of the sacred rivers of the ancestral homeland. Finally, the often elaborate post-cremation rites, which create a new ethereal body for the deceased and allow his or her safe transition to the world of the ancestors, are vastly curtailed and simplified in Canada (as in fact they have often become in India also).

Other challenges for Hindus practising their faith in Canada have included finding the needed items for rituals, not having extended family nearby to take their designated roles in rituals (or to help with the domestic work and parenting), constraints on time because of work schedules, and lack of recognition of Hindu holy days. Some women immigrants face special challenges of social isolation in the new country, while others have developed aspirations to assume religious ritual and leadership roles sometimes denied to them in India. Women are often part of a temple's board of directors, although usually in the minority. And then there are the ongoing concerns about how to adequately transmit Hindu religion and culture to the next generations.

Adaptation of Hinduism in Canada

If religion is a key factor for retention of cultural identity by Hindus in North America, and if women have been the primary conservators and transmitters of the Hindu family's religious heritage in the ancestral homeland, how is that role affected in the new cultural environment? Many first-generation Hindu women immigrants in Canada continue to place importance on their responsibilities for the maintenance of ritual practices and transmission of a wide range of traditional beliefs and values to the next generation. But, as noted earlier, one of the most significant changes that has occurred in the practice of Hinduism in Canada compared with India is the augmented role that temples have assumed as a locus of practice, as a major source of reinforcement of religio-cultural identity, and as a source of religious instruction. As one woman explained, "Here the temple is important to teach your kids mainly, and for us to have a focus in our life. In India you don't have to make such efforts to learn about the religion… you just pick things up and you believe in them" (personal remark to author, Hamilton, 2002).

In India, as we have seen, ritual fasts (vrats) are one of the most common types of domestic rituals

observed by Hindu women. These rituals, like domestic pujas, have always been allotted, in both text and practice, a certain flexibility in procedures and fasting requirements. Even so, in Canada the constraints of time and, to some extent, the unavailability of certain ritual paraphernalia and so forth have meant that less attention is given to the details of correct ritual procedure—such as the correct time for starting and ending the fast and other conventions—than would normally be considered acceptable in India. Further, some of the traditional reasons for women to keep ritual fasts, such as to ensure the long life of one's husband, the well-being of children, or family prosperity, or to solicit assistance from God to solve particular problems, appear to be less compelling to Canadian-born Hindu women. Instead they add, or even favour, such reasons as "It's good discipline" (spiritual and physical); "It's healthy" (restorative to digestive processes); or even "It's a way to diet." Other reasons echo what one might also hear in India: that observing such ritual fasts is a significant way (because it involves hardship) to express one's faith and to draw nearer to God.

Ritual fasts and their array of meanings and purposes are just one of the Hindu traditions being transmitted to younger generations in the Canadian setting. The performance of puja, the singing of bhajans with a gathering of friends in the home, the reading or recitation of holy texts, the significance of special festivals and holy days are being conveyed by parents through a variety of means. One important means is the personal example of the parents themselves. Others include taking the family to Hindu temples and enrolling them in children's classes or classical Indian dance and music classes, associating with other Hindus, and taking the children on visits to India and, while there, to pilgrimage centres. A common view is that the overarching value to transmit to one's children is that religion is important. "It is like the food you eat," commented one mother. "It provides sustenance."

Generational Issues

Young Hindus born and brought up in Canada often express a positive regard for the values that have been instilled in them by their parents, affirming, for example, that familial closeness as well as respect for and obedience to one's elders are important. At the same time, they may comment appreciatively about parents who allow their children at a certain age to choose for themselves whether and how to express their religiosity. Discussions this author has had with second-generation youth affirmed the views that Hinduism is "not a judgmental religion," that it is "open and accepting." "If you want to follow rituals like my mother," said one young woman, "you can, but I don't feel any less Hindu for not doing her sort of ritual practice." In contrast to her mother, who performed a daily two-hour puja and engaged in numerous fasts (while holding down a full-time job), this Canadian-born Hindu's practice was far simpler, consisting of a brief worship of her own chosen form of the Divine, followed by a period of meditation.

On the other hand, second and third-generation Hindus have also expressed concern that in the established temples the voice of youth is not heard, and their participation in any decisions is negligible. Further, if priests are speaking only in Hindi or Tamil, Canadian-born Hindus cannot always understand them. In short, they want a more participatory, meaningful, and informed experience of their religion.

There are also some aspects of Hindu traditions that young Canadian Hindus openly question or reject in a way that tends to be more decisive than their parents. For example, they question the sexist attitudes demonstrated in the preferential treatment of boys and menstrual taboos that prevent girls from going to the temple or participating in puja. Traditional explanations, especially those that appeal in a vague way to ancient tradition, are not always acceptable to young people. Thus, in their process of questioning and research, Hindus today often expect a more "rational" account of their religious practice.

Gender, Dating, and Marriage

There are other areas of negotiation that have been more contentious between the first and second generation of Hindu Canadians: such issues as dating, timing of marriage, and the degree of parental involvement in the choice of a spouse. Among first-generation Hindus it is often thought that the easiest way to ensure retention of Hindu identity for the second and following generations is to marry another Hindu. "If you want to make me happy," one woman told her daughter emphatically, "I would like you to marry a Hindu." And while many Canadian-born Hindus accept that parents should play a role in choosing a spouse for them,

as still largely remains the tradition in India, few accept total parental control in this choice. It has been argued that as an institution, arranged marriage "is tied to the notion of a harmonious Hindu family shielding young people from immodest, selfish, individualistic non-Hindu Canada" (Coward and Banerjee 2005, 43). Because females in many cultures are particularly implicated in upholding family honour, it is not surprising that in matters of dating much greater restrictions tend to be placed on girls than on boys. While dating is becoming more common in urban India, it is still not the norm in rural India (thus, in India as a whole). Ideals of female modesty, sexual respectability, and familial honour do continue to be important.

Caste and Class

Hindus who have grown up in Canada almost uniformly reject class and caste as a valid organizing principle of society, especially if they are understood hierarchically. In other words, they embrace the levelling egalitarian ideology of North American culture. Notions of purity and pollution are often confusing, if not repugnant, to second- and third-generation Hindus. Some argue that birth-based caste distinctions are a cultural, not a religious practice. Others look to interpretive strands in the history of Hinduism that allow for seeing the system of caste as a recognition that not everyone is born with the same temperament, abilities, and interests. What one ends up doing is thus determined in large measure by one's characteristics from birth, and so one can have a "brahmin" mother or a "kshatriya" brother and so forth, since these categories refer to types of work or careers related to natural aptitudes and predilections. Others see caste as part of one's natural social group—understood as determined by commonalities in language, customs, norms of social interaction—that is, more like the British class system of old. Thus, parental preference for finding a suitable marriage partner within one's jati/caste grouping would make sense in terms of the factors that enable successful marriage arrangements.

Hindu Students on Campus

Immigrants from South Asia tend to place a strong emphasis on the importance of higher education and professional training. This tendency, along with the growing Hindu population in Canada, means that colleges and universities in Canada often have significant Hindu student populations. Hindu students' associations are playing an increasingly important role in reaffirming Hindu identity and practice on campuses. Such associations, in addition to organizing social events and celebrations of major Hindu festivals, also sponsor **satsangs**, or religious meetings for meditation and talk that serve an educative function for youth, Hindu and non-Hindu alike. How to perform puja may be a topic, for instance, or discussion of a Hindu concept or text. There are also Hindu groups on campuses affiliated with particular gurus and Hindu organizations based in India—for instance, the Sri Sathya Sai Baba organization and the Swadhyaya ("self-study") movement that began in Mumbai in the 1950s. These groups in particular are also interested in providing opportunities for *seva*, or service to the larger community.

One prominent organization that has established chapters in North America and that often has links with campus Hindu student associations is Vishwa Hindu Parishad (VHP), a Hindu nationalist cultural organization founded in India in 1964, which offers an interpretation of Hindu identity located in the history and geography of India, the "fatherland." The organization is interested in perpetuating this identity and consolidating the Hindu community within the multicultural context of North America. VHP offices organize conferences and weekend gatherings for children and youth, and sponsor speeches by VHP leaders that celebrate Hindu heritage and also valorize Hindu nationalism.

HINDUISM AND THE INTERNET

If one wished to investigate Hinduism on the Internet, it would not be difficult to find a bewildering array of websites with a vast amount of sometimes conflicting information. Like people of other religions, Hindus have taken full advantage of the possibilities of presenting their faith to the world in an accessible manner, including on YouTube, where one can find clips on virtually any topic from Vedic sacrifices to how to apply *mehndi* (henna designs) on the hands and

Satsang: a religious gathering for singing hymns, meditation, and holding spiritual discussions.

feet to "live *darshan*" (see, for example, http://www.shrikashivishwanath.org). Unlike some other religions, however, there are no "official" institutional sites that hold authority in matters of doctrine or practice for all or even most Hindus. Thus, when researching information about Hinduism on the Internet, one may wish to keep in mind such questions as these: Who speaks for Hinduism and with what claims of authority? What are the scholarly credentials of the authors of the site? Who is sponsoring the site? To whom is the information on the site primarily directed? Does the site have a "byline"? For example, the Hinduism Today website's is "Inspiring Hindus and seekers to follow the path of Dharma." It is also important to note that there are few uncontested "facts" in the history of Hinduism.

The academic study of modern Hinduism in recent decades reflects attempts to dissect the essentializing frameworks of past Euro-American orientalists who constructed and packaged their own version of the religion of Hinduism. However, such analyses have also had to contend with the "empire striking back." Despite the tolerance ascribed to Hinduism, there are influential groups in India and abroad who are not very tolerant of views that do not conform to their versions of the "facts" of Hinduism. There are, therefore, accounts of Hinduism on certain websites that can be just as essentializing as their orientalist precursors. There one may find the "multiple Hinduisms" of social reality returned to a more monolithic Hinduism, but one authored by Hindus themselves.

CONCLUSION

To conclude, one might ask, Can there be such a thing as a Canadian Hinduism? There is surely a history of Hinduism in Canada that makes it distinct from any other history. The Canadian cultural context, itself in the process of change, has exerted its influence on the forms and expressions of being Hindu in Canada. On the one hand, in Canada the extraordinary diversity of Indian Hinduism was, initially at least, smoothed over by several factors. One factor was the early experience of Hindu immigrants' finding themselves a small religious minority. A second factor was the need for early temples built in Canada to satisfy a diverse community united primarily by their desire for a shared public sacred space and community centre. A third was the need to accommodate their own diversity as well as the Western business calendar and its expectations around work schedules and days off, which privileged Sunday as the main day for worship. Finally, there were (and are) the forces of neo-Hinduism, arising first in the nineteenth-century colonial milieu and carried on by organizations such as VHP, whose efforts to describe a more "pure" or pared-down Hinduism have also exerted their influence on the shape of Hinduism and Hindu identity in Canada. These and similar efforts are reflected in Internet sites that offer what one might describe as "streamlined" presentations of Hinduism.

On the other hand, efforts to establish a unitary discourse on Hinduism are continually challenged, if not thwarted, by other processes in Canada that work to reaffirm distinctive forms of Hinduism. While in the 1980s and 1990s many second-generation Hindu Canadians preferred a pan-Hindu identity over regional, caste, and sectarian affiliations—in part because the peers they encountered in temples and at festival celebrations emphasized their commonalities as Hindus—the picture today is more complicated. The rise of more distinctly sectarian and regional temples has allowed greater religious, linguistic, and cultural continuity among Hindu immigrant groups. Sri Lankan Tamil Shaiva Hindus, Sri Vaishnavas from Karnataka, and Bengali Shaktas of the second generation in Canada may regard their upbringing in the sub-traditions of Hinduism as comfortable and normal, and may not encounter much diversity in ways of being Hindu until later adult life. At the same time, Canadian-born Hindus continue to question and negotiate their own identities as Hindu Canadians. Hinduism, unlike most religions, does allow for such generational negotiation around freedom of thought to occur without much concern about creation of schism. Like a living tree, the religion is organic, growing and changing while still remaining recognizable, decade by decade and century by century.

NOTE

1. In 2001, of 250 346 immigrants who came to Canada, about 27 per cent were from the family class, 62 per cent from the independent class, and 11 per cent from the refugee class. By the 1990s, 73 per cent of Canadian immigrants were from visible minority groups, and by 2005 India was among the top three sources of Canadian immigrants (along with China and the Philippines).

KEY TERMS

Arati, p. 61
Artha, p. 43
Asana, p. 41
Atman, p. 40
Avatara, p. 54
Bhajan, p. 61
Bhakti, p. 53
Bindi, p. 66
Brahman, p. 38
Brahmin, p. 36

Darshana, p. 63
Deva, p. 35
Dharma, p. 32
Guru, p. 40
Jati, p. 46
Jnana, p. 52
Kama, p. 44
Karma, p. 40
Mandir, p. 76
Mantra, p. 33

Moksha, p. 40
Murti, p. 63
Pandit, p. 75
Pativrata, p. 47
Pranam, p. 76
Prasada, p. 63
Puja, p. 61
Rishis, p. 33
Sampradaya, p. 54

Samsara, p. 42
Samskara, p. 64
Sannyasin, p. 45
Satsang, p. 81
Sattva, p. 46
Shakti, p. 55
Vahana, p. 55
Vrat, p. 63
Yajna, p. 35

CRITICAL THINKING QUESTIONS

1. What is problematic about defining Hinduism? What do analogies used to express the complexity of Hinduism, such as a great tree or a palace added to over the centuries, convey to us about Hinduism? What characteristics have enabled Hinduism to develop in many directions? Does it make sense to speak of a singular Hinduism?

2. What is the Hindu understanding of reincarnation? How do the following terms relate to this

doctrine: *samsara, atman, Brahman, karma, yoga, moksha*? How does this doctrine compare with those of the Jewish, Christian, or Muslim religions?

3. Why did the practice of asceticism assume such prominence in Hinduism? What is its purpose and what are some of the forms that asceticism takes (including yoga)? What does asceticism tell us about notions of salvation, detachment, and purity in Hinduism? How can Hinduism reconcile the values of asceticism with the values of family life and an appreciation of the aesthetic and even the sensual world?

4. Why does ritual tend to be pervasive in Hinduism? Describe and discuss the nature of ritual with reference to several particular forms of Hindu ritual, including prasada, darshana, puja, and vrat. How does ritual help facilitate the goals of Hindus?

5. What is the ideal conception of the organization of society according to Hindu texts such as the dharma shastras? How is this vision expressive of the concept of dharma? (Consider what duties, if any, are shared across classes and castes in Hinduism, and how the system of the four main social classes is justified in Hinduism. Does this division of society have parallels in other cultures?)

6. How do Hindus understand the nature of the Divine or ultimate reality, beginning with the Vedas? How do views expressed in the Upanishads differ from those expressed in, for example, the Bhagavad-Gita or other theistic texts? How is the Divine honoured or worshipped in Hinduism?

7. Describe features of popular goddesses in Hinduism. Explain the concept of the female consort of a deity. If there are goddesses in Hinduism, why has women's religious and social status generally been lower than men's?

8. What challenges and opportunities have been presented to Hindus immigrating to Canada? What are the ways in which Hindu identity is negotiated?

RECOMMENDED READING

Bramadat, Paul, and David Seljak, eds. *Religion and Ethnicity in Canada*. Toronto: Pearson Education, 2005.

Doniger, Wendy. *The Hindus: An Alternate History*. New York: Penguin Press, 2009.

Eck, Diana. *Darshan: Seeing the Divine Image in India*, 3rd ed. Chambersburg, PA: Anima Books, 1998.

Falk, Nancy Auer. *Living Hinduisms: An Explorer's Guide*. Belmont, CA: Wadsworth, 2006.

Humes, Cynthia, and T. Fortshoefel, eds. *Gurus in America*. Albany: State University of New York Press, 2005.

Narayanan, Vasudha. *Hinduism*. New York: Oxford University Press, 2004.

Olson, Carl, ed. *Hindu Primary Sources: A Sectarian Reader*. New Brunswick, NJ: Rutgers University Press, 2007.

Pearson, Anne Mackenzie. *Because It Gives Me Peace of Mind: Ritual Fasts in the Religious Lives of Hindu Women*. Albany: State University of New York Press, 1996.

Rinehardt, Robin, ed. *Contemporary Hinduism: Ritual, Culture, Practice*. Santa Barbara, CA: ABC-CLIO, 2004.

Rodrigues, Hillary. *Introducing Hinduism*. New York: Routledge Press, 2006.

Sarma, Deepak, ed. *Hinduism: A Reader*. Oxford: Blackwell, 2008.

Sharma, Arvind. *Modern Hindu Thought: The Essential Texts*. New Delhi: Oxford University Press, 2002.

Younger, Paul. *New Homelands: Hindu Communities in Mauritius, Guyana, Trinidad, South Africa, Fiji, and East Africa*. New York: Oxford University Press, 2010.

USEFUL WEBSITES

Internet Sacred Text Archive

Somewhat dated (nineteenth-century) translations into English of key Hindu texts, including Vedas, Upanishads, epics, dharma shastras, compilations of Hindu myths, etc.

BBC Religions: Hinduism

This site from the British Broadcasting Corporation has a selection of scholarly and introductory articles on Hindu history, key concepts, and practices, with illustrations.

Hindu Universe

Calling itself the largest Hinduism site on the Net, this site offers links to numerous articles on all aspects of Hindu beliefs and practices, history, festivals, and deities, plus the complete text of eighty-five books and several scriptures and a listing of Hindu temples around the world. It also includes links to activism, shopping, and newsgroup archives.

Harappa
This site has extensive coverage in both essay and image form of the Indus Valley civilization, much of it prepared by leading scholars working at Indus sites.

Indira Gandhi National Centre for the Arts
This site has a cultural informatics division with pre-views of various CD-ROMs the group has produced. Included are image collections of prehistoric rock art, Vedic ritual, temple traditions, and more.

GaramChai
A site by and for Indo-Canadian communities, with a list of and links to websites of many Hindu temples and Hindu organizations in Canada.

Vedanta Society of Toronto
The Toronto branch of the Vedanta Society site, with links to the Ramakrishna Order of India site. Both offer a wealth of information on these modern movements.

Vishva Hindu Parishad
Offers the VHP's perspective on Hindu culture and the need to preserve and defend it.

hinduism.co.za
While no authorship is indicated, this neo-Vedanta site provides essays on many topics with reference to and excerpts from Hindu texts (such as the Mahabharata) and figures such as Swami Vivekanan-da, for whom there is a clear preference. Information on Hindu calendars, festivals, Hinduism and quan-tum physics, etc. is also provided.

About Hinduism
This site has numerous helpful short articles on a wide variety of topics written by one person, Sub-hamoy Das. It also has links for Indian cultural forms including music, dance, visual arts, how to wear a sari, and more.

Sri Devasthanam
The many short, often illustrated articles found at this site give information about all aspects of Hindu beliefs and practices, written by one author, Shukavak Dasa. They are fairly scholarly but with few citations.

A "Hindu Primer" page gives a table of contents for all the articles, organized topically.

Vedas Cultural Sabha, Inc.
Site of the largest Vishnu temple in Canada, with talks, a temple tour, and other helpful information.

REFERENCES

Brockington, John. 1998. *The Sanskrit Epics*. Leiden: Brill.

Coward, H., and Banerjee, S. 2005. "Hindus in Canada: Negotiating Identity in a 'Different' Homeland." In *Religion and Ethnicity in Canada*, ed. Paul Bramadat and David Seljak. Toronto: Pearson Education.

Doniger, Wendy, and Brian K. Smith, trans. 1992. *The Laws of Manu*. New York: Penguin Books.

Engineer, A. A., ed. 1997. *Gandhi and Communal Harmony*. New Delhi: Gandhi Peace Foundation.

Flood, Gavin. 1996. *An Introduction to Hinduism*. Cambridge: Cambridge University Press.

Fuller, C. J. 1992. *The Camphor Flame: Popular Hinduism and Society in India*. Princeton, NJ: Princeton University Press.

Gandhi, M. K. 1957. *From Yeravda Mandir*, trans. V. J. Desai. Ahmedabad: Navajivan Publishing.

Goldman, Robert, trans. 1984. *The Rāmāyana of Vālmīki: An Epic of Ancient India*. Vol. 1, *Bālakānda*. Princeton, NJ: Princeton University Press.

Hawley, J., and M. Juergensmeyer. 2007. *Songs of the Saints of India*. Oxford: Oxford University Press.

Jones, Kenneth. 1989. *Socio-religious Reform Movements in British India*. Cambridge: Cambridge University Press.

Klostermaier, Klaus. 2007. *A Survey of Hinduism*, 3rd ed. Albany: State University of New York Press.

Lopez, Donald, ed. 1995. *Religions of India in Practice*. Princeton, NJ: Princeton University Press.

Mascaro, Juan, trans. 1962. *The Bhagavad Gita*. New York: Penguin Books.

Müller, F. M. 1883. *What Can India Teach Us?* Lecture I. London: Longmans, Green.

Nanda, B. R. 1990. *Gandhi and Religion*. New Delhi: Gandhi Smriti and Darshan Samiti.

O'Flaherty, Wendy Doniger, trans. 1983. *The Rig Veda: An Anthology*. New York: Penguin Books.

Olivelle, Patrick, trans. 1996. *Upanisads*. New York: Oxford University Press.

Quigley, Declan. 1993. *The Interpretation of Caste*. Oxford: Clarendon Press.

Radhakrishnan, Sarvepalli. 1927. *The Hindu View of Life*. London: Unwin Books.

Raheja, Gloria G. 1988. *The Poison in the Gift: Ritual, Prestation and the Dominant Caste in a North India Village*. Chicago: University of Chicago Press.

Sharma, Arvind. 1996. *Hinduism for Our Times*. Delhi: Oxford University Press.

Spear, Percival. 1979. *A History of India*. Vol. 2. New York: Penguin.

Vishnu Purana. 1870. Book 6, chap. 1, trans. H. H. Wilson. London: Trübner.

Zimmer, Heinrich. 1951. *Philosophies of India*, ed. Joseph Campbell. New York: Bollingen Foundation, Princeton University Press.

Timeline

- **c. 850 B.C.E.** Parsavantha, the twenty-third Tirthankara.

- **599–527 B.C.E.** The traditional dates of Mahavira, the twenty-fourth Tirthankara.

- **c. 360 B.C.E.** Severe drought and famine in Maghada region, location of the first Jain sangha; group of Jain monks led by Bhadrabahu migrates southward to what is now Karnataka region.

- **c. 327 B.C.E.** First council of monks in Patliputra held in attempt to codify Jain canon (oral tradition); disagreement leads to first division within Jain community (Svetambara versus Digambara).

- **c. 82 C.E.** Shivakoti credited with establishing first officially separate order of naked monks; rift between Svetambara and Digambara becomes more entrenched.

- **2nd century C.E.** Digambara philosopher Acharya Kundakunda compiles text on nature of the soul, *Samayasara Sutra*.
  Acharya Umasvati, student of Kundakunda, authors prominent text *Tattvartha-sutra*, first Jain text written in Sanskrit.

- **c. 300 C.E.** Two simultaneous councils for compilation of Jain canon (Agamas): Mathura Council, headed by Acharya Skandila, and First Valabhi Council, headed by Acharya Nagarjuna.

- **c. 455** Second Valabhi Council headed by Devarddhi Ganin; final redaction and compilation of Svetambara canon.

- **4th century** First period of established Jain temple building.
  Beginning of development of Jain logic, philosophy, and yoga.

- **5th century** Notable philosophers Siddhasena Divakara and Akalanka.

- **6th–7th centuries** Philosophers Pujyapada and Jinabhadra.

- **8th–9th centuries** Philosophers Mallavadin, Haribhadra, and Prabhacandra.

- **9th–11th centuries** Digambara Jain community frequently supported by South Indian royalty. Colossal statue of Bahubali erected in Sravanabelagola, Karnataka (South India), in tenth century.
  Philosophers Hemacandra (1089–1172) and Vadideva.

- **15th century** Lonkashaha initiates reform in Svetambara tradition.

- **16th century** Banarsidass initiates reform in Digambara tradition.

- **17th century** Iconoclastic Stanakvasis sect emerges within Svetambara group.
  Notable philopher Yasovijaya (1624–88).

- **18th century** Emergence of Terapanthi as Svetambara sub-sect.

- **18th–21st centuries** Many Jain laity emigrate to East Africa, United Kingdom, and North America and, without presence of ascetics, tend to focus on building temples and community centres.

CHAPTER 3

Jainism

■

Mikal A. Radford

INTRODUCTION

For many students their first exposure to the Jain tradition is through a relatively broad description in an "Introduction to World Religions" text. Unfortunately, many earlier versions of these texts tend to describe Jainism as a philosophical offshoot—usually in the context of being an unorthodox "descendant"—of the Vedic/Hindu traditions of South Asia. Though most Jains (and many Jain scholars) do not accept the idea that Jainism "sprang forth" from the Vedic tradition, it is fair to say that Jainism—and also Buddhism to a great extent—is a **sramana** ("striver" or ascetic) religious tradition that countered the religious practices—particularly the principles underlying the need for animal sacrifice—and philosophical position of South Asian Vedic culture.

In this chapter you will be learning why and how Jain communities both past and present have rejected the authority of the Vedic and Hindu scriptures; the supremacy of the Brahminical (priestly) caste, or **varna** (Jains tend to reject all South Asian caste systems, for that matter); the efficacy of Vedic animal sacrifice; and, perhaps most important, the notion of a great cosmic god/goddess that creates and holds moral sway over the universe. It is important to understand that Jainism is a non-theistic religion with its own collection of sacred texts that tend to detail three basic assumptions about the nature of the universe:

1. The principle of **karma** is the primary law under which all living things within the universe operate.[1]
2. The practice of **ahimsa** (non-violence) is the only way to escape the karmic and worldly bonds of **samsara** (the cycles of reincarnation).
3. A Jain practices a religion of self-reliance in which individuals must free themselves from samsara without depending on a priestly caste, ritual sacrifice, fate, or the help of deities.

CENTRAL BELIEFS

To a great extent the term *Jain* (or, more correctly, **Jaina**, though the usual English form will be used in this chapter) is a quirk of the early Sanskrit and Prakrit languages. Literally, *Jain* translates as "follower of a **Jina**." So who or what are Jinas? Briefly, the Jinas (or **Tirthankaras**) are not gods or goddesses but enlightened spiritual teachers who have carried out great feats of meditation, conquered attachment to all worldly desires, and attained the infinite knowledge of the meta-universe, which ultimately leads to **moksha** (liberation, the final release from the cycles of reincarnation). The core to any Jain's life—whether that person be an ascetic monk or nun or a lay householder—is to imitate, as closely as possible, the life of renunciation lived by the Jinas.

Sramana: members of a community who follow the ascetic ideal of the Jain monks and nuns.

Varna: the Sanskrit term for the Portuguese word meaning the caste or class system developed in South Asia.

Karma: according to the Jain tradition, subtle particles of matter.

Ahimsa: non-injury to or interference with any living being (the opposite of *himsa*, harm).

Samsara: the cycles of transmigration and reincarnation.

Jaina: a follower of the Jaina (Jain) religion.

Jina: a spiritual victor.

Tirthankara: "the one who crosses the stream of existence"; an omniscient being.

Moksha: the attainment of complete freedom of the soul from karmic matter; salvation.

History and Development

Historically, most scholars agree that Jainism emerged as a formidable sramanic (ascetic) tradition during the latter years of the South Asian Vedic period (c. sixth century B.C.E.)[2] and that Vardhamana Mahavira (c. 599–527 B.C.E.) was the historical founder of the tradition (Dundas 1992; Folkert 1993; Jaini 1979/1990).[3] To put this in context, the dominant Vedic tradition of the period focused on the use of priests to conduct specialized rituals and sacrifice to seek favour with the gods and goddesses. For the most part, these sacrifices were external in nature. That is, an individual or community that wanted to seek favour with a god or goddess would go to a Brahmin priest and provide the priest (or, in many cases, several priests) with all the things necessary for the specific ritual. The priest would then perform a sacrifice to the gods on behalf of the individual or community.

The sramana tradition objected to these rituals, particularly the use of animal sacrifices, and suggested that they did very little to change the world. The ascetic philosophy argued that if you truly want to change the nature of the world, you must first begin by changing (and understanding) the nature of self. This tradition shifted the focus of sacrifice from the external to the internal—one didn't sacrifice animals (external sacrifice) but instead sacrificed the self, through fasting and meditation (internal sacrifice). In this sense, rather than being "founders of a religion," the omniscient ascetic

teachers—especially Jinas such as Parsvanatha and Mahavira—are regarded as "revealers" who continually reanimate an ever-present eternal truth: that salvation of the soul from the cycles of rebirth is not achieved by Vedic ritual and the sacrifice of animals, nor by divine providence, but rather by having faith in the fundamental principles underlying non-violence (*ahimsa*) and following a path of ascetic rejection of all worldly passion. For example, from the first text of the Jain canon, known as the *Asaraoga Sutra*, we find the following:

> The *Arhats* and *Bhagavats* of the past, present, and future, all say thus, speak thus, declare thus, explain thus: all breathing, existing, living, sentient creatures should not be slain, nor treated with violence, nor abused nor tormented, nor driven away. This is the pure, unchangeable, eternal law, which the clever ones, who understand the world, have proclaimed. ... Having adopted (the law), one should not hide it, nor forsake it ... and "not act on the motives of the world." ... Those who acquiesce and indulge (in worldly pleasures), are born again and again. (*Acaranga Sutra* 1.4.1.1–3, Jacobi 1884/1995).

Source: Jacobi, Hermann (English trans.) (1995 [1884]) *AcharangaSutra*. Vol. 22 of *The Sacred Books of the East*. (ed.) Max Muller. (Delhi: Motilal Banarsidass, 1995).

A vivid image emerges from this early text. In contrast to the polytheism and highly ritualized sacrifices of the Vedic traditions of the time, the central religious ideal developed by what was to become the Jain community was to lead an exemplary ascetic life of world renunciation, non-attachment, and non-violence to all living beings. To be Jain was to be an ascetic, or to live as closely as possible the life of an ascetic.

If the defining figure in the early Jain community was the ascetic renouncer—communities of monks and nuns—the texts also make it very clear that at the other end of the religious spectrum was the householder. According to these texts, which were primarily codes of conduct for the sramana monks rather than for both monks and nuns, contact with any householder (particularly women) was considered hazardous to the ascetic's spiritual welfare.

Words

The Story of Sagaradatta, Who Was Redeemed by a Clever Woman

Much like most of the traditional literature of India, whether it is Vedic, Hindu, Buddhist, or Jain, we find a rather unflattering picture of women. Females are often portrayed as fickle, treacherous, wicked beings or, at the very least, beings incapable of independence from a male guardian. Though few and far between, some stories connected with the hagiographies of Jain Tirtankaras and saints do attempt to cast women in a favourable light. As you read the following story, taken from an ancient Digambara source—*The Life and Stories of the Jaina Saviour Parsvanatha, the Twenty-third Tirthankara*—ask yourself what this story might mean to a culture that can at times be rather misogynist. Does it help to adequately counter the negative portrayals of women?

The Lord of the world (Parsvanatha), in the course of his progress in time arrived at Pundradesa. There, in the city of Tamralipti, lived a pious young merchant's son, Sagaradatta by name. In a former existence (life) he had been a priest, and had been poisoned by his lewd wife. Cast out of his house while unconscious, he was left to die, but was revived by a shepherd's wife. After gaining his strength, he became a wandering ascetic, and after death, was reborn as Sagaradatta. Owing to the

memory of his former birth as being a poisoned priest, Sagaradatta became a woman-hater.

The kind shepherdess who had revived the poisoned priest, and who also died in piety, was reborn as the beautiful daughter of a merchant. Sagaradatta cast longing eyes upon her, and his relatives, knowing his sentiments, chose her as his wife. But his eyes only were pleased with her, not his mind. For Sagaradatta now looked upon all women with fright and hate, as though they were swords.

The woman, undismayed by his fear, wrote him a *sloka* (verse) message: "Why, o wise man, dost thou neglect and fear a devoted lady? The full-moon day makes the moon shine; lighting the ocean, so too, a woman for the householder."

Sagaradatta replied with a *sloka* of his own: "Like a river, woman is by nature unstable, tends to fall downward, and she is ill-behaved, stupid, and destroys both partners."

Sagaradatta's betrothed, concluding that his mind was poisoned by the memory of a woman's corruptness in a former birth, sent him a second *sloka*: "Surely, the fault of a single woman must not be visited on her entire race: is the full-moon night to be shunned because of the dark night before the new moon?"

Then Sagaradatta, attracted by her insight and cleverness, married her, and the two enjoyed a life of full happiness together.

Source: *Life and Stories of the Jaina Savior Parasvanatha*, Maurice Bloomfield, trans. (Baltimore, MD: Johns Hopkins University Press, 1919). The text has been slightly modified.

SOURCES OF THE TRADITION

The Jain tradition holds that the first Tirthankara of the current period, Rishbha, lived about 100 000 years ago (some sources say more, some say less). Obviously there is great debate among scholars of South Asian history, and among Jains themselves, about the accuracy of this historical date of origin for Jain society. However, what the Jain community does agree upon is that a special spiritual reverence is given to Rishbha for first

These Svetambara and Digambara icons (murti) are both images of Mahavira, but they are quite different in appearance. For example, note that the eyes are open in the Svetambara icon (left) and that Mahavira is pictured wearing a crown. Members of the Svetambara sect in Toronto state that they want to show Mahavira as an "awakened" (enlightened) prince—hence the crown—who gave up all worldly desires, but also to demonstrate that he was of this world, and not some god. The Svetambara message is: "Mahavira was a very real person with a very real life, but renounced all those pleasures of a princely life to become our twenty-fourth Tirthankara. By showing him in a princely fashion, we are also saying that anyone can follow his path. In time, all people have the potential to become Tirthankaras." The emphasis of Digambara icons (right) is slightly different. Note that the eyes of the icon appear to be closed, as they would be in a state of meditation, and that it wears no adornments. These types of icons represent the purified naked ascetic in meditation—an image that demonstrates the state to which all Jains should aspire.

Sources: Mikal Radford (left), ASSOCIATED PRESS (right)

establishing the principles of ethics, community activity, and social interaction. In contrast, there appears to be a little more historicity to the last three Jinas of this time cycle (see the section below on Jain cosmology and time). For example, the twenty-second Tirthankara, Nemi, is given a little historical credence within the Jain tradition; unfortunately, however, historians can find very little evidence to support the claim that Nemi existed as a contemporary of Krishna. On the other hand, Parsvanatha and especially Mahavira (the twenty-fourth and final Tirthankara of the current age or time cycle) are accepted as being historical figures by both the community and Jain scholars. Parsvanatha appears to have flourished in Varanasi in about 850 B.C.E., and Mahavira ("the Great Hero") was born in about 590 B.C.E. in the kingdom of Vaisali, in the Magadha region near modern Patna in north-eastern India. Much as in the more familiar life story of the Buddha, Mahavira's father was a warrior chieftain and his mother was of

princely lineage, and Mahavira led a privileged life that he rejected in his thirtieth year.

AUTHORITIES

Unlike many other religious traditions, there is no single authority in Jainism other than the ascetic model established by the Tirthankara, and all Jain sects trace their spiritual authority back to these enlightened teachers. Over the course of its long history in India, however, there have been many sub-sects within the Jain community, the first being the major division between the Svetambaras and the Digambaras. Although there are no genuinely ancient sources to "explain how deviant tendencies arose within Jainism" (Dundas 1992, 41), the two traditions maintain that the first major schism occurred in the fourth century B.C.E., when a famine in north India drove one group

Though there are many sub-sects within Jainism, the two primary groups are the Digambara and the Svetambara. According to the Digambara tradition, all monks must remain naked, renouncing all possessions, including clothing. Women are not allowed to be naked ascetics, so the tradition holds that a Digambara nun must eventually be reborn as a male ascetic in order to gain final liberation. Note that the Digambara monk does have a peacock-feather broom. This is used to wipe the ground before he sits down in order to prevent harm to any insects or other organisms that might be in the seating area. Digambara monks and nuns will visit temples and learning centres for special festivals but will not actively participate in those festivals, other than to give religious instruction. For most of the year they travel from place to place in small groups, spending no more than three days in one location (to prevent attachment to a particular village or household). The monks and nuns (both Svetambara and Digambara) must beg for food daily, and they eat only one meal a day.

Source: © Hemis/Alamy

from a supposedly "unified Jain community" south to what is now Karnataka (Jaini 1990, 5). According to the Digambara tradition, those who fled south eventually returned to Paliputra (modern Patna, in Bihar) after a twelve-year absence. They discovered that the Jains who had remained in the north had assembled and attempted to codify the Agama texts (the ancient "oral texts") and, more importantly, that the ascetics had adopted the practice of wearing a simple white cloth around their body. The southern group declared the new canon and the practices adopted by this nascent Svetambara group to be backsliding and heretical practice. Meanwhile the Svetambara group maintained that their canon was an accurate transmission of the original oral texts and that the abandonment of clothes had "died out with Mahavira's disciple Jambu" (Dundas 1992, 41).

Interestingly, in light of the fact that the Digambaras refuse to accept Svetambara canonical literature, there is very little difference between the two sects from the perspective of spiritual authority, doctrine, ethics, and metaphysical prescription (Dundas 1992, 44; Folkert 1993, 157). There are, however, three major areas of concern that differentiate the two groups in India and hence overtly influence the North American community. First, the Digambara community maintain that omniscient Tirthankaras achieve such total detachment from this world that they no longer need to engage in any worldly activities—such as eating, sleeping, or wearing clothes—and that they preach "by means of a magical divine sound" (Jaini 1990, 39: Folkert 1993, 157). In contrast, the Svetambara community holds that Tirthankaras can simultaneously engage in the normal day-to-day human activities of an ascetic and at the same time enjoy omniscient cognition.

Sangha: a Jain community, made up of monks, nuns, laymen, and laywomen.

The second primary difference between the two communities concerns the issue of nudity. The Digambaras maintain that the practice of ascetic nudity is an absolute prerequisite to attaining moksha (liberation of the purified soul), and posit that the Svetambara monks—and, by implied association, the nuns—are attached to the possessions of clothing. In this sense, the Digambaras would argue, Svetambara monks and nuns more closely resemble observantly religious householders rather than "true" Jain ascetics in the tradition of Mahavira. The Svetambaras counter this philosophical perspective by maintaining that Mahavira did not renounce his clothing; rather, he lost his robe by rubbing against a thorn bush while in a state of walking meditation. From this perspective, they argue, the wearing of clothing is optional and is not an obstacle to salvation, as long as one does not become attached to the wearing of cloth (Dundas 1992,

41–43). Unfortunately the option of nudity does not apply to women, and this leads to the third major difference between the two major communities: the status of women as nuns within the **sangha** (community).

Although the origins of this third position are somewhat obscured by the mists of time, the Digambara community claims that a woman's very femaleness, and the karmic material that forms into such a being, creates a spiritual inequality between men and women. That is, unlike her male counterpart, it is the very nature of the female body to be in a constant state of impurity, for instance, because of menstruation—an indication of both her sexual nature and the bearing of children. It is maintained by the Digambara mendicants, therefore, that a woman is both physiologically and psychologically incapable of developing the pure body of a Tirthankara (Jaini 1991) or, for that matter, to be as pure as a monk (the clothing issue is again part of this position). Accordingly, a woman must be reborn as a man in order to accomplish the highest stages of asceticism and, ultimately, release from the cycles of reincarnation (moksha).

Svetambara monks and nuns are easily identified by their white cloth robes and the traditional mask over the mouth. In this sense, both the monks and nuns are equal in their renunciation, so both have the capacity (as male or female) to gain liberation. The Svetambaras wear the mask to prevent swallowing insects or other organisms—they take the principle of non-violence very seriously—and there is also another important reason: the mask prevents drastic changes of temperature in the mouth, which could kill the micro-organisms that live there.

Source: AFP/Getty Images

Cosmology and Time

Unlike the Western religious belief in a universe with both a created beginning and an ultimate, apocalyptic ending, the Jain scriptures maintain a cosmological position that both time and the universe are eternal and cyclical in nature. In the Jain universe, time can be imagined as a succession of large waves divided into two equal parts: the descending part of the wave (its trough) and the ascending part (its crest). Each of these components is further divided into six subsections, or epochs (ages). During the ascending component of the wave, the universe and all the beings within the universe are seen as making gradual spiritual progress. The opposite is true for the descending part of this wave or cycle, when the universe slips into gradual decline. During this period of decline, civilizations are subjected to spiritual deterioration. Ultimately comes destruction of the material universe and then the process starts again. In sum, the universe, through its own natural forces, creates itself, destroys itself, and regenerates itself eternally, and there is no divine mind or will directing the process.

According to the tradition, twenty-four Jinas or Tirthankaras ("builders of the river crossing" of samsara) appear in each half of the full wave cycle, in both its ascending and descending aspects. Each of the epochs within a cycle can last for hundreds of thousands of years. The Jinas appear in these different ages to help guide all living beings toward liberation from the cycles

PERSPECTIVES

The Jain Cycle of Time

Each wave of the Jain time cycle is divided into two major components, and each of these two components is further divided into six sub-components, or epochs, each of which can last thousands of years. According to the Jain scriptures, the third and fourth epochs of both the ascending and descending parts of the cycle are supposed to be best for the development of human civilization and culture, as there is a balance between misery and joy. As was explained at the Jain Mandir in Toronto, when people are too happy or too sad, they cannot focus on spiritual concerns; rather, they focus on (are attached to) their misery or their joy. When there is a balance between the two extremes, there is a chance of conquering the emotions and attachments of both. Therefore it is during these four epochs that human civilization produces the largest number of great spiritual personalities, including the twenty-four Tirthankaras who guide the community toward spiritual liberation.

Ascending Part of the Wave Cycle
1. The age/epoch in which most people are suffering great misery.
2. The age/epoch in which most people are suffering in misery.
3. The age/epoch in which most people are suffering in mostly misery with a bit of joy: Age of the Jinas.
4. The age/epoch in which most people are experiencing joy with a bit of misery: Age of the Jinas.
5. The age/epoch in which most people are experiencing joy.
6. The age/epoch in which most people are experiencing extreme joy.

Descending Part of the Wave Cycle
1. The age/epoch in which most people are experiencing extreme joy.
2. The age/epoch in which most people are experiencing joy.
3. The age/epoch in which most people are experiencing mostly joy with a bit of misery: Age of the Jinas.
4. The age/epoch in which most people are suffering mostly misery with a bit of joy: Age of the Jinas.
5. The age/epoch in which most people are suffering misery.
6. The age/epoch in which most people are suffering great misery.

> **Jiva:** soul, spirit, living substance.
>
> **Ajiva:** non-soul, non-living substance.

of reincarnation; however, it is important to note that it is still up to the individual to gain salvation (moksha) through the path of renunciation. As one Jain at a Toronto mandir (temple) stated, "Only the individual (soul) can awaken to this infinite knowledge. 'Infinite knowledge' is not received through divine revelation, magical formula, or ritual actions. Ultimately, it is only individuals who can 'save themselves,' not a god."

The Metaphysics of Parsvanatha and Mahavira

From a philosophical perspective that has developed since the time of Parsvanatha and Mahavira, the twenty-third and twenty-fourth Jinas, Jainism has come to view all of existence as consisting of three principal categories:

1. all those objects in the universe that have a soul (**jiva**) and therefore have some degree of sentience;
2. all those objects that do not possess a soul (**ajiva**) but have a material form consisting of matter (*pudgala*) and such qualities as colour, taste, smell, dimension, and palpability; and finally
3. those things that are characterized as having neither a soul nor a material form.

This last category includes such components of the cosmos as space, the principle of motion, the principle of rest, and the principle of time. This last category may seem a bit confusing at first, but it must be remembered that the Jain philosophers tend to be very thorough in describing both their physics and their metaphysics.

No Beginning and No End As mentioned earlier, Jainism asserts a metaphysical principle about the nature of the universe that is quite distinct from the other theistic traditions of South Asia. That is, all three categories of existence that make up the cosmos are eternal. The universe and all that it contains may constantly change form (thanks to space, time, motion, and so on), but the contents of the universe were never created—they have always existed and will always exist. There is no

theological entity akin to Aristotle's "prime mover" or Thomas Aquinas's "necessary being."

With this philosophical starting point—and if we set aside the third category, "things without a soul or form," for a moment—Jainism presents a unique dualistic worldview to its followers. Unlike in the philosophies underlying the more familiar theologically based traditions, the soul, and the soul alone, is the ultimate perfected state in Jainism; there is no union with a god or place in heaven. All other states are considered blemished. It is the matter of the universe—the deficient and the "soulless"—that encases and imprisons the soul within the physical universe. It is the materiality of the universe and the desires in our lives that prevent our souls from reaching their state of perfection and, ultimately, our release from the cycles of reincarnation. As long as the soul of any living being is ensnared within matter, it is bound to remain trapped in the endless cycles of birth, death, and rebirth.

Metaphysics Blends with Physics

According to such texts as the *Tattvartha-sutra* and the *Samayasara*, the three principal categories of existence outlined above can be further subdivided into the six categories or components that comprise the entire Jain universe. The primary component, as mentioned earlier, is the soul (more on this in the following section). As several members of the Jain community in Toronto explained, "The soul, once liberated from the bonds of karma, is in a state of pure bliss—there is no other way to describe it. The soul, once liberated, becomes fully aware of all that is pure soul and all that is not pure soul. The soul has no attachments to time, space, or the all that is contained within the universe . . . the soul just *is*-ness."

Unlike some of the other metaphysical traditions of South Asia, the Jain philosophers did not doubt that the universe exists as a very real entity comprising very real components. In this sense Jain physics is very similar to what we read in the texts of modern Western physics. For example, the Jains believe that one of the prime components of the universe is matter—matter that is composed of molecules, atoms, particles, and so forth. Matter comprises all things that can be scientifically measured by one or all of the five senses (or, in the modern context, by scientific instruments). In contrast to this category of matter, the Jains argue that the

Figure 3.1   The Jain Universe

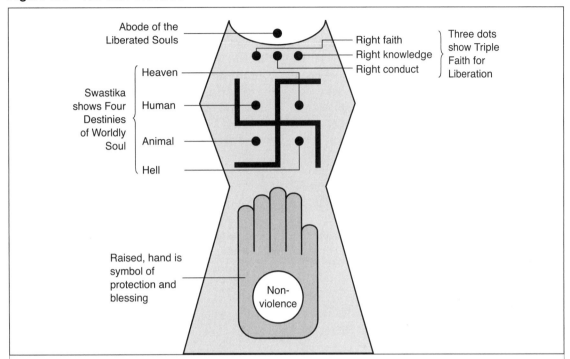

This symbol was adopted by the Jain community to commemorate the 2,500th anniversary of Mahavira's liberation (moksha) in 1969. It demonstrates the entire Jain universe and all the beings that occupy it. The swastika represents the four categories of living beings: (1) human beings, (2) heavenly beings such as gods and goddesses, (3) hell beings, and (4) all animals, birds, fish, insects, plants, bacteria, etc. that possess a soul. The hand represents ahimsa, the practice of strict non-violence. The three dots represent the "three jewels" or ideals of the Jain philosophy: right knowledge, which will lead one to right faith, and then both of these elements will lead to right conduct.

The single dot at the top is the abode of the liberated soul. Note that it is outside the symbolic representation of the Jain universe—no longer in contact with matter (the things that are contained in the universe). You will often see the Jain universe represented by a human-like form, with the abode of liberated souls in the head position and the material universe looking like the rest of the body. Human beings, animals, and plants live in the waist area, heavenly beings live in the shoulder area, and hell beings live in the legs and feet.

In order to gain liberation, all beings must return to the "waist" as human beings; even the gods and goddesses must be reincarnated as ascetics in order to gain liberation. Someone who becomes a Tirthankara will gain liberation by shooting straight through the heavens to the place where the liberated souls abide. It is important to note that they do not go to "heaven" first.

universe is also composed of components that *cannot* be measured by the five senses but that their effects are present and observable. For example, dharma is best described in the early Jain texts as the principle or law of motion, or, more precisely, the accompanying circumstance that makes motion possible. To borrow P. Jaini's example, consider the image of a bird in flight: the air represents the nature of dharma. Air does not make the bird fly but provides the circumstances for the bird to fly. As a counterpoint to dharma, or the principle of motion, the Jains hold that there is also a passive condition of non-motion, or "stationariness."

The final two categories, at least to the Jain philosophers, are components of the universe that can be simultaneously both scientifically measurable and not. For example, space accommodates a place for everything to exist, including all possible dimensions (many of the medieval Jain texts on metaphysical speculation mention other universes and other dimensions), but space can also represent a state of emptiness, a state that does not contain matter or have characteristics that can be scientifically measured. Time is another such element. It has no taste, sound, colour, smell, or texture. It has only its own attributes and the attribute of helping in the modification of other substances. That is, the Jains maintain the basic philosophical principle that matter is not static; matter is constantly changing, and both space and time perform their roles to allow this changing to take place.

The Nature of the Soul and the Principle of Karma

In the *Tattvartha-sutra* we see the Jain philosopher Umasvati[4] describe the human being as comprising three possible combinations: the soul/non-soul, the non-soul, and the pure soul (jiva). The soul/nonsoul is the state of union between the pure soul and that which comprises non-soul, such as the body of the being. The pure soul is timeless and has no beginning or creation point. Although the soul is sometimes described as a finite entity in each body, the duration of each individual soul is eternal.

One of the questions I had to ask members of the Jain community in Toronto was, of course, how does pure soul become "defiled" by karmic matter in the first place? Unfortunately, no answer is provided in the

canonical texts, nor could I discover any speculation on this subject within the contemporary Jain community. The texts usually state simply that the soul has always been corrupted by karmic matter. The soul in its pure state is totally blissful and uninterested in external matter; however, it does come into contact with matter from time to time, and so it can become "infused" or obscured by a covering of "material dust," or defiling karma. This material, depending on the types of defiling karma experienced in previous lives, then forms into a living being that can be anything from a plant to an animal, a god or goddess, a hell being, or a human being.

Therefore, according to Jain metaphysics, the soul and consciousness are not simply the domain of human beings and gods or goddesses (note that in the Jain tradition even the gods and goddesses are affected by the principles of karma, in which sense they are like human beings). Even the lowliest being that has only one of the five senses has a soul—in some cases it may actually contain several souls within its makeup—and consciousness of any type means the presence of soul. An example of an object consisting of several souls is a pomegranate. Although there is just one fruit, that fruit contains many seeds, and each seed has a soul; the same would be true of a tomato. A mango, on the other hand, has just one seed. Jains are forbidden to eat pomegranates, but they may eat mangoes as long as they haven't been picked from the tree. Technically fruit should fall to the ground before being eaten, in order to reduce any harm that might be done to the plant. Remember, harming any living creature leads to karmic material forming around and bonding to the pure soul, and this karmic material forms the next series of incarnations or rebirths.

Words

The Nature of Right Knowledge

The following is an excerpt from the first chapter of Kundakunda's *Samayasara*. It describes the nature of right knowledge, the soul as the pure self, and the relationship this soul has to the bondage of matter. The Jain acharyas (spiritual teachers) argue that the

pure soul (jiva) is in possession of the "infinities of conation, knowledge, power and bliss," and that it is karmic matter that obscures the pure soul. Karmic matter clings to and saturates the soul, thus changing the pure soul to a state of soul/non-soul (*jivajiva*).

2. Know ye that the *jiva*, which rests in its own intrinsic purity, rests on Right Conduct, Right Faith, and Right knowledge, is the real Self. That which is conditioned by karmic materials is other than the real.

3. The Self which has realised its oneness, and is uncontaminated by alien conditions, is the beautiful ideal in the whole Universe. To associate the bondage of karmic material with this unity is therefore self-contradictory.

4. The proposition that all living beings are characterised by desire for worldly things, enjoyment of the same and the consequential bondage has been heard about, observed and personally experienced by all. But the realisation of the unity of the Higher Self, which is free from all such empirical conditions [i.e., matter], is not an easy achievement.

5. The path to that Higher Unity differentiated from all alien conditions I will try to reveal as far as I can. But if I fail in my description, you may reject it....

9. Whoever realises the absolute and pure nature of this Self through the knowledge of the scripture is a light of the world illuminating the true nature of Self to itself and others....

13. Right belief is constituted by a clear comprehension on the correct point of view of the nature of the following categories: *jiva* (soul), *ajiva* (non-soul), *punya* (virtue), *papa* (vice), *asrava* (inflow of karmic matter onto the soul), *samvara* (how to stop the inflow of karmic matter), *nirjara* (the shedding of karmic matter), *bandha* (bondage), and *moksha* (emancipation/liberation)....

15. He who perceives the Self as that which is not bound, not other than Self, steady and without any difference understands the whole Jain doctrine which is the kernel of all the scriptures....

23. In the case of the soul that is characterised by various emotions such as desire and lust, there are physical objects, some of which intimately bound to it (like the body), and some not so intimately bound (such as wealth). "These material objects are mine" so declare one whose intellect is deluded by wrong knowledge....

34. The discriminative knowledge of the Self leads to discarding all alien dispositions, knowing them to be entirely foreign to the nature of the Self.

Source: *Samayasara: The Soul-Essence. Shri Kunda Kunda.* Vol. 8 of *The Sacred Books of the Jainas* (verses 1, 2–34) Trans. by J.L. Jaini. (New York: AMS Press. [1930] 1974).

The Community

By the time of Umasvati's *Tattvartha-sutra*, in the early years of the Common Era (Tatia 1994, 4), we witness a discernible change in the recorded relationship between ascetic and householder. Although the complexities of this relationship are still in the process of re-examination by contemporary scholars, it is clear that the period from about 200 B.C.E. to 300 C.E. was one of extraordinary fluidity in Jain history. In contrast to the monastic content of the Agamas, other textual

Sadhu: a male ascetic

Sadhvi: a female ascetic.

evidence of this period and the remnants of material culture at sites developed during the Kusala period (Folkert 1993, 111) and the Mathura site (Smith 1901) indicate a complex social interdependence between what was to become the four components of the Jain sangha: monks (**sadhus**), nuns (**sadhvis**),

Sravaka: a male householder; layman.

Sravika: a female householder; laywoman.

Mahavratas: the five great vows of renunciation made by monks and nuns.

Anuvrata: a small vow.

Sallekhana: the ritual of fasting to death.

laymen (**sravakas**), and laywomen (**sravikas**). For the most part, this symbiotic relationship has sustained itself until the present day in South Asia. In the most elementary of terms, the laity provide young monks and nuns for the monastic community, support the socio-religious activities of the ascetic renouncers, and fund the building of religious institutions. Meanwhile the ascetics provide religious instruction for the community and spiritual guidance for the conduct of business affairs and statecraft, and act as "living icons of the ascetic ideal," as revealed by the twenty-four Tirthankaras (Babb 1988; Carrithers and Humphrey 1991; Humphrey 1985; Laidlaw 1995; Vallely 1999; Zydenbos 1987).

RELIGIOUS PRACTICES
The Five Great Vows of Jain Monks and Nuns

After receiving permission to do so from his or her family, the community at large, and the leader of a mendicant order, an individual may wish to leave the life of a householder behind and become an ascetic (a monk or a nun). Upon entering the order of mendicants, the individual must make five great vows known as the **mahavratas** to guide their lives. The Jains believe that the soul can be freed from the cycles of life, death, and rebirth only by the actions of the individual. That is, to keep the soul from coming in contact with karmic matter—the matter that accumulates on the soul because of one's actions— all Jains must do as little as possible to harm any living being. Though there are five vows, they all tend to focus on the first vow, of non-violence or non-injury.

1. *Ahimsa*: to follow a path of non-violence and non-injury for all living beings.
2. *Satya*: to always speak the truth.
3. *Asteya*: to never take what is not given.

4. *Brahmacharya*: to renounce all pleasures, particularly sexual pleasure.
5. *Aparigraha*: to renounce all attachment to family and possessions.

The Twelve Vows of the Jain Householder

There is no special initiation ceremony needed to practise Jainism, and therefore no conversion to the religion. As was explained at the Jain mandir, "Although an individual may not know it at the time, everyone is a Jain by nature. They just have to realize it." In other words, once one understands the reality of karma and the nature of the soul, one starts to become a Jain and will begin to live a life of non-violence. By performing these twelve vows, called **anuvratas**, a lay follower may live a righteous life of non-violence and advance toward a fuller, more perfect life by conquering desire and the need for violence. The first five vows are similar to the monastic vows, and the Jain laity are encouraged to follow them as closely as possible. The more closely one follows the twelve vows, the more likely one is to get closer to liberation.

1. Never intentionally take life or destroy a soul-being.
2. Never lie or exaggerate.
3. Never steal.
4. Never be unfaithful to one's spouse or think unchaste thoughts.
5. Limit the accumulation of wealth, and give away all extra possessions (e.g., contribute to maintenance of the temple, community centre, or animal hospitals).
6. Limit the chances of hurting someone or something by limiting one's travel.
7. Limit the number of personal consumable and non-consumable possessions.
8. Guard against unnecessary and avoidable sins.
9. Observe periods of meditation (hopefully at least once a day).
10. Observe special days of limitation (e.g., avoid drinking tea for three days).
11. Spend some time living as an ascetic.
12. Provide alms to a monastic community.

There is one final vow that both ascetics and householders may observe, and this is the vow of a "peaceful death"—in other words, fasting to death (**sallekhana**). The peaceful death is characterized by non-attachment to all worldly objects and the suppression of all passions through a state of deep meditation and, ultimately, calm renunciation of the body, which is considered to be the seat of all desire and passions.

Sallekhana

In order to perform the Jain ritual of fasting to death, an individual must first seek the permission and authority of a Jain teacher, usually the head of a monastic order. The individual should also attempt to seek spiritual and moral support from members of the family and community. It is the responsibility of the teacher, or **acharya**, to ascertain whether the individual requesting to take the vow is spiritually developed and sufficiently experienced and disciplined to endure the rigours of sallekhana.

In short, this ritual process gradually reduces to the point of elimination all physical sustenance such as food, water, and creature comforts. It is intended to be the final act of non-violence (ahimsa) at the end of one's life, in which all worldly aspirations and desires—those things that constituent karmic matter—are eliminated. The philosophical theory is that fasting "burns away" the karmic matter of this life, and to fast to death ensures that one burns away as much karma as

Acharya: the head of a group of monks (sadhus).

possible and stops any further karmic material from accumulating on the soul. The Jain logic on this matter is quite clear: if one does not eat anything, one does not harm anything, so no karma.

Though the original prescription for this ritual was for only the most learned and practised ascetics—usually males—by the medieval period we find examples of both monks and nuns performing this uncommon Jain ritual, especially in such sacred sites as Sravanabelgola, in Karnataka. We also find some examples of householders performing the ritual during this period. A modified form is still performed by the contemporary Jain community in both India and the diaspora. As several Jains told me, the modification for laypeople is that they will perform the ritual if death is already approaching, rather than taking a vow to fast in order to bring about death prematurely. That is, if a person is in a terminal state of illness or very old and infirm, he or she will vow not to take any food or water in the final stages of life. The purpose is the same: to stop more karma from being produced. Though rare, the ascetic version of the ritual is still performed in India today.

Practices

Fasting to Death

The following are excerpts from one of the early texts of the Jain canon describing the different kinds of religious deaths that can be performed. The ritual is to be performed at the end of a twelve-year period during which the ascetic has thoroughly mortified the flesh in preparation for the final act of fasting to death.

The wise ones who attain in due order to one of the unerring states in which death is prescribed, [that is] those who are rich in control and endowed with knowledge, and know about the incomparable religious death, should continue their contemplation to this end.

Knowing the twofold obstacles to moksha, the body and the mind, the wise ones, having thoroughly leaned the law, perceive in due order that the time has come to die, to get rid of karma....

Without food he should lie down and bear the pains which attack him. He should not, for too long a time, give way to worldly feelings which overcome him.... When crawling animals or such as live on high or below, feed on his flesh and blood, he should neither kill them nor rub the wounds.

Though these animals destroy the body, he should not stir from his position.

After the asravas have ceased, he should bear the pains as if he rejoiced in them.

(continued)

> When the bonds [of karma] fall off, then he has accomplished his life....
>
> Intent on such an uncommon death, he should regulate the motions of his organs. He should raise himself above attachments and bear all pains.... He should mortify his flesh, thinking: There are no obstacles in my body.
>
> Knowing as long as he lives there are dangers and troubles, the wise and restrained ascetic should bear them as being instrumental to the dissolution of the body.

> He should not trust in the delusive power of the gods; a good ascetic should know of this and cast off all inferiority.
>
> Not devoted to any of the external objects he reaches the end of his life; thinking that patience is the highest good, he should choose one of the described good methods of [fasting to death and] entering moksha.

Source: Jacobi, Hermann (English trans.) (1995 [1884]) *AcharangaSutra*. Vol. 22 of *The Sacred Books of the East*. (ed.) Max Muller. (Delhi: Motilal Banarsidass,1995).

Sravanabelgola

Of all the Jain pilgrimage sites in India, Sravanabelgola—situated in Karnataka in South India—is perhaps one of the most famous because of its colossal statue of the Jain saint Bahubali. In ancient times this site was known primarily as a meeting place for Jain monks and nuns, and tradition holds that this was where the first Maurya emperor, Candragupta, performed the ritual of fasting to death around 300 C.E. However, from the ninth to the twelfth centuries, Jain rituals, temples, and associated pilgrimage sites specifically developed for the lay community were becoming more prominent in both Karnataka and other regions of India, perhaps because of the rise and influence of the Hindu bhakti cults.

Commissioned in about 980 C.E. by Camundaraya, a famous general of the Hoysala empire, the colossal statue of Gommateswara Bahubali stands a little over seventeen metres high, is sculpted from a single rock, and is considered one of the largest stone sculptures in the world. The image shows Bahubali standing upright, arms by his sides, unclothed except for the jungle vines creeping up his legs, and with a countenance of deep meditation as he remains detached from the world. Every twelfth year, thousands of Jains gather at the site and perform the Maha-abhiseka, or "Great Anointment." This ritual lasts several weeks as hundreds of Jains climb a ceremonial scaffold erected around the statue and pour sacred substances such as milk and powdered sandalwood over the huge image. Many Jains pay large sums of money for the honour of taking part in the unction; this money is then redistributed back to the community by building such things as schools, temples, hospitals, animal sanctuaries, and rest houses. The most recent ceremony took place in 2005.

PEOPLE & PLACES

Bahubali

According to the Jain tradition, the first Tirthankara had a son whom he made king after he had renounced all his kingly possessions. His son, Bharat, ruled the kingdom with great justice and peace, and the people were very happy. One day a magical *cakra* (a circular throwing weapon) appeared in the young king's armoury, and the king's advisors said this was a sign that Bharat would be the first world emperor and that he should start out on a large military campaign. However, before this was to take place, one of the king's advisors reminded Bharat that his brothers had not come by to pay homage to the new king.

One of the brothers, Bahubali, said that rather than paying homage to Bharat, he would meet him on the battlefield. To avoid a huge loss of life, advisors on both sides suggested that the battle should be between the two brothers in single combat. Both agreed to this and began to wrestle. Bahubali, though younger than Bharat, soon had the upper hand and was about to deal a final death blow to his older brother when the vision of non-violence came upon him. Bahubali then stopped the combat with his brother. His brother was humiliated by this act of kindness and, according to some sources, threw the magic *cakra* at Bahubali in order to kill him. The *cakra* missed him completely and fell harmlessly to the ground. Bharat was greatly ashamed by this cowardly act of anger.

Bahubali made it clear to his brother that he no longer wanted to contend for the throne. Instead he chose to give up all kingly claims and retreated to the forest to become a naked ascetic. It was noted by the sages of the time that he gained enlightenment while meditating in the traditional Jain standing pose. Both sects consider Bahubali to be a great spiritual teacher, but the Digambara hold a slightly different position: that Bahubali was the first member of the Jain lay community to gain liberation (moksha).

Religious Practices of the Lay Community

Paryushana Parva (for the Svetambara, whose monks and nuns wear white) or Daslakshana Parva (for the Digambara, whose monks are naked) is the most auspicious time of the year in the Jain lunar calendar, especially for the laity in both India and the diaspora. In India this event coincides with the end of the rainy season. Traditionally it is a special time when the monks and nuns preach to the community. Of course, that practice has changed a bit here in Canada. As one Jain member said, "We don't have the luxury of the monks' or nuns' advice here—their strict ascetic vows will not allow them to travel outside India—but this means that the other aspects of the celebration and the gathering together of members of the community are all that more important. It is that time of year when all Jains in the community, even those who are a bit tardy in attending their local temple or centre during the rest of the year, participate by taking on some form of restraint such as fasting, perform ritualized confession, and get to hear special spiritual lectures."

The Most Sacred of Jain Prayers

The most revered of Jain prayers in the contemporary lay community is called the Namokara Mantra. It is chanted at the beginning of all religious ceremonies and is also often used to begin most non-religious events within the Jain community. Interestingly, this prayer does not request the aid of a divine being or ask to receive some special grace; rather, it allows the Jain devotee to pay respect to all spiritual leaders, both past and present, and to inspire followers to continue their quest for purification of the soul. Although this is not a direct word-for-word translation, the meaning of each component is given below.

Namo arahamtanam
I bow and seek inspiration from those souls who have gained total victory over themselves and have shown us the path to liberation *moksha*.
Namo siddhanam
I bow and seek inspiration for the perfect, pure, and liberated souls.
Namo ayariyanam
I bow and seek inspiration from the heads of the religious orders.
Namo uvajjhayanam
I bow and seek inspiration from the teachers of the scriptures.
Namo loe savva sahunam
I bow and seek inspiration from all the ascetic monks and nuns in the world.
Eso pancha namokkaro savva pava panaasano mangalanam cha savvesim padhamam havai mangalam
Salutations to these five types of great souls will help diminish my inauspicious karma. These salutations are most auspicious—so auspicious as to bring everyone happiness and peace.

For the entire period (eight days for the Svetambaras and ten days for the Digambaras), members of the community have the option—depending on their spiritual and physical fortitude—of fasting every other day, eating only one meal a day, giving up certain food items, and so on. As described to me, all members of both communities fast to some extent on the last day of the festival. The Svetambaras mark the end of the period with a public confession, in which each member of the community confesses his or her transgressions over the past year and begs forgiveness from the community for those transgressions. A local pilgrimage is also performed by both communities. In India this can be to a local shrine; in the case of the North American community, temporary shrines are established for the festival, usually in the homes of volunteer families.[5]

Unlike the more pious festival mentioned above, the two other major celebrations on the Jain calendar are Mahavira Jayanti, the celebration of the birth of Mahavira held in the month of *ciatra* (March/April), and Divali, which represents the lunar new year (November/December). Unlike the Hindu tradition, in which Divali represents the return of Lord Rama to Ayodhya, the Jain community see it as the time when Mahavira gained full knowledge of everything in the universe and the true nature of the soul.

RELIGIOUS IDENTITY

As we have seen, the primary difference between the two major sects of Jainism is the practice of *aparigraha*, or minimization of possessions. The Digambara sect maintains that a monk must renounce all possessions, including clothes. Because of the ritualization of nudity within the Digambara ascetic community, women cannot fully observe the vow of non-possession, and therefore cannot achieve moksha. On the other hand, the Svetambara sect maintains that the white cloth is not a possession, and suggests that draping the body with a functional piece of cloth does not mean that the monk or nun is emotionally attached to it; attachment, they argue, is a state of mind, not something intrinsic to the object itself.

The other major debate in the possession versus non-possession issue is over the building of temples. Originally one of the major rules for both the Svetambaras and Digambaras was that temples were to

be for the laity only. That is, the ascetics were never to spend more than three days in one location (to prevent attachment to a specific area). By the fourth century C.E. this attitude had changed and many temples were built; as the historical record indicates, in some cases monks began to live in the temples. These monks were accused of becoming attached to one dwelling place.

As well there was disagreement over displaying icons of the Tirthankaras within these temples. The Digambaras have unadorned icons portraying the ascetic ideal of sitting or standing in meditation, whereas the Svetambara icons are adorned like kings. As was explained at the Jain mandir in Toronto, the Digambara icons are to show us what we should become; the Svetambara icons are to show that the Tirthankaras were people, not gods, and that everyone has the potential to become a Tirthankara. Though the two sects continued to subdivide into different strands, ultimately they both maintained a similar philosophical approach to the major metaphysical issues.

One other development that was to become an important discussion topic within the Jain tradition concerned the position of the *bhattaraka*. In the south of India, with the growth of royal patronage in the medieval period, many of the Digambara monks, rather than following the path of the wandering ascetic, began to spend more time within the lay community. This practice drew bitter criticism from other religious orders within the larger Jain community and forced a situation in which there was even less contact between the ascetics and laypeople. The community, feeling somewhat abandoned by the ascetics, developed a new religious authority, the *bhattaraka*. To some extent this position was situated somewhere between a layperson and an ascetic. That is, *bhattarakas* studied the scriptures and remained celibate but they could remain within the lay community to conduct religious rituals, provide education and spiritual guidance, and administer religious institutions such as the temples and ashrams. Though they have dwindled in number over the past few centuries, the position of *bhattaraka* is still present and well respected within the Digambara sect.

The question of whether ascetics should live in the towns and villages and interact with the lay community or stay in the forests was the other major concern that was to plague both the Svetambaras and Digambaras. Some sub-sects said it was acceptable for the ascetics to preach to the lay community in meeting halls, but that they should not participate in any lay rituals involving image worship. Another group agreed with this position, but in time several members broke away from this group and declared that they found had image worship to be justified in the scriptures. The debate over the two types of ascetics—forest-dwelling and temple-dwelling—continued from the fourth century until the eleventh century. In the Digambara tradition there were forest-dwelling monks and the *bhattarakas*; the Svetambaras came up with a compromise that has prevailed to date, whereby Svetambara monks and nuns are not required to retreat to the forest but are also not allowed to stay in one place for any length of time.

The Position of Women in Jainism

The Digambara community maintains that to achieve the highest stages of asceticism, the mendicant must renounce all possessions, including clothing. As Jaini notes, to retain the use of clothing "is functionally equivalent to retaining *all* possessions, that is, to remain a householder" (1979/1990, 39). Compounding this situation for the female ascetic, of course, is that the majority of societal rules forbid women to practise naked asceticism. The Svetambara community, on the other hand, maintains that women are just as capable of attaining omniscience and moksha as men, and suggests that there have been examples of both naked and "white-clad" nuns throughout Jain history who have been great ascetics. In support of this claim, they maintain that the nineteenth Tirthankara was a woman named Mallinath (Jaini 1979/1990, 39–40).

However, as Goldman states in his introduction to Jaini's text *Gender and Salvation*,

> Some arguments on the Digambara side derive from postulates that echo the generally misogynistic and patriarchal attitudes of the [South Asian] society as a whole…that women are not only physically weaker than men, and hence unable to endure the harsh asceticism regarded as necessary for liberation, but are intellectually, ethically, and morally inferior as well.…[T]he Svetambaras, although they steadfastly argue for the possibility of women entering the mendicant life and attaining moksha, rarely categorically refute the misogynistic claims of the Digambaras *per se*. Although they may tend to soften these claims by, for example, pointing out famous women from literature and scripture who showed great spiritual or moral courage, or by asserting that men too may share some of the moral defects ascribed to women, they seem generally willing to accept the negative characterizations, contenting themselves merely with asserting that these do not in and of themselves preclude the possibility of moksha for all women. (Jaini 1991, xvii)*

As we have seen, traditional views on the status of women are neither singular nor monolithic in their scope. The question arises of why women were not permitted to achieve salvation, when it appears somewhat obvious in many of the life stories of Mahavira that he made no explicit discrimination between men and women, or according to caste, creed, or colour. And in point of fact, according to the Svetambara tradition, when the first few thousand males took *diksa* (the vow to become an ascetic) under the guidance of Mahavira, this act was quickly followed by three times that number of women taking vows to become nuns, a ratio that has remained fairly consistent throughout the history of the Jain community. Though there is no official explanation for this ratio, one can certainly speculate, at least from a pragmatic point of view, that the status for a woman in the South Asian context would certainly be improved if she became a spiritual leader. And though her status would not be as great as that of a monk—at least according to the early texts—it would certainly be greater than that of both the female and male householder. In a society that may marginalize women to the outside borders—particularly women who are widows—becoming a nun places a woman at the very centre of the Jain spiritual community.

Interestingly, the ironic twist to the religious diatribe against women is that the historical record shows that many women were both admirable ascetics and great spiritual teachers of the tradition. It has to be admitted that to consider nudity a prerequisite to achieving salvation created some real problems for women. However, despite this there were instances, such as in Karnataka from the second to fifteenth centuries, when women were given the same freedoms as men to pursue the ultimate spiritual life (Jain 1992). Not only were women poets and administrators who donated land and money to the people, but it was recorded that they also participated in battles.[6]

Chandanbala: The First Jain Nun

Chetak, the chief of the Vaishali republic, was the brother of the brother of Trishala, the mother of Lord Mahavira. Chetak had seven daughters, and of these, Padmavati married King Dadhivahan of Champapuri. They were very happy with each other and had a daughter named Vasumati. Vasumati was beautiful and obedient, and though she was brought up in royal comfort and luxuries, she was exposed to religious tenets as well.

Once it so happened that King Shatanik invaded Champapuri. Dadhivahan fought bravely, but he was killed in the battle and Champapuri fell into the hands of Shatanik. Padmavati, the wife of Dadhivahan, did not want to surrender herself. She tried to escape with her young daughter, Vasumati, but unfortunately the pair fell into the hands of some soldiers of Shatanik. Attracted by her beauty, the soldiers wanted to molest Padmavati. In order to save herself from sexual assault, Padmavati committed suicide. The soldiers were scared by this horrible scene, and were afraid that Vasumati may try to follow her mother's actions, so they treated her well and took her to Koshambi, where they intended to make money by selling her into slavery.

In Koshambi there was a kind-hearted and wealthy merchant named Dhanavah. He saw Vasumati in the market and decided to get her because he was childless, and thought she could help his wife, Muladevi.

How strange for Vasumati that within a short period of time she had gone from being a princess to a captive, and finally to a maidservant. She had been raised with some spiritual thinking, and therefore accepted all the changes in her life as consequences of her earlier karma. She had decided not to disclose her original identity and adopted her new role without grumbling. She took all possible care of Dhanavah and his wife, and he developed a fatherly affection for her. He used to call her Chandanbala, meaning "Sandalwood Girl," because, like sandalwood, she scattered fragrance in his life by her sweet, obedient, and accommodating nature.

Unfortunately, as Dhanavah's affection for her grew, his wife, Muladevi, started harbouring suspicions about their relations. She was aware that she could not give him a child and was worried that her husband might marry Chandanbala in order to have a child.

Once Dhavanavah had to go on a business trip for three days and Muladevi decided to make use of his absence. She called for a barber and a locksmith. Chandanbala's beautiful long hair was the immediate cause of Muladevi's jealousy, so she had the barber completely shave Chandanbala's head. Then Chandanbala was put in chains by the locksmith and locked in a dark, remote room without any food or water. Muladevi thought the girl would die of thirst and hunger.

True to her religious orientation, Chandanbala did not fight back, but accepted her situation as the consequence of her earlier karma. Amazingly, she did not harbour any bad feeling toward Muladevi, and decided to use the period of confinement for fasting and spiritual mediation on the nature of the soul.

After four days away, Dhanavah returned to his home but did not find Chandanbala waiting for him. He thought she might be sick but could not find her anywhere in the home. When asked, Muladevi replied that he had spoiled her and she had run away. It has hard for Dhanavah to accept what his wife was stating. He knew his "daughter" very well, and knew that she would not run away. He could not eat, and continued to look in all the rooms of the home, but he neglected to go to the dark, remote room. Failing in his search, his heart began to sink and he began to cry. He asked one of the maidservants if they had seen Chandanbala, but Muladevi had sworn her to secrecy and she was watching the maidservant all the time.

The maidservant respected Danavah; she even had a soft spot for Chandanbala. In time, when she finally got out of sight of Muladevi, she pointed out the remote room to her master. He burst open the door and found the half-starved body of Chandanbala. Luckily for him she was not dead. He picked her up in his arms and brought her to the living quarters. To his astonishment he found that all the rooms were locked.

In the meantime, as Muladevi saw Dhanavah rushing to the remote room, she became very frightened that her secret was out and that her husband would punish her for her wickedness. In order to escape his wrath, she hurriedly locked all the rooms and sped to her parents' home. And because she had locked all the rooms, Dhanavah could not find any food for Chandanbala. In desperation, Dhanavah searched high and low, but all he could find was a pot of black peas soaking in water. He put the peas in a bowl and then rushed to call on a locksmith to remove Chandanbala's chains.

Chandanbala took the bowl of peas and for a moment thought about the changes that had come into her life. From being a princess she was reduced to the position of a miserable, starved girl who had nothing to eat but soaked peas. She laughed at her fate. Before putting the peas in her mouth, however, she remembered that she was on a religious fast for three days. *Would it not be possible for me to offer food to a monk before I terminate my fast?* she thought.

As it happens, Mahavira was in a renounced state. In his endeavour to seek truth and ultimate bliss, he was continually meditating and observing severe austerities. In that process he went without food for days and weeks. That year he had imposed upon himself an apparently improbable stipulation for accepting food. He had vowed that he would accept food only if it was soaked black peas offered to him in a bowl by a princess in chains with a shaved head, who had fasted for three days and who had tears flowing from her eyes. For months he went from place to place and came back without food because his stipulations could not be fulfilled.

So it came to pass that Mahavira came to look for alms where Chandanbala was thinking to offer food to some monk. In the moment of a twinkle of an eye he saw that all his stipulations for breaking his fast were coming true. Here was a princess in chains with a shaven head, having fasted for three days and offering black peas in a bowl—but

there were no tears. Mahavira had to decline Chandanbala's offering, and turned to leave.

Chandanbala felt intensely miserable that the sage did not accept her offering of food, and she started to cry terribly. Tears began to roll from her eyes as she repeatedly entreated the great ascetic to accept her humble offer. Turning around, Mahavira saw the tears rolling down her cheeks, and as all of his stipulations to break his fast had been met, he willingly accepted the food offered by Chandanbala.

With the acceptance of this offering there was a great roar of thunderous cheering by the people following the great ascetic. For months the people of Koshambi had been watching the great spiritual teacher moving from place to place and going without food. This concerned a great many of his followers, as they thought he would starve to death. All those admirers were filled with joy as he ultimately accepted food from Chandanbala. They rushed to surround her and showered her with flowers and perfumes and offered her good food and fancy clothes. There were some artisans in the crowd and they broke her chains. There was joy and pleasure everywhere.

When Dhanavah came back, his pleasure knew no bounds as he learned about the miraculous event. Almost the whole city had turned out for this occasion. Even Muladevi dared to come back to see the miracle event and to ask her husband for forgiveness. Though Dhanavah was too angry her to forgive her, Chandanbala asked that he forgive his wife for her transgressions. She asked Dhanavah to think that perhaps fate had prompted Muladevi to do what she did, and that it was because of this twist of fate that Chandanbala could help Mahavira break his long fast. Dhanavah did forgive Muladevi.

Chandanbala was now happy in every respect. She had not forgotten, however, the role of karma and how it played into her life. She was eager, therefore, to eradicate all karma. When Mahavira gained omniscience, Chandanbala renounced all worldly life and became a nun. And when Mahavira established the religious order, Chandanbala was made the head of all nuns.

Source: Doshi, Manubhai, *Jain Stories of Pre-Christian Era*. Boston: Indira Mansukhlal Doshi Memorial Trust (Jain Center of Greater Boston).

Historians have clearly identified this statue as being of Jain origin and produced in the tenth to eleventh centuries; however, there is a great deal of controversy over what this icon represents. The Digambara sect has always stated that there were no female ascetics and that all Digambara nuns have to be reborn as males in order to become full ascetics (i.e., those who renounce all possessions, including clothing). Despite this position, this statue appears to indicate that there were some naked female ascetics during the medieval period or, at the very least, that it was an ideal to which women could aspire during that period. The problem with identifying this particular icon is that the symbol usually located in the square on the base is difficult to decipher (each Tirthankara has a specific symbol). However, most Jain art historians have stated that this is not just an icon of a female ascetic but a figure of Malli (her symbol is the water jar), the nineteenth and only female Tirthankara within the Svetambara tradition.

Source: Photograph Courtesy of the State Museum in Lucknow. Photographer: Ravinder Singh Bedi.

Also the tradition contains two interesting components in its religious lexicon. The first concerns the many stories about Risbha, the first Tirthankara. According to both the Digambara and Svetambara traditions, Risbha was the first to establish the rules of society, a society that contained both monks, nuns, and the laity. And, more interestingly, according to the Svetambara tradition, prior to becoming a Tirthankara, Risbha enjoyed married life, raised children, and ruled over the earth looking after the welfare of the subjects. In other words, Risbha chose to recognize the importance of all four components of the sangha rather than condemning two-thirds of it (that is, the nuns and, to a certain extent, the laymen and laywomen of the community).

Reinforcing the position of the householder in the community is a tiny story about Mahavira contained within one of sacred texts. In this story we find Mahavira in a spiritual struggle against Gosala Mankhaliputta. Gosala claims to be a Jina and has been recognized as such by his community; however, Mahavira tries to convince Gosala of the error of his ways. Gosala finally succumbs to the struggle (and, of course, to the realization that Mahavira was correct to say that he, Gosala, was not a Jina), and just before his death he tells Mahavira that he too will die. Mahavira responds that his mission to his community is not complete and that he will live another fifteen and half years. Gosala dies, and then Mahavira is suddenly struck by a "bilious fever" that should lead to certain death. Mahavira reassures his disciples that he won't die as long as they follow his instructions and acquire a special meal made by the laywoman Revai. Once he eats the meal he immediately regains his health and lives for another fifteen years (*Vyahapannati* 15, Ch. 8–11). In this story we find that a householder—and, more important, a woman—saves the life of the Jina with the purity of her special food.

Although this might be stretching the point, I think this story contains an important message for the Jain community (it was actually a member of the Jain community in Detroit who first pointed me toward it). First, it stresses the importance of the householder to the ascetic community. For example, Mahavira's ascetic disciples do not know how to save the dying Jina; it is knowledge of "food medicine" by a householder that saves the day. And second, it posits a positive image of women within the community. Instead of being presented as a seductress who tempts the monk from his metaphysical quest, the woman in this story is presented as a person who creates opportunity for Mahavira to pursue his spiritual path. This could be read as a powerful message, especially in light of the contemporary Jain community in the North American context.

The New Role of the Jain Laywoman in Medieval Literature

Between the seventh and fifteenth centuries we begin to see a wealth of Jain literature in which the focus shifts from the practices and doctrine of the ascetic to the interactions between all four components of the Jain sangha. Though most writings tend to continue painting the lay community in a dark light, there are many that show the laity, and women in particular, as devoted to the cause of the Jain religion. As Phyllis Granoff states, "Jain women in these stories are beautiful, desirable, intelligent and resourceful, and they use their gifts to insure the triumph of their religion. In the story of Revati (Revai), the Jain lay woman is singled out for praise even at the expense of a Jain monk . . . . Revati knows the Jain doctrine and remains firm in her faith, while the monk succumbs to heretical doubts on certain points" (1998, 13).

The Story of Revati

Now there was in the land of the Pandyas a city called South Mathura. It was rich in grain and money and adorned with many Jain temples. There reigned King Pandu intent upon protecting his subjects; he had charmed everyone in the world by his many excellent virtues. His wife was named Sumati, "the Clever," and indeed she was thought to be quite smart. She was chaste, beautiful and soft-spoken, and her fame reached the very corners of the world. An ascetic, a teacher named Munigupta, also lived there. He was a veritable ocean of virtue and knew all of the sacred texts; he possessed supernatural knowledge and practised severe austerities.

One day some Vidyadhara prince endowed with magical power came to the city of South Mathura; his name was Manovega, "Swift as Thought," and indeed he dashed to the city with uncustomary speed. Filled with devotion, he circumambulated the most excellent Jain temple three times and said a prayer to the Jina; such prayer puts an end to all suffering. He worshipped the ascetic Munigupta with all the devotion due one's guru, and then bowed down to the other ascetics. Finally he sat down near Munigupta. The wise Manovega was silent for a few moments, listening to the discourse on the Jain doctrine; then he bowed his head in

(continued)

reverence and said to Munigupta, "Blessed One! I wish to go to the city of Sravasti to pay respects to the Jina; tell me what I may do for you when I get to the sacred city."

When he heard Manovega's words, Munigupta spoke to him, with a voice so deep that it made the peacocks think the clouds were rumbling and set them dancing. "If, oh lay disciple, you go to the lovely city of Sravasti to worship the Jinas, who are worthy of being worshipped by hosts of gods, then you must carefully convey my words of blessing to the lay disciple, the lady Revati, whose mind is totally permeated with thought of the Jain doctrine."

Having heard those words of the ascetic, the lay disciple was surprised. Not understanding the monk's intention, he thought to himself, "This monk takes special care to send his blessings to the lay disciple, the Lady Revati, but does not have any special words of reverence for the monks nor for the male lay disciples." So he thought to himself for awhile, and then, desirous of testing the ascetic, he said to him again, "I will go to the city of Sravasti." The ascetic heard what the lay disciple said; he told Manovega, who had a crooked mind and was definitely operating under false impressions, "If you are going to that city to worship the Jinas, then you must convey my blessing to the lay disciple, the lady named Revati."

Manovega was even more surprised and angry too. He asked, "Blessed One! Tell me, what makes that Lady Revati so special that even when I asked you three times you still sent your blessings all three times to her and not to any of the male lay disciples? Furthermore, in that city there is a great Jain ascetic named Bhavyasena, who practises severe austerities; he knows from memory the eleven texts and is a leader of the four-fold Jain community, the monks, nuns, and lay disciples, male and female. He is the best of the monks and removes all doubts concerning the verities of the Jain doctrine, the soul and other entities. Why did you not send your respects to a noble ascetic like him?"

When he heard these words of the Vidyadhara, the lord of ascetics replied with a voice so deep that it made all the world echo with the sound. "That Bhavyasena of whom you spoke is deluded and does not believe in the existence of earth-souls. Not to believe in the categories as they have been expounded is an example of false belief, and the soul that is sullied by false belief wanders endlessly in the cycle of rebirths. That is why I did not exchange respectful greetings with him, oh Vidyadhara, nor did I send him any friendly words. And as for what you have asked me, why I would send words of blessing to the Lady Revati and not to any of the male lay disciples, listen to me as I explain why that is so. Revati is endowed with right belief; she adheres to the doctrine propounded by the Jinas, and her mind is repulsed by the actions of heretics and those who are monks but adhere to wrong doctrines. She accepts only the Jina and the renunciation of all possessions as the path to release; she believes that the highest religious action is non-violence and that true asceticism is control of the senses. She accepts as her teachers only those steadfast ones who follow the correct code of conduct and observe total chastity, those ascetics whose bodies are adorned by the virtue of forbearance. It is for this reason that I send my blessings to Revati and not to the others, whose souls are sullied by false belief."

When the Vidyadhara heard these words of Munigupta, that were destined ultimately to result in happiness, he raised his eyebrows and thought to himself, "See how even monks can be afflicted by passion; otherwise why would he say that a lay woman is the best of all, pure in her right belief, and that a monk who knows all the sacred texts and is a great ascetic has succumbed to false belief? What use is it to argue with him like this? I will go to that city, and as soon as I get there I will make my own test to determine the truth."

Manovega bowed down to the Jina and to that ascetic and then angrily rushed away. In an instant he reached the city of Sravasti. With his magic powers he made himself appear as the Hindu god Brahma in the east; the fine likeness of Brahma was seated on a royal swan and holding a water pot; he had four faces. With his magic powers he took on the form of Vishnu appearing in the south; Vishnu was seated on the bird Garuda and held the conch and club and wheel. With his own magic powers he took the form of Rudra appearing in the west; Rudra held the skull club and the snake Vasuki was in his hair; he was mounted on his bull. With his magic powers he quickly made a very handsome likeness of the Buddha appear in the north; the Buddha was seated in meditation and was calm in appearance. The devotees of each of these were delighted when they saw the gods, Rudra and the others. The foolish Jain lay disciples, men and women, also went to see what was going on; only Revati stayed home. Then Manovega used his magic powers to make twenty-five Jinas appear in the middle of the city, along with the eight wondrous signs that accompany them, which include things like haloes, the sound of drums, and a rain of divine flowers. Bhavyasena, the leader of the Jain monks, when he heard that the twenty-five Jinas had appeared, went to see them along with the nuns, the male lay disciples and the female lay disciples.

A group of women then said to the lay disciple Revati, "See, twenty-five Jinas have all come to the centre of the city. The monks and nuns, the male lay disciples and the female lay disciples, filled with devotion, have all gone to see them, bearing flowers in their hands for worship. Let us take flowers and rice grains, fruits, and incense, sandalwood and lovely lamps and go quickly, my friend, to worship them, too."

The lay disciple Revati then said to the pious women, who were contentedly gazing on her lotus-face, "I am busy here in the house and cannot go now." Her friends, filled with affection, replied, "This city alone of all cities is blessed with the protection of the gods like Brahma; you do not believe in the religions devoted to these gods and so it was right that you did not go to see them. But

if you do not go when the Jinas have come down here, too busy with tasks that only occasion sin, you will surely go to hell!"

With those words, her friends made ready to go. Revati told them, "The lords of the monks clearly told me that there are only twenty-four Jinas, including those of the past, the present and the future. There is no twenty-fifth Jina, there never has been and there never will be. I know that this is some magician's trick. Don't bother me; go home." When they heard these words of Revati, the women were utterly taken aback. They left Revati's house and went about their business.

Bhavyasena with great devotion bowed down to the twenty-five Jinas and then with the other Jains went back to his residence. Manovega saw the entire Jain community there, but he did not see Revati. Then he abandoned the form of the Jina and took on the guise of a novice monk. Afflicted by fake pains, he fell on the road. He vomited and had diarrhea and groaned; shouting out the name of the lay disciple Revati, he rolled on the ground. Some woman went to Revatis's house and told her, "Friend! There is a young monk lying on the road who is calling out your name." When she heard this, Revati asked, "Where is he?" The other woman replied, "He is lying on the main road." Revati then went to the monk. She took him by the hand and brought him home with her.

When the monk got to Revati's house, he said to her, "I am starving. Hurry, give me something to eat." Ravati first made sure the monk was seated comfortably and then she joyfully offered him some food, for she considered any monk to be worthy of her gift. No sooner had she brought him some tasty beans to eat, than with his magic power he devoured them all. No sooner had Revati brought him some rich butter, than that one who used magic powers gobbled that up too. In one swallow, with his tricks . . . . When he had eaten all that she gave him and was still not sated, he boldly said to Revati, who was undaunted, "Mother! When I heard how famous

(continued)

you are for your firm belief in the Jain doctrine, I came to see you, tormented though I was by hunger and thirst. But the food you have given me has left me still hungry; I have to say that I am not satisfied with what you have served me. Bring me tasty food and lots of it. See to it that I am satisfied at last!"

When she heard these words of the novice monk, Revati was taken aback. But she did not let herself be discouraged and hastened to give him more food. She made all kinds of things to eat, sweets, sweetmeats, cakes with ghee, dumplings, and delicacies, fried snacks, sweet and savoury. She made him heaping mounds of candies and sweetmeats and she offered them all to him with respect and devotion. And he gobbled everything up. He drank hundreds and thousands of pots of water that she brought for him, gulping them down in a split second. Then that sorcerer began to have diarrhea and to vomit up everything that he had eaten and drunk, not once, but again and again. Revati cleaned his stinking vomit and faeces with her own hands and threw it all outside. When he saw Revati's humility and how she took care of him so carefully and single-mindedly, the Vidyadhara Manovega dropped his appearance as a novice monk and revealed to her his true form as a Vidyadhara. When Revati saw his divine form, with his godly earrings; when she saw how the many light rays that streamed from his shining teeth whitened the very sky itself, she asked him, "Who are you? Why have you come here?" In answer to Revati's questions, the Vidyadhara replied, "Know me to be a Vidyadhara named Manovega, oh lovely lady! I came here to test you, using my magic to create the gods and to turn myself into a novice monk. The monk Munigupta told me that seeing you was even more auspicious than seeing the ascetic Bhavyasena, and now I have seen for myself that what he said was true. Oh Revati, the monk Munigupta, who guards his thoughts, words and deeds, sends to you his blessing." Noble Revati took five steps towards the Vidyadhara and then gently bowed her head at his feet. Having explained himself to her and having told her how he had come to test her, Manovega, his mind at ease, then vanished.

The Vidyadhara Manovega circumambulated the lofty temple to the Jinas; he praised the Jina and the excellent monk Bhavyasena, leader of the monastic community. He then sat down to listen to Bhavyasena's discourse along with other lay disciples, who had mastered the meanings of all the sacred texts and who accepted the Jina. When the discourse was over, Bhavyasena went outside with the speedy Manovega to move his bowels. The Vidyadhara, with his magic, made these three things disappear from the vicinity: ashes, potshards, and bricks. When Bhavyasena had finished, he ordered the lay disciple, "Quick, quick. Go find some ash, or brick or potsherds." Instead, the lay disciple brought a good-sized clod of earth. Curious to see what would happen, he showed it to the monk. "I could not find any one of the three things you asked for, oh monk! So take this pure piece of earth I have brought you; it has no living creatures on it." The king of monks looked carefully at the clod of earth and then took it in his hand; since he doubted the existence of earth-souls, he then said to the lay disciple, "Some teachers say that without exception all the elements like the earth contain living souls, but Manovega, I do not accept that." With these words, the monk, who did not believe in the existence of earth-souls, took the clod of earth and used it to clean his hands.

Manovega now knew that the lay disciple Revati was adorned with the true right belief and that the monk indeed did doubt the existence of earth-souls. He went back to the monk Munigupta and bowed down before him again and again. He then told him everything that had happened. That done, he went home.

One should never praise a monk who is not a true Jain monk; praising false monks destroys true faith in the Jain doctrine. After all, poison and the nectar of the gods will never be the same. There are six things that are worthy of respect: knowledge, an ascetic possessed of knowledge, those who have attained release, a Jain temple, proper conduct, and an ascetic possessed of such conduct.

Other than these things that lead frightened souls to turn to religion, there is nothing worthy of devotion. Revati loved to bow down at the lotus feet of the Jain ascetics, as a bee yearns for the taste of lotus pollen. She was not deluded by the magic tricks of the Vidyadhara.

Source: Brhatkathakosa of Harisena, no. 7, in Phyllis Granoff, *The Forest of Thieves and the Magic Garden: An Anthology of Medieval Jain Stories* (Toronto: Penguin Canada, 1998).

THE CANADIAN CONTEXT

The first Jains to come to North America in any large numbers—at least to live in Canada and the United States—did so during the 1960s. According to discussions with members of the Jain community who immigrated during this period, many of the first Jains to this continent first came here on student visas and had to return to India or Africa after the visas expired. Although a few individual Jains settled in North America prior to 1950, the first families began to arrive in Canada during the mid-1960s (Kumar 1996). As traders, merchants, engineers, and professional administrators whose families had established themselves within the remnants of the British empire, the majority (approximately 50 per cent of the North American population) immigrated from East Africa; they came as well from India, England, Burma, Southeast Asia, and Hong Kong (Kumar 1996). The majority of Jain immigrants from East Africa are image-worshipping Svetambaras who trace their roots back to the Indian state of Gujarat. Political unrest in Africa—particularly in Kenya and Tanzania in 1967–68 and Uganda in 1971 (Kumar 1996, 101)—and the new provisions of Canada's Immigration Act (1962), which prohibited using race, colour, or national origin as criteria for selection of immigrants (Petros 1993), greatly accelerated Jain migration to Canada.

By the early 1970s the Jain community in Ontario had grown to become a recognizable group that actively participated in non-governmental community organizations (NGOs) alongside other South Asian groups, societies, and religious organizations. However, Jains soon realized the need for an organization that would promote and encourage specifically Jain spiritual and cultural concerns, particularly as ascetic community leaders are not allowed to travel outside India (their vows of ahimsa do not allow them to travel by any mechanical device, as the vehicle might kill an insect or other living being; therefore they must walk to wherever they travel). In this sense, the Jain community of North America consists of only two components of the traditional community: the laymen and the laywomen.

On February 10, 1974, the first organizational meeting of the Jaina Society of Toronto was held at the home of J. D. Shah. Its mandate was to create a non-sectarian community in which all aspects of the Jain faith could be developed and maintained for future generations in Canada, and North America more generally, and to formulate a strategy in partnership with the larger Canadian society through which Jainism could be promoted as a world religion actively participating "as part of the diversity of the Canadian mosaic" (Jain Society of Toronto 1999, 33).

As the number of Jain families in Ontario had grown to three hundred by the late 1980s, the Society agreed to buy a former Christian church and its property at 48 Rosemeade Avenue in Etobicoke. Possession of the building was obtained on September 4, 1990, and the opening ceremonies for the present Jaina centre were performed on September 23. The Ontario Jaina community is one of the oldest in North America; it presently has a membership register of more than five hundred families.[7] Annual International Mahavira Jain Mission (IMJM) youth and adult summer camps, the youth group known as Young Jains of Toronto (YJOT), the Young Jain Professionals group, and many support groups for Jain women who have recently immigrated to Ontario are among the activities and

A *Pujari* at the Digambara Jain Mandir in Toronto

The position of *bhattaraka* was developed by the Digambara sect during the medieval period. Although they took most of the vows of an ascetic, the *bhattarakas* were considered neither full monks nor householders. They studied the scriptures and remained celibate, but they could remain within the lay community to conduct religious rituals, provide education and spiritual guidance, and administer religious institutions such as the temples and ashrams. To an outsider visiting a temple they might appear to be akin to a priest in the Hindu tradition; however, there are some differences, such as the celibacy and no-marriage rules. Over the years, especially within the diaspora, the *bhattaraka* has been somewhat modi-fied to become a position often called the *pujari*. Though they are very learned men—these positions are always held by males—their prime function in the temples is to perform puja (ritual worship) rather than scriptural instruction.

Jain rituals may look very similar to Hindu rituals, but there are significant differences. One major point is that when one offers something before the icon, unlike in the Hindu ceremony, one does not expect a blessing in return. When a Jain makes an offering, it is an act of renunciation—one gives an offering to symbolize the giving up of something, not to seek something in return. Jain images are not the "seat of the god" but are icons of the ascetic on whom the Jain may focus their ritual meditations.

Note that in these rituals a small image made of metal is used. I asked the *pujari* why this was done. His pragmatic answer: "Some of the sandalwood paste and water we use in the rituals acts a bit like an acid and would eventually destroy the larger marble icons [in the background]. The metal icons are immune to this effect."

Source: Mikal Radford

organizations that are sponsored by the Jain Society of Toronto. It is worth noting the importance of women within the diaspora community. Many of the spiritual retreats or camps are organized by women and, more important, the presidents of many Jain societies in North America have been or presently are women. In this sense the laywomen are very much equal to their male counterparts within the diaspora community.

It is important to note that as Jains migrate to North America, the growth of their communities is marked by consecration of temples and establishment of lay soci-eties, rather than the initiation of ascetic mendicants that takes place in Jain communities in India. In other words, although there is among North American Jains a vibrant social, ritual, and textual discourse around the ascetic ideals of ahimsa (non-harming), renunciation of material goods, following strict rules for food consumption (vegetarianism in conjunction with temporary vows of restraint such as vrats and fasts), and sexual restraint, as established by the founding Tirthankaras of the tradition,[8] as mentioned earlier, the direct influence of monks and nuns within the lay community of North America is severely diminished, and to a great extent the traditional modes of spiritual communication by the monks and nuns—or at least their teaching and advice—have been replaced by use of the Internet.

JAINISM AND THE INTERNET

Rather than seeing it as a rupture with the past, the Jain laity outside South Asia were quick to embrace the new technology offered by the World Wide Web, particularly from the early 1980s to the present. And though it was never stated officially, many Jains have communicated privately to the author that they love the Internet, as it helps bring together the global Jain family (especially the diaspora) to celebrate Jain culture and religious principles and, as in the old tradition (with a modern twist), to communicate the ideals of Jainism to both Jain and non-Jain alike.

What is particularly interesting about this phenomenon is its appearance of having a common goal, but with little to no unified leadership or hierarchical structure to direct the establishment of the many websites and their content. In general terms,

the websites are set up as either social networks or, more important, sites to create awareness among Jains about the origins of their religious tradition, to build a trustworthy knowledge base of the Agamas and the canons of both the Digambara and Svetambara traditions, and to preserve the literature and teachings of the Jain acharyas (spiritual leaders of the various monastic orders)—in a virtual sense, to help keep the sramana tradition alive. As well, many of the websites also concentrate on worldwide campaigns in support of vegetarianism and the ethical principles of non-violence.

CONCLUSION

As the Jains left India and migrated to North America, their socio-religious ethos shifted from a core centred on the initiation of ascetic mendicants to one that centred wholly on building temples and Jain centres and establishing lay societies. In other words, although there is among North American Jains—particularly first-generation Jains, who often delight in having "rediscovered their religion though their children"—a vibrant social, ritual, and textual discourse around Jain ascetic ideals, the interdependent dynamics of monks and nuns as "living icons of asceticism" within the lay community (Babb 1996, 62–63) is severely diminished within the North American experience. But to some extent this absence of "living icons" has also meant a decrease in the sectarianism that the youth of the diaspora want to challenge. For the Jains of the diaspora it has meant reassessment of the Jain tradition, how that tradition and the community are to move forward, and, finally, what it truly means to be a Jain.

NOTES

1. The inflow (*asrava*) of karmic matter into the soul is best described by Matilal in "The Jaina View of Karma":

   > For Jainism karma does not [mean] merely a "deed or work" or a mystical invisible force. Here it stands for an exceptionally subtle form of matter that flows into *jiva* (soul) and the activity of the latter acts in much the same way as some medicine injected into the (human) body changes the chemistry of and is assimilated by the latter. (Matilal 1981, 25)

2. The term *sramana* ("striver") is used to distinguish those who practised the Jain and Buddhist ascetic traditions—traditions that necessarily entailed a "life devoted to the minimizing of the performance of external action and an accompanying control of inner activity" (Dundas 1992, 14)—from the Brahmin sacrificers whose locus was the highly ritualized Vedic tradition(s). For material on Vedic sacrifice, see J. C. Heesterman (1993) and Stephanie Jamison (1996).

3. For more discussion on the historical context of the twenty-third Tirthankara, Parsvanatha, who lived in the ninth century B.C.E., see Cort 1998; Folkert 1993; Jaini 1979/1990; Dundas 1992; etc.

4. Acharya Umasvati (c. second century C.E.) is credited with systematizing the Jaina canonical teachings into an integrated philosophical treatise (*Tattvarthasutra*) that is acceptable to both Svetambaras and Digambaras, the two major sects of the Jaina tradition. Acharya Kundakunda (c. second to third century C.E.) was a Digambara teacher who is considered to be the foremost writer on Jaina mediation and the nature of the soul.

5. For more on this ritual observance and *pratikraman*, see Cort 2001, 147–62; Humphrey and Laidlaw 1994, 38–39; Jaini 1979/1990, 216; Laidlaw 1995; and Sangave 1980, 234.

6. In comparing other traditions to Jainism, Goldman notes:

    Women, specifically the wives of religious thinkers, are depicted as early as the Upanisads as engaged in metaphysical debate with their husbands. In the epic literature such women are frequently shown as the spiritual companions of their husbands . . . In a few instances individual women ascetics are mentioned and occasionally they play independent roles in the epic narratives and may even be shown to attain spiritual liberation. (Jaini 1991, xiv)

7. Although the 2001 census figures for Canada include members of the Jain community under the category of "Other," it is estimated by the community's own accounts that approximately 3,000 Jainas live in Canada, and three-quarters of those live in the Greater Toronto Area of southern Ontario. This number tends to be substantiated by the number of families registered in the *Jain Directory of North America*, produced by the Jain Center of Greater Boston. From my calculations, the number of Jains in the United States is probably closer to 50,000 in number. Why more Jains in the United States than Canada? From my discussions with both Canadian and American Jains, the reason is not solely the immigration policies of either country; rather, much is due to such concerns as family migration patterns (where relatives first settle, as they in turn sponsor other family members), economic opportunities, educational ties (where they go to get their higher education), preferred forms of governmental systems (Canadian versus American), and quality-of-life issues.

8. For this discussion, see Carrithers and Humphrey 1991; Chapple 1991; Cort 1995; Folkert 1993; Granoff 1998; Humphrey and Laidlaw 1994; Jaini 1991; and Ryan 1999.

KEY TERMS

Acharya, p. 99	Sadhu, p. 97
Ahimsa, p. 87	Sadhvi, p. 97
Ajiva, p. 94	Sallekhana, p. 98
Anuvrata, p. 98	Samsara, p. 87
Jaina, p. 87	Sangha, p. 92
Jina, p. 87	Sramana, p. 87
Jiva, p. 94	Sravaka, p. 98
Karma, p. 87	Sravika, p. 98
Mahavratas, p. 98	Tirthankara, p. 87
Moksha, p. 87	Varna, p. 87

CRITICAL THINKING QUESTIONS

1. In the relatively recent past religion was often defined as an entity that holds the belief in an ever-living God, that is, a belief in a Divine mind and will ruling the universe and having a moral relationship with humankind. Ask yourself as you read through the chapter on Jainism, "Must religion have a god or goddess or something akin to a 'Divine Mind' in order to be a religion?"

2. With all the translations of its sacred texts, the increased presence of Jainism on the Internet, and the fact that the monks and nuns can't leave India to preach directly to the laity (which is one of the main functions in the Jain community), do you envision the possibility that Jainism in the diaspora will eliminate the need for the ascetics?

3. Some young Jains in North America actively support social organizations that fight for the rights of animals. And although they don't support some of the more radical elements of the animal rights movement, as you understand the term *ahimsa*, do you think these actions are non-interfering and non-violent?

4. Two atheistic religions have their foundations in India: Buddhism and Jainism. What do you think are the major differences between the Jain understanding of the soul and its relationship with the universe, and your own understanding of these concepts?

RECOMMENDED READINGS

Babb, Lawrence. *Absent Lord: Ascetics and Kings in a Jain Ritual Culture.* Berkeley: University of California Press, 1996.

CΠ+©※▮☆CΠ+♱※▮☆CΠ+©※▮

Carrithers, Michael, and Caroline Humphrey, eds. *The Assembly of Listeners: Jains in Society*. Cambridge: Cambridge University Press, 1991.

Cort, John E. *Jains in the World: Religious Values and Ideology in India*. New York: Oxford University Press, 2001.

Dundas, Paul. *The Jains*. New York: Routledge, 1992.

Humphrey, Caroline, and James Laidlaw. *The Archetypal Actions of Ritual: A Theory of Ritual Illustrated by the Jain Rite of Worship*. Oxford: Clarendon Press, 1994.

Israel, Milton, and Narendra K. Wagle, eds. *South Asians in Ontario*. Toronto: Multicultural Society of Ontario, 1991.

Jaini, Padmanabh S. *The Jaina Path of Purification*. 1979. Reprint, Delhi: Motilal Banarsidass, 1990.

Laidlaw, James. *Riches and Renunciation: Religion, Economy, and Society among the Jains*. Oxford: Clarendon Press, 1995.

O'Connell, Joseph T., ed. *Jain Doctrine and Practice: Academic Perspectives*. Toronto: University of Toronto Centre for South Asian Studies, 2000.

Stevenson, M. S. *The Heart of Jainsim*. 1915. Reprint, New Delhi: Munshiram Manoharlal, 1970.

Tatia, Nathmal, trans. *Tattvartha Sutra (That Which Is)*. San Francisco: HarperCollins, 1994.

Wagle, Narendra K., and Olle Qvarnström, eds. *Approaches to Jaina Studies: Philosophy, Logic, Rituals and Symbols*. Toronto: University of Toronto Centre for South Asian Studies, 1999.

RECOMMENDED VIEWING

Ahimsa: Nonviolence. 1987. One of the first documentary films produced in North America to examine Jainism, this one-hour film portrays various aspects of Jain religion and philosophy, including its history, teachers, rituals, politics, law, art, and pilgrimage sites.

The Frontiers of Peace: Jainism in India. 1986. This forty-minute film explores Jainism by showing the interrelationship between all four elements of the sangha, or community of monks, nuns, and laypeople. Set in Ahmedabad, Gujarat, the film first establishes the central religious tenets of the religion, that impure actions prevent the soul from achieving liberation and liberation can be achieved only by practising ahimsa (nonviolence). The implications of these assumptions for each element of the Jain community are also explored.

Trip to Awareness: A Jain Pilgrimage to India. 1971. This half-hour documentary is about Gurudev Chitrabhanu's annual pilgrimage to Jain sites in India with his Western students. Gurudev is an enlightened spiritual teacher who came to North America to enlighten seekers in search of truth and self-realization. JMIC (the Jain Meditation International Center) was founded by Gurudev in 1971.

Nirmala: Diksha of a Jain Nun. c. 1992. This forty-five-minute film is a wonderful examination of a laywoman named Nirmala taking her vows to become a Digambara nun. It is an extremely difficult film to get one's hands on, but well worth the search.

USEFUL WEBSITES

YJA (YoungJainsofAmerica.org)

Young Jains of America (YJA) is a non-profit organization parented by the Federation of Jain Associations in North America (JAINA). Its membership consists of Jain youth from fourteen to twenty-nine.

Jain Society of Toronto

A non-profit religious institution dedicated to fostering and preserving Jain culture and providing a forum for information and discussion related to Jainism.

JAINA Organization and Young Jain Professionals

JAINA is the umbrella organization for local Jain associations (sanghas) in North America. YJP is a network of young Jain professionals concerned with teaching and promoting Jain principles.

jaindharmonline.com

This site's goal is to publicize Jain dharma and the teachings of the Tirthankaras. Administered by the Ganeshmal Patni Memorial Trust, this website houses contributed articles and information about Jainism in both English and Hindi.

International School for Jain Studies

A worldwide association of scholars of Jainism that offers comprehensive study resources and emphasizes the need for academic study of Jainism.

Jain Study Circle

Dedicated to propagating the Jain religion, particularly among young people, this group organizes seminars and other study events and publishes the *Jain Study Circular*.

Jainworld.com

Aims to spread the word of Jainism across the world and create a global online community. This site contains scriptures, radio lectures, quotes, photos, information about global Jain events, and much more.

Anekant Education Foundation

Educational website about Jain philosophy and Indian culture that emphasizes education of the young and alternative approaches to the study of Jainism.

Jain Center of Northern California
A non-profit organization serving the Jain community in Silicon Valley and the San Francisco Bay area.

Jainism Global Resource Center
Offers online resources related to Jain philosophy, practice, and communities worldwide.

Jain Animal Rights/Vegetarian Jiv Daya Resource Center
A lifestyle website that offers guidance in adapting the Jain principle of ahimsa to life in the United States.

REFERENCES

Primary Sources
Shri Kunda Kunda. 1930/1974. *The Sacred Books of the Jainas*. Vol. 8, *Samayasara: The Soul-Essence*, trans. J. L. Jaini. New York: AMS Press.

———. 1931/1974. *The Sacred Books of the Jainas*. Vol. 9, *Niyamsara: The Perfect Law*, trans. Uggar Sain. New York: AMS Press.

Shri Nemichandra Siddhanta. 1927/1974. *The Sacred Book of the Jainas*. Vol. 5, *Gommatsara Jiva-Kanda: The Soul*, trans. J. L. Jaini. New York: AMS Press.

Suri, Amrita Chandra. 1933/1974. *Purushartha-siddhyupaya*. New York: AMS Press.

Umasvami. 1920/1974. *The Sacred Books of the Jainas*. Vol. 2, *Tattvarthadhigama Sutra: The Essential Principle of Jainism* trans. J. L. Jaini. New York: AMS Press.

Secondary Sources
Alsdorf, Ludwig, trans. 1966. *The Arya Stanzas of the Uttarajjhaya: Contributions to the Text, History and Interpretation of a Jaina Canonical Jaina Text*. Mainz: Verlag der Akademie der Wissenschatter und der Literatur.

Babb, Lawrence. 1988. "Giving and Giving Up: The Eightfold Worship among Svetambar Murtipujak Jains." *Journal of Anthropological Research* 44: 67–85.

———. 1993. "Monks and Miracles: Religious Symbols and Images of Origin among Osval Jains." *Journal of Asian Studies* 52, no. 1: 3–31.

———. 1996. *Absent Lord: Ascetics and Kings in a Jain Ritual Culture*. Berkeley: University of California Press.

———. 1998. "Ritual Culture and the Distinctiveness of Jainism." In *Open Boundaries: Jain Communities and Cultures in Indian History*, ed. John E. Cort, 139–62. Albany: State University of New York Press.

Balbir, Nalini. 1994. "Women in Jainism." In *Religion and Women*, ed. Arvind Sharma, 121–38. Albany: State University of New York Press.

Bloomfield, Maurice. 1919. *Life and Stories of the Jaina Savior Parasvanatha*. Baltimore, MD: Johns Hopkins University Press.

Caillat, Colette. 1977. "Fasting unto Death According to the Ayarangasutta and to Some Painnaya." In *Mahavira and His Teachings*, ed. A. N. Upadhye. Bombay: Navjivan Press.

Caillat, Colette, A. N. Upadhye et al. 1974. *Jainism*. Delhi: Macmillan of India.

Carrithers, Michael, and Caroline Humphrey, eds. 1991. *The Assembly of Listeners: Jains in Society*. Cambridge: Cambridge University Press.

Chapple, Christopher. 1991. "Non-resistant Death." *Jinamañjari* 2, no. 2: 51–61. Mississauga, ON: Bramhi Jain Society.

Cort, John E. 1986. "Recent Descriptive Accounts on Contemporary Jainas." *Man* 66, no. 2: 180–87.

———. 1995. *Defining Jainism: Reform in the Jain Tradition*. Toronto: University of Toronto Press.

———, ed. 1998. *Open Boundaries: Jain Communities and Cultures in Indian History*. Albany: State University of New York Press.

———. 2001. *Jains in the World: Religious Values and Ideology in India*. New York: Oxford University Press.

Coward, Harold, John R. Hinnells, and Raymond Brady Williams. 2000. *The South Asian Religious Diaspora in Britain, Canada, and the United States*. Albany: State University of New York Press.

Deleu, Jozef, trans. 1996. *Viyahapannatti (Bhagavai): The Fifth Anga of the Jaina Canon*. Delhi: Motilal Banarsidass.

Dixit, Krishna Kumar. 1974. "The Problem of Ethics and Karma Doctrine as Treated in the Bhagavati Sutra." *Sambodhi* 2, no. 3: 1–13.

Doshi, Manubhai, trans. 1994. "Lord Mahavir and Chandanbala." In *Jain Story Book*. Boston: Indira Mansukhlal Doshi Memorial Trust, Jain Center of Greater Boston.

Dundas, Paul. 1992. *The Jains*. New York: Routledge.

Folkert, Kendall. 1993. *Scripture and Community: Collected Essays on the Jains*. Atlanta: Scholars Press.

Granoff, Phyllis. 1998. *The Forest of Thieves and the Magic Garden: An Anthology of Medieval Jain Stories*. Toronto: Penguin Canada.

Heesterman, J. C. 1993. *The Broken World of Sacrifice: An Essay in Ancient Indian Ritual*. Chicago: University of Chicago Press.

Herberg, Edward N. 1989. *Ethnic Groups in Canada: Adaption and Transitions*. Scarborough, ON: Nelson Canada.

Hoernle, A. F. Rudolf, trans. 1989. *The Uvasagadasao, or the Religious Profession of an Uvasaga Expounded in Ten Lectures, Being the Seventh Anga of the Jains*. Calcutta: Asiatic Society.

Humphrey, Caroline. 1985. "Some Aspects of the Jain Puja: The Idea of 'God' and the Symbolism of Offerings." *Cambridge Anthropology* 9, no. 3: 1–19.

Humphrey, Caroline, and James Laidlaw. 1994. *The Archetypal Actions of Ritual: A Theory of Ritual Illustrated by the Jain Rite of Worship*. Oxford: Clarendon Press.

Israel, Milton. 1987. *The South Asian Diaspora in Canada: Six Essays*. Toronto: Multicultural History Society of Ontario and University of Toronto Centre for South Asian Studies.

Israel, Milton, and Narendra K. Wagle, eds. 1993. *Ethnicity, Identity, Migration: The South Asian Context*. Toronto: University of Toronto Centre for South Asian Studies.

Jacobi, Hermann, trans. 1884/1995. *The Sacred Books of the East*. Vol. 22, *AcharangaSutra* ed. Max Muller. Delhi: Motilal Banarsidass.

———. 1895/1995. *The Sacred Books of the East*. Vol. 45, *The Uttaradhyayana Sutra*, ed. Max Müller. Delhi: Motilal Banarsidass.

Jain, Jagdishchandra. 1988. "The Position and Status of Women in Jain Literature." In *Studies in Early Jainism: Selected Research Articles*, 164–71. New Delhi: Navrang.

Jaini, J. L., trans. 1920/1974. *The Sacred Books of the Jainas*. Vol. 2, *Tattvarthadhigama Sutra: The Essential Principle of Jainism* [Umasvami]. New York: AMS Press.

Jaini, Padmanabh. 1979/1990. *The Jaina Path of Purification*. Delhi: Motilal Banarsidass.

———. 1985. "The Pure and the Auspicious in the Jaina Tradition." In *Purity and Auspiciousness in Indian Society*, ed. J. B. Carmen and F. A. Marglin, 84–93. Leiden: E. J. Brill.

———. 1991. *Gender and Salvation: Jaina Debates on the Spiritual Liberation of Women*. Berkeley: University of California Press.

Jain Society of Toronto. 1999. "Souvenir Address." Jain Society of Toronto 25th Anniversary Celebration.

Jamison, Stephanie W. 1996. *Sacrificed Wife/Sacrificer's Wife: Women, Ritual, and Hospitality in Ancient India*. New York: Oxford University Press.

Johnson, W. J. 1995. *Harmless Souls: Karmic Bandage and Religious Change in Early Jainism with Special Reference to Umasvati and Kundakunda*. Delhi: Motilal Banarsidass.

Kamala, K. 1984. *Life in Ancient India as Depicted in Prakrit Literature*. Hyderabad: Prakrit Academy.

Kumar, Bhuvanendra. 1996. *Jainism in America*. Mississauga, ON: Jain Humanities Press.

Laidlaw, James. 1995. *Riches and Renunciation: Religion, Economy, and Society among the Jains*. Oxford: Clarendon Press.

Lalwani, Kastur Chand, trans. 1973. *Dasavaikalika Sutra*. Delhi: Motilal Banarsidass.

———. 1979. *Kalpa Sutra of Bhadra Bahu Svami*. Delhi: Motilal Banarsidass.

Matilal, B. K. 1981. *Central Philosophy of Jainism*. Ahmedabad: L. D. Institute of Indology.

O'Connell, Joseph T., ed. 2000. *Jain Doctrine and Practice: Academic Perspectives*. Toronto: University of Toronto Centre for South Asian Studies.

Radford, Mikal Austin. 1995. "Sallekhana, Ahimsa, and the Western Paradox." *Jinamanjari* 11, no. 1: 23–39.

Reynell, Josephine. 1991. "Women and the Reproduction of the Jain Community." In *The Assembly of Listeners: Jains in Society*, ed. M. Carrithers and C. Humphrey, 41–65. Cambridge: Cambridge University Press.

Ryan, James. 1999. "Jainas in Context: Tirthankaras, Siddhas, Arhat, Nun and Layperson in the Civakacintamai." In *Proceedings of the International Conference on Approaches to Jaina Studies: Philosophy, Logic, Rituals and Symbols*, ed. N. K. Wagle and Olle Qvarnström. Toronto: University of Toronto Centre for South Asian Studies.

Sain, Uggar, trans. 1931. *Niyamsara by Shri Kunda Kundaa Acharya*. Lucknow: Central Jain Publishing.

Sangave, Vilas. 1980. *Jaina Community: A Social Survey*. Bombay: Popular Prakashan.

Schubring, Walther. 1962. *The Doctrine of the Jainas: Described after the Old Sources*. Delhi: Motilal Banarsidass.

Shah, Pravin K. 1998. *Jain Fundamentals, Jain Compassion, Jain Scriptures, and the Essence of World Religions*. Boston: Jain Center of Greater Boston.

Smith, Arthur Vincent. 1901. *The Jain Stupa and Other Antiquities of Mathura*. Allahabad: Government Press.

Stevenson, M. S. 1915/1970. *The Heart of Jainsim*. New Delhi: Munshiram Manoharlal.

Tatia, Nathmal, trans. 1994. *Tattvartha Sutra (That Which Is)*. San Francisco: HarperCollins.

Vallely, Anne. 1999. *Women and the Ascetic Ideal in Jainism*. Toronto: University of Toronto Press.

Wagle, Narendra K., and Olle Qvarnström, eds. 1999. *Approaches to Jaina Studies: Philosophy, Logic, Rituals and Symbols*. Toronto: University of Toronto Centre for South Asian Studies.

Williams, Robert. 1963. *Jaina Yoga: A Survey of the Mediaeval Sravakacaras*. London: Oxford University Press.

Zydenbos, Robert J. 1987. "The Jaina Nun Kavunti." *Bulletin d'études indiennes* 5: 387–417.

Timeline

- **1469–1539** Guru Nanak.

- **1581–1606** Guru Arjan (born 1563).

- **1675–1708** Guru Gobind Singh (born 1666).

- **1699** Creation of Khalsa order.
  Inauguration of Sikh scripture as the Guru Granth Sahib.

- **1780–1839** birth and death of Maharajah Ranjit Singh

- **1849** Annexation of Punjab by the British.

- **1860s** Sikhs begin migration out of India.

- **1873** Singh Sabha (Society of the Singhs) established.

- **1919** Jallianwala Bagh Massacre.

- **1920** Shiromani Gurdwara Parbandhak Committee established.

- **1925** Punjab Gurdwara Act.

- **1947** Partition of Punjab as a result of India's independence.

- **1980s** Agitation for Khalistan.

- **1984** Operation Bluestar: attack on Harimandir Sahib and other gurdwaras by Indian army.

- **2004** Dr. Manmohan Singh sworn in as the first Sikh prime minister of India.

CHAPTER 4

Sikhism

Doris R. Jakobsh

INTRODUCTION

In major cities across Canada, as well as throughout the world, Sikhs celebrate the Vaisakhi festival, gathering in great numbers in a procession that winds its way through the streets. While standing amid the assembled crowd, you might first hear the loud beating of a drum, then see five males with turbans and long beards leading the procession, wearing traditional Punjabi garb, carrying swords, and holding flags before them. Immediately following these five you might see a large float carrying what is most sacred to Sikhs, the **Guru Granth Sahib**, the revealed scripture of the Sikhs. Large crowds of Sikhs follow, taking part by singing hymns of devotion (**kirtan**) as they walk along the streets.

In this chapter you will come to understand the significance of this festival and the various components that make this an important occasion for Sikhs. You will discover that the Guru Granth Sahib must always be carried higher up than anything or anyone else in the procession, for Sikhs understand their scripture to be a living guru to which one must show utmost respect and dignity. For this reason the **granthi** (custodian or reader) waves a fly whisk over the pages: in India, whisks were used to keep flies away from royalty or particularly holy men or women.

The historical development of the Sikh tradition will be covered in this chapter and you will come to know and understand important terms used by Sikhs within their religion. Central Sikh tenets will also be examined and explained. You will learn that that Sikhism, like any other religion, is not a monolithic entity. There are many kinds of Sikhs and various ways of "being Sikh." You may have Sikh friends who never cut their hair or wear turbans or scarves; you will likely know other Sikhs who do cut their hair. Sikh family and societal structures will become clearer to you as you read this chapter. You will also come to know some of the joys and challenges facing Sikhs within the Canadian context.

Sikhs welcome all to join their public celebrations and also to enter their houses of worship, which are called gurdwaras. This chapter will explain various features of what takes place within the gurdwara ("the Guru's door") as well as help you understand proper etiquette when entering a gurdwara for the first time. If you have not yet met a Sikh, it is very likely that you will at some point in time. Sikhs form an important part of the Canadian mosaic and are generally very open to speaking about their religion and customs.

Sikhism is one of the youngest of the world's religions, but in terms of numbers of adherents it has gained increasing importance, becoming the fifth largest religion worldwide, with about twenty-three million followers. Sikhs trace their tradition to the Punjab, in the northwest of India, where the founder of the Sikhs, Guru Nanak, was born in the fifteenth century. This area was once a part of India, but with the partition of India and the creation of Pakistan in 1947, western Punjab was divided from its eastern counterpart. The birthplace of Guru Nanak is now situated in Pakistan.

Guru Granth Sahib: the confessional designation of the Adi Granth, the Sikh sacred scripture, as the eleventh guru of the Sikhs. Often, the prefix Siri is added as an additional term of respect, namely, Siri Guru Granth Sahib.

Kirtan: devotional congregational hymn singing.

Granthi: the custodian of a gurdwara, who often serves as reader of the Guru Granth Sahib.

Akal Purakh: "Eternal Being" or "Timeless One"; the Divine.

Vahiguru: "Wonderful Lord" or "Sovereign"; the Divine.

Nam-simran: the Sikh discipline of meditation on the divine name or divine essence.

CENTRAL BELIEFS

The Divine

Central to Sikh teachings is belief in the oneness of the Divine. However, Sikh Gurus used a variety of names for this ultimate reality, some stemming from the Hindu and Muslim traditions. Their hymns upheld an understanding of the Divine as Nirgun ("Formless One") or **Akal Purakh** ("Eternal Being"). However, Akal Purakh is understood to be manifested in the world as well as within the human heart. From this perspective, Akal Purakh can be understood as both having attributes and being utterly without form (N. Singh 1995, 2). The Gurus taught that while the essence of the Akal Purakh is beyond human comprehension, divinity can be found everywhere, in every place, in every experience, in every relationship. While many translations generally utilize masculine language to denote the Divine, importantly, the Gurus did not, using instead both male and female concepts that reflected a personal, loving relationship with the Divine (N. Singh 1995, 3). This chapter will generally use the terms Akal Purakh (Eternal Being), Nirgun (Formless One) or **Vahiguru** (Wonderful Sovereign) to refer to the Divine.

Humanity

The Sikh Gurus taught that the human soul originates from the light of Akal Purakh. As such, humanity is essentially good. But there is a problem with the human condition in that human beings are unaware of who they really are—namely, that the light or presence of Akal Purakh is within them and surrounds them at all times. This problem, which the Gurus called *haumai*, manifests itself in self-reliance as opposed to recognizing one's ultimate dependence on Akal Purakh. Humans are also *manmukh*: ego-bound or self-centred. This concept is related to another important term, *maya*, which means "illusion" or "attachment." Within Sikhism the notion of *maya* refers to worldly attachment, or having a materialistic view of the world. While being attached to one's child, one's home, or one's job is not necessarily evil, when combined with *haumai* (self-reliance), attachment takes on negative qualities. Sikhs speak of five main "evils" while acknowledging that many other evils exist as well. These are lust, covetousness or greed, attachment, wrath, and pride. *Maya* is love turned into possessiveness. *Maya* is divinely blessed attraction to another turned instead to lust (Cole and Sambhi 1995, 76–85).

Karma and Transmigration

The Sikh Gurus taught that the destiny of each individual is directly tied to actions that have taken place in past lives as well as within one's present lifetime. As in other Indian religious systems, this is known as karma. Transmigration refers to the cycle of birth, death, and rebirth as a result of one's karma. While being born as a human is understood to be a great privilege, rebirth can also take place in the form of an animal or insect. However, an individual who becomes increasingly attuned to the will of Akal Purakh, a *gurmukh*, can overcome the bonds of karma and be released from the wearisome circle of rebirth.

The Spiritual Quest

The Gurus did not just expound on the human condition but also offered a clear solution to the problem facing humanity. The goal is to move away from self-reliant and ego-bound attitudes and become *gurmukh*, or focused on Akal Purakh in everyday living. The path to enlightenment is to be found through the discipline of **nam-simran**, meditation on the divine name or divine essence.

Through intentional focus on Akal Purakh, the human will and the Divine will begin to converge. For the Sikh Gurus this did not mean that one has to give up one's occupation and house and family; nam-simran can and should be practised within the ordinary course of events. While sowing the fields, while mending, while churning butter—all images utilized by the Gurus—one can practise the discipline of meditation. Congregational devotional singing (kirtan) of praises to Akal Purakh is also essential to the spiritual quest, for in the company of like-minded people, the personal quest for liberation is enhanced.

Five Stages of Liberation

The Gurus also taught that there are stages or realms through which humans must pass before attaining enlightenment. The first stage, into which all humans are born, is Dharam Khand, the stage of duty or piety. In this realm, humans act according to notions of dutiful behaviour based on basic levels of responsibility and piety. They are then enabled to reach the second stage, Gyan Khand, the realm of awareness or knowledge. This awareness goes beyond simply doing for duty's sake. In this stage, devotees become aware of the mystery of being and the vastness of the universe. The realm of effort, Saram Khand, is the stage whereby the mind and natural intellect become increasingly attuned to Akal Purakh. This realm is also the last stage of human effort and insight; movement to the fourth stage, Karam Khand, or stage of grace, comes only as a gift from Akal Purakh. While positive actions are important, true liberation can come only through the grace of Akal Purakh.

The last stage is the realm of truth, Sach Khand, the realm where the essence of the Divine exists in its formless state. This realm cannot be described in words; it can only be experienced. Within this realm, the individual no longer perceives the world from a human perspective but from the perspective of Akal Purakh. This is true liberation, *jiwan mukti*, achievable in this present life. The individual will no longer experience the negative effects of karma (cause and effect) that leads to repeated rebirths. The cycle of transmigration is thus broken and the seeker will rest in union with the Divine upon her or his death.

Practices

The Three Cornerstones of Sikh Practice

1. Remembering the Divine at all times, based on the Sikh meditative discipline of nam-simran as well as through kirtan (devotional singing) or simply through listening to sacred text.
2. Making an honest living without exploitation or fraud (based on the householder ideal put in place by Guru Nanak in opposition to a life of asceticism and begging for one's daily food).
3. Sharing with others or helping those in need, which may be in the form of feeding the hungry but can also refer to offering *seva* (service) to other Sikhs or to humanity as a whole.

SOURCES
Adi Granth/Guru Granth Sahib

To come to an understanding of the very essence of Sikhism, we must turn to the Sikh scripture known as the Adi Granth. *Adi* means "original" and *granth* means "book." However, Sikhs understand their scripture to be much more than a mere book; it is in fact recognized as the embodiment of the eternal living Guru of the Sikhs. From a confessional standpoint, Sikhs call their scripture Guru Granth Sahib Ji or Siri Guru Granth Sahib. The term *Siri* is used in the Indian context when referring to one who is exalted—generally an enlightened teacher—and the honorific terms *Sahib* and *Ji* also denote respect. This chapter will mainly use the term Guru Granth Sahib when referring to the sacred scripture of the Sikhs.

When entering a gurdwara, one can see the exalted position of the Guru Granth Sahib being maintained. The Guru is carefully carried on the head of an individual when it is being transported and is then respectfully placed on an elevated platform, ensuring that the Guru Granth Sahib is always physically higher than everyone in the congregation.

Gurmukhi: the script of the Guru Granth Sahib, which stems from that used by the merchant classes during the time of the Gurus.

The main content of Sikh scripture is understood as *gurbani* (utterance of the Guru) or *shabad* (divine word), the latter referring to the revelation of scripture by Akal Purakh through the Gurus as well as through other, like-minded poet-saints. The language of the Guru Granth Sahib is a vernacular language—the language of the common people—that is similar to modern Punjabi and Hindi. It was written in **Gurmukhi**, a script that was widely used among the merchant classes at the time of the Gurus. Significantly, the Guru Granth Sahib was not written in Sanskrit, the holy language of the priestly classes; this choice of the Sikh Gurus is important—they wanted their words to be accessible to all.

An earlier version of the Guru Granth Sahib was compiled by the fifth master of the Sikhs, Guru Arjan (1581–1606), and completed in 1604. It included the hymns of his four predecessors alongside his own, as well as carefully chosen hymns by a number of other poet-saints, called *bhagats*, from both the Hindu and Muslim traditions, including hymns by Kabir, Namdev, and Ravidas. To this collection Guru Gobind Singh added the compositions of his father, Guru Tegh Bahadur. The Guru Granth Sahib thus contains the writings of six of the ten Sikh Gurus and numerous other writers; it totals 1,430 pages. The Guru Granth Sahib is organized systematically and chronologically, beginning with the hymns of the Sikh Gurus and ending with the compositions of the *bhagats*. Sikhs believe that the same light that shone within the first master, Guru Nanak, was present within all subsequent Gurus. This is given practical evidence in that the compositions of each of the six Gurus in the Guru Granth Sahib are labelled according to his number within the Guru succession, not by his name.

The Guru Granth Sahib is not a series of stories, parables, or philosophical statements, nor is it a set of ethical precepts or arguments or an account of Sikh history. Instead, the scripture is a collection of hymns praising Akal Purakh alongside a message of spiritual liberation for all through loving devotion to Nirgun (Formless One) and through the practical meditative techniques taught by the Gurus. It does not contain a great deal of information about the daily lives of the Gurus or the historical development of the Sikh tradition.

Guru Granth Sahib and Granthi, Chandigarh, India
Source: Harjant Gill

While their words are very often translated or interpreted using masculine-dominated language and imagery instead of being gender neutral, it is important to note that the Sikh Gurus employed both male and female imagery to describe the characteristics of the Divine and the mystical union between God and the devotee. They were clear that Nirgun cannot be understood or bound by gendered language (N. Singh 1993, 243–44).

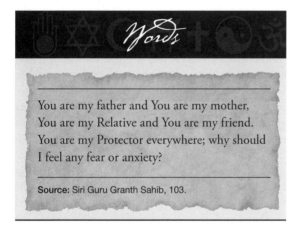

Words

You are my father and You are my mother, You are my Relative and You are my friend. You are my Protector everywhere; why should I feel any fear or anxiety?

Source: Siri Guru Granth Sahib, 103.

Dasam Granth

Another important text for Sikhs is known as the **Dasam Granth** (*dasam* means "tenth"), which contains the writings of a tenth master, Guru Gobind Singh. By many accounts it also includes compositions by other writers from the Guru's court. The Dasam Granth is in many respects more varied in content than the Guru Granth Sahib; it contains, alongside devotional hymns, ancient legends, popular anecdotes, and even a letter addressed to the Mughal emperor Aurangzeb, who reigned over much of India during the lifetime of Guru Gobind Singh. While much of the Dasam Granth plays a lesser role in the devotional lives of Sikhs, specific hymns within it are recited daily, especially those that are clearly attributed to Guru Gobind Singh.

Janam-sakhis

Other important texts are called **janam-sakhis** (literally "birth stories"), which are hagiographic (idealized) collections of narratives focusing on the life of the founder, Guru Nanak. Their form and style were reproduced in stories of the later Gurus as well, in what is called the

Dasam Granth: sacred writings attributed to Guru Gobind Singh.

Janam-sakhis: hagiographic (idealized) stories of Guru Nanak.

Sikh Reht Maryada: the Sikh code of conduct.

janam-sakhi genre. The janam-sakhis are questionable as reliable historical sources, since they were written well after the death of the Gurus and various versions exist that are not consistent with one another. But they do offer glimpses into a developing Sikh tradition and how early Sikh followers understood the life and mission of their Gurus (H. McLeod 1997, 8).

Sikh Reht Maryada

Another important, though more recent, text that plays a central role in Sikh religious life is known as the **Sikh Reht Maryada**. This is the code of conduct that provides definitions for Sikh religious identity, correct Sikh behaviour, things to avoid, how to conduct specific rituals, and other personal and community disciplines. It also outlines prescribed behaviours, ethics, correct attitudes, and beliefs for Sikhs (Dharam Parchar Committee). The version that is considered authoritative for Sikhs today stems from 1950; it incorporates a number of earlier codes.

SIKHISM IN HISTORY
The Guru Period
Guru Nanak (1469–1539)

The study of Sikhism begins with the boy Nanak, who was born into a relatively peaceful and stable society in North India. According to the janam-sakhis, his birth was accompanied by auspicious and miraculous signs that indicated his was to be an important life (H. Singh 1994, 63–71). He grew up in a Khatri Hindu family, that is, an upper-caste family that was involved in commerce. His mother was named Tripta and his father was Kalu, a village accountant. Nanak also had an elder sister named Nanaki, who is credited as being one of the first people to recognize her brother's important life mission.

Following the custom of the time, Nanak was educated to allow him to follow in his father's footsteps. He was trained in Sanskrit, Persian, and basic Arabic, but he showed little interest in the life of business for which he was being prepared. Often lost in religious musings, Nanak was keenly interested in the teachings of travelling holy men, both Hindu sadhus and Muslim Sufi masters. When he was eleven years old, he was to be invested with the *janeu*, the sacrificial cord that was and still is worn around the neck and over the shoulder by Hindu males of the upper castes, those known as the "twice born." It is the janeu that distinguishes upper-caste Hindu boys from those within lower castes. However, narratives tell us that Nanak refused the janeu, insisting that all humanity was equal. His actions caused a great stir in the village, and some were alarmed that Nanak was disregarding honoured traditions (H. Singh 1994, 76–78).

When Nanak was a teenager, he married, according to traditional customs, a young girl named Sulakhani. The couple then moved to the town of Sultanpur, where Nanaki and her husband lived. There Nanak's brother-in-law got him a job with a local official. Soon two boys were born to Nanak and Sulakhani, named Srichand and Laksmidas.

According to the janam-sakhis, Nanak arose every morning to bathe in the nearby River Bein and then spent the rest of the time before and after work in meditation and singing praises to the Divine. His boyhood friend Mardana, a low-caste Muslim musician, accompanied Nanak's hymns on his *rabaab*, a simple stringed instrument.

When Nanak was around thirty years old, tradition tells of a life-transforming experience. Upon entering the river for his morning ablutions, he mysteriously disappeared. His family began fearing the worst, but after three days he reappeared. Nanak later described what had happened to him: he had had an overwhelming mystical experience of union with Akal Purakh. His first words after emerging from the river, according to the janam-sakhis, were, "There is no Hindu, there is no Muslim," a statement that was to become the formula for his life's work and message (H. Singh 1994, 97). He recognized that humans tend to rely on the teachings and rituals of their respective traditions that separate them, while it is in fact only the truly loving relationship with Akal Purakh that ultimately matters. From that time forward Nanak was known as Guru Nanak, and word travelled quickly of his great piety and enlightened teachings.

Soon thereafter Guru Nanak left his family behind and began to travel extensively, accompanied by the minstrel Mardana, preaching and singing his message of praise and devotion to the Formless One, throughout India and the neighbouring countries.

After twenty years of travel, Guru Nanak returned to his family to establish a community in the village of Kartarpur. Daily life revolved around the presence and charisma of the Guru and his message. The Sikhs (literally, "learners") were to rise early in the morning—that mysterious time known as the "ambrosial hour" as the sun's rays are just beginning to light up the world—then bathe in preparation for the day ahead. Throughout all their daily activities the Sikhs were to remember or meditate on the divine name. This spiritual discipline, as taught by Guru Nanak, was nam-simran (that is, meditation on the divine name or divine essence). Then, as now, it is the central form of meditative practice for the Sikhs.

Meditation on the divine name had far greater implications than simply mindless repetition. Followers were to sincerely focus on the many and varied attributes and characteristics of the Formless One. The Gurus had numerous names for the Divine, including those of Hindu gods and Muslim designations, but no one name could sufficiently capture that divine essence that is beyond all names, all words, all conceptions. Guru Nanak also taught that over time, through nam-simran, the characteristics of the Divine would become deeply internalized. Those who consciously meditated and became ever more attuned to Akal Purakh were *gurmukhs*; those who were self-centred or ego-driven were *manmukhs*. For the Gurus, the ultimate purpose of human life was divine union through the Divine's indwelling within the soul—*jiwan mukti* (liberation in one's lifetime).

Religious Influences Guru Nanak's message had numerous influences, particularly what scholars today call the Sant tradition of North India. The term *sant* relates to the word *sat*, or "truth"; the sants were "seekers of truth" and they were known to combine various elements of the religions of the day. Most important of all was the bhakti movement, which began in South India in the sixth century and moved westward and northward through to the fourteenth century. The bhaktas (poet-saints) stressed above all devotion and love toward the Divine. While the movement initially centred on the gods Shiva and Vishnu and is generally called *saguna bhakti* (devotion to the Divine with attributes), it later came to include devotion to the Formless One, *nirguna bhakti*.

Other influences on the Sant tradition were Nath yogis, who emphasized the possibility of experiencing union with the Divine through meditative disciplines (McLeod 1987). The Sufis (Muslim mystics) also influenced Sant thought in their focus on the absolute oneness of God. They emphasized "remembrance of the Name," which is so prominent in Guru Nanak's teachings. The sants composed their poetry and hymns in vernacular languages instead of Sanskrit, which was considered a priestly language.

While the message of Guru Nanak contains elements of both Hinduism and Islam, Sikhism must be understood as a distinct religion, independent from both. The subsequent development of the community and its representative teachings came together innovatively in the creation of a distinct though always developing tradition. Along with individual meditation while pursuing daily activities and following routine prayers, known today as *nitnem*, the Guru's followers were to come together in the house of the Guru, then known as the *dharmsala*, or "place of assembly," to sing the praises of the Creator (kirtan) with other like-minded people. The term *dharmsala* was eventually replaced by *gurdwara*, "the Guru's door," and it is this term that today denotes Sikh sacred space.

The community of devotees, or congregation, was known as the *sangat*. Clearly Guru Nanak believed that his followers were to be defined by the company they kept. The compositions (*gurbani*) of Guru Nanak were well-known to his disciples; they were meant to be sung, accompanied by musical instruments, as in the Guru's early ministry with the minstrel Mardana. An initiation ritual distinguished the early community from surrounding groups. The Guru—and later, when the community had grown, a deputy of the Guru—would dip his right toe into a bowl of water; the initiate would then drink the water as a token of his or her submission to the Guru. This was significant in a society highly focused on ritual purity and avoidance of pollution.

More than any other reason, however, the early followers of the Guru gathered to receive the blessings, or darshan, of their Guru. *Darshan* means both "seeing" and "being seen" (Eck 1998, 5–6), and in the context

of the Sikhs and their Guru it referred to a reciprocal process of devotees seeing their master but also being seen by him. Simply by being in Guru Nanak's presence, through verbal or even nonverbal exchange, or by being within the community of those surrounding him, a devotee received the Guru's darshan. This was at the heart of devotees' longing. Today Sikhs gather to receive the darshan of the Guru Granth Sahib in much the same way as the early Sikhs gathered around their living guru.

Guru Nanak was understood as one who had a mission to redeem a corrupt society (Cole and Sambhi 1995, 15). Rigid religious affiliations, according to him, had led to societal discord. Shortly before his death it is said that members of the Muslim community gathered to honour Guru Nanak and later to claim his body as their revered *pir* (Sufi master), to be buried in accordance with Muslim traditions. Hindu followers also gathered around the Guru and they believed that since Guru Nanak had been born a Hindu, he should instead be cremated. The janam-sakhis give various versions of the following story.

As those surrounding him began to argue about which community the Guru belonged to, he opened his eyes and requested his disciples to surround him with sweet-smelling flowers. He told his devotees that if after his death the flowers on his left side were still fresh, then the Muslims could claim his body. If, however, the flowers on his right were fresh, he was to be cremated according to the tradition of Hindus. After the Guru died and the sheet covering his body was raised, nothing remained but flowers, as fragrant as the moment they had been picked (H. Singh 1994, 196–97). This beautiful narrative was an attempt to come to terms with the variety among those who held Guru Nanak's message to be their own. It underscored the lesson that had been at the core of his teachings: "There is no Hindu. There is no Muslim." All become equal through loving devotion to the Divine.

Subsequent Gurus

Guru Angad As Guru Nanak neared the end of his long life, he began the important process of finding a successor to lead the community. Often spiritual leaders would turn to their offspring, especially the eldest son, to succeed them. But Guru Nanak broke with that custom and chose instead a devotee named Lehna, known for his pious living, humility, and dedication. This choice

> **Langar:** the free communal meal offered at Sikh gurdwaras worldwide.
>
> **Harimandir Sahib:** also known as the Golden Temple, the holiest Sikh shrine, located in Amritsar, Punjab.
>
> **Akal Takht:** the Sikh religious and political centre that faces the Harimandir Sahib, representing Sikh temporal authority.

started an important tradition of the Guru period of Sikh history, namely that new successors were chosen based on merit. Lehna was renamed Angad, from the word *ang*, or "limb." While the name and the body were different, Guru Angad (1504–52) was as close and connected to his beloved teacher as Guru Nanak's own limbs, and henceforth their teachings were to be understood as one.

Guru Amar Das and Guru Ram Das Guru Angad was followed by Guru Amar Das (1479–1574), who is known for institutionalizing a practice that had begun earlier with Guru Nanak: **langar**. *Langar* refers to the sharing of a common meal, irrespective of caste, class, or any form of societal hierarchy. Visit any gurdwara worldwide today and you will see this practice still being followed today. Guru Amar Das's daughter was Bibi Bhani, who is held up as a model of piety and goodness for Sikhs. She was married to a devotee of her father's named Jetha, later called Guru Ram Das (1534–81) when he succeeded Guru Amar Das.

According to popular tradition, the Mughal emperor Akbar, while visiting Guru Amar Das on a diplomatic mission, was so impressed by Bibi Bhani's piety that he presented her with a large parcel of land. But women did not generally own land, and so, as the story is told, she in turn gave the land to her husband (Macauliffe 1901/1993, 97). On this parcel of land her husband, Guru Ram Das, founded a new centre known as Ramdaspur, later to be known as Amritsar. There he began excavation of the sacred pool that was later to house the **Harimandir Sahib**, the holiest shrine of the Sikhs, which is commonly known today as the Golden Temple.

Guru Arjan From this time onward, a significant change took place with regard to the line of succession: the guruship henceforth stayed within the family lineage of Guru Ram Das. However, instead of choosing his eldest son as

his successor, as was the custom, Guru Ram Das turned to his youngest son, Arjan (1563–1606). In some ways, then, the spirit of the tradition of a merit-based line of succession was upheld.

The community had grown significantly, and important institutional changes were instituted by Guru Arjan. He completed the pool that his father, Guru Ram Das, had already begun and built a gurdwara in its centre, thus providing his followers with a sacred shrine. He also compiled the compositions of the preceding Gurus into one volume; this was later, upon the death of the tenth and last Guru, known as the Guru Granth Sahib. The Mughal authorities, aware of the ever-growing following of Guru Arjan—one that included Muslims as well—had Guru Arjan arrested, and he was put to death while in their custody. He is remembered today as the first martyr of the Sikhs (P. Singh 2005).

Guru Hargobind The relationship between the Sikhs and the Mughals was becoming increasingly charged, especially after Guru Arjan's death while in their custody. When Guru Arjan's son Guru Hargobind (1595–1644) succeeded him, a number of important changes were instituted; most important was that the Guru was to represent both spiritual and worldly, or temporal, authority. According to tradition, as a symbol of this altered role, the eleven-year-old Guru wore two swords, one representing spiritual authority and the other political authority. During this time the **Akal Takht** was built near the Harimandir Sahib in Amritsar, which was also indicative of these changes. The Harimandir Sahib was the spiritual centre for Sikhs, while the Akal Takht represented (and still represents today) the Sikh community's temporal concerns.

Guru Har Rai, Guru Hari Krishan, and Guru Tegh Bahadur The seventh Guru was the grandson of Guru Hargobind, the gentle, nature-loving Guru Hari Rai (1630–61). Stories tell of Guru Har Rai's open heart to all living things; on one occasion he was hurrying to reach his beloved grandfather, Guru Hargobind, and in his haste his robe got caught in a bush and broke several flowers. He was overcome by the realization that he had hurt the plant. Numerous narratives bespeak his gentle and loving demeanour toward both the natural world and his devotees. His second son, the child Guru Hari Krishan (1656–64), succeeded Guru Hargobind

Harimandir Sahib, the Golden Temple

Harimandir Sahib (the Golden Temple), Amritsar
Source: Doris Jakobsh

The Harimandir Sahib (from *hari*, "the Divine," and *mandir*, "temple") is the most sacred place of worship for Sikhs and reflects their heritage and philosophy. Guru Ram Das founded the city of Amritsar and excavated a pool that was believed to have healing properties, creating a place of pilgrimage for the developing Sikh community. Guru Arjan built a gurdwara in the centre of the pool and installed within it a complete version of the Sikh scripture of the time: the writings of the first four Gurus and of like-minded bhagats (poet-saints), as well as his own compositions.

While traditional Hindu temple architecture is built higher than other buildings, the Guru constructed the Harimandir Sahib at a lower level so that devotees would have to go down steps in order to worship, emphasizing humility as they entered this sacred abode. As well, instead of the traditional single gate of most temples, the Harimandir was accessible through four gates, representing entry to all. The Harimandir Sahib was repeatedly destroyed by invaders in the eighteenth century. It was rebuilt and later came to be known as the Golden Temple, reflecting the gilding and embossing of the upper storeys of the shrine carried out by Maharajah Ranjit Singh in the nineteenth century.

Panj piare: the "five beloveds" who were originally initiated into the Khalsa order by Guru Gobind Singh; also signifies the five males who may administer the Khalsa initiation ritual today.

Khalsa: Khalsa, a term used originally by the Mughals to designate lands under the emperor's direct supervision. In the Sikh context, Khalsa referred to Sikhs whose were loyal to Guru Gobind Singh as opposed to his rivals.

Khande di pahul: the Khalsa initiation ritual of the sword, inaugurated by Guru Gobind Singh.

Singh: "lion," the name given to Sikh males at birth.

at the age of five but died within three years after succumbing to a smallpox epidemic. Guru Tegh Bahadur (1621–75), the ninth master, was the youngest son of Guru Hargobind. In 1675, near the end of his life, Guru Tegh Bahadur was summoned to Delhi by the Mughals on a charge of instigating rebellion against the government; he too was executed by the authorities. The community was stunned by this, the second execution of one of their Gurus. Relations between Sikhs and Mughals were increasingly deteriorating.

Guru Gobind Singh With the succession of Guru Tegh Bahadur's only son, Gobind Rai (1666–1708), as the tenth Guru, the community underwent its most significant transformation. Gobind Rai became the Guru when he was nine years old, under the guidance of relatives and family friends. He was well-trained in martial arts and loved to hunt and ride his beloved steed. He was also educated in the manner of the royal court of the time, in languages, astronomy, botany, and medicine. He was well versed in the varied religious philosophies that surrounded him.

Tensions had increased between the Mughals and Guru Gobind Rai, and there were occasional confrontations between the Guru's army and those of local Hindu chieftains in the Shivalik Hills, foothills of the Himalayas where Guru Gobind Rai had settled. A number of rivals within the wider Guru lineage had also staked their claim to leadership of the Sikh community, while some of the Guru's deputies had become corrupt in their positions of power.

The Khalsa

In 1699, during the Baisakhi festival (New Year's celebrations), a time when Sikhs traditionally gathered together in great numbers, Guru Gobind Rai made a special call to his followers to join him at Anandpur, his new centre in the Shivalik Hills. His devotees were expected to answer the call of loyalty to their one true Guru and their sole leader, as opposed to the numerous rivals who also claimed authority. As the crowd gathered, Guru Gobind Rai suddenly called upon a Sikh to come forward and offer his head in devotion to his Guru. The assembly was stunned. Finally one Sikh came forward. The Guru called for four more heads, and four devoted Sikhs answered his call. Importantly, each of the five that came forward stemmed from a different caste. According to one source, the five followers actually offered their lives to their Guru, and he came out from inside the tent with his sword dripping with the blood of their sacrifice—and then he miraculously healed them again. Another tradition had the Guru sacrificing five goats instead of his five devotees, as a ruse to test the will of those assembled (H. McLeod 1997, 52).

Regardless of the actual events that took place, it is clear that five disciples were called forward, and they were henceforth designated the "five beloveds," or **panj piare** (*panj* means "five" and *piare* means "beloved"). The Guru then administered a novel ritual of initiation to these five, called the **khande di pahul** (sword ritual), whereby water sweetened with sugar was stirred in an iron bowl with a double-edged sword. This nectar (*amrit*) was then sprinkled five times with the Guru's sword, onto each initiate's face, cupped hands, eyes, and hair. Sanctified food known as *karah prasad* was then offered to each of the five from the same iron bowl. The new initiates were henceforth to be part of the **Khalsa** order, *khalsa* being a common term used by the Mughals to designate lands that were under direct supervision of the emperor, as opposed to any other political entity (Grewal and Bal 1987, 113–15). The new Khalsa represented Sikhs who came under the direct authority of the Guru, as opposed to any of the Guru's rivals. The Guru himself was then initiated by khande di pahul. All those inaugurated into the Khalsa were given the name **Singh** ("lion"), and Guru Gobind Rai was henceforth known as Guru Gobind Singh.

The Singhs were required to adopt aspects of what were then part of the uniform of the warrior, with important additional elements. They included a call to arms, symbolized by the military uniform that included a *kirpan* (dagger); a *kara* (steel bangle), worn to protect the sword-wielding right wrist; and *kachh* (above-the-knee breeches), which were necessary for warriors who needed to mount and dismount horses easily and thus move quickly in times of battle (this was in contrast to the traditional *dhoti*, a long cloth wrapped around the lower body). The injunctions in time also came to include an important focus on the body with *kesh*—uncut or unshaved hair that signified the body in its pristine form—and the *kangha*, a small circular comb meant to be both used and worn in the hair, which emphasized tidiness and cleanliness (Mann 2004, 44). These five elements are known as the **five ks** (*panj kakar*), since each of the symbols begins with the letter *k*. The five ks, along with the turban, whose function is to keep the uncut hair in place, today remain distinctive marks of the Khalsa Sikh.

According to tradition, at the inauguration of the Khalsa order the Guru also prescribed a set of rules of conduct based on what are known as the four **kurahits**,

Five ks: the five symbols of the Khalsa Sikh that begin with the letter *k*—*kirpan* (dagger), *kara* (steel bangle), *kachh* (short breeches), *kesh* (uncut or unshaved hair), and *kangha* (a small circular comb).

Kurahits: the four cardinal sins for Sikhs, which are uncut hair; the use of intoxicants such as drugs, alcohol, or tobacco; ingesting *halal* meat (from animals killed according to Muslim slaughter rituals); and involvement in an adulterous relationship.

or cardinal sins. Sikhs were never to cut their hair, they were not to smoke or chew tobacco or consume alcohol, they were not to eat *halal* meat (meat from animals killed according to Muslim slaughter rituals), and they

Practices

This photograph shows a Sikh male wearing all 5ks. The *kangha,* or comb, is neatly fitted into the topknot and is just barely visible. Here, the beard is flowing; in this instance, this Sikh would then normally cover his hair with a turban (see photo at left on page 130).

Source: Capt Suresh Sharma/THE GREEN FRAMES

The Five Ks

The five external symbols that are worn by some Sikhs begin with the letter *k* in Punjabi. The are *kesh* (uncut hair), *kangha* (comb), *kachh* (short breeches), *kara* (steel bracelet), and *kirpan* (dagger). While Sikh tradition maintains that the five ks stem from the time of Guru Gobind Singh's inauguration of the Khalsa, there is a great deal of obscurity surrounding these symbols. The earliest texts name only three—*kesh*, *kirpan*, and *kachh*—but do make reference to five weapons that were to be carried by the Khalsa. By the nineteenth century, explicit mention is made of five items beginning with the letter *k*.

Various meanings are attributed to the five ks. Uncut hair (*kesh*) has been a symbol of holiness and strength in a number of traditions. For Sikhs, hair is a gift from Vahiguru that must be left in its natural state; hair on any part of the body must remain uncut, which makes unshorn Sikhs highly visible as a religious group. The comb (*kangha*) is a practical implement that keeps uncut hair tidy and in place, representing both bodily and spiritual purity. Moreover, it is a symbol that distances the Sikh emphasis on uncut hair from that of a great number of ascetics in India, whose long hair is often left matted. Short breeches (*kachh*), worn above the knee, are symbols of chastity that also had important practical implications, in that they

(continued)

enabled warriors to quickly mount and dismount their horses in times of battle. The steel bracelet (*kara*) is a useful wrist protector for a sword-wielding arm but is also understood to represent Akal Purakh in the form of a circle, without beginning or end. The dagger (*kirpan*) can be from a few centimetres to a metre long and represents the Sikh struggle against injustice. *'Sarab Loh' or 'All-Steel'* is also a name used by Guru Gobind Singh for the Divine. Some Sikhs wear only some of the five ks, usually the *kara* and the *kirpan*, which is often worn as a symbol on a bracelet or necklace.

Here is an example of a Sikh male with a turban which neatly covers the hair and comb. In this case, the beard is neatly trimmed, indicating at least a partial rejection of the Khalsa identity.

Source: Photos.com

When visiting a gurdwara, or, simply being in the presence of the Guru Granth Sahib, the head must be covered. This is an example of a more informal head-covering that is often used by Sikh men who cut their hair.

Source: Photos.com

were not to have sexual relations with Muslim women (W. H. McLeod 2003, 97). In time this last injunction evolved to prohibit adulterous relationships of any sort.

The Guru then called on other volunteers to join the Khalsa order. The Sikhs were now set apart, clearly identifiable from their Hindu and Muslim counterparts, and henceforth known as a community of warrior-saints. However, many continued to follow the practices and precepts of the earlier Gurus and still remained devoted Sikhs. This included women, who were not initiated into the brotherhood, given that the Khalsa were to be armed and ready for battle at all times. While there were a few exceptions to the rule, military roles were not open to women in the seventeenth and eighteenth centuries (Jakobsh 2003, 37–44).

The Sikhs after Guru Gobind Singh

The Mughals were alarmed at the growing militancy of the Sikhs and took action against them. Two elder sons of Guru Gobind Singh died fighting a united front of local chieftains and Mughal forces, and his two youngest sons were later executed. Guru Gobind Singh was heartbroken and wrote a letter of admonishment to the Mughal emperor Aurangzeb, which is known as the Zafar-nama. Soon thereafter, in 1708, Guru Gobind Singh was assassinated, possibly by a Mughal agent, in the town of Nander in the present state of Maharashtra.

With the Guru's death and those of his sons, the Guru lineage ended. Henceforth, Sikh authority was to reside in

---

PERSPECTIVES

Sikh Emblems and Symbols

Ek Oankar symbol
Source: Dorling Kindersley/
Getty Images

Ek Oankar

The Ek Oankar emblem comprises the first two words in the Guru Granth Sahib, which mean "The Divine is one reality." It combines the number one in Gurmukhi (the script of the Guru Granth Sahib) and the letter O. For Guru Nanak, together they described most completely the essence of Akal Purakh and formed the cornerstone of Sikh belief. Ek Oankar forms the first two words of the Sikh creedal statement known as the Mul Mantra, which in turn is the beginning stanza of the first hymn of Sikh scripture, which is recited by Sikhs in the morning. The notion of Ek Oankar is similar to that of *om* in Hinduism.

The Mul Mantra

The Mul Mantra is the Sikh creedal statement. It comes from the Japji, the first verses of the Guru Granth Sahib:

One Universal Creator God [Ek Oankar].
The Name is Truth.
Creative Being Personified.
No Fear.
No Hatred.
Image of the Undying,
Beyond Birth,
Self-Existent.
By Guru's Grace.

Chant and Meditate:
True in the Primal Beginning.
True throughout the Ages.
True here and now.
O Nanak, Forever and Ever True.

Source: Siri Guru Granth Sahib, 1. Translation courtesy Sant Singh Khalsa

Khanda symbol
Source: Nicolas Raymond/Shutterstock

Khanda

The Sikh Khanda emblem consists of three parts: a solid circle, two interlocking swords, and a double-edged sword in the centre. The two-edged sword, also known as a *khanda*, represents the sword used for the initiation ritual into the Khalsa. It sits within a *chakkar*, a circular shield that represents the oneness of Akal Purakh, without beginning and without end. The two interlocking swords signify the spiritual and temporal leadership of the Sikh Gurus, the sword on the right representing spiritual sovereignty (*piri*) and the sword on the left representing temporal authority (*miri*). The Khanda symbol is found on Sikh gurdwaras and on the saffron-coloured Nishan Sahib (flag) that flutters above gurdwaras worldwide. Together, Ek Oankar and the Khanda reflect fundamental concepts of Sikhism.

the Guru Granth Sahib, the sacred scripture of the Sikhs, and the Guru Panth, or Sikh community. Day-to-day leadership of the Sikhs was to be based in the local congregation, known as the sangat, led by an executive called the panj piare (modelled on the "five beloveds" who offered their heads in devotion to their Guru) and guided by the wisdom and insight of the Guru Granth Sahib. This form of leadership is still followed by Sikhs worldwide today.

In South India, shortly before his death, the Guru had met an ascetic known as Madho Das, who became his devotee and was renamed Banda Bahadur. Aware of the political unrest in Punjab and anticipating that he would soon be returning, the Guru sent Banda Bahadur ahead of him to begin organizing his Sikhs to be ready for battle.

Since Banda Bahadur was the bearer of the Guru's final command, he was received as the new warrior chief of the Sikhs. Banda Bahadur led a number of successful uprisings against the authorities, but he was soon overcome by the massive Mughal army and was executed in 1716. A time of intense persecution of Sikhs followed, first by the Mughals and then by Afghan invaders. Those Sikhs who resisted and died in battle are still named and celebrated today on a daily basis in a Sikh prayer of remembrance, the Ardas, as the greatest of Sikh martyrs. The ideal of martyrdom became firmly entrenched in the Sikh psyche; it was understood then, as now, as a righteous fight to the death and as the upholding of faith in the face of intolerance and persecution (Fenech 2001).

Practices

Martyrdom

The concept of martyrdom (shahidi) has Islamic roots in the notion of death's "giving witness" to a righteous cause; it became an important institution with the development of the Sikh tradition. As the early Gurus of the Sikhs gained increasing political power within their spiritual domains, they began to draw the ire of the dominant systems surrounding them. According to Sikh tradition, Guru Arjan, the first martyr, was gruesomely burnt alive on a griddle at the hands of his captors. When Guru Hargobind took up arms during his reign, it was because of his father's horrific death at the hands of the Mughals. Sikh accounts also maintain that Guru Tegh Bahadur was beheaded when he interceded to the authorities on behalf of a group of Brahmins who were being coerced into conversion to Islam. Today a gurdwara in Delhi called Sis Ganj (sis means "head") commemorates the ultimate sacrifice made by the Guru in the name of justice. His death is understood as a significant factor in the creation of the militaristic Khalsa order by his son, Guru Gobind Singh, who believed that Sikhs not only should be able to fight injustice but also should be visible as Sikhs in the defence of righteousness.

After the death of Guru Gobind Singh's sons, two of whom are believed to have been bricked up alive for refusing to convert to Islam, the concept of dying for a righteous and noble cause took on added significance. In the warfare against Mughal and Afghan forces, Sikhs were believed to have offered their lives as the supreme sacrifice for the larger cause of righteousness. One Sikh warrior, Baba Dip Singh, was known for his miraculous powers; he is pictured with one hand holding his own severed head after receiving a fatal blow from his Afghan assailant, while the other hand continues to wield a sword.

In modern times, Jarnail Singh Bhindranwale, the charismatic leader of a group of armed Sikhs in the 1980s, took a stand against the central Indian government from within the precincts of the Harimandir Sahib, where he was killed. Today he too is honoured as a martyr by many Sikhs. Martyrdom has become an established institution within Sikhism through the retelling of these and other heroic events and is perceived as an ideal to inspire piety and bravery in Sikhs. As an institution, martyrdom continues to hold a fascination for and even to inspire reverence among many Sikhs. Some gurdwaras contain pictures depicting memorable scenes of martyrdom that are meant to inspire Sikhs today.

By the mid-eighteenth century, Sikhs had begun to organize themselves into twelve confederacies. Ranjit Singh (1780–1839), a young and ambitious chieftain, soon rose to prominence through his political astuteness, but also through the guidance of his equally ambitious mother-in-law, Maharani Sada Kaur. Under Maharajah Ranjit Singh, the Sikhs entered nearly four decades (1801–39) of relative peace and prosperity. It is a time remembered as one of Sikh glory, for although the Sikhs were a small minority among Hindus and Muslims, it was a Sikh who ruled a significant portion of northern India.

The Sikhs, the British Raj, and Sikh Reform

Two Anglo-Sikh wars (1845–46 and 1848–49) followed soon after the death of Maharajah Ranjit Singh. The Sikh kingdom was annexed by the British in 1849, and from that point onward, British rule was established over the entire Indian subcontinent. The Sikhs fared well, as the Raj had grudgingly admired the leadership of Ranjit Singh and the military prowess of his armies. The Sikh aristocracy and religious elite were offered land grants and special rights to ensure their loyalty to the British Crown. Sikhs were given considerable autonomy, offered educational initiatives, and welcomed to serve in the British army.

As in other parts of India, reform movements in Punjab gained momentum as the British-educated elite middle class came to assess and re-evaluate its religious beliefs and practices. Among the Sikhs, the **Singh Sabha** (Society of the Singhs) reform movement was inaugurated in the late nineteenth century. Earlier Christian Orientalist scholars had been diligent about discovering the "pure" teachings of the religions of India. Practices that did not fit into what they considered "true" religion were labelled as mere superstitious belief or simply perceived as rural customs. Stung by the criticisms of their religious practices, Singh Sabha reformers too began a thorough evaluation of Sikh customs, many of which were labelled "superstitious" or even "anti-Sikh." Another important goal of the Singh Sabha was to conclusively distinguish Sikhs from Hindus and Muslims. Particularly in rural Punjab, where the majority of Sikhs resided, the peasantry shared many of their religious and cultural festivals, sacred shrines, and other rituals with their Hindu and Muslim neighbours. New Sikh rituals and festivals

> **Singh Sabha:** the Society of the Singhs, a reform movement of late-nineteenth-century Punjab.
>
> **Kaur:** the Sikh female second name, given at birth, originally meaning "prince" but today given at birth generally translated as "princess."

were instituted in an attempt to separate Sikh and Hindu identities in particular (Oberoi 1994, 189–90).

While the Khalsa order initiated by Guru Gobind Singh had continued to thrive, other varieties of Sikh identity were also prevalent at the time. Singh Sabha reformers worked diligently to promote a single, homogeneous Sikh identity—that of the Khalsa Sikh. Newspapers and tracts were published to put in place a new, reformed vision that focused on the Khalsa identity. In fact, many of the reforms put in place by the Singh Sabha continue to characterize the Sikh tradition today.

Sikh women's roles, religious practices, and identity markers became an important component of Singh Sabha reforms. Women had largely been excluded from being a part of the Khalsa identity, but the reformers increasingly believed that a full-fledged Sikh reformation would be impossible without Sikh women's "upliftment," as it was described. Women were initiated into the Khalsa order and given the name **Kaur** to distinguish them from Hindus and Muslims. *Kaur* in time became both ritually significant (like *Singh* for males) and significant in terms of Sikh female identity. Female education also became an important platform of reform (Jakobsh 2003, 210–37).

The Sikhs, Independence, and Punjabi Suba

Across India the call for independence from the British Raj was growing more strident. Sikhs too, though they had been largely loyal to the British Raj, increasingly raised their voices against foreign rule. In 1919 an incident took place in Amritsar that is remembered as the Jallianwala Bagh (park) Massacre. Following days of protest and general unrest over British policies, Brigadier General Reginald Dyer placed Amritsar under martial law. But large numbers of Sikhs had come to Amritsar and gathered at Jallianwala Bagh, near the Harimandir Sahib, for the annual Baiskahi festival. Under Dyer's command, riflemen began firing into the enclosed area. Official records indicate that 379 individuals were killed and many more

Nishan Sahib: the triangular saffron flag flown on a saffron-wrapped flagpole above Sikh gurdwaras.

wounded in the assault, most of whom were Sikhs. This incident clearly increased anti-British sentiment.

Sikhs began to realize that they needed to organize politically to best represent their interests. In 1920 the Shiromani Gurdwara Parbandhak Committee (SGPC) was inaugurated to govern the affairs of Sikh shrines in Punjab and the surrounding areas. A political party, the Shiromani Akali Dal, was also founded. In 1925 the Sikh Gurdwara Act was legislated; it gave custody of gurdwaras and shrines in Punjab, including the Harimandir, to Sikhs through the SGPC instead of through the hereditary proprietors, many of whom had not fallen in line with Singh Sabha reforms.

The Second World War played a role in stemming the tide of Indian independence for a short while. Sikhs played an important and valorous role in the war because their numbers were disproportionately large in the Indian Army. After the war, on August 15, 1947, at the stroke of midnight, Indian independence from British rule was achieved. But the victory came at a great price for the Sikhs, for with independence came the geographic partition of India. Punjab, the homeland of the Sikhs, was split into East and West Punjab; East Punjab was allotted to India and West Punjab became part of Pakistan.

A great exodus took place. Sikhs and Hindus moved to India and Muslims left for Pakistan. Great riots took place in the midst of this mass migration, eventually leading to massacres on both sides of the new border (K. Singh 2006). As a community, Sikhs suffered greatly from the loss of homes and land in the resettlement process. Partition also meant leaving behind the erstwhile capital of the Sikh kingdom, Lahore, and shrines and gurdwaras associated with a number of their Gurus.

1980s to the Present

The 1980s were a significant decade for Sikhs. They believed that as a tiny minority group they were being discriminated against by the central government of India. The charismatic militant preacher Jarnail Singh Bhindranwale called for a new nation called Khalistan within India, to be run by Sikhs and built upon Khalsa ideals. He urged Sikhs to reject all identities except what he considered the essence of true Sikhism—the Khalsa Sikh identity. He and his armed followers fortified themselves

within the precincts of the Harimandir Sahib. Prime Minister Indira Gandhi, alarmed by Bhindranwale's increasing power, sent troops into the Harimandir Sahib in an effort to subdue the militants. The result was one of the most painful episodes in modern Sikh history. Bhindranwale was killed and the sacred shrine became the site of a great deal of bloodshed and violence. Sikhs were outraged, and many who had until then rejected the militant Khalistani movement increasingly aligned themselves with its aims and objectives.

The political situation intensified after the murder of Prime Minister Gandhi by her two Sikh bodyguards, who were avenging the sending of troops into the Harimandir Sahib. Radical Hindu groups in turn called for revenge. In Delhi, the capital of India, mobs began roaming the streets, especially in areas with large numbers of Sikhs. Many Sikh homes and businesses were burned to the ground, and thousands of Sikhs were killed, maimed, or burned.

The Sikhs were horrified that their entire community was being blamed for the actions of the bodyguards. Moreover, these acts of violence were taking place despite a significant police and army presence. Sikhs were faced with the realization of their precarious minority situation in India. While much of the anguish surrounding this tumultuous time has subsided, 1984 will always be remembered as a year when the Sikh community and Sikh identity were cause for violence and bloodshed.

Punjab has long since returned to an orderly state, with Sikhs, Hindus, and Muslims living in peaceful coexistence with one another. Moreover, Sikhs all over the world take great pride in the fact that in 2004, Dr. Manmohan Singh, a renowned economist, scholar, and politician—and a turbanned Sikh—was sworn in as India's fourteenth prime minister. The election of a member of a tiny minority to India's highest political position has been seen as symbolically significant for all other minority groups in India, and in particular for Sikhs.

SIKH WORSHIP
The Gurdwara

Congregational worship for Sikhs takes place in a gurdwara. Gurdwaras were originally built on sites associated with the Gurus, the most sacred being the Harimandir Sahib in Amritsar. Gurdwaras can be found in all parts of the world today, and most are recognizable by the triangular saffron flag called the **Nishan Sahib**, which is held high by a saffron-wrapped flagpole outside the building. On the flag is the Sikh Khanda symbol, the double-edged sword that serves as one of the emblems of the Khalsa.

The daily routine of congregational worship is prescribed in the Sikh Reht Maryada. When the Guru Granth Sahib is taken from its nightly resting place, it is carefully carried on the head of a devout Sikh to a raised platform in the main hall of the gurdwara. Morning services begin with specific prayers, which are followed by additional hymns. Services are conducted almost exclusively by male granthis, the custodians of the gurdwara who also serve as readers of scripture. The term *granthi* is often translated as "priest," but this term is misleading—there is no ordained priesthood in the Sikh tradition. Anyone who is literate can serve as granthi.

Another important role in gurdwaras is played are trained musicians called *ragis*, who sing hymns accompanied by a harmonium, a mini-organ whose bellows are pumped by hand, and tabla, a small Indian percussion instrument that beats out the rhythms of the hymns. Kirtan (devotional singing) occupies a major portion of congregational worship. The service comes to a conclusion with a routine prayer of remembrance, the Ardas. A randomly chosen hymn from scripture is read, and then sanctified food, *karah prashad*, is distributed to all who are assembled, irrespective of caste or creed.

Practices

What to Do in a Gurdwara

Throne for the Guru Granth Sahib, Gurdwara Shillong, Assam, India
Source: Karam Bharij

Anyone is welcome to visit a gurdwara. Upon arrival, you must take off your shoes and cover your head as a traditional sign of respect to the Guru Granth Sahib. Women generally wear a light scarf as a covering; men wear kerchiefs or turbans. Tobacco should never be taken into a gurdwara; this would be construed as clearly disrespectful of Sikh tenets, as tobacco use is understood as one of the four cardinal sins in Sikhism.

(continued)

Upon entering the main hall housing the sacred scripture, Sikhs will touch the palms of their hands together as a sign of devotion, then walk toward the Guru Granth Sahib, which is kept on a raised canopied platform, supported by cushions and beautiful cloths. The granthi stationed in front of the Guru Granth Sahib will be slowly swishing a fly whisk over the scripture, a tradition reminiscent of shielding royal personages from insects. Once there, Sikhs will get down on their knees, touch the forehead to the ground, make an offering of money or food, and then move to the right, to sit with the men of the sangat (congregation), or to the left, to sit with the women. As a visitor you are welcome to take part in this tradition; otherwise, respectfully enter the main hall and sit down quietly while the service is taking place. Some Sikhs will enter the main hall, pay obeisance to their Guru, and then leave again; others will sit for as long as they wish to take part in the service.

Most of the service consists of kirtan being sung, but it will also include a sermon by the granthi or another respected male (generally). The service comes to an end after the sangat takes part in singing and responding to specific verses from particular hymns and communal chanting of salutations: *Vahiguru ka Khalsa! Vahiguru ki fateh!* ("Hail to the Guru's Khalsa! Hail to the Guru's victory!") and *Sat Sri Akal* ("Truth is immortal"). When the service concludes, *karah prasad* (sanctified food) is handed out to all assembled. *Karah prasad* is a sweet pudding-like substance that is accepted in cupped hands, then eaten with the right hand, echoing the traditional Indian injunction against eating food with one's left hand.

After leaving the main hall, everyone is welcome to partake of the communal meal called langar. This generally takes place in a separate hall and consists of a simple vegetarian meal. While the majority of Sikhs are not vegetarian, all food offered at the gurdwara must be vegetarian to meet the needs of those who are vegetarian, both Sikhs and non-Sikhs. In India and in most gurdwaras within the

Whether Sikh or non-Sikh, one is required to cover one's hair when entering into the presence of the Guru Granth Sahib, whether that be in a gurdwara or within a home. This is a sign of respect toward Sikh scripture. Sikh women generally cover their head with a light shawl or scarf, while men will wear a turban or a kerchief.

Source: © Pascal Deloche/Godong/Corbis

Sikh diaspora, the meal is eaten while sitting within marked lines on the floor and is served by members of the sangat. In some gurdwaras in the diaspora, langar is shared at tables with chairs.

Sikhs will greet and take leave of one another with the words "Sat Sri Akal," and Sikhs are greatly appreciative if visitors also use this greeting when entering or leaving a gurdwara.

Personal Worship

The daily routine of a Sikh begins with rising early, bathing, and then reciting specific hymns from the Guru Granth Sahib. There are also prescribed hymns to be sung at sunset and just before bedtime. Many Sikh households, whether in India or in other parts of the world, have a special room reserved for a copy of the Guru Granth Sahib, which serves as the family gurdwara.

Sikh Festivals and Celebrations

Vaisakhi

Throughout the Sikh world, a celebration called the Vaisakhi (or Baisakhi) festival celebrates Guru Gobind Singh's inauguration of the Khalsa in 1699, as well as the New Year's celebrations marking the end of one agricultural cycle in Punjab and the beginning of another. The city of Amritsar is the central site for this event, but Vaisakhi is also celebrated worldwide. On this day the Guru Granth Sahib is taken out of the gurdwara and carried around the town or city in an open vehicle, in a procession called *nagar kirtan*, with the panj piare leading the procession. The gathered congregation follows the float in great numbers while singing kirtan.

Divali

The festival of Divali, known to Hindus as the festival of lights, is celebrated by Sikhs to honour the release of their sixth master, Guru Hargobind, from Gwalior prison by Emperor Jahangir. When the Guru finally arrived at the Harimandir Sahib, he was welcomed by his devotees, who had decorated it with lights. Today at Diwali the Harimandir Sahib is decked with lights and a massive display of fireworks delights onlookers. This celebration also takes place in gurdwaras in all parts of the world.

Hola Mohalla

The festival of Hola Mohalla, which is similar to Divali celebrations, was put in place as a Sikh version of the Hindu spring festival of Holi. It celebrates the summoning of Sikhs by Guru Gobind Singh to Anandpur, where the Khalsa order was inaugurated. Anandpur is the principal centre for this festival; it is there that Sikhs take part in martial arts competitions called *gatka* that

highlight weapons such as swords, bows and arrows, and chains. The festival also includes other sporting events and weapons training exercises.

Gurpurbs

Gurpurbs celebrate important anniversaries in the history of Sikhism. The most widely celebrated *gurpurbs* include the birthdays of Guru Nanak and Guru Gobind Singh, as well as the anniversary of the martyrdom of Guru Arjan. These special days are usually marked by processions carrying the Guru Granth Sahib through the city or town, accompanied by the singing of kirtan.

Sikh Rites of Passage

Birth and Name Giving

Sikhs regard children as a gift from Akal Purakh. When a child is born, the family will visit their local gurdwara, where thanksgiving prayers are said for the child. By randomly opening the Guru Granth Sahib, it is in effect "consulted," and the first initial of the first word on the left-hand page is used by the parents to choose the child's name. Names of girls are followed by the second name Kaur and boys are additionally given the name Singh.

In very devout Sikh families, the baby will be given *amrit*, a nectar made by dissolving sugar in water and stirring it with a kirpan. A drop of *amrit* is then carefully placed on the baby's tongue with the tip of the kirpan; the mother of the baby then drinks the rest of the sanctified water.

Patriarchy

By and large, Indian family systems, including those of Punjabi Sikhs, are highly patriarchal. The valuing of sons over daughters is generally the norm, for it is the son who carries on the family name, receives the family inheritance, and, importantly, performs the final funeral rites of his parents. For these reasons, the birth of a son is surrounded by a great deal of excitement and rejoicing, while the birth of a daughter is a much quieter affair. The January festival of Lohri, though not explicitly a Sikh festival, is one that many Sikhs take part in to rejoice the birth of sons. Though rare, in some instances the birth of girls has been included in Lohri celebrations as well (Kalsi 2004, 92).

A disturbing aspect of Punjabi Sikh society, as in much of South Asian society as a whole, is a clear imbalance in the male–female sex ratio, with males constituting a far greater number in the overall Sikh populace. Historically the practice of female infanticide was prevalent among certain Sikh castes. Today's sophisticated technology allows for using abortion as a sex-selection procedure, which has ensured that males significantly outnumber females within Punjab.

Turban Tying

The turban is understood as an essential aspect of male Sikh identity, though not specifically one of the five ks. The length of a turban varies from five to six metres, and in some families a special turban-tying ceremony takes place. There is no specific age for this ceremony. Families meet either in the gurdwara or at home, but always in the presence of the Guru Granth Sahib, before which prayers are said, accompanied by specific hymns. Parents and friends then give gifts to the young son. There is no similar rite of passage for girls within Sikh society. A fairly recent development among a small number of females in the diaspora has seen young women also choosing to wear a turban.

Marriage Practices and Rituals

For Sikhs, following the example of their Gurus, the life of the householder is the ideal and the foundation of Sikh society. Guru Nanak and the majority of subsequent Gurus were married and had children; in doing so, the Sikh Gurus rejected celibacy as an ideal. Sikhs today are expected to marry and have children to continue the family line. They are also required to marry other Sikhs, and this is particularly the case for Sikh women.

As in most Indian family systems, the joint family is the norm for Sikhs. If you speak to your Sikh peers or friends about their marriage practices, you will discover that often members of the wider family unit are very involved in finding a suitable marriage partner. Arranged marriages take the value systems of both families into consideration when young adults reach a suitable age, generally after their education is completed. Sikh society is firmly endogamous—that is, one must marry within one's own caste group—but it also follows rules of exogamy—marrying outside one's immediate village and sub-caste.

Tradition maintains that the eldest sibling, particularly among females, is married before her younger sisters. While historically marriages often took place without the spouses even meeting before their wedding date, today couples meet beforehand and increasingly have a say in the choice of a marriage partner. Dating is generally not approved of, but couples may meet and get to know one another in the company of relatives. Often the issue of dowry, or bride price, must also be taken into consideration, despite many attempts to curb the practice. Dowry debt historically has been high in Punjab, and it continues to constrain many families as they struggle to pay back debts incurred to ensure that their daughter is well placed and well received into her new family.

The marriage ceremony, called Anand Karaj, begins as normal congregational worship. After the initial morning hymn has been sung, the groom arrives, kneels before the Guru Granth Sahib, and then sits down cross-legged facing the sacred scripture. The bride, with her attendants, follows the same pattern, sitting to the left of the groom. The granthi then gives a brief sermon on the importance of marriage within Sikhism. Marriage is understood as a union of souls, similar to the spiritual journey or union of an individual with Akal Purakh. The bride and groom then make a public statement accepting these ideals by bowing before the Guru Granth Sahib. The marriage ritual begins with the bride's father coming forward to symbolically join the couple by placing the hem of the groom's shoulder scarf in the bride's hand.

While the first stanza of the wedding hymn is sung by the ragis (musicians), the groom leads his bride slowly around the Guru Granth Sahib in a clockwise direction, then the couple kneels before the Guru Granth Sahib. This takes place four times, once for each stanza of the hymn. After the service the congregation is offered *karah prashad*, which formally concludes the religious portion of the marriage.

The couple then departs for either for the bride's home or a marriage hall for a reception, after which they will leave for the groom's home, where his extended family will be waiting to welcome its newest member. In keeping with Sikh and Indian tradition in general, the bride will spend the rest of her life in her husband's family home. While in some cases this practice is changing because of weakening of the

Lavan Hymn

This hymn, written by Guru Ram Das, is sung to solemnize Sikh weddings while the bride and groom circumambulate the Guru Granth Sahib:

In the first round of the marriage ceremony, the Lord sets out His Instructions for performing the daily duties of married life.
Instead of the hymns of the Vedas to Brahma, embrace the righteous conduct of Dharma, and renounce sinful actions.
Meditate on the Lord's Name; embrace and enshrine the contemplative remembrance of the Naam.
Worship and adore the Guru, the Perfect True Guru, and all your sinful residues shall be dispelled.
By great good fortune, celestial bliss is attained, and the Lord, Har, Har, seems sweet to the mind.
Servant Nanak proclaims that, in this, the first round of the marriage ceremony, the marriage ceremony has begun.
In the second round of the marriage ceremony, the Lord leads you to meet the True Guru, the Primal Being.
With the Fear of God, the Fearless Lord in the mind, the filth of egotism is eradicated.
In the Fear of God, the Immaculate Lord, sing the Glorious Praises of the Lord, and behold the Lord's Presence before you.
The Lord, the Supreme Soul, is the Lord and Master of the Universe;
He is pervading and permeating everywhere, fully filling all spaces.
Deep within, and outside as well, there is only the One Lord God.
Meeting together, the humble servants of the Lord sing the songs of joy.
Servant Nanak proclaims that, in this, the second round of the marriage ceremony, the

unstruck sound current of the Shabad resounds.
In the third round of the marriage ceremony, the mind is filled with Divine Love.
Meeting with the humble Saints of the Lord, I have found the Lord, by great good fortune.
I have found the Immaculate Lord, and I sing the Glorious Praises of the Lord.
I speak the Word of the Lord's Bani.
By great good fortune, I have found the humble Saints, and I speak the Unspoken Speech of the Lord.
The Name of the Lord, Har, Har, Har, vibrates and resounds within my heart;
Meditating on the Lord, I have realized the destiny inscribed upon my forehead.
Servant Nanak proclaims that, in this, the third round of the marriage ceremony, the mind is filled with Divine Love for the Lord.
In the fourth round of the marriage ceremony, my mind has become peaceful; I have found the Lord.
As Gurmukh, I have met Him, with intuitive ease; the Lord seems so sweet to my mind and body.
The Lord seems so sweet; I am pleasing to my God.
Night and day, I lovingly focus my consciousness on the Lord.
I have obtained my Lord and Master, the fruit of my mind's desires.
The Lord's Name resounds and resonates.
The Lord God, my Lord and Master, blends with His bride, and her heart blossoms forth in the Naam.
Servant Nanak proclaims that, in this, the fourth round of the marriage ceremony, we have found the Eternal Lord God.

Source: Siri Guru Granth Sahib, 773–74. Translation courtesy Sant Singh Khalsa

extended family system in both India and new home-lands, the majority of Sikh families continue to live within joint families.

Family Honour

As already noted, Sikh marriages are generally understood to link two kinship groups rather than two individuals. This has led to a resolute emphasis on the cultural norm of honour (*izzat*) within Sikh society, and Punjabi society at large. Generally associated with notions of honour, especially for women, is modesty. Together, honour and modesty play an important role in maintaining the traditional patriarchal framework of Punjabi society. Loss of honour and modesty has traditionally been viewed as relevant to women's behaviour. Beyond the individual framework, loss of honour represents a loss of family honour, which in turn leads to a decline in the family's social standing in the community. For this reason, regulations surrounding females are generally more stringently upheld than for males within families (Mooney 2010). In extreme and rare cases, women have been killed because their behaviour was perceived as ruining family honour.

Divorce

For Sikhs, marriage is understood as a spiritual union that must be upheld at all costs; the Gurus described this union in mystical terms, as a single soul residing in two bodies. The Sikh Reht Maryada does not mention divorce. When marriage breakdown does occur, because Sikhs have no personal code in Indian law, they (along with Buddhists and Jains) are included in the stipulations for divorce under the Hindu Marriage Act of 1955. Sikhs are thus in a legal position to obtain support in the case of divorce.

Where Sikhs have migrated to other countries, the marriage and divorce laws within each country are followed. While divorce among Sikhs, as in other communities, is on the rise, it is generally understood as dishonourable to both the family system and the community at large. Women generally carry the weight of dishonour associated with divorce, in keeping with the patriarchal norms of Sikh society.

Homosexuality

Homosexual behaviour is generally not condoned within Sikh communities, although the Guru Granth Sahib and the Sikh Reht Maryada do not address this issue at all. In some instances, however, gay and lesbian activist Sikhs, largely in the Sikh diaspora, have interpreted this omission as allowing for the possibility of same-sex unions.

Death Rituals

Death, like birth and marriage, is understood as having a spiritual dimension. Much as for Hinduism, in Sikhism transmigration of the immortal soul (reincarnation) is understood as a movement into another state that is dependent on one's karma, or actions. Sikh doctrine stresses that death represents a transition from a life filled with worldly cares to the possibility of a joyous and ultimate union with the Divine. Sikh funeral rituals focus on this hope for spiritual fulfilment and also stress that in death, as in life, all must submit to the loving will of Vahiguru.

Sikhs practise cremation, which generally takes place on the day of death or as close as possible after death. Tradition maintains that women in the family do not take part in carrying the wooden frame (bier) holding the body or lighting the funeral pyre. They are also prohibited from entering the cremation ground (N. Singh 2000). A complete, continuous reading of Sikh scripture over forty-eight hours then begins, although in many families the reading is done intermittently over ten days. The ashes are collected within a few days of cremation and scattered in a river or the open sea.

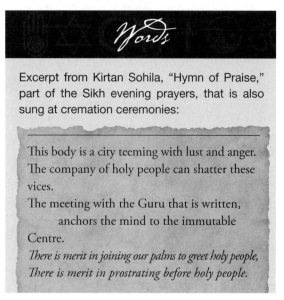

Words

Excerpt from Kirtan Sohila, "Hymn of Praise," part of the Sikh evening prayers, that is also sung at cremation ceremonies:

This body is a city teeming with lust and anger.
The company of holy people can shatter these vices.
The meeting with the Guru that is written,
    anchors the mind to the immutable Centre.
There is merit in joining our palms to greet holy people,
There is merit in prostrating before holy people.

The deluded have not tasted the elixir of love,
    they are pierced by the thorn of ego.
As they move on, the thorn pierces more
painfully,
    till the end where death awaits with staff
poised to strike.
But the devotees steeped in the Name
    are sundered from the suffering of life
and death;
They attain the Everlasting, the Supreme Being,
    and they are honoured in regions far
and beyond.
We are poor and low, but we still belong to You,
    Highest of the high, protect us and keep
us with You.
Nanak says, Your Name alone is my support
and sustenance,
    the Divine name along brings perfect joy.

Source: Siri Guru Granth Sahib, 12–13. Translation courtesy Nikky-Guninder K. Singh

> **Amritdhari Sikh:** a Sikh who has received the sword initiation (also known as *amrit sanskar*) into the Khalsa order.

AUTHORITY

The question of authority within Sikhism is an important one, largely because there is no one organizational hierarchy that applies to all Sikhs living in all parts of the world. It is best then to understand Sikhism as having various layers of authority embedded within it (Kalsi 1995).

Guru Granth Sahib

The Guru Granth Sahib, as the living Guru or living word, is the central scriptural authority for Sikhs. One manifestation of its divine authority takes the form of a divine order whereby a passage from the Guru Granth is chosen at random to guide the daily activities of Sikhs. In the age of the World Wide Web, this divine order emanating from the Harimandir Sahib can be accessed worldwide for all Sikhs to follow.

Administrative Bodies

Alongside the spiritual realms of authority are temporal authoritative structures, the most important known as the Akal Takht, which is adjacent to the Harimandir Sahib in Amritsar. There are four additional *takhts* that are recognized as authoritative and revered by Sikhs, in various parts of Punjab and India. Each *takht* is led by a *jathedar*, a male Sikh whose authority stems from his position as the chief officiate of that particular *takht*.

The Shiromani Gurdwara Parbandhak Committee (SGPC) is an elected administrative body that is in charge of maintaining Sikh gurdwaras and shrines. There has been one instance where a female was elected for a term as President of the SGPC in the 1990s. While it historically played a central role, the SGPC's authority does not actually extend far beyond gurdwaras and shrines in Punjab. Each *sangat,* or local congregation, for the most part acts as an entirely autonomous institution. Elected officials maintain each gurdwara separately, so the *sangat* is responsible for running its own affairs.

Sants

Another form of authority revolves around individual saintly persons, often known as "Sant" or "Baba Ji" (father or elder), who have a following because of their spiritual knowledge. They do not have the same status as a Guru, but some are believed to possess supernatural powers. These individuals exert a great deal of authority over the lives of their followers, both in India and in overseas Sikh communities. In some cases, *sants* lead their own gurdwaras and support beliefs and practices that differ from those of mainstream Sikhs.

SIKH IDENTITY

While the majority of Sikhs are not initiated members of the Khalsa order inaugurated by Guru Gobind Singh in 1699, those who have been initiated through the sword ritual are known as **amritdhari** Sikhs. The initiation ritual holds a special place within the religion, and the status of amritdhari is upheld as an ideal for Sikhs. However, only a small minority of Sikhs are amrit-dhari.

Keshdhari Sikh: a Khalsa Sikh who has not received initiation into the order but is recognizable as a Sikh through wearing the five ks, particularly *kes* (uncut hair).

Sahajdhari Sikh: a Sikh who is not a Khalsa Sikh, does not wear all of the five ks, and typically cuts his or her hair.

In India most Sikhs are **keshdharis**, which literally means "ones who wear hair." Keshdharis are Khalsa Sikhs in that they follow the injunctions of the tenth Guru in terms of the standard code of Sikh discipline, especially the rules of uncut hair and the rest of the five ks, but are not formally initiated into the Khalsa order.

Many Sikhs who do not follow the five ks, especially with regard to cutting their hair, but still profess to be Sikh call themselves **sahajdhari** Sikhs. *Sahajdhari* is often translated as "slow adopter" and generally refers to someone who, while still sporting short hair, is in the process of one day becoming a Khalsa Sikh. This notion of "slow adopter" is in some ways misleading and includes a value-judgement, as many Sikhs who cut their hair have no intention of being initiated into the Khalsa order.

Most Sikh families will include both Khalsa and non-Khalsa members. An amritdhari Sikh who subsequently cuts his or her hair is known as an apostate. Once wrongdoings have been confessed, an apostate will be assigned penance and can then be reinitiated into the Khalsa order (H. McLeod 1997, 207–27).

The Khalsa Initiation Ritual

According to the Sikh Reht Maryada, the Khalsa initiation, *amrit sanskar* (*sanskar* means "life-cycle rite"; *amrit* means "nectar")—which is also known as the *khande di pahul* ritual—is open to Sikhs who lead lives of devotion and follow the ideals of the Khalsa. Today both men and women are welcome to take part in this ritual. There are no age limits, but the new initiate must be able to understand the implications of becoming part of the Khalsa order. Before the actual ceremony, each participant must bathe, wash his or her hair, remove all jewellery, and be wearing the five ks. The initiation takes place before an open copy of the Guru Granth Sahib and in the presence of the panj piare (Dharam Parchar Committee). Because the original panj piare were male, females are generally not included in this role.

After a short sermon on the significance of Khalsa initiation, sweetened water (*amrit*) in an iron bowl is stirred with a double-edged sword. A small amount is poured into the cupped hands of the initiates and drunk and then *amrit* is sprinkled five times on the eyes and hair of the initiate. The greeting "*Vahiguruji ka Khalsa. Vahiguruji ki fateh!*" is joyously called out ("Hail to the Guru's Khalsa. Hail to the Guru's Victory!"). The creedal statement—the Mul Mantra—is chanted and a brief sermon on the Sikh code of conduct follows. New names may be chosen from the Guru Granth Sahib and will include *Singh* for men and *Kaur* for women. The ceremony concludes with distribution of *karah prashad*.

The Khalsa initiation ritual abounds with symbols of equality for Sikhs. In the drinking of sweetened water and the eating of sanctified food from one bowl, the egalitarian ideals of the Sikhs are clearly being put into practice. While it stresses the importance of the Khalsa ideal, the definition of a Sikh according to the Sikh Reht Maryada is highly inclusive. It states that anyone who has faith in the One, the ten Gurus and their teachings, and the primacy of the Guru Granth Sahib, and does not adhere to any other religion, is a Sikh. It does continue, however, by saying that a Sikh is one who believes in the necessity and importance of initiation into the Khalsa. While attempts have been made to limit the definition of *Sikh* to one who follows the Khalsa order, the current definition continues to prevail, and this has allowed for diverse expressions of Sikh identity.

Caste and Sikhism

The issue of caste is problematic for many Sikhs. Very often, if you were to ask a Sikh friend or colleague about this issue, she or he would insist that the Sikh Gurus abolished caste. And clearly the Gurus did reject caste as an impediment to liberation, insisting in their hymns that Akal Purakh's love was accessible to all of humanity. A number of ritual practices, such as the Khalsa initiation rite, as well as practices such as langar (the communal meal), confirm this rejection. Yet caste is still firmly enmeshed in Sikh society as a social order or convention, something that the Sikh Gurus also seemed to sanction: all the Gurus and their offspring married within the Khatri caste, and thus in accordance with the caste regulations surrounding traditional Indian marriage customs. In other words,

the Sikh Gurus opposed the spiritual ramifications of upholding caste but appeared to accept it as a form of societal classification within their own social system (H. McLeod 1997, 230).

In India in general, caste is associated with religious and local boundaries as well as having tribal and occupational origins. The rules and social customs associated with each caste—of which there are many—allow for each individual, family, or group to be situated in some way within the caste hierarchy. How that caste hierarchy is assembled may vary from state to state or region to region.

For the majority of Sikhs today, family life is based upon important kinship and caste relationships. Every individual is a member of a larger joint family unit which is then divided into caste and sub-caste groupings. Most Sikhs take on the name of their sub-caste. As noted earlier, the majority of Sikhs today marry within their caste but outside their sub-caste, which is often associated with their village of origin. One of the reasons for marrying outside one's community has to do with rules of inheritance, which for the largely agrarian Sikh populace are tied to land ownership. This ensures that ancestral land need not be further subdivided. Descent is always patrilineal and inheritance is always through the male line; female Sikhs are generally understood as entering their husband's family in terms of inheritance laws. "Marrying outside" is also a way to ensure that marriages do not take place too close within a blood line.

Although historically and hierarchically classified as a low peasant caste, the dominant group in terms of numbers and power in Sikh society today is the Jat caste. However, the Khatri caste, the lineage of the Sikh Gurus, though relatively small in terms of numbers, continues to occupy an important place within Sikh society. Ramgarhias form another important Sikh caste group. There are also Sikhs who fall within that larger classification known as Dalits (previously called "untouchables") or who do not fulfil even the minimum requirements for fitting into the caste system. These Sikhs are known as Mazhabi or Ravidasi Sikhs. Dalits, whether Sikh, Hindu, Muslim, or Christian, experience the worst prejudices associated with the caste system and in some cases are not even welcome to enter traditional centres of worship (Pettigrew 1975, 44). They typically work as sweepers or leatherworkers, occupations traditionally associated with

pollution and impurity. Intermarriage between Sikh castes is rare, and virtually unthinkable between upper castes and Dalits.

DIVERSITY IN SIKHISM

There have been differences within Sikh identity and in Sikh loyalties since the time of the living Gurus (Takhar 2005). These differences in identity have largely been downplayed: Khalsa Sikhs have been successful at presenting their own tradition as the only authentic expression of what constitutes Sikhism. The term *sect* is often applied to Sikhs who operate outside mainstream Sikhism, but the word is viewed as pejorative by the Sikhs in these different systems. Other terms such as *orthodox* and *unorthodox* are also problematic. For this reason, the term *Sikh groups* is utilized here instead. While there are many groups within Sikhism, only a small number are described below.

Namdhari and Nirankari Sikhs

Two historically important groups within Sikhism are the Nirankari and Namdhari Sikhs. They were originally part of Sikh reform movements stemming from the mid-nineteenth century, and were forerunners of the Singh Sabha reformers. The Nirankaris are followers of Baba Dayal (1783–1855), a Sikh reformer who criticized many of the practices followed by Sikhs after the time of Maharajah Ranjit Singh. Baba Dayal believed that Sikhs had lost their moorings in the disciplinary practice of nam-simran and were instead far too focused on acquiring political stature and wealth. Baba Dayal did not emphasize the Khalsa form of Sikhism.

Some of the reforms introduced by the Nirankaris, such as the *anand karaj* marriage ritual (earlier Sikhs were married according to Hindu rites), have been assimilated into the mainstream community. Another important, though divisive, practice is that the Nirankaris uphold a lineage of living gurus—one that goes beyond the ten Sikh Gurus—continuing through the successors of Baba Dayal. For many mainstream Sikhs, a living guru lineage is anathema and contradictory to the message of Guru Gobind Singh, who installed the Guru Granth Sahib as the sole and eternal Guru of the Sikhs.

The Namdharis are another group that played an important role in Sikh history. Another name for Namdharis is Kuka Sikhs, *kuk* or "shriek" deriving from their loud, ecstatic cries during some of their rituals. Namdharis emphasize the practice of nam-simran. Where they differ from the Nirankaris is that they believe the Guru lineage continued in an unbroken line from the time of Guru Gobind Singh. Namdharis believe that Guru Gobind Singh did not die in 1708 but continued to live anonymously for some time. The Guru is then believed to have passed his mantle on to Balak Singh, the founder of the Namdharis. They also differ from the Nirankaris in that they wholeheartedly support the Khalsa identity. They see themselves as adhering to a purified form, however, which is reflected in their own code of conduct.

Namdharis are easily recognizable among Sikhs in that they dress in all-white Punjabi clothing. They are strict vegetarians and are vehemently against consumption of alcohol, thus also differing from the majority of Sikhs. Further, they solemnize marriages by circumambulating around fire, thus conforming to Sikh marriage practices before the changes introduced by the Nirankaris and later adapted by the Singh Sabha reformers. Another important contribution of the Namdharis was that historically they initiated both men and women into the Khalsa, a practice that was not put in place among mainstream Sikhs until the time of the Singh Sabha movement. Namdharis played a central role in the struggle against British rule in India, and in their practices they foreshadowed a number of the initiatives of Mahatma Gandhi, who later became the primary spokesperson against the British. Though historically important, their numbers have been dwindling in the twenty-first century.

Akand Kirtani Jatha

Akand Kirtani Jatha, also known as the AKJ, is a group that followed the leadership of a pious Sikh named Bhai Randhir Singh (1878–1961). The AKJ is known for its rigorous Khalsa discipline, strict vegetarianism, and unique forms of kirtan, especially its all-night performance. Another feature of the AKJ is the practice of disciplined rapid repetition of the word *Vahiguru* ("Wonderful Sovereign") as a meditative technique. Akand Kirtani Jatha interprets the five ks differently from mainstream Sikhism, insisting that one of them is *keski* (a small underturban) instead of *kesh* (hair), since hair is part of a person's

natural condition. In contrast to mainstream Sikhs, both men and women must wear the *keski*. Akhand Kirtani Jatha devotees also follow their own distinctive code of conduct (H. McLeod 1997, 199–201).

Sikh Dharma of the Western Hemisphere (3HO Sikhs)

In the 1960s, a Punjabi Sikh customs official named Harbhajan Singh Puri (1929–2004) arrived in California after initially settling for a short while in Canada. Within a few years he had changed his name to Yogi Bhajan and founded an ashram for his organization, the 3HO, or Healthy, Happy, Holy Organization. His followers were almost exclusively white, middle-class, counterculture seekers longing for insight into the ancient spiritual wisdom of India. Yogi Bhajan offered his students a unique blend of Eastern and Western ideas and lifestyles, especially focusing on kundalini yoga and healthy living practices. He taught that through a rigorous routine of meditation, dormant energy (*kundalini*) resting at the base of the spine could ascend through centres called *chakras* and, upon reaching the top of the head, climax and enter union with the inner Divine. Devotees were known as yogis and yoginis, and initially they had little connection to Sikhism.

Over time, Sikh tenets were introduced, and in 1973 the group was officially registered as Sikh Dharma of the Western Hemisphere (alternatively, 3HO). Yogi Bhajan changed his name again, to Siri Singh Sahib Bhai Sahib Harbhajan Singh Khalsa Yogiji.

Members of the group see themselves as full-fledged Sikhs and strictly follow the Sikh Reht Maryada, despite introducing a number of significant changes. All members, male or female, take on the name Khalsa with their new Sikh names and wear all-white Punjabi clothes and white turbans. They have an ordination process for leaders, who are then called ministers (Elsberg 2003, 75).

For the most part, 3HO and Punjabi Sikhs rarely congregate together (Dusenbery 1990, 334–55). Members of the Sikh Dharma of the Western Hemisphere have increasingly learned Punjabi, but unlike the majority of Punjabi Sikh gurdwaras, they also include English for kirtan and sermons. 3HO ragis include instruments such as guitars in their musical accompaniment. 3HO Sikhs are adamant in their belief in the inherent egalitarianism of Sikhism and insist that men and women must play equal roles in all aspects of Sikh religious life. Although the

Sikh Dharma of the Western Hemisphere has remained a small group of perhaps a few thousand adherents, they exert a significant influence on Sikhism in the West, particularly in the United States and Canada. They can best be understood as a Sikh New Religious Movement, given their melding of Eastern and Western ways of living. Yogi Bhajan died in 2004, and it remains to be seen what new directions the 3HO will take without his charismatic leadership (Jakobsh 2008).

Sikhs and Other Religious Practices

Alongside the mainstream religious practices in India, many individuals, especially in rural areas, have beliefs and practices that fall outside their primary religious identity. These beliefs and practices have often been described as part of what has been dismissed as "popular religion," "folk traditions," or, even more pejoratively, "superstition," but aspects of these practices are integral to the lived realities of many Indians, regardless of their dominant religious affiliation. Many of these practices contribute to an understanding of lived religion that is far more diverse than the normative religious traditions generally outlined, and this translates into acknowledgment that issues pertaining to a specific religious identity are not nearly as neat and tidy as often presented in religious studies textbooks.

Within the North Indian context, religious practices that are not purely Muslim, Hindu, Christian, or Sikh are followed by adherents from a variety of religions. These include worshipping relics and ancestors, wearing amulets (which contain special stones believed to have spiritual properties), and placing specific objects around homes to ward off evil spirits (for example, blackened pots perched on rooftops). If you ever travel to India, you may see bunches of chilies fastened to the rear bumpers of trucks, cars, or rickshaws. It is believed that chilies protect those within the vehicle from wayward or evil spirits. They are similar to the good-luck charms worn by many people all over the world.

Such alternative practices do not mean that Sikhs are confused about their primary religious identity, but instead point to a complexity and multiplicity that is in many ways a hallmark of rural Punjabi religion (Bhatti and Michon 2004). However, many of these practices have long been condemned by Sikh religious authorities as anti-Sikh, most particularly in the time of the Singh Sabha during British rule. The fact that these ancient observances continue, especially in rural areas, attests to how deeply they are ingrained in wider Punjabi religious practices.

THE CANADIAN CONTEXT

Any major urban centre in Canada has evidence of Sikhs. Sikhs wearing turbans and the colourful Punjabi outfits known as *salwar kameez*—loose-fitting trousers and long tunics for women—can be found

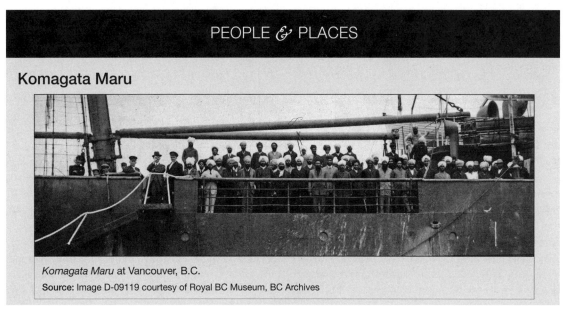

PEOPLE & PLACES

Komagata Maru

Komagata Maru at Vancouver, B.C.
Source: Image D-09119 courtesy of Royal BC Museum, BC Archives

(continued)

The British viceroy in India and the Canadian government did not wish to be perceived as openly discriminatory against Indians, so they did not issue a point-blank restriction on Indian immigrants. However, the Continuous Journey Regulation introduced by Canadian legislators in 1908 effectively halted all immigration from India until after the Second World War (Johnston 1989). Immigration officers had the right to refuse entry to immigrants who arrived in Canada on tickets that had not been booked in their native country. Not applicable to Europeans, this regulation was applied in full force at the Pacific ports of Vancouver and Victoria to stem the tide of Indian immigrants. Another restriction put in place to further limit immigrants from South Asia was that they had to arrive with a minimum of two hundred dollars, in contrast to the fifty dollars required of Europeans entering Canada.

In 1914, *Komagata Maru*, a Japanese ship, was chartered in Hong Kong to carry 376 Indians, 340 of whom were Sikh, who wished to immigrate to Canada. When the ship arrived in Vancouver, except for twenty returning residents of Canada, immigration officials refused to allow the passengers to disembark. The Continuous Journey Regulation stipulated that all people entering Canada were required to have travelled non-stop from their country of origin; of course, continuous travel from India to Canada was simply not possible at the time. The passengers argued that, since they were British subjects, the two-hundred-dollar entry fee did not apply. Moreover, as subjects of the British Crown, they believed they had the right to travel without restriction throughout the British empire.

As the courts set about deciding the passengers' fate through that summer, local Sikhs raised funds to finance their legal costs and provided the basic necessities for the passengers. Despite their generosity, at times the situation on *Komagata Maru* became dire: they completely ran out of water and food. After numerous legal battles, the British Columbia Court of Appeal, with the blessing of the government of Canada, supported the Immigration Department's initial decision. After sitting in Vancouver Harbour for more than two months, *Komagata Maru* and its passengers were escorted out of Canadian waters by the former Royal Navy ship *Rainbow*.

Some of the passengers on board *Komagata Maru* were sympathizers of the Ghadr Party, a revolutionary movement that advocated overthrow of the British in India. Further, some members of the shore committee that organized on behalf of the passengers were actually involved in Ghadr Party initiatives. Canadian officials were aware of these connections, and this provided them with additional reasons not to allow these passengers to disembark on Canadian soil. Upon arriving in India, these passengers were again detained. When skirmishes broke out between them and the police, a number of them were killed. The Ghadr rebellion was soon put down by the British, and some of the party's members were executed.

The *Komagata Maru* incident plays a significant role in the collective memory of Sikhs in Canada. In 1994 a plaque commemorating the eightieth anniversary of the incident was installed at Vancouver Harbour by the City of Vancouver. In 2008 the prime minister issued a long sought-after apology for the overtly discriminatory actions of the Canadian government.

in cities and towns across Canada. Punjabi cuisine is widely available in most urban centres, and Sikh gurdwaras dot the Canadian landscape. There are more than 300 000 Sikhs in Canada today. It is believed that their earliest presence in Canada was in 1897, when the Sikh Lancers and Infantry Regiment visited Vancouver after celebrating Queen Victoria's Diamond Jubilee. In 1997, in celebration of the centennial year of Sikhs arriving in Canada, pins and T-shirts could be seen sporting an intertwined symbol of the *khanda* (double-edged sword) and the Canadian maple leaf to honour Sikh contributions to Canadian society.

Sikhs in Canadian History

In 1904 a group of about thirty Punjabi immigrants arrived in Canada to work in the lumber industry in British Columbia. Although the majority of the new immigrants were Sikhs from Punjab, they were falsely identified as "Hindoos," a term that was used to identify all immigrants of Indian origin. However, Punjabi Sikhs at the beginning of the twentieth century were not nearly as concerned about clear-cut distinctions between Sikhs and Hindus as many became in the coming years. During the first decade of the twentieth century, about five thousand Indian men, most of whom were Sikh, entered Canada. These South Asian immigrants faced a great deal of discrimination during the early years after their arrival in Canada. They could not vote and had difficulty getting access to housing, education, and public services. Canada was increasingly being understood as a "white man's country," with official government policies and less formal discriminatory attitudes effectively discouraging non-white individuals from calling Canada home. By 1911 many South Asians had returned to India or had moved to California, where a larger group of Indian immigrants lived. By 1921 just over a thousand Indian immigrants remained in Canada.

The vast majority of early Sikh immigrants were males who had left their families behind in Punjab. The 1911 census shows that there were only three South Asian women out of a total of about two thousand. These initial immigrants often sponsored other male relatives in an effective pattern of chain migration. Given the overtly discriminatory attitudes toward them of their fellow Canadians, as well as deeply held cultural and religious values that discouraged marriage outside their racial, ethnic, and religious boundaries, very few Sikhs intermarried with the broader Canadian society. Most saw themselves as settling in Canada for the short term only and then, upon acquiring sufficient wealth, returning to India. Eventually, however, a number of early Sikh migrants brought over their wives and children as thoughts of a permanent return to Punjab began to fade against the increasing opportunities in their new country of residence.

After the Second World War and India's independence in 1947, Canada's doors once again opened to Indian immigrants. With new policies in place to select newcomers based on level of education and job qualifications, different classes began arriving in Canada. While these policy changes applied to all immigrants from India, Sikhs figured prominently among the newcomers. Unlike the earliest Sikh labourers, who settled in small towns in British Columbia that offered agricultural and forestry job opportunities, this new wave of immigrants was largely urban professionals; they settled in the major cities, especially Toronto, Montreal, and Calgary (Johnston, "Sikhs").

The most recent wave of Sikh immigration to Canada took place in the 1980s and 1990s, after deepening conflict between the Indian government and a small number of Sikh separatists intent on establishing a sovereign Sikh state called Khalistan. Many Sikhs at that time, realizing their fragile position as a tiny minority in India, decided to immigrate to other parts of the world. These included separatists who became asylum-seekers in Canada.

Sikh Gurdwaras in Canada

The first wave of Sikh immigrants arrived in 1904, which was also the year that the first Guru Granth Sahib was brought to Canada; it was housed in a home in Port Moody, British Columbia. The first gurdwara built in Canada was the Vancouver Sikh Temple in 1908, and by 1920 there were at least seven other gurdwaras in British Columbia. Today many gurdwaras dot the Canadian landscape. While there have been attempts to bring them all under a unitary national religious organization, these attempts have thus far failed. Gurdwaras exist as independent entities, each controlled and managed by an elected executive board. The number of gurdwaras is increasing yearly in the major cities that are home to the greatest numbers of Sikhs.

Canadian Sikh gurdwaras play important roles beyond that of communal worship. They serve as community centres, teach Punjabi language and religious education, and are meeting places for elderly Sikhs, women's groups, and youth groups. Some gurdwaras have built adjacent gymnasiums to support sports activities. They also contribute to the Canadian health system by offering their facilities as blood donor clinics.

One important issue that is increasingly taking centre stage in many South Asian centres of worship in Canada has to do with language. Many second- and third-generation Sikhs cannot speak Punjabi or read the Gurmukhi script, and they are increasingly opting out of attending services at gurdwaras. Some gurdwaras are attempting to reach out to youth by including English translations of the hymns, which are projected onto screens in front of the congregation.

Gurdwara Politics

Given the very real discrimination early Sikh immigrants faced upon arrival in Canada, many of them made attempts to blend into Canadian society. Most wore Western clothes and many began cutting their hair and rejecting other parts of the Khalsa Sikh identity. With the arrival of new immigrants after the Second World War, many of these practices were challenged. The 1950s witnessed the first split within the Canadian Sikh community. While most gurdwaras had consisted largely of clean-shaven Sikhs, newly arrived members began to argue that gurdwara management committees should be restricted to Sikhs who followed the Khalsa form.

These divisions intensified with the heavy immigration of the late 1960s and 1970s. Many of the new immigrants from India were keshdari Sikhs who viewed the practices of earlier Sikh immigrants as far too lax. For example, many members had long been entering their gurdwara bare-headed, something that would be considered highly disrespectful in India (Johnston 2004, 1080). In some gurdwaras, langar was being served on tables with chairs, instead of on the floor, which proved to be a point of great contention for many Sikhs. Moreover, during the radicalized time of the Punjab disturbances in the 1980s, many new immigrants had brought with them their political perspectives and dreams of a separate state of Khalistan. Conflicts between Sikhs became increasingly tense, even within gurdwaras, at times breaking out in violence. The Canadian media began to focus on these confrontations, and the negative publicity led to Sikhs in Canada becoming less known for their peaceful spiritual practices than for the political battles waged in gurdwaras by a small minority.

Sikh Attitudes to Gender and Caste

Many second- and third-generation Sikhs have been raised with the belief that Sikhism is at its core an egalitarian religion, yet they are faced with very different realities, especially when it comes to marriage and caste observance, as well as gender inequality in both their homes and their gurdwaras. Perceiving any form of discrimination within Sikh society as hypocritical and anti-Sikh, some Canadian Sikhs

are making efforts to confront various instances of gender and caste bias within gurdwaras.

Some of the discriminatory attitudes toward women stem from ancient Indian prohibitions regarding impurity or pollution associated with women's menstrual cycles, despite the Gurus' exhorting their followers not to perceive anything in Akal Purakh's creation as having an inherent ability to pollute. These and other attitudes are increasingly being challenged by Sikhs who have been raised to believe that their religion is unparalleled in terms of its egalitarian principles, with regard to both gender and caste. For example, Sikh women from overseas communities, including Canada, have challenged discriminatory practices even within the Harimandir Sahib (Jakobsh 2006a).

Marriage and Kinship Patterns in Canada

As in India, family and kinship patterns continue to be important elements of Sikh society in Canada. While changes are taking place in the traditional extended-family patterns in India, they are being especially challenged among immigrant groups outside the homeland, including among Sikhs in Canada. Many Canadian Sikhs live and work within a largely self-contained Punjabi Sikh society (often bound to a particular local gurdwara) that operates within the bounds of traditional Sikh and Punjabi value systems. For many Sikhs, notions of *izzat* (honour) and other fraternity rules, especially with regard to family prestige and status, continue to be effective family and kinship and caste group control mechanisms. For the majority there is a strong emphasis on living within the bounds of expected behaviour and ensuring that actions taken are beyond reproach with regard to keeping up the good name of family and kinship and caste group.

Arranged marriages or, as they are sometimes called today, assisted or guided marriages, continue to be the norm in Canadian Sikh families. But while families are still heavily involved in their children's marital choices, the suggestions and preferences of the prospective bride and groom play an increasingly large role in the search for a suitable partner. Some Sikh families turn to their homeland to find a suitable mate for their children, especially for their sons (Walton-Roberts 2004, 366–67). Young Sikh women from India are often perceived as less tainted by "loose" Western societal norms and more able to ensure that the Canadian family's *izzat* is upheld. What are known as "love marriages" are also on the increase within the Sikh community, especially in cases where Sikh youth leave the extended-family home to work elsewhere or for post-secondary education and take upon themselves the responsibility of finding a marriage partner.

Words

Feminism and Sikhism

A small number of feminist scholars of religion have begun examining Sikhism and Sikh scripture through a feminist lens (Jakobsh 2003; N. Singh 1993). Here is a traditional translation of an excerpt from the first page of the Adi Granth and a recent translation of the same verses by Nikky-Guninder Kaur Singh, who stresses the need to move beyond traditional male-dominated images and terms in Sikh scripture. You will notice that the pronoun *he* is conspicuously absent in the second translation.

Translation 1

By thinking, He cannot be reduced to thought, even by thinking hundreds of thousands of times. By remaining silent, inner silence is not obtained, even by remaining lovingly absorbed deep within. The hunger of the hungry is not appeased, even by piling up loads of worldly goods. Hundreds of thousands of clever tricks, but not even one of them will go along with you in the end. So how can you become truthful? And how can the veil of illusion be torn away? O Nanak, it is written that you shall obey the Hukam of His Command, and walk in the Way of His Will.

Source: Siri Guru Granth Sahib, 1.

Translation 2

Thought cannot think,
nor can a million thoughts.
Silence cannot silence,
nor can seamless contemplation.
Greed is not made greedless,
not by the wealth of all the world.
Though a thousand mental feats become a million,
not one can go with us.
How then to be true?
How then to break the wall of lies?
By following the Will.
Says Nanak, this is written for us.

Source: Adi Granth, 1. Translation courtesy Nikky-Guninder K. Singh

Khalsa Schools and Gurmat Camps

Another important development in Canada, as well as in other countries where large numbers of Sikh reside, is independent schools specifically designed to fit the needs of Sikh children. Khalsa schools are funded either exclusively through private money raised by Sikhs or through a combination of private and public funding available to faith-based schools in some provinces. While the number of Sikhs attending these schools has remained small, they offer Sikh children a religion-based education, Punjabi language training, and Sikh martial arts, while at the same time following the provincial ministry's curriculum guidelines.

Other important initiatives among Sikhs are the growing number of camps for children, youth, and women organized by Sikh *sangats* throughout Canada. These are often known as *gurmat* camps, in reference to the teachings of the Gurus. Many of these camps are based in local gurdwaras.

Practices

Sikhs and the Courts

Many important legal battles have been fought in Canadian courts to win Khalsa Sikhs the right to maintain their external Sikh identity markers. Following practices adopted by the army and police long ago in India, in 1986 the Metropolitan Toronto Police began to allow Sikh officers to wear their turbans as part of their uniform. Another important case involved a Sikh officer in the Royal Canadian Mounted Police (RCMP). Some Canadians felt that the turban, as an accompaniment to the religious symbolism of uncut hair, should not overshadow the time-honoured and distinctive dress uniform of the RCMP. Canadian law, however, deemed the religious right of Sikh RCMP officers to wear turbans as overriding any historical or cultural norms. In 1991 Baltej Singh Dhillon became the first Sikh RCMP officer in Canada to proudly serve his country while wearing a turban.

Other court cases involved Sikh parents, students, and school boards when children were prohibited from bringing specific Sikh insignia such as the kirpan (dagger) onto school property. Many non-Sikhs understand the kirpan to be a weapon and not just a religious symbol (Stoker 2007, 814–39). In Ontario the issue came to a head between the Peel County Board of Education and the local Sikh community. In 1990 the Ontario Human Rights Commission ruled that while Sikh students and teachers could wear the kirpan, it had to be securely fastened inside their clothing and could not be longer than 7 inches (18 centimetres) in length. In 2006 the Supreme Court of Canada overruled a Montreal school board's ruling, which had been backed by the Quebec government, banning a Sikh student from wearing his kirpan to school. The Supreme Court did, however, establish some restrictions, namely that the kirpan had to be sheathed and worn underneath clothes (Johnston 2004, 1080).

Sikhs and 9/11

The time immediately following the events of 9/11 ushered in a new era for Sikhs in North America. In the United States, the first casualty of the distrust of all foreigners was a Sikh, mistakenly identified as a follower of Osama bin Laden because of his turban. North American Sikhs once again realized they were in a precarious situation and, fearing a continued backlash against their community, began a successful campaign to educate the general public about Sikhism. Post-9/11 has seen a proliferation of organizations operating within the domain of "Sikh rights." Though largely centred in the United States, groups such as SALDEF (Sikh American Legal Defense and Educational Fund), the Sikh Coalition, and United Sikhs may be found advocating for Sikhs beyond North America as well.

Sikhs and Politics

Sikhs are becoming increasingly involved in Canadian politics, on both the provincial and federal levels. In 2000 Ujjal Dosanjh became the first Sikh to reach the highest level of provincial politics, when he became the thirty-third premier of British Columbia. Another Sikh, Herb (Harbance Singh) Dhaliwal, was the first Sikh to serve as a Cabinet minister in federal politics. Many Sikhs understand religion and secular politics to be inseparable.

SIKHISM AND THE INTERNET

Scholars of religion are increasingly paying attention to the significance of the World Wide Web in the study of religion. Sikhs, along with other religious communities, have embraced this technology and are using it as a useful learning tool and resource. Specific hymns or verses from Sikh scripture can be found using sophisticated search engines, and Sikh baby names can also be found online. Sites offer online courses in learning to write Gurmukhi along with effective tools for Punjabi language acquisition. Sikhs make extensive use of YouTube and other video- and audio-sharing sites to broadcast kirtan, share turban-tying techniques, and publicize *gatka* (martial arts) events. Maps pinpointing ancestral villages can be posted, and daily communication can take place between family members in rural Punjab and in metropolitan cities in Canada and elsewhere. The worldwide Sikh community has never in its history been so connected through mass communication, nor has there ever been as much information so readily available to anyone interested in learning about the Sikh tradition.

Scholars who focus on religion and the Internet have looked at the various ways in which this new media is changing Sikhism. One effect, as already noted, is that online information on Sikhs is growing in leaps and bounds. While many sites simply reproduce material found elsewhere, others make concerted efforts to post information that offers a novel perspective on a specific issue. Perhaps even more important is the issue of who speaks for Sikhs online. The Internet is the ultimate democratic tool for those who have the resources necessary. Anyone who has the technological expertise to construct a website focusing on Sikhism can do so. And certainly if one peruses the most popular sites on Sikhism in particular, one realizes that they are not the handiwork of scholars in Sikh studies, nor are they associated with the traditional religious authority structures. While there are indeed official sites for the SGPC, the Harimandir Sahib, the Akal Takht, and various gurdwara managements around the world, it becomes quickly evident that many of these sites lack the sophistication, reliability, and ease of interchange foung in those constructed by deeply engaged Sikhs outside the bounds of traditional authority (Jakobsh 2006b).

Moreover, the majority of the most sophisticated sites on Sikhism originate outside India, dominated by webmasters in the United States, Canada, and the United Kingdom who view their online work as a useful service (*seva*) to the Sikh community. They have become in some ways the new "authorities" or intermediaries of Sikhism, not because of their great knowledge of things Sikh but because of their expertise in technology. To this they add their own devoted interest in Sikhism. Because of the democratic properties of the Internet, these new authorities are able to take on powerful roles as creators of knowledge and mediators in the online transfer of knowledge about Sikhism.

Often Sikhism is presented through the liberal and humanistic lenses with which these Web creators have been raised outside India. The values of the vast majority of Sikhs who live in rural Punjab, many of whom are illiterate and who adhere to practices and attitudes considered superstitious or "un-Sikh," are generally not acknowledged by online presentations of Sikh tradition. In many ways, then, attempts are being made to present a far more homogeneous tradition that is more in line with the liberal, humanistic values of the host country than actually exists within the Sikh homeland. This issue of perspective is becoming increasingly important as more and more people, including university students, turn to the Internet for information about religion in general and about Sikhism in particular.

If one turns to images of Sikhs online, it quickly becomes clear that the forces of homo-genization are at work. For example, while outside Punjab—and increasingly within the region—the majority of Sikhs do not wear turbans, the majority of pictures posted online are of turbaned Sikhs. The issue becomes even more startling when one looks up images of Sikh women: turbaned women quickly come to the fore, despite the fact that only a minuscule number of women in the Sikh diaspora wear turbans and even fewer do so in Punjab. Moreover, many of these most easily accessible images show white Sikh women in turbans, who are largely converts to Sikhism through 3HO. While this group's numbers are small—likely less than a few thousand among a total of roughly twenty-three million Sikhs worldwide—they appear to be playing an increasingly significant role in defining Sikhism, using their websites and their excellent communication skills. They have become important spokespersons for the Sikh religion online, despite their small numbers and unique practices, which many Punjabi Sikhs in fact reject.

The Internet has also become an important religious space for young Sikhs who, perhaps as a result of generational differences or because of highly publicized negative gurdwara politics, choose not to attend local gurdwaras. Many youths have turned to the Internet to learn about Sikhism. Others use virtual space, often anonymously, to express their dissatisfaction with how Sikhism is being interpreted or practised within their local communities. Frank online discussions of taboo subjects generally not addressed within traditional Sikh homes or gurdwaras, including homosexuality, abortion, dating, and domestic abuse, are utilized by young Sikhs to make sense of what may appear to be clashes between the two cultures they live in, between their minority Punjabi culture and dominant Western values.

CONCLUSION

The Sikh tradition has in a relatively short time moved from being a little-known and scarcely understood regional religion of Punjab, India, to an expanding and continuously developing tradition with adherents who can be found in virtually all parts of the globe. As a result, gurdwaras have become familiar sights in far-flung cities and towns worldwide. Within centres of higher learning, Sikh studies is an exciting field of inquiry, and a number of universities in North America, through individual or community donations, have established chairs in Sikhism that lead to graduate degrees in Sikh studies. Moreover, Sikhism, as with other religious traditions, has bene-fitted greatly from revolutionary changes in communication and globalization, although it has also been challenged by these same forces. Traditional attitudes rooted within Punjabi Sikh culture are being eroded as ties to the homeland continue to diminish while increasingly diverse value systems challenge many of those same traditional assumptions and ideologies. Many Sikhs of the diaspora are no longer literate in Punjabi, the language of the Guru Granth Sahib, and, given the language barrier, are less inclined to frequent gurdwaras. Nonetheless, Sikhs have proved to be remarkably resilient when it comes to change. The timeless truths found in the Eternal Guru, the Guru Granth Sahib, continue to stand as the foundation that informs, sustains, and inspires Sikhs worldwide.

KEY TERMS

Akal Purakh, p. 120
Akal Takht, p. 126
Amritdhari Sikh, p. 141
Dasam Granth, p. 123
Five ks, p. 129
Granthi, p. 119
Gurmukhi, p. 122
Guru Granth Sahib, p. 119
Harimandir Sahib, p. 126
Janam-sakhis, p. 123
Kaur, p. 133
Keshdhari Sikhs, p. 142

Khalsa, p. 128
Khande di pahul, p. 128
Kirtan, p. 119
Kurahits, p. 129
Langar, p. 126
Nam-simran, p. 120
Nishan Sahib, p. 134
Panj piare, p. 128
Sahajdhari Sikhs, p. 142
Sikh Reht Maryada, p. 123
Singh, p. 128
Singh Sabha, p. 133
Vahiguru, p. 120

CRITICAL THINKING QUESTIONS

1. The development of the Sikh tradition took place within the context of Hinduism and Islam. How have these traditions influenced Sikhism?

2. Sikhs believe that while each Guru responded to changing circumstances, the core of Sikhism remained the same. Describe the significant events that led to major changes in the Sikh tradition's development. What has remained consistent during its development?

3. Sikhism has been characterized as a militant tradition. Is this true or false? Expand on your conclusions.

4. Sikhs view their tradition as inherently egalitarian in terms of gender and caste. Discuss.

5. What are some major issues facing Sikhs in the diaspora? Comment especially on generational and gender issues.

6. Discuss the role of the Internet within the context of Sikhism in the twenty-first century.

RECOMMENDED READING

Bains, Tara Singh, and Johnston, Hugh. *The Four Quarters of the Night: The Life Journey of an Emigrant Sikh.* Montreal: McGill-Queen's University Press, 1995.

Ballantyne, Tony, ed. *Textures of the Sikh Past.* Delhi: Oxford University Press, 2007.

Basran, G. S. *The Sikhs in Canada: Migration, Race, Class, and Gender.* Delhi: Oxford University Press, 2003.

Juergensmeyer, Mark. *Terror in the Mind of God: The Global Rise of Religious Violence.* Berkeley: University of California Press, 2000.

Mann, Gurinder Singh. *The Making of Sikh Scripture.* Delhi: Oxford University Press, 2001.

McLeod, W. H., ed. and trans. *Textual Sources for the Study of Sikhism.* Chicago: University of Chicago Press, 1984.

————. *Who Is a Sikh? The Problem of Sikh Identity.* Oxford: Oxford University Press, 1992.

Nayar, Kamala Elizabeth. *The Sikh Diaspora in Vancouver: Three Generations amid Tradition, Modernity and Multiculturalism.* Toronto: University of Toronto Press, 2004.

Shackle, Christopher, and Arvind-pal Singh Mandair. *Teachings of the Sikh Gurus: Selections from the Sikh Scriptures.* New York: Routledge, 2005.

Singh, Khushwant. *A History of the Sikhs*, 2nd ed., 2 vols. Delhi: Oxford University Press, 1999.

Singh, Pashaura. *The Guru Granth Sahib: Canon, Meaning and Authority.* Delhi: Oxford University Press, 2000.

Tatla, Darshan Singh. *The Sikh Diaspora: The Search for Statehood.* Seattle: University of Washington Press, 1999.

RECOMMENDED VIEWING

Continuous Journey. Dir. Ali Kazimi, 2004. The story of *Komagata Maru* and the challenge to Canada's racist immigration laws in 1914.

Runaway Grooms. Dir. Ali Kazimi, 2005. Documentary looking at marriages in the South Asian community in Canada, including Sikhs, and the disturbing trend of men abandoning their brides once the dowry has been collected.

Mistaken Identity: Sikhs in America. Dir. Vinanti Sarkar, 2003. Documentary looking at how the lives of Sikh Americans have changed since 9/11.

Building Faith: Gurdwaras. Prod. Angus Skeene and Catherine Drillis, 2005. Part of a larger documentary series, this episode explores the architecture of Sikhism, with a focus on Sikh gurdwaras in Canada.

My Sikh Wedding. Dir. Iqbal Mahal, 2007. Documentary focusing on *anand karaj*, the Sikh wedding ceremony and rituals, in Canada.

USEFUL WEBSITES

PHILTAR
One of the best scholarly sites on Sikhism, from the University of Cumbria's Department of Religion and Philosophy. PHILTAR stands for "Philosophy, Theology, and Religion."

British Broadcasting Corporation
An excellent comprehensive site on Sikhism.

Ontario Consultants on Religious Tolerance
An important site focusing on all aspects of religion, including controversies within various religious traditions.

Preface to the Sikh Reht Maryada
Offered by the Shiromani Gurdwara Parbandhak Committee (SGPC).

Shiromani Gurdwara Parbandhak Committee and Golden Temple
The SGPC is responsible for maintenance of gurdwaras, including the Harmandir Sahib, or Golden Temple.

Siri Guru Granth Sahib
English translation of the foundational text, endorsed by the SGPC.

Internet Sacred Text Archive: Sikhism
A major online resource that includes links to Max Arthur Macauliffe's *The Sikh Religion*, first published in 1909, and Siri Guru Granth Sahib.

Sikhism Homepage
Created by Canadian Sandeep Singh Brar in 1994, this site is claimed to be the first devoted to Sikhism.

SikhNet
Website of the 3HO/Sikh Dharma of the Western Hemisphere, inaugurated in 1986.

Sikh Missionary Society of the U.K.
This site offers a vast array of resources focusing on Sikhism.

Sikh Heritage site
An important site focusing on Sikh heritage in the broadest sense.

The Encyclopedia of Canada's People: Sikhs in Canada
Simon Fraser University's online version of the encyclopedia originally created by the Multicultural

History Society of Ontario. This site offers the most comprehensive history of Canadian Sikhs, by Dr. Hugh Johnston.

Namdhari Sikh Homepage
Resources related to the Namdhari sect of Sikhism, also known as Kukas.

Sikhchic
Sikh art and culture of the diaspora.

REFERENCES

Bhatti, H. S., and Daniel M. Michon. 2004. "Folk Practices in Punjab." *Journal of Punjab Studies* 11, no. 2: 139–54.

Cole, W. Owen, and Piara S. Sambhi. 1995. *The Sikhs: Their Religious Beliefs and Practices*. Brighton, UK: Sussex Academic Press.

Dharam Parchar Committee (Shiromani Gurdwara Parbandhak Committee). *Sikh Reht Maryada*. http://www.sgpc.net/sikhism/sikh-dharma-manual.asp (accessed May 2009).

Dusenbery, Verne A. 1990. "Punjabi Sikhs and Gora Sikhs: Conflicting Assertions of Identity in North America." In *Sikh History and Religion in the Twentieth Century*, ed. Joseph T. O'Connell et al., 334–55. Toronto: University of Toronto Centre for South Asian Studies.

Eck, Diana. 1998. *Darśan: Seeing the Divine Image in India*. New York: Columbia University Press.

Elsberg, Constance. 2003. *Graceful Women: Gender and Identity in an American Sikh Community*. Knoxville: University of Tennessee Press.

Fenech, Louis. 2001. *Martyrdom in the Sikh Tradition: Playing the "Game of Love."* Delhi: Oxford University Press.

Grewal, J. S. 1990. *The Sikhs of the Punjab*. Cambridge: Cambridge University Press.

Grewal, J. S., and S. S. Bal. 1987. *Guru Gobind Singh*. Chandigarh: Panjab University.

Jakobsh, Doris R. 2003. *Relocating Gender in Sikh History: Transformation, Meaning and Identity*. Delhi: Oxford University Press.

———. 2006a. "Sikhism, Interfaith Dialogue and Women: Transformation and Identity." *Journal of Contemporary Religion* 21, no. 2 (May): 183–99.

———. 2006b. "Authority in the Virtual Sangat: Sikhism, Ritual and Identity in the Twenty-First Century."

Heidelberg Journal of Religions on the Internet 2, no. 1: 24–40. http://online.uni-hd.de/.

———. 2008. "3HO/Sikh Dharma of the Western Hemisphere: The 'Forgotten' New Religious Movement?" *Religion Compass* 2, no. 1: 1–24.

Johnston, Hugh. 1989. *The Voyage of the* Komagata Maru: *The Sikh Challenge to Canada's Colour Bar*. Vancouver: University of British Columbia Press.

———. 2004. "Sikhs in Canada." In *Encyclopedia of Diasporas: Immigrant and Refugee Cultures around the World*, ed. M. Ember et al. Vol. 2, 1075–83. Springer Reference.

———. n.d. "Sikhs." In *The Encyclopedia of Canada's Peoples*. http://multiculturalcanada.ca/Encyclopedia/A-Z/s4.

Kalsi, Sewa Singh. 1995. "Problems of Defining Authority in Sikhism." *DISKUS* 3, no. 2: 43–58.

———. 2004. *Simple Guide to Sikhism*. Delhi: Alchemy.

Leonard, Karen. 1989. "Pioneer Voices from California: Reflections on Race, Religion and Ethnicity." In *The Sikh Diaspora: Migration and the Experience beyond Punjab*, ed. N. Gerald Barrier and Verne A. Dusenbery, 120–40. Delhi: Chanakya.

Macauliffe, Max Arthur. 1909/1993. *The Sikh Religion: Its Gurus, Sacred Writings and Authors*. Vol. 2. Delhi: Low Price Publications.

Mann, Gurinder Singh. 2004. *Sikhism*. Upper Saddle River, NJ: Prentice Hall.

McLeod, Hew. 1997. *Sikhism*. London: Penguin.

McLeod, W. H. 1987. "The Development of the Sikh Panth." In *The Sants: Studies in a Devotional Tradition of India*, ed. K. Schomer and W. H. McLeod, 229–50. Berkeley, CA: Berkeley Religious Studies Series.

———. 2003. *Sikhs of the Khalsa: A History of the Khalsa Rahit*. Delhi: Oxford University Press.

Mooney, Nicola. 2010. "Lowly Shoes on Lowly Feet: Some Jat Sikh Women's Views on Gender and Equality." In *Women in Sikhism: An Exploration*, ed. Doris R. Jakobsh. Delhi: Oxford University Press.

Nesbitt, Eleanor. 2005. *Sikhism: A Very Short Introduction*. Oxford: Oxford University Press.

Oberoi, Harjot. 1994. *The Construction of Religious Boundaries: Culture, Identity and Diversity*. Delhi: Oxford University Press.

Pettigrew, Joyce. 1975. *Robber Nobleman: A Study of the Political System of the Sikh Jats*. London: Routledge and Kegan Paul.

Singh, Harbans. 1994. *Guru Nanak and Origins of the Sikh Faith*. Patiala: Punjabi University.

Singh, Khushwant. 2006. *Train to Pakistan: 50th Anniversary Illustrated Edition*. Delhi: Roli Books, Lotus Collection.

Singh, Nikky-Guninder Kaur. 1993. *The Feminine Principle in the Sikh Vision of the Transcendent*. Cambridge: Cambridge University Press.

———. 1995. *The Name of My Beloved: Verses of the Sikh Gurus*. San Francisco: HarperSanFrancisco.

———. 2000. "Why Did I Not Light the Fire? The Refeminization of Ritual in Sikhism." *Journal of Feminist Studies in Religion* 16: 63–85.

Singh, Pashaura. 2005. "Understanding the Martyrdom of Guru Arjan." *Journal of Punjab Studies* 12, no. 1: 29–62.

Siri Guru Granth Sahib. English translation endorsed by Shiromani Gurdwara Parbandhak Committee (SGPC). http://www.sgpc.net/files/English%20 Translation%20of%20Siri%20Guru%20Granth%20 Sahib.pdf.

Stoker, Valerie. 2007. "Zero Tolerance: Sikh Swords, School Safety and Secularism in Québec." *Journal of the American Academy of Religion* 75, no. 4: 814–39.

Takhar, Opinderjit Kaur. 2005. *Sikh Identity: An Exploration of Groups among Sikhs*. Farnham, UK: Ashgate.

Walton-Roberts, Margaret. 2004. "Transnational Migration Theory in Population Geography: Gendered Practices in Networks Linking Canada and India." *Population, Space and Place* 10: 361–73.

Timeline

- **6th–5th century B.C.E.** Life of the Buddha (traditional dates: 566–486 B.C.E.; proposed dates: c. 480–400 B.C.E.).

- **3rd century B.C.E.** Emperor Asoka sends Buddhism to Sri Lanka.
Third Council (Theravada Buddhism).

- **2nd century B.C.E.** Rise of Mahayana Buddhism.

- **1st century B.C.E.** Sri Lanka: Pali canon committed to writing.

- **1st century C.E.** China: Buddhism arrives.

- **2nd century C.E.** Nagarjuna (circa 150); Madhyamaka.
India: Nalanda University founded.

- **3rd century** China: fall of the Han Dynasty.

- **4th century** Yogacara (Asanga and Vasubandu).

- **5th century** China: Sri Lankan nuns establish order (433/434); Pure Land Buddhism begins; Kumarajiva carries out major translation project.

- **6th century** China: Bodhidharma arrives (Zen Buddhism); Chinese schools of Buddhism begin to develop. Japan: Buddhism arrives.

- **7th century** Tibet: king's wives establish Buddhist temples.
Japan: King Shotoku establishes first constitution (604), enshrining Buddhism, Confucianism, and Shinto as state religions.

- **8th century** Tibet: first monastery (Samye); debate between Indian and Chinese Buddhist masters (720).

- **9th century** Japan: Tendai (Saicho) and Shingon/Tantric (Kukai) Buddhism established.

- **10th century** Tibet: Buddhism persecuted and goes into eclipse with murder of king (945).

- **11th century** Tibet: revival of Buddhism.
India: decline of Buddhism.

- **12th century** India: Nalanda destroyed; Buddhism rapidly disappears in India.
Japan: Honen beginning of Pure Land Buddhism; Eisai founds Rinzai Zen school.

- **13th century** Japan: Shinran establishes True Pure Land school; Dogen establishes Soto Zen;

Nichiren establishes Nichiren school.
Tibet: Mongolians convert to Tibetan Buddhism (Sakya Pandita).
Sri Lanka: last record of nuns.

- **15th century** Tibet: Geluk school founded (Tsongkhapa).

- **17th century** Tibet: Great Fifth Dalai Lama of Geluk school becomes political and religious head of country.
Japan: Tokogawa period begins (1603–1867).

- **18th century** Japan: Hakuin (1685–1769) revives Rinzai.
Sri Lanka: monks' lineage "refreshed."

- **19th century** Japan: period of state Shinto (1868–1945).
Sri Lanka: Buddhism challenged by colonialization.
China: Chinese begin migrating to North America for gold rush and railway work.
The West: Buddhism becomes known through Theosophical Society, World Parliament of Religions, and scholarship.

- **20th century** Buddhism comes West.
Kerouac's *Dharma Bums*, (Ginsberg, Snyder literature) and pop culture, films, and music.
Study of Buddhism, mostly texts, enters the university.
Groups (San Francisco Zen Centre) and temple/ churches (Pureland temple, B.C., 1905) formed.
Monasteries established (Scotland and Cape Breton Island).
Thich Nat Hahn exiled from Vietnam and establishes Order of Interbeing.
Tibet: China invades (1950) and assumes full control (1959); Western scholars have access to Tibetan texts; Dalai Lama goes into exile and awarded Nobel Peace Prize (1989).
Western women begin to be ordained as nuns.
Sri Lanka: order of nuns re-established.
Sakyadhita, the International Organization of Buddhist Women, formed (1987).

- **21st century** Buddhism established in mainstream Western society.
Buddhists begin to come together across traditional lines to work together on common causes.

NEL

CHAPTER 5

Buddhism

◼

Mavis L. Fenn

INTRODUCTION

We walk slowly down a rural road in Lumbini, Nepal, our faces bathed in the spring morning sun. A small girl plays in a puddle at the side of the road. We are walking back through time, to about 2,500 years ago, around 483 B.C.E. Lumbini is the birthplace of Siddhartha Gotama Sakya, the **Buddha**, the Awakened One. People come here for many reasons. We have come to attend a conference, a most unusual conference of Buddhist women: nuns and laywomen, Western and Asian, wealthy and poor. Some of us come to a newly completed nunnery to present academic papers. Others will take workshops on women's health and how to practise the **dharma** (teachings) within family life. All of us, Buddhist or not, have come to learn about each other. The location of this conference at the dawn of the new millennium has not been chosen at random. This place in the middle of rural Nepal, surrounded by farmer's fields, is considered by Buddhists to be a holy site. Because of this, the countryside is dotted with monastery complexes and hotels for the convenience of tourists.

The specific spot known traditionally as the Buddha's birthplace is set apart from the surrounding fields, and even at this early hour a steady stream of tourists and devotees walk the path. The site has a small monastery residence and cone-topped structures called **stupas** (relic containers). Hanging above a large tree and pool are waving prayer flags. The tree is where the Buddha's mother braced herself as she gave birth, and the pool is where she bathed. Each prayer flag has a **mantra** (sacred chant) written on it and sends a wish for peace and happiness to all living beings.

A short distance from the tree is a large pillar surrounded by wire. On the pillar are written ancient words indicating that it was constructed by Emperor Asoka, who had sent a delegation to find the spot where the Buddha was born. Because this was the Buddha's birthplace, Emperor Asoka gathered fewer taxes from the surrounding area and erected the pillar for all to come and marvel at.

Buddhism is a "founded" religion. That is, scholars attribute its origins to a specific person and his/her thought. This differs from religions such as Hinduism, which is believed to be without human origin. Thus the Buddhist narrative begins in rural Nepal with Siddhartha Gotama Sakya's birth. Traditionally the dates for his life have been estimated as 566–486 B.C.E., but more recent scholarship has suggested that 480–400 B.C.E. is more accurate.

In this chapter you will learn about the life of Siddhartha Gotama Sakya, a young prince who "had it all" but left it all behind in the search to find an end to suffering of all kinds, and who became a buddha—one who awakens to the nature of reality and discovers how to deal with it. You will learn the truths he discovered as summarized in the central concepts of Buddhism. You will learn how Buddhism distinguished itself from the other religious traditions of India, of its doctrinal development into the three strands known as Theravada, Mahayana, and Vajrayana, and the important role played by

Lumbini, Nepal, where the Buddha was born
Source: Mavis L. Fenn

Buddha: a person who discovers the truth about reality and becomes enlightened on his or her own.

Dharma: the truth about reality—that it is impermanent, without essence, and ultimately unsatisfactory—and the Buddha's teachings about this.

Stupa: a structure that contains a relic of an important religious figure; something associated with that person, such as clothing or a begging bowl; or some sacred text or verse; a site to which pilgrims come and worship.

Mantra: a sacred sound; like a mandala, often a focus for meditation.

the Emperor Asoka in propelling Buddhism from being just another new religious movement to becoming a major force in India and subsequently throughout Asia. You will also come to understand Buddhism's continued development in more recent times throughout the world. You will learn how it has managed to adapt to the needs of many people through time and across cultures. You will learn about Buddhist practices that encompass body, speech, and mind, practices on a path that everyone may follow according to his or her needs and abilities. In short, then, you will learn about and be able to explain to others the Buddhist assessment of the human dilemma—suffering—and how to live a contented life in the face of that dilemma.

PERSPECTIVES

The Three Strands of Buddhism

To begin learning about central Buddhist beliefs and practices, it is important to identify the three major strands of Buddhism: Theravada, Mahayana, and Vajrayana Buddhism.

The term **Theravada** refers to the type of Buddhism traditionally practised in South and Southeast Asia. It means "the speech or words of the elders," and the tradition considers itself the repository of the original words of the Buddha and the arhats (those enlightened through hearing a Buddha teach). For scholars, the matter is more complex. There were about eighteen Buddhist schools in India, perhaps more. Only fragments of their texts remain and none of the schools exist today. Theravada developed from one of these schools, and the Pali Canon is the only complete set of texts from those early schools that we have.

Mahayana Buddhism developed in India after the death of the Buddha, sometime around the second century B.C.E. It began as a movement centred on the production of texts containing a variety of new concepts and interpretations. In China and Japan separate schools of Mahayana Buddhism developed: Pure Land, Ch'an (Zen), and Tiantai (Tendai), for example.

Vajrayana Buddhism was the last major form of Buddhism to emerge in India, around the third or fourth century of the Common Era. It is an esoteric tradition; that is, some teachings and practices are considered to be secret and are passed along only between student and teacher. It is also called Tantric Buddhism for its emphasis on ritual as a means to enlightenment. It too spread throughout the Buddhist world. It did not become prominent in South and East Asia but is found in Japan as Shingon Buddhism. It is most identified with Tibet, where it arrived in the late eighth century.

CENTRAL BELIEFS
Buddha

The term *buddha* is actually a title. It means "awakened one," that is, a person who has attained insight into the nature of reality: that it is impermanent, without self-existence, and ultimately unsatisfactory. That insight puts an end to suffering and rebirth. The three main divisions of Buddhism—Theravada, Mahayana, and Vajrayana—understand *Buddha* somewhat differently. For the Theravada, the Buddha was a man, Siddhartha Gotama Sakya, whose successful spiritual quest for meaning transformed him into a buddha. As such, he was removed from the cycle of death and rebirth and was no longer accessible except in his teachings, which were safeguarded by a community of monks and nuns. Anyone following the path initiated by Siddhartha can also become a buddha. But the notion of the Buddha as a man was rooted in a particular historical era, the sixth and fifth centuries B.C.E., and India changed over the centuries. Before we examine those changes, we need to examine the basic account of the Buddha's life because it has been a paradigm—an example and model—for Buddhists through the centuries.

At first glance, discussing the Buddha would seem to be an easy matter, given our comment above that

Buddhism is a founded tradition. But while we know that such a person existed, we know little about him from a modern historical perspective. Even the dates of his birth and death are not agreed upon by scholars; they vary among the various Buddhist traditions and Buddhist scholars. The generally used dates in Western scholarship until about twenty-five years ago were 563–483 B.C.E. More recently, some scholars have come to believe that the date of the Buddha's death was closer to 400 B.C.E., with some room for error on either side of that date (Cousins 1996).

Even if there were a consensus regarding the Buddha's dates, little is known about the historical details of his life. While there is mention of some events in the early texts, full biographies of his life were not written for centuries, until roughly between 200 B.C.E. and 200 C.E. While many accept these biographies and traditional narratives at face value, some find the references in them to magical or supernatural events, gods intervening in human events, and prophecies to be problematic. For example, the Buddha and other religious figures are said to have possessed the thirty-two marks of a great man, marks that include golden skin, wheel patterns on the feet, and other significant signs. How can such improbable things be accepted without discounting the historical value of such narratives?

Scholars of the history of religion make distinctions between history and "sacred history." When dealing with a history, they pursue the "facts" of what occurred, then analyze them for patterns, actors' intentions, other relevant factors from previous events, current politics, and personalities. Finally the historian comes to a conclusion about the meaning of the event within the broader historical context. In a sacred history, the matter of overriding importance is meaning—the ultimate meaning in religious terms—so pattern takes priority. This notion is reinforced by the idea that all the Buddha's former lives (in Theravada, twenty-five) follow a pattern. The pattern is sacred in that it reveals something important about the religious dimensions of life, not just for the religious figure but for the devotee as well. It provides a pattern for believers to identify with and emulate. Undoubtedly "real" events and facts are included, but they are woven into the larger, more important spiritual narrative.

These approaches must be kept in mind in examining the traditional narrative of the Buddha's life. The overarching theme or pattern is of a man who had all the material benefits and social status one could hope

Jataka Tales: a collection of stories, many of them older folk tales, that have been shaped into Buddhist morality tales.

Bodhisattva: a person heading for enlightenment; in Theravada Buddhism, used only of the Buddha before his birth; in Mahayana, both a person who has taken a vow to attain full enlightenment for the benefit of all living beings and a celestial bodhisattva, who does not become a buddha but continues to use his merit and skill to help others.

for and a personal life blessed with wife and son, who found all this unsatisfactory because it could not prevent suffering and death. It is the story of a man who prepared, over countless lives, to leave his parental home as Siddhartha Gotama Sakya in order to find an end to suffering, and who died at about eighty years of age as a buddha. His teachings, ultimately, are centred on putting an end to suffering. The thirty-two marks, while having traditional meanings, are within modern scholarship understood as a literary means of stating that spiritually advanced people can be identified as such.

The story of the Buddha's life began many lifetimes earlier, when a young man, Sumedha, influenced by the teaching of a former buddha, vowed to become a fully enlightened buddha for the benefit of all living beings. Thus begins the preface to the **Jataka Tales**. What follows is a series of stories, many of them originally non-Buddhist fables, that tell about the previous lives of the Buddha. In these stories, whose characters are frequently animals, the character identified with the **bodhisattva** (a person who is on the path to becoming a buddha) is almost always the wisest character and displays a valuable quality such as compassion that foreshadows his future as a buddha. One of the most compelling of these tales is of a man who comes upon a tigress dying of exhaustion after having just given birth. If she does not get food, she and her cubs will die. The man slits his throat at her feet so that she can be nourished.

There are also morality tales that encourage the reader to develop certain qualities such as generosity and faith. In one tale a poor man stands all night so that he can be first in line to offer food to the Buddha. Although he has only a small bowl of sour porridge to offer, he does so with a pure heart, receiving great benefit while others attempt to buy his merit, and a better rebirth in the future. Finally, the stories encourage people to learn from their mistakes. Each narrative begins in the present, which sets the stage for telling a story of the past as a teaching device, and ends with identification of the main characters in the story of the past. For example, people complain to the Buddha about a greedy monk. In response, the Buddha tells a story in which a greedy bird (later identified as the monk) gets into trouble because of his greed. The message to the reader is clear: do not be like the greedy monk who continues to repeat his mistakes lifetime after lifetime.

The last of the tales is the story of Prince Vessantara, whose desire for enlightenment and development of the virtue of generosity are so great that he gives away everything he has, including his wife and family. Prince Vessantara is widely accepted as the last incarnation of the Buddha before his rebirth as Siddhartha. In the story, rather than experiencing immediate rebirth, the bodhisattva remains in the highest heaven until the time is suitable for his birth. When the time is right, his mother, Maya, is impregnated when she dreams that a white elephant has entered her womb. Elephants are regal symbols in India and white elephants are extremely rare: certainly this would be an exceptional child. Sages predict that the child will be either a world conqueror or a buddha. All the versions of his birth are accompanied by fractures in nature, such as earthquakes, water flowing from the sky, or the intervention of gods, which alerts the audience to the cosmic significance of this miraculous birth (these fractures in the natural order also occur at the point of the Buddha's enlightenment and death).

The world into which the historical Buddha, Siddhartha Gotama Sakya, was born was one of great change. He was born into the Sakya clan and his father, Suddhodana, likely one of the clan rulers, is traditionally presented as a king. Given the nature of the prophecies concerning his son and his own position as a king, it is not surprising that Suddhodana wanted his son to become a world conqueror. Warned by a sage that he should keep Siddhartha away from unpleasantness in case that might lead to his turning to religion, Suddhodana spent his life trying to protect his son from anything unpleasant, providing him with the best that life had to offer and making a good marriage for him with the beautiful and intelligent Yasodhara. While some texts talk about a growing dis-ease gradually developing within the prince and disturbing the atmosphere created by his father, the more usual telling of his confrontation with the realities of the human condition occurs in the story of the Four Sights. On three different occasions

Siddhartha is confronted by an old man, a diseased man, and a corpse, representing old age, disease, and death. Siddhartha questions his charioteer on each occasion and is horrified to discover that old age, disease, and death are universal, that they happen to everyone. On the fourth trip Siddhartha sees a **sramana**, a wandering philosopher. The root of the word means "to strive," so sramanas were those who strove to find answers to the fundamental questions of existence. The man had a calm demeanour, and Siddhartha, curious as to how someone could be calm in the face of the reality of the human condition, determined to find the answer to the question of suffering. And so, in the traditional language of the time, "he left home for the homeless life."

Initially he studied under two of the most famous teachers of the time, practising very sophisticated levels of meditation. Having learned everything these teachers had to offer, he still had not achieved the end to suffering he sought. He struck out on his own, practising ever more stringent ascetic practices—that is, practices that severely restrict physical or mental aspects of a person in order to attain an altered state of consciousness. It is said that Siddhartha was able to live on as little as a jujube fruit a day and that he was able to suspend his breathing for long periods of time. These practices brought him five disciples who were impressed by his abilities, but they resulted only in near starvation and headaches rather than enlightenment. Recognizing that this was not the way, he accepted food from a laywoman, and the five disciples, horrified at such indulgence, left him in disgust. As he recovered his physical strength, he thought about a time when he was a child and had seen a field being tilled. At the time he had spontaneously gone into a trance, so perhaps this, rather than the traditional methods of the time, should be explored. He sat down under a tree—now called a bodhi tree (*bodhi* meaning "enlightenment")—and vowed not to move from that spot until he had conquered the mystery of suffering.

Siddhartha's resolve attracted the attention of the god Mara, who is commonly understood as the god of death. While not incorrect, this understanding is, however, limited. Mara represents all the obstacles that prevent humans from seeing things as they really are, waking up to reality, and ending suffering. In a sense he represents the ordinary world, where people are motivated by self-centredness, lust, hatred, and delusion. As the god of this realm, he has an interest in keeping people ignorant. In one version of the story he sends

> **Sramana:** a wandering philosopher, a mendicant who lives on the donations of others.
>
> **Karma:** act; in Buddhism, moral acts.
>
> **Arhat:** a person who has attained enlightenment through following the teachings of a buddha.

armies against the Buddha. When that fails, his daughters attempt to seduce the Buddha; they are usually interpreted as various temptations, emotions such as jealousy and anger, and flaws such as self-centredness. This also fails to shake his resolve. A final challenge from Mara himself questions Siddhartha's worthiness for enlightenment. In response, Siddhartha calls upon the Earth as his witness, who validates his merit and readiness. He returns to his meditation, and over the course of the night achieves enlightenment.

What does it mean to achieve enlightenment? What did the Buddha learn? The process is described as the attaining of three knowledges. First, the Buddha saw all his past lives, his karmic chain. Next he was able to see the karmic chain of other beings. In short, he was able to see that he and others had come to be where they were as a result of **karma** (act or deed). Having fully grasped karma, he meditated on how to end the karmic chain, and gained insight into *dependent arising* (how things such as suffering come to be). By doing so, he was able to figure out how to break the chain of suffering. The consequence of these three knowledges was that he no longer had to suffer rebirth.

The Buddha was anxious to share his knowledge with his two former teachers but, now also possessed of supernormal powers, he intuited that both had already died. He also came to know that his former disciples had become residents of the deer park at Sarnath, and he travelled to meet them there. His disciples, however, tried to ignore him, still disappointed that he had discontinued his ascetic practices. Eventually, sensing that their teacher has changed, they asked for a teaching. This first sermon is known as the "Wheel-Turning" sermon, in that it turns the wheel of dharma for the first time in this eon, making an end to suffering possible. Over the course of the next few days, the Buddha taught his disciples the Four Noble Truths and the Eightfold Noble Path. In turn, each disciple was enlightened and became an **arhat**, one who has attained enlightenment through hearing the teachings.

The Buddha continued to teach for another forty-five years. His teachings were called *dharma*, and they present the Dharma, the truth of reality as impermanent, without essence, and ultimately unsatisfactory.

Mahayana

Mahayana Buddhism was a later development of Buddhism that came to be known through the production of new texts. The Mahayana understanding of a buddha differed from that of the Theravada in that the emphasis shifted from the personhood of the historical Buddha to the wisdom that made him a buddha. This wisdom was called **prajnaparamita**, the Highest Wisdom. It was understood to be ever-present and able to generate a multitude of buddhas in multiple realms of the cosmos. These buddhas were accessible through visions and through meditative practice. Thus the whole notion of the Buddha shifted from a human paradigm to a cosmic one. Through these developments, the Buddha of the Theravada, Shakyamuni (an ascetic of the Sakya clan), was understood simply as one of a pantheon of buddhas. Perhaps the best known of the Mahayana buddhas is Amitabha, the Buddha of the West, who created a pure land where those who call on him can be reborn and where enlightenment is easier to attain than in this realm.

Vajrayana

The final turning of the Buddhist wheel came to be known as Vajrayana or Tantra Buddhism. *Tantra* means "weave" or "thread," and it was called Tantric Buddhism because its texts interwove rituals and meditative practices that centred on a particular deity, for example, Hevajra. Vajrayana followed Mahayana in its understanding of the nature of a buddha and added its own Tantric deities. One of the most prominent of the buddhas is a female buddha, Tara.

Bodhisattva

Theravada, Mahayana and Vajrayana also have different understandings of the *bodhisattva*, a being headed for enlightenment. When the term is used in Theravada Buddhism, it refers to the historical Buddha prior to his enlightenment, both in his life as Siddhartha and in his previous lives. For Mahayana, there are two types of *bodhisattva*. There are ordinary *bodhisattva*, men and women who have taken a vow to reach full enlightenment for the sake of all living beings. There are also what have been termed celestial *bodhisattva*, very advanced, worthy of worship and to whom one can appeal for assistance. The best known of these is Avalokitesvara, the *bodhisattva* of compassion, known as Kuanyin in China and Kannon in Japan.

Four Noble Truths

The Context

The Four Noble Truths are a summary of insights into the nature of reality, the arising of suffering, the origins of that suffering, and the way to end suffering. These insights transformed Siddhartha Gotama Sakya, an ordinary man, into a buddha, an "enlightened one," someone who has awakened from ignorance to truth. The Four Noble Truths are accepted by all traditions within Buddhism. In order to get a good grasp on these teachings, it is necessary to have some understanding of the context within which they originated. While we may not know the precise dates of the Buddha's life, we do know that the time he lived in was one filled with uncertainty.

The sixth century B.C.E. was a time of great change. This change encompassed every aspect of life, from new technologies to a crisis of religious identity. The use of iron in agriculture for plowing fields does not sound like much of change to those of us who have seen the invention of television and travel to the moon, but its influence on daily life on the Ganges plain of India was massive and extensive. With an iron plow, one person could do much more in less time, and fewer people were needed to till the fields. Many of these people were displaced into the large cities that had begun to spring up. Crowding produced disease and violence. People took up new occupations: where previously individuals would make baskets as they needed them, now guilds of basket-makers formed to serve the needs of a new class of people, the traders who ventured along the dangerous routes into Central Asia and China. Trade requires financing, so banking began; the first coins made in India were produced by the guilds.

The social order also began to change. The area where Buddhism arose, in the east of India, had a tribal system. That is, each family was part of a larger social unit called a clan. The tribe was made up of many clans and ruled by a council of high-ranking individuals from each clan. Land was held in common, owned by the tribe, and decisions were made by the council. The Buddha's father was likely one of those nobles. As this system began to break down, land began to be controlled by individual families within a limited geographic area. A system of kingship began to emerge, with standing armies and a bureaucracy to support it.

Further complicating the social situation was the rapid expansion of the Indo-European peoples in India. Their religion, Brahmanism, which was founded on the Vedas, focused on sacrifice as a means to ensure one's welfare in this life and the next. Sacrifice was becoming a more specialized field and priests could command large fees for performing the rituals. But questions arose both within the tradition and outside it as to whether or not these sacrifices were even effective. Complaints about the suffering of animals and the waste of resources grew, and the priests came to be viewed as greedy and far too powerful.

Large numbers of men and women left the social order, leaving behind their worldly goods and families in order to wander the country and debate with one another about the issues of change and suffering, the human dilemma, and solutions to these problems. These were the wandering mendicants called sramanas, religious "strivers," and they tended to form groups around charismatic teachers. The Buddha was one such teacher, and there were many more, the most well-known of whom was Mahavira, the founder of the Jain religion. Their debates with the Brahmanical religious priests and the wandering mendicants—about the nature of truth, the existence of a soul, the way to live a meaningful life now and in future lives—produced Hinduism, Buddhism, and the Jain religion.

The Buddha was a sramana, and his thought developed within this atmosphere of intellectual debate. Asked on one occasion what he taught, the Buddha replied that he taught suffering and an end to suffering. The Four Noble Truths are (1) there is suffering, (2) there is a cause of suffering, (3) there is an end of suffering, and (4) there is a path to the end of suffering. It is important to note that, while all the major divisions of Buddhism accept these truths, and all forms of Buddhism hold wisdom and compassion as universal values, understanding and practice vary greatly. The Buddhism of Tibet differs from that of Japan or Sri Lanka or North America. Indeed, even within these areas, one will find variations due to geography, culture, class, or gender.

The First Noble Truth

The First Noble Truth is deceptively simple: there is suffering. According to Buddhist teaching, there are three types of suffering. The first is "ordinary" suffering. Things like old age, disease, and death constitute ordinary suffering, as each and every human being experiences them. The second type of suffering is due to impermanence, for all things are impermanent. For instance, in *The Songs of the Elder Nuns*, the enlightened nun Ambapali talks about how the beauty of her youth faded into old age. It is not just matter that is impermanent. Emotions too are impermanent—people fall into and out of love. Social status too can change, and drastically. One moment one is a trader on the Toronto Stock Exchange—the next, one is unemployed.

Ambapali Reflects on the Impermanence of Beauty

Glossy and black as the down of a bee my curls once clustered.

They with the waste of years are liker to hempen or bark cloth.

Such and not otherwise runneth the rune [verse], the word of the Soothsayer [the Buddha].

Fragrant as casket of perfumes, as full of sweet blossoms the hair of me.

All with the waste of years now rank as the odour of hare's fur.

Such and not otherwise runneth the rune, the word of the Soothsayer. ...

Flashing and brilliant as jewels, dark-blue and long-lidded the eyes of me.

(continued)

> They with the waste of the years spoilt utterly, radiant no longer.
> Such and not otherwise runneth the rune, the word of the Soothsayer.
> Dainty and smooth the curve of the nostrils e'en as in children.
> Now with the waste of years seared the nose is and shrivelled.
> Such and not otherwise runneth the rune, the word of the Soothsayer.
>
> Source: *Poems of the Early Buddhist Nuns,* trans. C. A. F. Rhys Davids and K. R. Norman (Oxford: Wisdom Books, 1989).

No soul: the idea that a person is not an essence but a relationship.

Finally there is suffering caused by "conditioned states." This notion of suffering arises from the Buddhist view of causation, and focuses on ideas about the nature or construction of the person. In short, how do things, especially people, come to be, and is there some eternal, unchanging essence at the core of a person—a soul? The questions of causation and soul are philosophical questions, and they were hotly debated in the religious circles of the Buddha's time. The predominant religious tradition of the time was the Veda-based Brahmanism noted above, and Buddhism developed some of its key concepts—dependent origination (multiple causes) and no soul (*anatman*)—in direct opposition to Vedic Brahmanical notions. Brahmanical philosophers believed that there was a central essence to the cosmos and that that essence could also be found in the human soul (*atman*). Buddhism rejected this essentialist view in favour of a relational view.

In Figure 5.1, the drawing on the left reflects Brahmanical understandings of *atman*, or the human soul—an unchangeable, eternal essence. On the right is the Buddhist view of the self: an ever-changing relationship between the five factors of which we are constituted. Each of the five—name and form (our material self), sensation, perception, mental formations, and consciousness—can be broken down into more elements within each category. For example, *mental formations* contain our karma (acts, deeds) and *sensation* includes six senses, mind being the sixth sense. Each of these five main factors of the self is changing all the time. Think about this for a moment. Are you the same person you were ten years ago? No, of course you are not. There is some continuity, but within Buddhist understanding, there is no permanent, eternal core, **no soul**.

What does this have to do with suffering? According to the Buddhist tradition, the view that humans possess

Figure 5.1   The diagram on the left shows how we think of ourselves, while the one on the right shows how we really are.

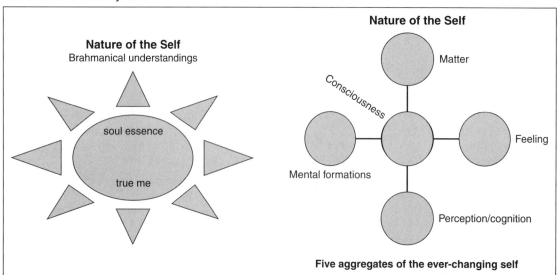

an eternal soul leads to promotion of self-centredness in one's attitude as well as in actions with others; it also promotes attachment to both people and material goods. Self-centredness means that everything, including other humans, is perceived in terms of one's own needs. This mistaken notion of one's self as the centre of the universe also causes individuals to cling to things, to try to make stable things that are by nature ever-changing. For example, parents' desire to protect their children can become controlling or smothering. Buddhist notions of desire and clinging come to the forefront through the Second Noble Truth.

The Second Noble Truth

The Second Noble Truth is that there is a cause of suffering. This truth ties directly in to the Buddhist notion of causation. Put briefly, everything has a cause and all causes are multiple. This is called dependent arising or **dependent origination**. Each person has a cause: their mother and father. Each of them has a cause, and so on back through the mists of time. When this notion

> **Dependent origination:** the notion that everything comes into existence through a multitude of causes.
>
> **Dukkha:** literally, "suffering," but best translated as "ultimately unsatisfactory."

is applied to the question "How does suffering arise?" a series of cyclical events takes place (see Figure 5.2). In theory, the circle could start or end at any point.

Basically, suffering arises because of ignorance about the nature of reality. All of reality, like human beings, is impermanent, without an essence, and is ultimately unsatisfactory. "Ultimately unsatisfactory" is a better translation of the term **dukkha** than "suffering," which is often used, because Buddhism also acknowledges the great joy of life. It is the desire to make permanent that which by its very nature is not permanent that causes us problems. This ignorance of reality leads to the development of thoughts and desires and will (psychic constructions), which in turn

Figure 5.2   This diagram shows how our actions based in ignorance lead to endless rebirth.

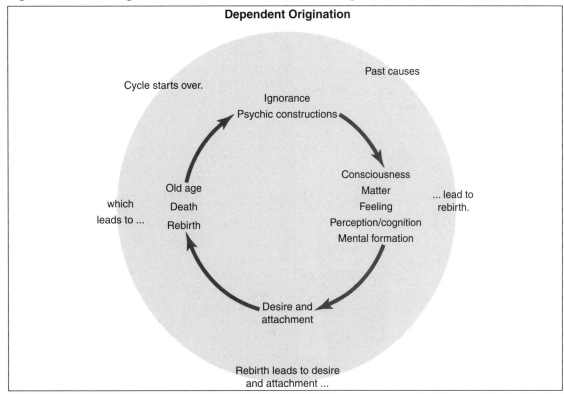

Samsara: the wheel or cycle of rebirth that is pro-pelled by karma.

causes action based on those desires. Act is karma, and it is karma that propels **samsara**, the wheel of birth and rebirth, the wheel of suffering. Further, it is karma that provides the continuity from one life to the next.

In Buddhism, the quality (negative or positive) of karma is conditioned primarily by two factors: inten-tion and overall character. At times intentions can be good but the results are not. The second factor is overall character. Even the most virtuous of people commit bad deeds from time to time. Figure 5.3 shows two glasses with salt suspended in them. The salt represents negative acts and the water denotes overall character. The glass on the left has very little salt in it, and adding another grain or two is not going to make much dif-ference. But the one on the right already has a lot of salt in it, so much so that adding any more will cause it to settle out on the bottom. Settling to the bottom in karmic terms means that the next rebirth will be qualitatively less than this one.

Figure 5.3 Salt added to the glass on the left remains suspended, while salt added to the glass on the right settles out. This demon-strates the importance of overall character in the workings of karma.

The Buddhist view of karma differs somewhat from the Jain and Hindu notions. Thought "counts" in Buddhism, as much or more than the act itself, whereas in the Jain religion it does not. Further, Jains believe karma to be a subtle material that coats and weighs down the soul and can change its shape. Hindus believe that karma dictates one's place in society and one's social duty. Neither Jains nor Buddhists accept that the social hierarchy is also a moral hierarchy. The Buddha did not reject caste as a means of organizing the division of labour in society. What was rejected was the notion that members of the priestly class, for example, were morally superior to the servant class simply because they were members of a higher class.

In summation, ignorance of the ways things really are (impermanent, without essence, and ultimately unsatisfactory) leads to actions that continue the cycle of rebirth and, ultimately, suffering. The ques-tion then arises, If Buddhism does not believe in an eternal soul, what is there to reincarnate? Several metaphoric answers are given. One is of a potter's wheel. When the potter stops turning the wheel, it still spins once or twice, throwing off some clay. In the same way, in death karma is thrown forward into a new being with physical, emotional, mental, and, to some extent, social attributes that are consistent with that karma. A more technical answer is that there is a special type of consciousness that operates only between death and rebirth, and it is the medium of transmission. It is karma that provides continuity between the being that was and the one that is reborn. It "conditions" the new life. And it conditions rather than determines, because in Buddhism karma is "the beginning." It is the baggage of abilities and limita-tions that are brought into the next life. Then we must make our own choices that will influence how karma will play out in this life and subsequent ones. In short, all have free will, although if bad choices were made in the past, it becomes harder to break those habits and begin to make new choices. While karma affirms our responsibility for the choices we make in life, it has also been used to explain congenital illnesses or physical deformities, a difficult concept to accept for those not born into a culture that uses karma as part of its explanatory system.

To phrase this according to Figure 5.2, one's current state of being is the present effect of past causes. "Present effects" are the constituents of the person: name and form (the material self, or matter), sensation (feeling), perception, mental formations, and consciousness. These five elements are often referred to as the self. While "the self" is one way to understand this relationship, it must be kept in mind that in Buddhist thought there is no essence (soul) included, just the relationship between the five components. The traditional illustration of how this works is a chariot, or in a contemporary situation, a car. The wheels of a car are essential for it to operate but, important as they are, the wheels are not "the car." The same is true for the frame, the transmission, and even the engine. We need each component but none on its own constitutes "the car." Every being is like that car. The body is part of one's self-identity but each individual is far more than just a body. Mental processes of reason and analysis are very important to the self but they are not all that constitutes "the self." No one of the five elements on its own can constitute the totality of selfhood. Similarly, one's name or *me* or *I* are simply means of referring to the package of five elements that constitute each human being.

Let us return to Figure 5.2. Who one is today is a combination of thoughts and actions carried forward from previous lives, and it continues to be shaped by the thoughts and decisions made today. Unfortunately, many of today's decisions are clouded by the **Three Poisons**: desire, aversion, and delusion. Decisions are not based on the reality of the situation but on what "I" want to possess (desire) or dislike and want to avoid (hatred/aversion). The decisions made create karmic energy that propels into the next lifetime and the endless march toward old age, disease, and death. How can this cycle of suffering be stopped? Within the Buddhist worldview, karma is the energy that propels the wheel of rebirth. Karma needs to cease—all karma. Even positive energy is still energy. But how can one think and act without creating karma?

The Third Noble Truth

The Third Noble Truth states simply that there is an end to suffering. While Figure 5.2 shows that dependent origination is cyclical, its dynamism comes from ignorance about the real nature of the self and from wilful actions generated by the Three Poisons, desire, aversion, and delusion. Understanding the true nature of things and eliminating the Three Poisons leads to action in a

> **Three Poisons:** desire, aversion, and delusion.
>
> **Nirvana:** enlightenment; the end of suffering; the ultimate goal of all Buddhists.

manner that is, karma-wise, neutral, in accordance with the way things *are* rather than the way we perceive them to be from our self-interested perspective. The term *buddha* means "one who has awakened"—one who has awakened to the nature of reality (that everything, including the self, is impermanent, without substance, and ultimately unsatisfactory) and who lives life in light of that knowledge. To live such a life means to act out of compassion and insight. This is **nirvana**.

Nirvana means literally "to blow out," in this context to blow out the fires of desire, aversion, and delusion. There are two types of nirvana: with support and without support. Nirvana with support simply means that you still have a body. A body is the result of karma and that energy must be exhausted. Nirvana without support means that an enlightened person has died. What happens to the enlightened person after death? The Buddha refused to comment on that; it was one of ten questions he refused to answer. In one text he was asked why he would not answer this question about the state of an enlightened person, called an arhat in the Theravada Buddhist tradition. He replied that the question needed to remain unanswered because any description of it would be misunderstood by an unenlightened person. In short, nirvana is so unlike our current experience that we have nothing to relate it to in order to help us understand it. Although the Buddha says nothing about nirvana after death, if we draw on general Indian notions of the highest spiritual goal, it seems to be characterized by great bliss, insight, and an unending state of being. Initially the enlightenment of an arhat (one enlightened through hearing a buddha teach) and a buddha were considered the same, but over time a buddha's enlightenment came to be considered as qualitatively fuller than that of an arhat.

The Buddha was often compared to a physician. He studied the symptoms and made a diagnosis—suffering; he looked for a cause of this suffering—ignorance and desire; and he discovered a cure—nirvana. The Fourth Noble Truth is considered the medicine necessary to put an end to suffering.

The Fourth Noble Truth

The Fourth Noble Truth is the path to the end of suffering. It is also known as the Eightfold Noble Path because is made up of eight "rights": understanding, thought, speech, conduct, livelihood, effort, mindfulness, and meditation, which are divided into three categories: morality, meditation, and wisdom. These categories are likened to a three-legged stool; you need to develop all three for balance and stability. These are practices to develop good habits of body, speech, and mind. A quotation from the Dhammapada (see "Words" box) provides a good summary of how the three categories work together.

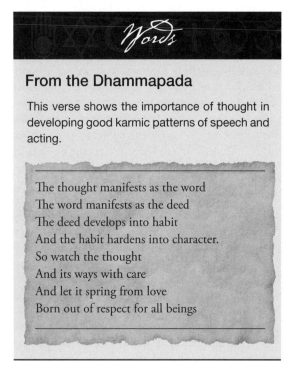

Words

From the Dhammapada

This verse shows the importance of thought in developing good karmic patterns of speech and acting.

The thought manifests as the word
The word manifests as the deed
The deed develops into habit
And the habit hardens into character.
So watch the thought
And its ways with care
And let it spring from love
Born out of respect for all beings

All Buddhists, be they laypeople or religious specialists, follow the same path of morality, meditation, and wisdom. Laypeople and religious specialists differ in the amount of time they have to devote to serious study and meditation and in their desire to attain enlightenment as soon as possible. People also differ according to their abilities and motivations. Prior to the modern era, laypeople in Asia did not generally meditate, although they did engage in what has been called "mental culture," spending some time thinking about the virtues of various sacred personages such as the Buddha. Lay morality consisted primarily in making donations to the monks and nuns (giving) and following the ethical guidelines called the Five Precepts. Monks and nuns have an additional five precepts specific to them, and they must follow the monastic code of their school of Buddhism. They also must assist the laity in their religious progress by preaching to and teaching them and accepting gifts from them so that the laypeople can gain spiritual merit. Giving is discussed in the section on the monastic community, so only the precepts are presented here.

The Five Precepts

The Five Precepts are the basic ethical guidelines for Buddhists. The term *guidelines* is helpful because Buddhist ethics are what is known as situational. In other words, one applies ethical values in accordance with a particular situation. For example, one of the precepts is that one should not lie, but there are different ways of understanding this. Imagine this scenario: One sees a woman run away from an abusive husband into a building. A few minutes later the husband runs up, asking, "Did she go in there?" One replies, "No, she didn't." While the precept has been broken, in this situation the breaking of the precept is viewed as a lesser evil.

Sometimes the situational aspect of Buddhism makes moral decisions difficult. Abortion, for example, is always a difficult situation, and a violation of the first precept, to do no violence. If a woman is pregnant with her sixth child and has been recently widowed or abandoned, she must take into consideration her own health and her ability to feed her family, and the situations of her other children and their future as well. It is here that Buddhism's factoring in of intent in ethical situations comes into play. There will be negative karma in the case of an abortion, but the final weighting of that karma depends upon a multitude of factors. This is a good place to note that ordinary humans do not assess karma and its complications and implications; only a buddha knows how it works. Moreover, as in all religious traditions, Buddhists may disagree about what is or is not violation of a precept and may disagree as to how narrowly the precepts should be applied.

Each precept has broader and narrower interpretations. Further, they are phrased in the negative; that is, they are listed as things one should not do. The assumption is that as one stops doing things that are wrong, one will begin to actively engage in things that are good and produce a positive outcome, both for oneself and for others. The five precepts are to refrain from murdering, stealing, lying, inappropriate sex, and intoxicants. The narrower interpretation is self-evident, the broader more encompassing. Murder is the extreme end of violence, but more broadly, the first precept is to refrain from abusive behaviour. Stealing would also include taking what is not given; an example might be manipulating others to give you something or do something they do not really want to do. Honest dealing in all your affairs and not lying would mean honesty of speech. Cultural opinions vary about what is considered inappropriate sex. Finally, Buddhism is a path of purification of body, mind, and speech, so intoxicants of any kind can impede one's progress on the path.

Meditation

Practices of meditation vary. Several types are discussed below under "Practices": mindfulness, stabilizing, and analytic meditation. It is important to note that what counts as meditation is quite varied and includes mindful practices in one's daily life. It is not just a practice of religious specialists but one done by many ordinary people in a variety of ways. A monk or nun might spend many hours in various forms of meditation and mindfulness practices, whereas a layman in Asia might visit a pilgrimage site associated with the Buddha's life and think about the Buddha's virtues as he circumambulates (walks around the site in a clockwise direction). Meanwhile, a woman in Burlington, Ontario, might eat her dinner slowly and mindfully as she thinks about the web of interconnection that brought the food to her table.

Wisdom

In the same way that other aspects of the path such as morality and meditation vary, so too does wisdom. At its most basic, it is learning the teaching and putting it into practice. Through study and meditation and life experience one begins to have a deeper grasp, an insight, into the nature of reality and how one should respond to that knowledge. This wisdom is expressed differently in the various traditions: dependent origination for

> **Sangha:** community; initially the community of monks and nuns.
>
> **Four Requisites:** what monk or nuns are allowed to have under the monastic code: food, shelter, robes, and medicine.

the Theravada and emptiness and prajnaparamita for the Mahayana, for example. The ways in which these philosophical notions are developed in the various traditions are discussed below in "Sources of the Tradition," below.

Sangha

The term **sangha** means "community" and was originally applied to the community of monks and nuns, the religious specialists. The community was the place where the Dharma was to be preserved and where men and women came to become arhats. In effect they were the body of the Buddha after he died. This point is made very clear in the narrative that deals with the First Council, which was reportedly held soon after the Buddha's death. In this text, the assembled group is a community of arhats, or enlightened beings. They chant the Dharma (teachings) and Vinaya (monastic code) together, effectively taking possession of it from the Buddha who spoke it. From this point onward, access to enlightenment came to be understood as through the sangha. The sangha came into being with the Buddha's first five disciples at the deer park in Sarnath. When the number of arhats in that community reached sixty, the Buddha sent them out to teach others and ordain people into the monastic community. This brought into being the Fourfold Sangha, the community of monks and nuns and male and female devotees.

There is a reciprocal relationship between the monastic sangha and the laypeople. Traditionally the laypeople provided the monastic community with everything they needed: food, clothing, shelter, and medicine. These are known as the **Four Requisites** for monks and nuns, what they need to sustain life and pursue enlightenment. One reason that Buddhism is known as the "Middle Way" has to do with its attitude toward these necessities of life: it outlines the way between having too much and having too little; the extremes of both affect one's ability to pursue enlightenment.

> **Vinaya:** monastic rules for monks and nuns, which are divided into two sections—rules for individuals and rules for the community (sangha).

But what did the laity get out of this arrangement? The answer is rooted in the ancient Indian notion that giving to spiritual people provides a type of positive spiritual or karmic return called merit. The notion of merit allows people who are not able or willing to devote themselves full-time to the religious quest to still make progress toward that goal. Giving is spiritually meritorious. The amount of merit that may accrue to a person for their gift varies according to a wide variety of things—the attitude of the giver, for one. Does the person give with a pure heart? Does he or she give meaningfully? This is often expressed in the texts as wealthy people giving "with their own hand" or poor people giving whatever they have with faith. A very important criterion is the worthiness of the recipient in spiritual terms. A gift to a monk or nun who studies hard, meditates, and lives simply and compassionately provides more merit than a gift to a monk or nun who took up the religious life because they had no other career options. But often one does not know who is living up to their vows. People are flawed, monks and nuns included. What assurance does one have that a gift is not wasted?

This brings us to a discussion of the Sangha of the Four Quarters. This sangha, composed solely of arhats, is an ideal one—it does not exist in reality but lays down the notion of monastic perfection. It is to this sangha that the laity's gifts are given, so quality of merit is ensured for the laypeople. Monks and nuns use but in theory do not own the clothes, food, and other items given by the laity; the Sangha of the Four Quarters owns them. This ideal sangha is ritually recreated before any major gift-giving occasions, such as the end-of-the-rains retreat. New robes are distributed after communal chanting of the main monastic rules found in the **Vinaya**, the code of discipline that forms one of the three sections of the Pali canon, or in other monastic codes used by the Mahayana and Theravada. The monks of the ordinary sangha are encouraged in their religious life through use of the donated items and are inspired to bring their behaviour into conformity with the ideal through periodically chanting together the rules that define the ideal monk.

This ideal Sangha of the Four Quarters also manages another problem. Because merit is tied to the worthiness of the monk or nun, forest monks—monks who practise in isolated retreats—are often given many and lavish gifts because of the perception that they are more spiritual. They cannot refuse these gifts because they have a responsibility to help the laity progress on the path by acting as a "field of merit," allowing the laity to plant seeds of giving that will blossom in a future life. But as monastics they have renounced wealth as an impediment on the spiritual path. The Sangha of the Four Quarters provides the buffer they need to maintain a balance between their vows and the laity's needs. While this is presented as the ideal, historically we know that individual monastics and the sangha itself did own property and material goods (Schopen 2004).

The sangha and the laity have what is known as a symbiotic relationship with one another. That is, the spiritual progress of each depends on the other. Buddhism is rooted in this relationship. The Buddha is reputed to have said that as long as there is a sangha, the teaching will last. He is also reputed to have said that as long as the monastic discipline (Vinaya) lasts, so long will the sangha last. It is not too much to say that without the monastic discipline there would be no Buddhism.

The Vinaya contains two categories of rules: those for individual monks and nuns and those that govern the life of the community and its relationship with those outside it. These rules are laid out within a framework of stories in which something untoward occurs and it is reported to the Buddha, often by a layperson. The Buddha questions the monk concerned and lays down a rule. This is followed by a list of clarifications and exceptions provided by an early commentator. The rules for individual monks and nuns try to provide some control over their environment in ways that lead to detachment from things of the world and the negative attitudes they often provoke. For example, the rules on clothing allow for decent, serviceable robes but do not allow for fancy cuts or expensive cloth. This minimizes opportunities for desire or envy of what others may have. So too, each rule provides an opportunity for mindfulness, for the outer rule mirrors the intent. The combination is designed to produce thoughtful action not based upon desire, aversion, or delusion, that is, non-karma-producing behaviour. Psychologically, the rules are based on ideas one would associate with behaviour modification. If a person learns how to dress, walk, and behave like an arhat, at some point that person will be transformed into an arhat.

The rules for the community are concerned with purity. As noted above, the community must do its best to conform to the ideal of the Sangha of the Four Quarters for the benefit of the laity. In order for teaching to continue and for arhats to continue being created and for the end of suffering to be available to all, the sangha must maintain itself as a pure community.

The account of the First Council does not mention any female arhats, although we know from early texts that they existed. In fact, there is one work, *The Songs of the Elder Nuns*, devoted to the stories of these early female arhats; the story of Ambapali (see "Words" box, pp. 163–164) is one of these. The order of nuns was founded about five years after that of the men. While there have always been individual women who became religious mendicants, the Jains and the Buddhists were the first to establish an organization of religious women. In the narrative that establishes this order, the Buddha is seen as being initially reluctant to ordain women. The request from his stepmother and aunt Mahaprajapati is initially denied quite firmly. Mahaprajapati does not give up, however, and Ananda, the Buddha's attendant and cousin, acts as an intermediary on their behalf. Initially Ananda's request is also denied. Ananda then asks the Buddha if women are capable of enlightenment. The Buddha replies that of course they are. Ananda then argues that if they are as capable of enlightenment as men they should be given the same opportunity as men to pursue it. The Buddha agrees, and he then establishes a set of eight extra rules for the nuns' order. Each of these rules essentially puts nuns under the supervision of monks. For example, one rule states that a nun may never correct a monk in public but a monk may correct a nun. While the only rule Mahaprajapati asked to be changed was the rule on seniority, her request was denied. In essence this means that a monk bows to any monk who is his senior, that is, who has been ordained longer than he has, even by minutes. Nuns must always bow to monks, regardless of how long either of them has been ordained.

Why was the Buddha reluctant to ordain women, and why the Eight Rules? Many scholars point to a likely lack of support from the broader society for such an initiative. People were reluctant to accept the notion that either men or women would abandon their traditional roles as householders, wives, and mothers. As the monks depended on laypeople for their food, they had to consider the laypeople's concerns. And many of the men who became monks were likely opposed to introducing women into the sangha because of the strong patriarchal culture of India. Finally, despite the ambivalence toward women in the order that the textual Buddha appears to display, the affirmation of women's spiritual capacity is very strong. Subsequently women joined the order in large numbers. They joined for many of the same reasons that men did, but it is also clear that many saw it as a way of escaping the rigidity of India's patriarchal culture and establishing some independence.

The nuns' order appears to have declined and died out in India before the male order did, likely because of a belief that birth as a woman is an inferior birth, so donations made to nuns bring less merit than donations to monks. Further, women were denied access to education, and as Buddhist monasteries also became large universities, women were deprived of an opportunity to get the education they needed to develop the sort of social respect that would enable them to receive major donations (Falk 1989). They remained largely uneducated, limited to performing ritual services and blessings in order to survive and having little time to study or meditate. In many parts of Asia this remains the case today. While female ordination spread from India to other parts of Asia, it never reached Tibet or Thailand, and it has died out in some countries such as Sri Lanka and Burma (Myanmar). There has been a controversial movement to re-establish nuns' orders, a matter that will be discussed in some detail later.

Practices

Five Precepts for All Buddhists

1. Refrain from harming living beings.
2. Refrain from taking what is not given.
3. Refrain from sexual misconduct.
4. Refrain from false speech.
5. Refrain from intoxicants.

(continued)

Ten Precepts for Monks and Nuns

1. Refrain from harming living beings.
2. Refrain from taking what is not given.
3. Refrain from sexual misconduct [i.e., no sexual relations allowed].
4. Refrain from false speech.
5. Refrain from intoxicants.
6. Refrain from eating at inappropriate times.
7. Refrain from entertainments [shows, dancing, singing].
8. Refrain from adornments [cosmetics, jewellery, flowers].
9. Refrain from high beds.
10. Refrain from handling gold and silver.

Three Refuges/Jewels: Buddha, Dharma, and Sangha, usually chanted at the beginning of Buddhist services.

Pali canon: the sacred texts of Theravada Buddhism; accepted by the Mahayana and Vajrayana in addition to their own sacred texts.

The Three Jewels

The Three Jewels refer to the Buddha, the Dharma, and the Sangha. The Buddha discovered the truth about suffering and the way to end it. The Dharma is that truth and the Buddha's teachings about it and the path to ending suffering. After the Buddha died, access to that teaching and the truth to which it leads was preserved by the Sangha, the community of monks and nuns who had committed themselves to following in the Buddha's footsteps. Buddha, Dharma, and Sangha are also known as the **Three Refuges**, as one takes refuge from suffering. The taking of the Three Refuges precedes all Buddhist ceremonies.

SOURCES OF THE TRADITION

In this section some of the textual sources of the Buddhist tradition will be discussed, the texts accepted as authoritative by the three major traditions Theravada, Mahayana, and Vajrayana, or Tantra. Importantly, all Indian religious traditions place great emphasis on the spoken word. The word has power—power to spiritually transform. Even when writing was available, texts were not written down but passed on orally by groups of monks who memorized vast quantities of material. The names Four Noble Truths, Eightfold Noble Path, and Three Poisons are no accident. These numbers are used as memory devices. So too, talks were adapted to the audience. It is said that when the Buddha spoke to kings, he used examples that kings

would easily understand, and when he talked to wandering ascetics like himself, he used metaphors that they would understand. This flexibility tends to be lost when things are transcribed to text. The written word tends to seems more solid, less open to a variety of interpretations depending on the context in which it is used. One's understanding of text is often driven by the "letter" rather than the spirit. This is part of the reason why teachers are so important in Buddhism. The teacher's discussion of the Dharma is informed both by his or her personal experience of the spiritual dimension of the text and by his or her knowledge of the student or audience.

Theravada

The oldest and only complete group of texts is called the **Pali canon**. This is the body of texts accepted by the Theravada tradition as the authoritative word of the Buddha. The initial canon contained texts on the teachings and the monastic discipline; later a section on philosophy was added. So the Pali canon is composed of three groups of texts: teaching, monastic code, and philosophy. There are also other texts: collections of stories and fables that are considered important but not authoritative. The Pali canon was not written down until the first century B.C.E. in Sri Lanka, and then only because the monks were afraid it would be lost because of wars, famine, and political strife.

The teaching section of the Pali canon contains the teachings of the Buddha. As scholars, we cannot definitively state that these are the words he used (for the reasons stated above), but there is a great deal of consistency between texts in regard to key concepts. Thus it is traditional to accept the whole as authoritative. Each teaching is prefaced by the phrase "Thus have I heard." The speaker is Ananda, the Buddha's cousin and attendant for most of his teaching career.

At the First Council, the meeting held by senior monks after the Buddha's death, Ananda recited the teachings, setting out the time, place, and context where he had heard them. Upali, a monk noted for his knowledge of the monastic rules, recited the monastic code at the same council. When Ananda and Upali had finished their recitations, the whole group of five hundred enlightened monks chanted it together. This established consistency and orthodoxy, that is, everyone was clear about what was the correct teaching of the Buddha, and it also established orthopraxy, or proper monastic practice. Scholars, however, believe that there has never been just one version of what the Buddha taught.

The philosophy section noted above was added later to the canon. The fact that it was added at all indicates its importance to the tradition. These texts systematize and discuss the implications of teachings found throughout the teaching texts and attempt to account for any seeming discrepancies or contradictions. The Pali version of this section provides a detailed analysis of the elements of a person and the workings of the mind and is the foundation of Buddhist philosophy in South and Southeast Asia. In Chinese translation we have an incomplete

philosophical text from another early Buddhist school, the foundation for philosophy in East Asia and Tibet.

The canon also includes texts that, while not authoritative in the narrow sense, have been influential in the development and spread of Buddhism. The two most important collections are the Jatakas and the Avadanas. Both are what are called popular tales, narratives, or stories. Stories are an effective means of communicating religious truths or ideas to a broad range of people. Historically, most ordinary people would have been illiterate, and many people, even today, are neither interested in nor equipped to handle sophisticated philosophy. These stories explore the qualities, or perfections, of the bodhisattva. The perfections are things that a bodhisattva (a being headed for enlightenment) must perfect in order to complete the path to becoming a buddha. Some identify six perfections, others ten. Examples of perfections are things such as generosity, patience, courage, and insight. In Mahayana Buddhism these develop into the stages of the bodhisattva.

Architecturally, stupas developed from ancient memorial mounds built for heroes. The mound developed into an egg-shaped formation called an *andha* ("egg" or "womb") on a foundation, with an umbrella shape—a royal symbol—topping the structure. Originally stupas held the relics of a sacred person, which later evolved to include fragments of texts. While there is cultural variance, the basic form remains the same.

Source: Mavis L. Fenn

Some stories encourage giving to religious figures by presenting the karmic benefits of such acts, both present and future. Others tend to focus on devotion to a particular buddha or his relics. One who does an act of devotion or service now will be rewarded in the future. The metaphor is an agricultural one: one plants a seed (a service or gift) in the merit field of a Buddha or other great being, and it will later bear fruit. Stupas become important pilgrimage sites for acts of devotion and making vows, because it was believed that the bones of and items that had touched a great being, such as a robe or bowl, retained that person's power even after the person had died. The notions of Buddha fields and the benefits of devotion are also developed in Mahayana, and the idea was extended to texts.

While the texts above tend to be responses to the question "How does one attain a better rebirth and perhaps become a Buddha in the future?" texts of the early Buddhist monastic schools tend to ask questions perhaps stimulated by the death of the Buddha and related to the question of what it meant and what would happen next. Let us list just a few of them: Is the path that the Buddha followed a path that everyone can follow or is it just for extraordinary people? Is the Buddha really gone, and if so have we lost access to his

teaching and thus nirvana (enlightenment, end of suffering)? Is there a difference between the Buddha and an arhat? What does it mean in concrete terms to be an arhat, an enlightened person? Simmering beneath the surface, these issues burst forth in the creation of new texts that were quite different in tone from the earlier ones. These are the texts of the Mahayana, the "Large Vehicle." A significant departure from the Theravada texts, they are often referred to as the Second Turning of the Dharma Wheel.

Mahayana

It is important to understand the religious context within which the new texts of the Mahayana were created. We do not know the exact dates of their composition but they appear to start around the second century B.C.E. and continued to be produced perhaps as late as the fourth century C.E. What distinguishes Mahayana Buddhism from Theravada is the acceptance of one or more of these new texts as the word of the Buddha, along with the new ideas and ideals put forward in them. If the Buddha died hundreds of years before, how can the Mahayana claim these texts are the words of the Buddha?

Table 5.1   Key Differences between Theravada and Mahayana Buddhism

Authority	Theravada	Mahayana
Scripture	Pali canon	Pali canon plus new texts
Buddha	Buddha as human	Buddha as cosmic principle
Bodies of the Buddha	Form Dharma	Form Dharma Enjoyment
Spiritual hero	Arhat	Bodhisattva
Bodhisattva	The Buddha before he became enlightened	Celestial: powerful figures who transfer merit and use skill-in-means Ordinary: one who has taken a vow to attain full enlightenment for the sake of all living beings
Means to enlightenment/salvation	Work out your own salvation	Can be assisted through worship and transfer of merit
Geographic distribution	South and Southeast Asia	East Asia

The Mahayana defended the authority of these new sutras by using guidelines found in the Pali canon of the Theravada regarding how to know what is to be considered dharma (teaching) and what is not (MacQueen 1981, 1982). The Pali canon contains texts that are not directly spoken by the Buddha but by one of the enlightened monks (arhats). These texts are authorized by the Buddha either before or after the fact, and he makes it clear that the authority to speak comes from the arhat's own enlightenment and is simply being validated by him. Thus the Mahayana claim that their texts are also enlightened speech. Sometimes the new text is defended as an extended explanation of an earlier teaching. Most interesting is the idea that they have been received from either the historical Buddha or other buddhas in other realms through visions and meditation. With this explanation, Mahayana Buddhism moves decisively away from the Theravada notion of authority.

For the Theravada, there was only one bodhisattva who became a buddha. He died and is inaccessible to us except through the community of monks and nuns he founded (sangha) and his teachings that they preserve. No new revelations can occur until the time of a future Buddha, who will rediscover the Truth (Dharma) when the Truth expounded by this eon's Buddha has been forgotten. How do the Mahayana address this? Again there is precedent within the early strata of Buddhist texts. The Buddha had said that whoever saw him saw the Truth, and vice versa. He also commented that whether or not there is a Buddha to discover the Truth, the Truth is still there. Through shifting the emphasis from the Buddha as a person to the wisdom that created him (Prajnaparamita, or Highest Wisdom), the whole notion of Buddha shifts from one rooted in the here and now to one of cosmic potential. There is a category of Mahayana texts (called "Perfection of Wisdom") that explore this Highest Wisdom. The earliest of these is likely Perfection of Wisdom in Eight Thousand Lines, which saw several expansions over the centuries to as many as a hundred thousand lines. Two other famous texts in this category are Diamond Cutter and the very short Heart Sutra. These texts tend to emphasize the wisdom that a bodhisattva needs to develop in order to attain the Highest Wisdom, referred to as "emptiness." These texts became the basis for development of a philosophical school called the

Skill-in-means: various means used by a bodhisattva in order to help living beings; may include teaching and encouragement and other strategies such as setting a task to accomplish.

Madhyamika, founded by Nagarjuna about the middle of the second century C.E.

Perfection of Wisdom in Eight Thousand Lines is an important text because it brings together a variety of themes found in early Mahayana texts and later developed by different branches of the Mahayana. It discusses the difficulty of taking on the path of the bodhisattva and the wisdom one must acquire. It also gives us some insight into the likely state of many in the Buddhist community after the Buddha's death. The text ends with the story of Sadaprarudita, whose name means "always weeping." He weeps because he feels hopeless about the possibility of enlightenment because the light (Buddha) has been removed from the world. He weeps so much that the heavens answer him, providing hope and sending him on a quest for his teacher, a bodhisattva. In doing so he must overcome obstacles in his path in order to receive teachings. This echoes the presentation of the path of the bodhisattva that we find in the narrative texts above, and it stresses the importance of the text itself, devotion to it, and service to its teacher. Great merit accrues to someone who writes down some of it, carries it, and does service for the teacher of the text. Perhaps most important, according to the text, we are not alone. Powerful figures exist who can assist us on this journey of life, namely buddhas and bodhisattvas.

The Lotus Sutra and the Larger and Smaller Pure Land Sutras are also worthy of note. The Lotus Sutra contains the first appearance of Avalokitesvara, the bodhisattva of compassion who plays a prominent role in Asian Buddhist practice, primarily in female form as Kuan Yin (Guanyin). The Lotus Sutra also presents us with the notion of **skill-in-means**, in the parable of a man who saves his children from a fire by pretending he has gifts for them; focused on the gifts, the children do not panic and readily leave the burning building unharmed. So too the bodhisattva uses a variety of means and strategies to save living beings from the flames of rebirth.

The Larger and Smaller Pure Land Sutras introduce us to Amitabha Buddha and the Pure Land. Eons ago the bodhisattva who would become Amitabha vowed to become a buddha to help all living beings. One part of his vow was to build a land in which it would be easier to attain enlightenment, and people could be reborn there. The specific criteria for rebirth in the Pure Land vary somewhat between texts, but the central point is the same: call upon the name of the Buddha Amitabha in faith ten times, relying on his power and merit to ensure your rebirth there.

Finally, there are Mahayana texts that focus on visualizations, something that becomes increasingly important in the Vajrayana tradition of Tibet and Japan. The Meditations on Amitayus Sutra, a Pure Land text, presents a series of visualizations. One of them is geared toward people who would normally be excluded from the Pure Land as they had been excluded from enlightenment in the Theravada tradition. These are people who have killed their mother or father, harmed a buddha, killed an arhat, or caused a split in the sangha. If they do this meditation they may be reborn in the Pure Land, but in a closed lotus, where they must remain for twelve eons before the lotus opens and they hear the teachings. One can also get a preview of the Pure Land. The Meditation on the Presence of Buddhas Sutra teaches

visualization of a buddha as a means to receive teachings from one. These texts stress the loyalty that a student must have for the teacher. The teacher provides a priceless gift, and the student should be prepared to serve the teacher unquestioningly in all things (Williams 1989; Robertson 2005) This too became an important part of the Vajrayana Buddhist tradition.

Vajrayana

The term *vajrayana* means "vehicle of the diamond or thunderbolt." This refers to the luminous wisdom that is hard as a diamond and spontaneous as a thunderbolt as it cuts through ignorance. As with the Mahayana texts, we need to know the religious context from which these texts, called tantras, arose. While dating is always a problem, the tantric movement may have begun around the fourth century, although texts do not appear until about the sixth century. It was believed to have arisen among non-monastic religious practitioners, and some argue that women initially played an important role (Shaw 1994). The basic idea is that through ritual and meditation one can access the sacred power that creates a buddha and use that power to become a buddha oneself. These texts, unlike earlier ones, are esoteric, which means that the full meaning of the text is not clear even when it

A mandala done on cloth from India. A mandala represents a variety of things and provides a focus for worship or meditation. It is at once a picture of the sacred universe, of the enlightened mind, and of the palace of a buddha.

Source: Mavis L. Fenn

seems to be. Something is missing, and to determine that hidden meaning one needs a teacher. The root text, called a **tantra**, will have both written commentaries and verbal ones from one's teacher, plus a set of practices, rituals, symbols such as sacred drawings (**mandalas**), and visualization meditations attached to it.

Vajrayana generally sees itself as the culmination of earlier practice, incorporating levels of earlier teachings and practice and adding levels beyond that. It is the Third Turning of the Wheel, more powerful than earlier practices and shortening the time necessary for enlightenment. This is another reason why one needs a teacher. Tantra may be a shortcut to enlightenment for compassionate people with a strong desire for enlightenment as soon as possible, but it is dangerous because the rituals may use elements that are considered forbidden or incorporate the power of desire. Representations of the main Tantric deities of the class of texts called the Highest Yoga Tantras show a male deity in sexual union with a female deity. Because of this, many students assume that Tantric Buddhism is about sex. It is not. While I do not wish to simplify matters too much, these figures generally represent the union of compassion and wisdom. There are some sexual rituals, but these are only for advanced practitioners and are either visualized or enacted with a similarly advanced consort, neither of whom has taken a vow of celibacy. Scholars sometimes distinguish between "right-handed" and "left-handed" tantra. The majority of the rituals and practices are right-handed and can be performed by anyone. Left-handed rituals, called that because they incorporate substances or practices normally considered unclean or forbidden (such as meat, alcohol, bodily products, parched grain, or ritual sex), are limited to a few practitioners. Remembering that these texts are not self-evident and require an enlightened teacher to assist one, translations are available of some tantras, such as the Hevajra, the Kalacakra, and the Guhyasamaj Tantra (Powers 1995).

HISTORY AND DEVELOPMENT

Buddhism was unlikely to have remained a religion of wandering mendicants for long. From the early texts we learn that the laity made gifts of location and shelter to the Buddha and other prominent monks early on. Many of these donations came from wealthy traders,

> **Tantra:** a text that is accompanied by oral and written commentaries and prescribes a set of rituals and meditations centred on a buddha; also the belief that ritual and meditation are the means to enlightenment.
>
> **Mandala:** a sacred drawing of the universe, enlightened consciousness, or the palace of a buddha and his retinue.

bankers, and businesspeople. These largely urban elites had no place within the Brahmanical religious and social system: they had money but no place in the social order, and thus little or no respect. So they increased their social status through gifts to various mendicant groups such as the Buddhists and Jains. The Buddha advised monks to live close to cities, far enough away to provide solitude for study and meditation but close enough to receive donations and teach the people (in one text the coming of the Buddha of the future, Maitreya, is presaged by the development of large, prosperous cities teeming with people). Travel within India during the rainy season was almost impossible and restricted by both the difficulty and the possibility of harm to the teeming water beings. Monks would frequently return to their home area during that time and make a retreat, focusing on developing their meditation and studying. Some of the most interesting living spaces donated to the sangha were caves, some for solitary meditators and others quite large, expanding deep into the rock.

The Buddha named no successor to take charge of the sangha after he died. He told the monks that his teachings and the monastic code should be their guide. The monk Mahakasyapa is reputed to have called the First Council to establish what precisely the words of the Buddha were, but we also know from that account that there were differences in the texts and probably their interpretation from early on. There are other reasons to believe that there was never just one oral account of the Buddha's teachings or interpretations of them. The Buddha sent the first sixty arhats to various parts of the country to teach. Geographic dispersion will produce different accounts, especially as local languages were used for teaching. Anyone who speaks more than one language knows that while words may be translated directly, the sense of them often cannot. Groups of monks specialized in memorizing certain parts of the teachings. Some memorized the teachings, some the discipline, others parts of both teachings and discipline. Finally, people do not hear things the same way; each adds his or her own sense to what is heard. As a consequence of all these factors, several schools of Buddhism developed fairly early on.

The first real disagreement between different monastic communities is reported to have been a breach between the monks of the east and the monks of the west regarding whether or not monks could receive cash donations from the laity as well as material goods. This occasioned the Second Council, which decided that monks could not handle silver and gold. But far more serious was a later issue concerning the state of an arhat. This dispute centred on what was called the Five Points of Mahadeva, which likely represent a compilation of ideas of the time rather than being specific to any one monk. Taken together they focus on questions that are still relevant and being debated today: What does it mean to be enlightened? Does it mean one knows everything about everything or just about the spiritual life? An enlightened person is often thought of as being perfect, but what does *perfect* mean? If an arhat has an erotic dream, is that a moral imperfection indicating he is not really fully enlightened or is that just the way the male physiognomy works?

The most important issue was that of the nature of a buddha and the path of the bodhisattva. Could anyone set out on the path of the bodhisattva, as the Buddha did so many eons ago, or was it an ideal for exceptional people only? And what of the man who became Buddha and died at about eighty years of age? Was he really gone? Despite the Buddha's admonition that this was a question that could not be answered, it must have been a topic for speculation. The Buddha was a well-beloved teacher and the texts reflect the grief his followers felt when he died. As the Perfection of Wisdom in Eight Thousand Lines story of Sadaprarudita shows, there must have been fear that without the Buddha there was no hope for enlightenment. It was questions such as these—the nature of buddha-hood and the arhat's level of enlightenment, along with the question of whether or not everyone could aspire to the bodhisattva path—that culminated in the division of Buddhism into Theravada and Mahayana. Regardless, because the unity of the sangha is based upon the monastic Discipline, which

differed little between them, they continued to reside in the same monasteries for some time after the rise of Mahayana.

The questions and issues of the Five Points of Mahadeva became the focus for a plethora of new texts that surfaced with the development of Mahayana from about the second century B.C.E. to perhaps as late as the fourth century C.E. As well, several new concepts emerged that defined the divide between Theravada and Mahayana. First, while Mahayana was a monastic movement, it incorporated an expanded notion of what the laity could achieve spiritually. Pilgrimage and devotion came to be thought of as meritorious rather than simply commemorative. While the early texts did list enlightened laypeople, the Theravada had come to believe that renunciation was necessary to attain enlightenment. The Mahayana did not, and made the point in texts such as the Vimilakirti Nirdesa, in which the layman Vimilakirti possesses insight far beyond that of the assembled arhats. People were encouraged to take the bodhisattva vow that they would seek full enlightenment for the sake of all living beings. It was believed that celestial bodhisattvas such as Avalokitesvara would help people by transferring merit to them. These celestial bodhisattvas had accumulated great quantities of merit and—like the Buddha Amitabha, who created the Pure Land so enlightenment would be easier to realize—they used it for the benefit of others.

The distinction between a celestial bodhisattva and a buddha becomes elusive at the upper levels of the Ten Stages of the Bodhisattva, hinging only on the fact that the bodhisattva continues to reincarnate for the benefit of beings while a buddha removes himself from the cycle. The shift in the Mahayana texts, from an emphasis on the historical Buddha to the wisdom that creates buddhas, produced numerous realms and Buddha fields where buddhas could teach the advanced bodhisattvas or visit them in visions. The Buddha was now said to have been possessed of three bodies: the Truth body (the essence of what all buddhas are); the enjoyment or bliss (spiritual) body possessed by advanced bodhisattvas, which allows them to enjoy various benefits such as travelling to other realms; and a form body, which a buddha uses to teach ordinary people. We have already noted the growing importance of visualization both in gaining access to buddhas and their teaching and as a means to acquire their characteristics.

The concept of skill-in-means—the various ways and strategies used by a bodhisattva to teach others, as in the parable of the burning house in the Lotus Sutra—was put into philosophical form by the second-century monk Nagarjuna. He was the first to develop a distinctly Mahayana philosophy. He did so by extending the Theravada concept of dependent origination and the Mahayana concept of skill-in-means. Nagarjuna said that if there is no self-existent thing because everything has multiple causes, then everything is "empty." Even the relationship between the five components of a person is empty of substance, because each of those five things is also a product of many other things. So what all things share, people included, is this emptiness.

Language provides a good example for explaining what Nagarjuna meant. Language is constructed and relative. Take, for instance, terms such as *up* and *down*: there is no *up* that exists independently of a *down*. Similarly, the notions of *male* and *female* are constructs; terms such as *race* or *gender* are artificial, simply invented terms. But because of the power of language, race and gender are often understood as being separate and different "things" rather than simply aspects of being human. Believing that these categories exist in some substantial way, rather than being flexible descriptions, often leads to conflict between men and women, blacks and whites, "us" and "the enemy."

Nagarjuna distinguished two levels of truth. Language belongs to the ordinary level of truth, that of daily life. This is the level of everyday communication that takes place between people. But at the higher level of truth—what really exists—one realizes that all things, including one's self, are merely an accumulation of aggregates or parts that work together to perform a certain function. While this extension of the concept of dependent origination does push beyond the philosophy of the Theravada, what was truly radical is that Nagarjuna applied this idea of the two truths to Buddhist teachings as well. Teachings such as the Four Noble Truths, according to Nagarjuna, are like all practical tools of language, a means of directing people to a higher truth, Emptiness. On their own, they are empty as well. They are examples of skill-in-means.

His major work, *The Root Verses of the Middle Way*, provides a demonstration of this. It consists of a series of arguments. For example, an opponent will put forward an argument and then Nagarjuna will deconstruct it. But Nagarjuna takes no position himself. When it

> **Buddha nature:** a Mahayana term for the potential within all beings for enlightenment, an idea also present in Theravada.

comes to key notions of samsara (the wheel of rebirth) and nirvana, he demonstrates that these terms make sense only when related to one another—there is no substance to either term. Again the consequences of this are that, if there is no samsara to get away from and no nirvana to run to, then what people are looking for must be here—right here in our daily life and accessible through all time. This was a major philosophical shift.

Many Buddhists in Nagarjuna's time and since found his thought too negative. The other major Mahayana philosophical school is called the Yogacara, traditionally said to have been founded by the brothers Asanga and Vasubandhu. The name itself indicates that this school is more contemplative, the term *yoga* referring to meditation. It was also called "Mind Only" because it believed that Mind was real and existed in a substantive way. Sometimes Yogacara thought is called idealist, meaning based on a belief that the mind creates the world outside us, but this is not accurate. Yogacara believes that things do exist outside the self, but not in the way that is generally understood. One's perspective colours one's view of reality. The way to get rid of this falsely constructed picture is to remove this personalized perspective through meditation. This then brings one to Mind. Terms such as *empty* are also utilized, referring to Mind, or consciousness, in its original state as empty of imperfections. This consciousness, empty of imperfections, is referred to as "suchness." The notion of suchness provides the basis for all views of the world. This consciousness is also understood as **Buddha nature**.

Buddhism continued to spread after the death of the Buddha, but it was still one of many religious groups of the time. This situation changed with King Asoka (ruled c. 273–232 B.C.E.). Asoka was a "world conqueror." He inherited a large territory from his father and grandfather (Mauryan dynasty) and increased the size of his empire through a series of wars, at one time ruling almost all of India. In one of the Rock Edicts he writes that it was his battle with the Kalingas that provoked in him disgust for the violence, death, and misery of war. He vowed to become a "righteous ruler" who would rule his people through the Dharma.

He instituted a variety of reforms in line with his policy of non-violence: he cut down the amount of meat used in his court, he established festivals where no animals were to be killed, and he sent out ministers of ethics and wrote moral edicts for the people. Although he did not abolish capital punishment, Asoka allowed a few days for the condemned to settle their affairs, and he retained the right to use force against any territories who sought to break away from his control. As a king, Asoka was committed to supporting the various religious groups of the time, but he appears to have had a special affinity with Buddhism. Through his support Buddhism became a major religious presence in India and beyond. Asoka is credited with convening the Third Council, which is recognized only by the Theravada. The purpose of the council was to settle matters of dispute between different groups and expel monks who were not living up to their obligations. It also resulted in sending a missionary expedition to Sri Lanka.

Asoka represents the ideal of Buddhist kingship. Such a king provides a stable society not only through keeping order but also through providing for the legitimate needs of his people for food and employment. He supports and encourages religious groups and keeps a watchful eye on them to ensure their purity. In return the sangha accepts his gifts and his authority. This represents a reciprocal legitimization of authority, the civil and the religious. This is a powerful affirmation of rulership or government in countries where Buddhism is the primary religious tradition. To refuse to accept the king's gifts is to symbolically state that his rule is not legitimate. This has occurred occasionally, most recently in Burma (Myanmar) in 2008, where monks protesting actions by the military junta marched through the streets with their bowls overturned.

While Buddhism continued to receive patronage from Indian kings after Asoka, it did have challenges. It was faced with a reinvigorated Hinduism, challenges from the Jain religion, and loss of royal patronage. Muslim invasions, beginning in the tenth century, put an end to Buddhism in India. This situation did not change until the middle of the twentieth century, with the conversion to Buddhism of B. R. Ambedkar (1891–1956). Dr. Ambedkar was a low-caste Hindu who was influential during the movement for independence and the primary author of the Indian constitution, which contains certain rights for the lower castes, called "scheduled classes." Still, he believed it was impossible for the scheduled classes to achieve equality while remaining Hindu, so he studied the world's religions and decided on Buddhism. He focused on the rational and egalitarian aspects of Buddhist teaching, and in 1956 he and about half a million of his followers converted to Buddhism. This trend of mass conversions still occurs, and Ambedkar Buddhists are still working to improve social conditions in India.

South and Southeast Asia

While Buddhism may have died out in India, it did not die out in other parts of Asia. At the time of the Third Council, around 250 B.C.E., Asoka authorized sending Buddhist missionaries to various places in Asia. His son, the monk Mahinda, established Buddhism in Sri Lanka. A year later, Mahinda's sister Sanghamitta established an order of nuns. Theravada Buddhism is the dominant Buddhist tradition in Sri Lanka. While other forms were not unknown, it was Theravada that was embraced. The first monastery, Mahavihara, was built at Anuradhapura. There was considerable chaos during the first century B.C.E., including an invasion from South India, a famine, and a split in the Mahavihara group. The new group, Dharmaruci, from the Abayagiri monastery, received financial support from a new king. Concerned that the teachings might be lost, the Mahavihara group committed them to writing in the Sinhalese language.

The fourth and fifth centuries were a productive time for Buddhism in Sri Lanka. The nuns' order went to China to establish a female sangha there, and one of the most learned monks in Buddhist history, Buddhaghosa, translated the commentaries into Pali and composed a work called *The Path to Purification*, considered to be the definitive Theravada discussion of the Buddhist path.

Sri Lanka also played an important role in shaping how Buddhism was presented to the West. The colonial period (from the sixteenth century), during which Sri Lanka was ruled by a series of foreign powers, culminating in British rule, saw the Buddhist sangha lose much of its traditional role in education and medicine because of loss of government funding and the establishment of Christian missionary schools. Christian missionaries were critical of Buddhism and the social order of Sri Lanka, as they had been of Hindu India. The sangha became marginalized and was losing support.

However, in a series of debates with Christian missionaries, a young monk who had been educated in their schools defeated the missionaries in a series of debates, drawing the attention of the Theosophical Society.

The Theosophical Society supported Asian religions such as Hinduism and Buddhism because it believed that Asian wisdom was an important component of the original universal religious knowledge of humankind. Its support sparked both a renewal and a reform of the tradition. The Theosophists' campaign to restore Buddhism as central to society was fuelled by use of the printing press for pamphlets and the development of a list of beliefs, a flag, and dharma schools. Western technology was thus used against the Christian critics of Buddhism. At the same time, educated Buddhists and their Western supporters felt that many traditional practices were superstitious and they discouraged them. Texts became important in response to the Christian emphasis on the Bible. The Buddhist laity were encouraged to study and meditate and take a more active role in temple life. These changes are referred to as "Buddhist modernism" because, traditionally in Asia, laypeople did not meditate and were not concerned with temple business, and monks were not to engage in political or secular matters.

Of all the reformers, Angarika Dhammapala was the most influential. Western-educated in Christian schools, he developed a type of Buddhist nationalism, drawing on Buddhist chronicles that spoke of Sri Lanka as an "island of dharma," a sacred trust to be preserved. This nationalist Buddhism grew during the movement for independence and has continued into postcolonial times. While religion as a human product has inherent political aspects, it is not unfair to state that the Buddhist sangha in Sri Lanka has been politicized to the extent that nationalist Buddhism excludes non-Buddhists from its vision of the nation. Combined with economic and social strains as well as the political ones, this notion of Sri Lanka as a sacred Buddhist island has been used to rationalize violence against non-Buddhists.

The order of monks in Sri Lanka was threatened with extinction twice, in the eleventh and eighteenth centuries, as it failed to meet the requirement that ordinations have at least five senior monks. In the first case the order was refreshed from Burma, and in the second from Thailand. The order of nuns, however, was not refreshed when it died out; there

Sakyadhita: the International Association of Buddhist Women, which works to improve the circumstances of all Buddhist women.

is no record of the order after about the thirteenth century. There were non-ordained religious women in Sri Lanka called the Ten Precept Mothers, who wore white robes and adopted the novice precepts (explained below). Although efforts had been made to improve their education and living conditions from time to time, until the late twentieth century they were primarily older, poorly educated women who were often widows.

Concerted efforts by educated laywomen such as Ranjani da Silva, some Ten Precept Mothers, and **Sakyadhita**, the International Association of Buddhist Women—founded in 1987 by a group of women that included da Silva and the German Theravada nun Ayya Khema—changed that. Training centres for novices were established with the dual purpose of education and public service. The notion of public or social service is another example of modernism. Because women could not be ordained in the Sri Lankan sangha, they went abroad to Taiwan, Korea, or India for ordination. But these early efforts failed. Nuns who did attain full ordination outside Sri Lanka were not accepted in Sri Lanka because the ordination had been made by nuns of the Mahayana tradition, even though the monastic code used was from an early Theravada school.

It would be a mistake to think that the disagreement was solely along gender lines, with the men against ordination and the women for it. Some of the Ten Precept Mothers were against reinstitution of the nuns' order as well. Some believed they must wait until the Buddha of the future came. Others, remembering the eight special rules for nuns, did not want to come under the control of the monks (Batholomeusz 1994). On the other hand, some monks believed that the sangha was not complete without all four categories of people: nuns and monks, male and female laypeople. While the matter is still controversial, nuns have been ordained in Sri Lanka since 1998 and have gradually been gaining social acceptance.

Ordination has also been an issue in modern Thailand. Historically, no nuns' order ever reached Thailand, and efforts to establish a female order in the twentieth century have been met with resistance and

Vipassana: analytic or insight meditation on the Four Noble Truths, a modern version of which is widely taught.

hostility from the Thai Buddhist sangha. Still, there is a steadily growing movement begun by the late Voramai Kabilsingh, the only fully ordained nun in Thailand until recently. Despite enormous difficulties she established a home and school for girls; when she died, it was taken over by her daughter Chatsumarn (renamed Dhammananda), a former university professor. As Chatsumarn Kabilsingh, the Venerable Dhammananda completed her M.A. in religious studies at McMaster University in Hamilton.

The pattern established by Asoka, whereby the ruler oversees and supports the sangha and the sangha supports his righteous rule, was maintained in other areas of Southeast Asia such as Burma (Myanmar) and Thailand. Theravada Buddhism became the Thai state religion in the fourteenth century. While Thailand was never directly colonized, it did come under pressure from the French and British. Richard Robinson states that external diplomacy and internal reform, of which religious reform was a part, allowed the Thai kings to maintain internal unity and thus the crown (Robinson 1997). A series of reforms produced a centralized authority and standardized monastic education.

Venerable Dhammananda is one of the most prominent leaders in the movement for establishment of a nuns' order in Thailand.

Source: Gakuro

In Burma Buddhism continued to play a role in politics after the colonial period. The first prime minister of Burma, U Nu, attempted to construct a modern version of the ideal Buddhist state. Although Burma (renamed Myanmar by the junta) is currently under military rule, Buddhism continues to play an important role in politics, with demonstrations by Buddhist monks and world support for Aung San Suu Kyi, who was under house arrest for many years, unable to form a government even though her party won the election of 1990. Significantly, a modern form of **vipassana** (insight) meditation was developed in Burma for laypeople and has since spread throughout the world.

Buddhism also spread throughout Cambodia and Laos. In Cambodia, the massive Angkor Wat complex, a popular tourist destination, shows both Hindu and Buddhist influences. And while Indonesia is a Muslim country, it is also the site of Borobudur, on the island of Java. This huge stupa complex is said to be a metaphorical map of the spiritual universe. The minority population in Malaysia is Chinese and mostly Buddhist.

Although it is part of Southeast Asia, Vietnam's Buddhist history contains a mixture of influences. The history of Buddhism in Vietnam has tended to follow the traditional divisions of what is now one country: the northern areas were influenced by China and the southern areas by India. Thus Mahayana Buddhism was a force in northern areas and Theravada in the south, with mixing in the middle. Over time, Chinese-style Mahayana became predominant, although Theravada remains. Buddhist practice is a mixture of Zen and Pure Land Buddhism. Many people may know of Vietnamese Buddhism because of the long war in that country. Vietnam was colonized by the French in 1839, which resulted in Catholicism's being added to the religious scene. After the Vietnamese gained independence from France, there was a civil war between the north and the south. The north received assistance from China and its allies and the south received help from the United States and its allies. The war was complicated by the anti-Buddhist stance of the Catholic president of South Vietnam. As a result, several monks and nuns, following a devotional tradition developed in China during the medieval period, and drawing on the notion of the bodhisattva who takes upon himself the suffering of the people, set themselves on fire (self-immolation) to draw attention to this persecution.

The war in Vietnam also brought Thich Nhat Hanh to the attention of the West. One of the best-known Buddhist teachers in the world, he coined the phrase

"Engaged Buddhism." This is Buddhism that brings together Buddhist principles and social activism, and it is another example of the modernist Buddhism developed in Asia. During the Vietnam War he founded the Order of Interbeing and was active in aiding those who suffered because of the war. These efforts made him unpopular with both sides in the conflict, and he has lived in exile in France for many years. The communist government that took power in North Vietnam in 1975 allowed him to return in 2005 for a visit. However, in 2009 his remarks on religious independence were criticized by the government, and members of his Order of Interbeing were expelled from their temple. Buddhism in Vietnam is basically divided between the official state-sponsored Vietnamese Buddhist Church and the United Buddhist Churches of Vietnam, which attempts to coordinate the efforts of temples who wish to maintain their independence.

China

While most of the countries in Southeast Asia follow the Theravada tradition, this was not the case in China. While China received all forms of Buddhism, it was the Zen and Pure Land schools that thrived and dominated Buddhist discourse. Initially Buddhism seemed antithetical to Chinese culture, and the Chinese were highly suspicious of outsiders and non-Chinese thought. Confucian thought was very pragmatic and valued a hierarchical social order. Nirvana seemed very unworldly and the Buddhist notion of karma was deemed offensive because it placed animals on an equal footing with humans. Most offensive of all was the fact that Buddhist monks and nuns left their families, were celibate, and did not work. As an agrarian culture, the Chinese relied on family to till the fields, carry on the line, and care for the older people. Confucius built his whole notion of the state on the foundations of the family: each member must make a contribution to society and the state.

Yet there were aspects of Buddhist thought that did appeal to the Chinese. The doctrine of karma, for example, could be used to explain why one person was born a peasant and another one an emperor. Buddhism fit nicely with Daoism, and many Buddhist terms were translated into Chinese using Daoist terms. The compassionate bodhisattvas and buddhas were a comfort to the ordinary people, whose lives were—and in most countries of the world today continue to be—difficult. As for the family, Buddhists argued that the

merit accumulated by parents who gave a son to the sangha or transferred by a monk to his family benefited them not only now but in the future. And in the thought of Zen Buddhism, work is understood as a virtue. The breakdown of the Han dynasty (221 C.E.) ushered in a long period of instability, invasion, and weak rulers, and this provided an opening for Buddhism. While its position has never been comparable to that of Theravada in Sri Lanka or Vajrayana in Tibet, it was a major force in China for some time, and through reform movements in mainland China and Taiwan in the middle of the twentieth century, it has become influential worldwide.

Until the monk Kumarajiva set up a translation team in the fifth century, the Chinese had a plethora of Buddhist texts but they were poorly translated, and they did not have access to the traditional Indian commentaries. Many of the teachings seemed contradictory or confusing to the Chinese. They developed a system of categorizing Buddhist texts and thought into distinct stages, making their ideas seem less contradictory. They surmised that when the Buddha first taught, he kept it simple because the ideas were new to people—this is how they understood Theravada. As people became better able to grasp the basics of Buddhism, it was believed that he then taught the early Mahayana teachings and eventually the more sophisticated teachings of Madhyamaka and Yogacara. His teaching culminated in whatever text was central to a particular Buddhist school. So the Tiantai school, noted for its meditation, held the Lotus Sutra as the culmination of the Buddha's teaching, and the Huayan school placed the Garland Sutra at the top of the system. Neither of these schools lasted in China, but the thought of both influenced the development of Buddhism in China and the balance of East Asia.

Around the sixth century, separate schools of Buddhism began to emerge, creating a Buddhism that reflected Chinese culture and indigenous ideas. Of all the Buddhist traditions, it is Ch'an (Zen) that is often presented as the central Chinese school. This is in large part because of the writings of D. T. Suzuki and Alan Watts and the influence of post–Second World War writers in the United States such as Jack Kerouac, themselves practitioners of Zen. But what we know through this interpretation of Zen is often quite divorced from its historical Chinese and Japanese context (McRae 2003.) Zen traces its lineage back to one of the Buddha's most distinguished arhats, Mahakasyapa, renowned for his meditation and as the convenor of the First Council.

The narrative has the Buddha about to give a sermon. Instead of speaking, however, he simply holds out a flower, and Mahakasyapa smiles. The implication is that Mahakasyapa "gets it" and the Buddha knows this as well. It emphasizes a central Zen doctrine of "mind-to-mind" transmission from master to student.

Mahakasyapa becomes the first of the Indian patriarchs of Zen. The last Indian patriarch and first Chinese patriarch, Bodhidharma, is said to have brought Zen to China. There are many stories told of Bodhidharma. He sat in front of a wall meditating for nine years, until his legs fell off; he cut off his eyelids so he could be meditating all the time and not fall asleep; he told the emperor there was no merit in building temples. From a historical viewpoint the line of patriarchs in India is not factual, but it is significant in that it shows an attempt to establish legitimacy. The same is true of a statement attributed to Bodhidharma, that Zen is

> A special transmission outside the scriptures;
> Without depending on words and letters;
> Pointing directly to the human mind.
> Seeing the innate nature, one becomes a Buddha. (Harvey 1999, 154)
>
> **Source:** Peter Harvey, *An Introduction to Buddhism*. (UK: Cambridge University Press, 1990). Reprinted with the permission of Cambridge University Press.

If one combined the statement above with stories of Zen masters burning sacred texts, you would think that Zen was against scripture altogether. This is not entirely accurate, although there was tension between those who favoured a scholarly approach and those who preferred meditation. While the statement does imply that Zen has something the other traditions do not, the statement about texts and the stories of masters burning them conveys a traditional message: one can get attached even to sacred texts, and even this form of attachment blocks one's efforts at transformation. Zen masters insisted that their followers were not to cling to the texts but instead to test their truths through experience. This is similar to the stories about Bodhidharma. Remember the earlier discussion about narrative as history and as sacred history. It is necessary not to take such stories as historically factual but to

seek for an answer to their religious meaning within the historical context of the story. The message is that the spiritual quest is not easy. If one wants it, one must want it completely and be willing to give up anything for it. It is a story of commitment and dedication.

The primary text for the Zen tradition is the Platform Sutra of the Sixth Patriarch. The sixth patriarch was Hui-neng, about whom we know little historically. He is the paradigm of the Zen master, and his story vividly illustrates the notion that one has inherent Buddha nature to which one can suddenly awake. Hui-neng is presented as an uneducated rural boy whose interest in receiving teaching has brought him to the monastery of the fifth patriarch. He is set to work in the monastery kitchen. Meanwhile the fifth patriarch is preparing to hand on his robe and bowl, the sign of transmission to a successor. The fifth patriarch indicates that he wishes the pupils to demonstrate their level of insight by composing a poem. The most advanced student writes this poem anonymously on the wall:

> The Body is like the Enlightenment (Bodhi) tree;
> The mind is like a clear mirror.
> At all times we must strive to polish it,
> And must not let the dust collect. (Harvey 1999, 155)
>
> **Source:** Peter Harvey, *An Introduction to Buddhism*. (UK: Cambridge University Press, 1990). Reprinted with the permission of Cambridge University Press.

The Fifth Patriarch knows who wrote the poem. He also knows that the student is not yet enlightened. Seeing the writing, Hui-neng asks someone to read it to him and then in turn to write this poem:

> Enlightenment originally has no tree;
> The mirror also has no stand.
> Buddha-nature is always clear and pure;
> Where is there room for dust? (Harvey 1999, 155)
>
> **Source:** Peter Harvey, *An Introduction to Buddhism*. (UK: Cambridge University Press, 1990). Reprinted with the permission of Cambridge University Press.

The master sees this poem and recognizes that it represents an enlightened mind. Later he calls Hui-Neng to him, teaches him the Diamond Sutra, turns over the robe and bowl, and sends him away. We will not address the details of the Mahayana philosophy represented in the poem but will highlight its teachings about enlightenment. Hui-neng is uneducated and rural. One does not have to be educated or sophisticated to attain enlightenment, because all beings have within them the Buddha nature. The fifth patriarch knows that Hui-neng is enlightened because they possess one mind. As one scholar notes, it is more a recognition of the student's spiritual maturity on the part of the teacher than an actual transmission (McRae 2003). The two primary schools of Ch'an/Zen in China and Japan are sometimes referred to as the "sudden" and "gradual" schools. This refers to their belief that enlightenment is either a sudden awakening or a gradual unfolding. The "sudden" school in Japan is the Rinzai, and the "gradual" school is the Soto.

There is a stark absence of women in Chinese Buddhism. Women seem to have been active in the early centuries of Buddhism, but by the sixth century, when distinctly Chinese schools began to appear, we no longer hear from them. An eleventh-century teaching refers to the irrelevance of sex in terms of Dharma, and we do have the collection called *Lives of Eminent Nuns* written in the sixth century, but that is all. Several recent books have attempted to redress this situation (see "Recommended Reading" at the end of the chapter).

Zen also developed, from about the eighth century on, unique techniques for encouraging enlightenment in its students. The first was encounter dialogues, exchanges between teacher and student. Some of these dialogues may appear nonsensical to those outside the cultural setting of the time. Some are a play on words, but all of them are designed to force the student to think in new and unusual ways. Such an encounter would then be used as the basis for commentaries. These were called public legal cases, known in their most common form by the Japanese term *koan*. Longer koans soon came to be augmented by catch-phrase koans that removed the context of the encounter and left only a cryptic phrase. "What is 'Buddha'?" is answered by "Three pounds of flax" (Robinson 2005). This cryptic phrase could be reduced even further, to its key term, and that term would become the student's meditative focus. That is, the student would try to keep the term

> **Nien-fo:** the Chinese term (in Japanese, *nembutsu*) for a recitation in honour of and in thanks to Amitabha (Amida) Buddha, the Buddha of the Pure Land.

attentively in his mind without trying to figure out any possible meaning.

Pure Land Buddhism, which is in numbers of practitioners the largest Buddhist tradition in Asia, may have had its roots in India with the Larger and Smaller Pure Land Sutras and the Meditation on Amitayus Sutra, but it is in China that the tradition flowered. It began to take shape with the creation in the fifth century of a lay society dedicated to devotees' gaining rebirth in the Pure Land. The influence of three patriarchs on both Pure Land practice and doctrine created a structure for the organization of a separate school, which occurred in Japan. Tanluan (476–542) developed the meditative device of concentrating on the name of the Buddha Amitabha (Omito in Chinese, Amida in Japanese), which developed into a recitation called the **nien-fo** (*nembutsu* in Japanese), in which one recited the name of the Buddha Amitabha ten times in faith.

The concept of faith in Buddhism has far-reaching dimensions. The definition of faith we see in Theravada is faith *that*—that enlightenment exists, that the Buddha discovered it, and that if we follow in his footsteps we will attain enlightenment as well. In Pure Land Buddhism, faith is *in*—in the former bodhisattva, now Buddha Amitabha, who created the Pure Land as part of his vow to attain full enlightenment for the benefit of all living beings. The shift is usually referred to as a shift from *own* power to *other* power. Why this shift? It is the culmination of the idea that things and people are in decline, that they are not as capable or good as they used to be, not living as long, because of wars and disease. In other words, this age is a degenerate age. There might be some who could follow the traditional path, but most people were simply not capable of following the path of the elders.

This fits in with the general Buddhist feeling found in Indian texts that after the age of Dharma there would be a decline of Dharma. But in Mahayana the buddhas and celestial bodhisattvas could be asked for help because of their great compassion and merit. This understanding is taken further in Pure Land Buddhism: through the recitation of Amitabha's name, one is asking for rebirth in the Pure Land, where everything

> **Humanistic Buddhism:** a Buddhism that focuses on everyday life, developed in Taiwan and especially associated with Fo Guang Shan.

reminds devotees of Dharma and makes enlighten-ment possible again. The goal now becomes the Pure Land rather than enlightenment directly. This was an understanding and practice that attracted people on a massive scale.

While Buddhism flourished from about the sixth to the middle of the ninth century, a devastating perse-cution followed. In 845 a Daoist emperor confiscated monastery land and destroyed most of the monasteries. Only certain Zen schools and Pure Land remained, the latter continuing because it was embedded throughout the population. Many Zen monasteries were isolated in the mountains and were self-sufficient. This, plus the respect in which they were held, made them less open to persecution.

The period from about 1850 to 1950 was also one of great challenge for Buddhism. The Christian-inspired Taiping rebellion (1850–64) saw Buddhist monasteries looted and destroyed (Robinson 2005). These were eventually rebuilt, and in a movement sim-ilar to that in Sri Lanka, Buddhists responded by devel-oping printed materials and starting schools. When the Manchu dynasty was overthrown and the Nationalist government took power (1912–49), Buddhism was again targeted, but it was able to recover in some areas. When the Communists took over in 1949, Buddhist monastic lands were confiscated, monks and nuns were persecuted, and many were forcibly disrobed. This was nothing, however, compared to the destruction that occurred during the Cultural Revolution of the 1960s, which lasted about ten years. The purpose of the Cultural Revolution was to destroy the old ideas, values, and institutions of China in order to build a new order for a new time. Not just Buddhism but all religion was seen as part of a repressive past that needed to be swept away. From 1949 until the late 1970s many Chinese masters left for Taiwan. In mainland China today Buddhism has made something of a recovery but, as in Vietnam, there is an official Buddhist church that is expected to follow government policies.

A major Buddhist reform movement developed in Taiwan with the influx of Chinese masters. It began in China with Taixu (1890–1947), who believed that the sangha needed to modernize, purify itself of Daoist and folk practices, and help people in their daily lives. He also wanted Buddhism to be accessible to non-Buddhists and saw it as a way of resisting the forces of materialism. He believed that Buddhists should work toward creation of the Pure Land on earth. This style of Buddhism, with educated monks and nuns serving society along with a highly motivated and active lay association, is called **Humanistic Buddhism**. Several of the monks who fled to Taiwan from China were influenced by Taixu's thought, including Master Hsing Yun, the founder of Fo Guang Shan; Sheng Yen, founder of Dharma Drum; and Cheng Yen, founder of the Tzu Chi Relief Organization. Also inspired by Taixu was Master Tanzu, whose disciples founded the Cham Shan temples. All four of these Chinese Buddhist groups have a strong presence in the West generally and in Canada specifically.

Japan

Buddhism arrived in Japan from Korea in the middle of the sixth century, when a Korean king sent a Buddha image and texts to the emperor along with a recom-mendation: countries that practised Buddhism had done well and it would protect the nation. There was some resistance to the adoption of this new religion, fear that the kami, the native divinities of Japan, might object to worship of this foreign god. But one of the generals felt positive about it, and he and his family built a shrine and began worshipping the image. A plague broke out that was attributed to the wrath of the kami, and so the first entry of Buddhism into Japan ended with the image being thrown into the harbour.

About fifty years later more images and texts arrived, along with monks to interpret them. But it was really the sponsorship of Buddhism by Prince Shotoku (592–628) that put Buddhism on a firm foundation. Shotoku established Japan's first constitution in 604, and in it he recommended the practice of all three religions current at the time: Buddhism for its ethical benefit, Confucianism for its social order, and worship of the kami (Shinto) for the balance of natural forces. Since that time, with little exception, religious expres-sion in Japan has involved an interweaving of all three traditions. The first Japanese to be ordained was the nun Zenshin, who with two other nuns was sent to Korea to study the monastic code, returned, and set up an ordination centre for nuns. However, because the number of nuns required to provide full ordination is set at ten, technically the nuns were novices.

When the Japanese adopted Buddhism, they also adopted much of Chinese culture, initially through Korea but soon through direct contact. The Buddhist texts were in Chinese, and the Japanese adapted the language for their use, along with Buddhist schools imported from China. From the beginning of its introduction until the late eighteenth century, Buddhism was seen as a means of protecting the nation. It was also regulated by the court or state, so from the beginning Buddhism was associated with politics, and monks were political actors. Identification with the court was strengthened when the Cosmic Sun Buddha was identified with the Sun Kami from whom the emperor is traditionally believed to be descended. From about the ninth century, kami were understood to be bodhisattvas, Bliss or Enjoyment bodies of the Sun Buddha.

While the early period in Japan seemed to support a strong female presence in Japanese religion and positions of authority, it was not long before nuns began to face obstacles. For example, unlike monks, nuns received no state financial support. In the ninth century the two most powerful Buddhist schools, Tendai and Shingon, refused to allow women access to some mountain temples on the grounds that they were ritually polluted and, given that monks were in charge of ordination, they refused to ordain women. One of the contributing factors to this decline was undoubtedly the embedding of Confucianism in Japanese society, although there were other factors, including negative Buddhist attitudes toward women. Women persevered, however, in some cases establishing new practices for Japanese nuns.

The ninth century also saw the beginning of the process by which the Japanese made Buddhism their own. Saicho (767–822), who had studied in China, blended elements of Shinto with various elements of Zen and Tiantai. Saicho also wanted to depoliticize Buddhism, so he developed a rigorous twelve-year training program to discourage those who were not serious about Buddhism. Tendai (Japanese for Tiantai) was known for its discipline, meditation, and study. The other major figure of the time was Kukai (774–835), who had also studied in China and developed a Japanese tantric Buddhism called Shingon. Shingon is based upon the yoga tantras and is concerned with development of the identification between the practitioner and the Cosmic Sun Buddha through practices of body, speech, and mind. Kukai also developed a system to simplify reading and writing in Japanese and influenced Japanese art. Both of these schools were not open to women.

One of the most important periods for the development of Buddhism in Japan was the Kamakura period (1185–1333). Japan was ruled by provincial warrior-nobles who moved the centre of government to the city of Kamakura. There was still an emperor and court in the city of Kyoto but it had no political power. This was the beginning of the era of the samurai, the class of warriors idealized in film. The samurai were responsible in part for Rinzai Zen's becoming established as a separate school in Japan. The monk Eisai (1141–1215) of the Tendai school had brought Ch'an to Japan from China. The Tendai hierarchy did not approve, but he received the protection of the samurai class, who liked his disciplined style and meditation on fearlessness in the face of death. These qualities of discipline and fearlessness, combined with unwavering loyalty to one's lord, came to be known as the code of the warrior (*bushido*) after the end of the seventeenth century (Robinson 2005).

While Rinzai Zen appealed to the emerging middle class and the samurai, the Soto style of Zen had a much broader influence. It was introduced by Dogen, another Tendai monk. Dogen (1200–53) was a Japanese monk-scholar who was highly revered for his thought. While he wrote commentaries on koans, he was critical of sole reliance on them and also stressed that scriptures were a guide to enlightenment. Dogen believed in a simple, strict life. He took few students and demanded much. Some of those students were women; Dogen was very critical of the practice of denying women entry to certain temples and dharma halls.

The Soto Zen tradition through Master Dogen was highly supportive of women during the Kamakura period. This encouragement did not continue long after his death, however, and by the beginning of the twentieth century all that remained was the nuns' memory of his support and their own determination. According to Buddhist scholar Paula Arai, it took the nuns only three generations to remove the obstacles in their path (Arai 1999). The primary problem was, and still is in many countries, education. Prior to the early twentieth century, nuns had access to some schooling

Kensho: insight into one's own nature, that is, Buddha nature, in Japanese Zen Buddhism.

but not secondary education. In the late 1900s the government established monastery schools that granted both academic and Buddhist degrees. It also established monasteries for women, and eventually they gained entrance into the prestigious Komazawa Soto University. They lobbied for institutional equality, such as the right to pass on dharma transmission and to engage in service projects, and while doing this they maintained a strict monastic life of celibacy, study, meditation, and social service.

Dogen pondered difficult questions such as, if everything has Buddha nature, why do we need to practice? His conclusion was that meditation was not per se a tool to achieve enlightenment but was instead a demonstration of enlightenment. When sitting in meditation, one sits in awareness but does not think about anything. Dogen called this non-thinking. This concept is not as difficult as it may seem. When people run, for example, at times they may lose track of things for a while. Although they feel alert, they are often surprised by how far they have gone or how long they have been running. At such times one just *is*. When one sits in *zazen* ("sitting meditation"), one simply sits in awareness. So, in essence, one meditates as an expression of one's Buddha nature.

The period following the Kamakura period was the Muromachi period (1336–1603). During this time Zen became associated with an aesthetic sensibility. Koans were studied as literature; there was flower arranging and the development of the "way of tea." This emphasis on aesthetics rather than meditation and enlightenment led to the reforms of the great Zen master Hakuin (1686–1769) in the Tokugawa period (1603–1868). Hakuin felt that Zen had lost its focus. One could not achieve enlightenment through art, only through meditation. He developed the use of koans as a system of training in which students worked their way through five levels of koans designed to provoke and then enhance their awakening. This took years of dedicated effort. The students were supervised by a teacher who met with them frequently to assess their progress. Efforts to "figure out" the koan could be endless, and failure as swift as the master ringing his bell. Eventually the students would come to doubt that they could ever

solve the koan, yet so much time and self-identity had been invested in the process. This great doubt was part of the process. It is said that one then gave up and just lived on the meditation mat with the koan until it became an integral part of oneself. Then one might be prepared for an awakening called **kensho**, or insight into one's own nature. Hakuin said that the deeper the doubt, the deeper the experience of enlightenment. This system is still practised today.

The Kamakura period also saw developments in Japanese Pure Land Buddhism. Unlike in China, in Japan Pure Land became a separate school through the influence of Honen (1133–1212) and his disciple Shinran (1173–1262). While neither started out to create a separate school, their influence made it a reality. Honen believed that in the so-called degenerate age, chanting the *nembutsu* would produce not only rebirth in the Pure Land but also realization of one's buddha-hood. It could also provide worldly protection. Honen's views on the recitation as being able to wipe away sins and save the dead were perceived as a threat to Japanese notions of morality, and he was banished from the city. Exiled to the countryside, Honen continued teaching there.

One of the disciples sent into exile with Honen was Shinran. He both changed the shape of the monastic order and extended the notion of "other" power, that is, the power of Amida Buddha. Shinran believed that the notion of chanting the recitation to gain entrance to the Pure Land was wrong, because it implied that one could influence rebirth. It was an example of "own" power. Rebirth in the Pure Land was possible only through the grace of Amida Buddha. What the recitation did was acknowledge one's faith in Amida's grace and acceptance of it. One sincere repetition would do this; other repetitions were simply thanks to Amida for this grace. Shinran had a clear sense of his own sinfulness and wilfulness and saw that part of sinfulness is wilfulness in self-reliance. In reality, the only power of salvation belonged to Amida. If that was so, then the monastic habit of celibacy in order to focus only on enlightenment was in fact useless, another example of "own" power. Shinran married, establishing a married clergy and the passing on of temple authority to one's eldest son.

The Nichiren school of Buddhism is unique to Japan. It is named after its founder, Nichiren (1222–82). He believed that the problems of the nation and the imperial family stemmed from their having fallen away from the true Buddhist teachings of the Lotus Sutra and allowing false forms of Buddhism, particularly Pure Land, to prosper. The nation would face defeat from foreign invaders if it continued on this ruinous path. The recitation favoured by Nichiren was not of Amida's name but of the **daimoku**, the title of the Lotus Sutra. This was to be recited in front of a mandala (sacred artwork) constructed by Nichiren. If his teachings were followed, Japan would become a Buddha field on earth, reviving and spreading the true Buddhism to the world. He was uncompromising and argumentative and ended up being exiled twice.

The school continued to grow after his death. The most significant development in Nichiren Buddhism occurred in the late 1930s with the creation of Soka Gakkai, or the Value-Creation Society. Initially it was an educational society meant to promote values that would lead to both personal and public happiness and prosperity. In 1951 Josei Toda (1900–58), who had a religious experience while imprisoned during the Second World War, registered Soka Gakkai as a lay society of Nichiren Buddhism. Toda felt that people should chant for what they needed, including material objects such as a car or a job. He believed that when these immediate needs were met, people would begin to chant for the benefit of others as well. It was also necessary to convert others so that the Pure Land on earth could be realized. Soka Gakkai proselytizing was initially very aggressive. Under Daisaku Ikeda the organization grew into an international one with branches all over the world, and eventually the aggressive methods of conversion were stopped or moderated. The focus on education as a means to create value, especially peace, has come to be further developed. A falling out between the Nichiren priesthood and Ikeda in the early 1990s resulted in excommunication of the group, but this does not seem to have had much impact on the organization, at least internationally. In a recent study of Buddhism in the United States, Soka Gakkai membership was the most diverse in terms of race and gender compared to other forms of Buddhism (Hammond and Machacek 1999).

Religion in Japan has been tied to the nation through the kami, the deities of the land and its people. Buddhism was later included in this picture with the comingling of kami and bodhisattvas. However, beginning in the Tokogawa period and extending to the end of the Meiji Restoration (1868–1945), nationalism—that

Daimoku: a recitation of honour to the Lotus Sutra in Nichiren Buddhism.

is, identity as a nation that excludes others and sees itself as qualitatively different—began to emerge. For example, the early part of the Meiji era saw a concerted effort to separate the practices of Buddhism and Shinto, to restore a pure Shinto, devoid of foreign elements. Buddhism was persecuted, its lands taken and its temples converted to Shinto temples. Monks of all schools could marry and they were forced to teach the new State Shinto. Since that time, Buddhist monks in Japan have generally married after their training period. As well, Buddhism was forced to confront Christianity, science, and modernism as Japan was forced to open up to the West. As Japan embarked upon militaristic expansion throughout Asia, beginning in the late nineteenth century, Buddhism was able to contribute to the ideology of imperialism and regain a position of favour.

How these varied encounters and transformations took place is highly complex and the result of a whole range of factors: encounter with the West, challenges of Christianity and science, a loss of power and prestige. They come together in Japanese Buddhism in the nineteenth and early twentieth centuries in a complicated way. For example, we noted briefly above that the code of the warrior did not exist per se when the samurai were at their peak. Its compilation and strong identification with Rinzai Zen came later, in the seventeenth century. Writings about the code and samurai warriors do not appear in the West until the twentieth century. This warrior ethic became generalized to the populace at large in order to support the imperialist project. Zen masters also taught that Zen was the fullest expression of Buddhism; in fact, Zen was enlightenment itself. The artistic nature of Japanese Zen was taken as evidence that only in Japan was it possible to fuse art and Buddhism in that way, and only because of the special sensitivities of the Japanese people. In short, Zen was enlightenment and it was Japanese (Sharf 1993). When combined, these ideas fuelled the war effort through encouraging a belief in the nation's superiority. Some Zen masters refused to participate in such teaching, but others did not.

This understanding of Zen has also heavily influenced perceptions of Zen in the West, where it is seen as a type of mysticism without historical or cultural context. Zen has form, ritual, ceremonies, texts, and traditions. For example, when one understands that there was concern about people becoming too attached to textual study, one can also understand the story of the Zen master who burned his texts. Without that context, the Zen master could be conceived as a madman.

Tibet

In speaking of Buddhism in Tibet, the Tibet referred to is not simply that part invaded by China in 1950 and governed directly by it since 1959. Tibet was a broad territory in the Himalayan region where Tibetan culture exerted its influence, including Sikkim, Bhutan, and Ladakh and as far afield as Mongolia. The Buddhism practised in all these areas has come to be placed under the umbrella term Tibetan Buddhism.

Religious practice in these areas tends to be oriented toward three ends: the practical, rebirth, and enlightenment (Samuel 1993). Religion directed toward practical ends such as a good harvest, safe childbirth, or good health is found in all religions, though these beliefs and practices are often referred to as folk religion. Practices frequently involve the pleasing of potentially harmful spirits, exorcism of malevolent influences, and divination to discover what sort of ritual is required to attain a good result or prevent a negative one. The rebirth orientation tends to focus on attaining a better rebirth. The focus of these practices is often Buddhist gods and goddesses imported along with Indian Buddhism; they include merit-making, pilgrimage, and other acts of devotion. The final orientation, enlightenment, focuses on specific tantric texts, deities, and practices. Practices in this category include visualization of oneself as a deity as part of a process to become that deity, or the worship of one's teacher as such a deity. Tibetan Buddhist monks and teachers deal with all three orientations.

Visualization in Tibetan Buddhism is understood as being a means of restructuring one's consciousness (Powers 1995). The deity is ultimately oneself in one's enlightened state, a state that needs to be made one's own. Part of that process is identifying with that deity in such a strong and detailed manner that one in essence becomes that deity. This does not mean that suddenly one is visually transformed, but it does refer to attempting to live the enlightenment the deity represents. Everything is viewed differently, from an enlightened perspective, and so too are individual lives changed in this way.

Tibetans see the history of Tibet and the history of Buddhism as one and the same thing. It is the story of how the bodhisattva Avalokitesvara progressively brought Buddhism to Tibet and made it a Buddhist enclave in the world. Historically the process is believed to have begun during the reign of King Songtsen Gampo in the seventh century. Tibet was the central power in Asia at that time and up to about the middle of the ninth century. The best way of solidifying authority was to make alliances with surrounding powers, and marriage was one of the foremost means for creating such alliances. It is said that Songtsen Gampo had two wives, both Buddhist. One was from Nepal and practised Indian Buddhism and the other was from China and practised Chinese Buddhism. Both wives are seen by Tibetans as emanations of the bodhisattva Tara bringing Tibet to Buddhism.

The next king, Trisong Detsen (c. 755–97), sponsored the translation of Chinese Buddhist texts into Tibetan and invited Buddhist scholars to his court. King Trisong Detsen was also responsible for building the first monastery in Tibet, at Samye, which was completed in 775. As Buddhism is rooted in the monastic community, it is not unfair to say that the king thus established Buddhism on Tibetan soil, but he did so with great difficulty. A series of natural disasters was interpreted by non-Buddhist religious specialists as evidence that Buddhism was not wanted by the native deities of Tibet, and the Indian scholar-monk who was supervising the building was forced to flee. The king then requested the help of Padmasambhava, an Indian *siddha*—a man with supernatural powers and abilities acquired through advanced yogic practice. He swept through Tibet pacifying the local demons and deities, binding some with vows to become guardians of Buddhism in the future. Through his efforts, the monastery came to be completed.

The story of the two queens of the King Songsten Gampo is one way of explaining the two predominant styles of Buddhism in Tibet at that time, Indian and Chinese. These two types of Buddhism are also explained in terms of their sudden or gradual approaches to enlightenment. According to tradition a debate was held at Samye monastery in 720 to decide which approach would be adopted in Tibet. According to Tibetan sources, the Indian view (gradual) prevailed.

The end of the Tibetan empire and its support for Buddhism came in the tenth century with the assassination of an anti-Buddhist king by a monk. A period of political chaos followed and Buddhist practice became fragmented and monasteries were abandoned. The eleventh century scholar-monk Atisha (982–1050) finally established an organized and stable Tantric Buddhism in Tibet. He was able to integrate tantric rituals into a Mahayana philosophical framework and established Tibet's first monastic order, the Kadam, known for its adherence to monastic discipline.

The Sakya lineage came next and was a major power in the thirteenth and fourteenth centuries. A third school, the Kagyu, developed out of a combination of Kadam discipline and a type of meditation called Mahamudra. But remnants of early Buddhist practice had been maintained by a few after the fall of the empire; those practitioners did not necessarily approve of these newer schools, and gradually another school evolved. They did not accept the new translations, naming themselves Nyingma, or the "old school." So the four schools of Tibetan Buddhism were initially the Kadam, Sakya, Kagyu, and Nyingma. The lines between them were not rigid, as they shared a great deal and practitioners tended to seek teachings and initiations from a variety of teachers.

Tibet also has the Bon tradition. Bon combines elements of Buddhism and earlier pre-Buddhist deities and shamanist practice. Robinson argues that Bon's response to the new translations and reforms was to declare itself a separate tradition, rejecting Buddha Shakyamuni's lineage and stating that Bon's lineage was from the land west of Tibet rather than from India, and based on the teachings of the Buddha Shenrab (Robinson 1997). Bon is sometimes referred to as a fifth school of Buddhism and has shared Buddhism's fate both in Tibet and in exile.

The school that most students associate with Tibetan Buddhism, the Gelug school—the one to which Tenzin Gyatso, the fourteenth Dalai Lama, belongs—came shortly after. It was founded by Tsongkhapa (1357–1419), who developed a course of study that included the vigorous debating style with which Tibetan philosophy is identified. The focus was primarily on scholastics; after completion of a degree, monks could take studies in higher tantric practice and long retreats. This method of study and practice became so popular that the Kadam school was absorbed into the new Gelug school, which was known for both scholasticism and virtue.

It is with the mention of the Dalai Lama that we turn to the next major historical development in Tibetan Buddhism. This is the institution of incarnating teachers. A teacher is known as a lama, and a teacher who chooses to be reborn is called a *tulku*. This idea first arose in the Kagyu school but spread to others as well. The notion is this: As a lama comes to the end of his life, he leaves instructions for his followers concerning the likely place of his rebirth. They will seek out a child that fits the criteria and raise him to an age at which he can assume his position. At first glance this seems to solve the problem of succession, as there is only one authority. But in the same way that the Buddha's refusal to name a successor led to arguments about just exactly what the teaching and the monastic code were and what it really meant, so too rebirth succession could cause a host of problems. Different groups within a monastery composed of thousands of monks could easily disagree about the signs left or about the child eventually chosen. As well, the child could not assume authority immediately because of his age. In some cases the interim ruler did not wish to give up his power, which also led to intense disagreements and political wrangling.

The monasteries grew in land and power through what is known as the priest–patron relationship. In return for services, religious, political or diplomatic, a patron would donate land or rights to the products of that land without taxation, so the monastery in effect ruled the land and the people of that area. Monasteries of the different schools competed for power. The consequences of this became quite clear when Kodon Khan, a Mongolian ruler, threatened to invade Tibet in the thirteenth century. The ruling clans sent the respected scholar-monk Sakya Pandita to negotiate. He convinced the khan not to invade and to allow his school to rule Tibet. The Sakya used Mongol assistance to attack other monasteries, which in turn looked to make alliances with other Mongol khans.

Another important development was the creation of the institution of the Dalai Lama and the merging of political and religious authority in Tibet. In the sixteenth century the Gelug monk Sonam Gyatso and the Mongolian ruler Altan Khan re-established the priest–patron relationship that had been instituted under the Sakya. The Mongolian adopted Buddhism and gave the monk the title of Dalai Lama, "Ocean of Wisdom." A century later, with the backing of the Mongols, the "Great Fifth" (1617–82) consolidated his power over Tibet. He also made concrete an idea about the Dalai Lama that had been slowly developing, namely that the Dalai Lama was an emanation of the bodhisattva of compassion Avalokitesvara. He also instituted another category of reincarnating lamas, the Panchen Lama, recognizing his teacher as an emanation of Amitabha. The relationship between the Panchen and Dalai Lamas is very close, similar to that of a president and vice-president, each having a final say on the choice of the other. While this relationship is meant to be mutually supportive, there have been cases where they disagreed.

When the thirteenth Dalai Lama, Thupten Gyatso (1874–1933) came to rule, Tibet was beginning to be beset by foreign influences. He realized that Tibet needed to modernize its system of education and develop international alliances; he also raised a standing army. These reforms did not sit well with the monasteries, as they led to taxation and the introduction of Western-style education. Many feared that sending students abroad might lead to weakening of their Buddhist practices. At the end of his life the thirteenth Dalai Lama warned that if Tibet did not modernize, it would find itself ruled by others. That threat hung over Tibet until 1950, when the Chinese invaded, stating that it was reuniting Tibet with China. The fourteenth Dalai Lama, Tenzin Gyatso (b. 1935) assumed control shortly before the invasion and tried unsuccessfully to negotiate with the Chinese about the future of Tibet. In 1959 he went into exile in India, followed by thousands of Tibetans. While there was tremendous damage, destruction, and violence against monks and nuns during this period, it was far more severe during the Cultural Revolution (1966–76).

The effect of this on Tibetan Buddhism both within and outside Tibet has been tremendous. Most of the senior monks went into exile, taking their wisdom and many texts with them. Some monasteries in Tibet have been rebuilt for tourist purposes, but getting proper training in them can be difficult, since they are tightly controlled by Chinese authorities. On a short walk through Dharamsala in India, where the Dalai Lama resides, one sees walls plastered with pictures of monks and nuns who are imprisoned in Tibet. Outside Tibet, the initial challenge was to survive. Acclimatizing to India's heat, food, and lower elevation proved difficult.

For the first time, however, non-Tibetan Buddhist scholars had broad access to the Tibetan Buddhist tradition and teachers who were eager to have their texts and teachings translated. Gradually communities grew in northern and southern India and Tibetan teachers migrated throughout the world. Tibetan Buddhism has become popular worldwide. In Canada, for example, there are few ethnic Tibetans but numerous Tibetan Buddhist practitioners.

Alongside the chaos and suffering, sudden and violent change can also challenge people to see things in new ways and to try new things. This has been the case for women in Tibetan Buddhism. The full nun's ordination did not reach Tibet, although women were regularly ordained as novices—which, until recently, was all they received. Tibetan nuns rarely had an opportunity to study at the level that monks were able to achieve and, as for all Buddhist women, they have had a more difficult time getting donations from lay Tibetan Buddhists. This has changed somewhat, in large part because of the efforts of the Dalai Lama and a few senior monks. Increasingly nuns are given the opportunity to study in all areas and disciplines within Tibetan Buddhism, including debating and the creation of mandalas. There are also several senior nuns who have advocated for other nuns across the Himalayan area and who have worked closely with Sakyadhita, the International Association for Buddhist Women, to improve the conditions of all Buddhist women.

But once again there is an issue of ordination, in that the Tibetan Buddhist monastic code in which the nuns are ordained differs from that of the monks. While both are monastic codes of Theravada lineages, they stem from different schools. Some nuns are striving for a fully Tibetan order of nuns, ordained in the same monastic code as the monks. A recent (2007) conference in Germany put forward several suggestions in this regard to the Dalai Lama, who, while supportive, simply cannot make such a decision on his own. Until recently the Dalai Lama has traditionally been the head of the government in exile, but he does not have the same authority as the pope in Roman Catholicism. Other leaders and senior monks of all the schools must meet and discuss matters pertaining to Tibetan Buddhism as a whole. As the monastic code that governs the nuns' order affects the whole sangha, this must be a decision of the larger group of Tibetan spiritual leaders.

As in Sri Lanka and Thailand, so too in the case of Tibetan Buddhism: not all men and women agree on these matters. There have been other internal stresses as well since the Tibetan exile. The starkest example of this occurred in the Gelug school, in a dispute over practices associated with a guardian deity known as Dorje Shugden. This dispute led to a break between the Dalai Lama and one of his former teachers and also resulted in a fracture of the Gelug school, in effect creating another school. This new school of Buddhism is called New Kadampa and is headquartered in England.

RELIGIOUS PRACTICES

Some religious practices cut across the various traditions within Buddhism, others are limited to specific traditions, such as Theravada, Mahayana, or Vajrayana (Tantric), and others occur in one geographic location, for example, East Asia, but not another, say North America. There are also practices that may be done by the laity but not monks or nuns, and vice versa, or done to different degrees. There are also practices carried out by individuals that are expressive of a personal desire or connection to Buddhism.

The Noble Eightfold Path to the end of suffering is divided into three categories: morality, meditation, and wisdom. Monastics and laypeople follow the same path with some differences. In Asia traditionally, lay morality consisted primarily of giving and following the Five Precepts, while in the West meditation has been the primary lay practice. Within each category we find practices designed to purify body, speech, and mind. This provides a good outline for us to follow.

Practices of the Body

Ideally, practices of the body are accompanied by mindfulness and sometimes by speech as well. The two most common Buddhist religious practices are bowing, as a sign of respect or devotion, and giving, as a means of mental purification and merit-making. Bowing is a sign of respect: the laity bow to monks and nuns, monks and nuns bow to those senior to them, and nuns bow to monks as well. Religious bowing is usually done while holding the palms together and touching the head, the lips, the throat area, and the chest, symbolizing body, speech, and mind. There is also a full body prostration

in which one kneels and then lies fully extended on the ground. In Tibetan Buddhism one of the preliminary practices requires 100,000 full body prostrations. In pre-Chinese Tibet it was common for people to do these prostrations while circling the Potala Palace in Lhasa at the Tibetan New Year. Bowing at a sacred site or before a sacred object or image such as a Buddha statue is done three times, symbolic of the Three Jewels (Buddha, Dharma, Sangha).

Giving is another important religious practice that takes many forms, such as religious objects, for example. Donations keep a monastery or a shrine or a temple functioning. It is common in a large temple to see a row of golden Buddha images donated in memory of deceased loved ones. A family will donate or transfer the merit from such gifts to the deceased family member or to all living beings. Monasteries are often thought of as isolated buildings where peace and tranquility are the order of the day. This is not so in Buddhism. Monasteries are often very large complexes that provide a variety of services, educational and medical as well as spiritual. One large complex in Thailand has a monastic school, an elementary school, and a Thai massage school on its grounds, as well as signs giving instructions about when foreigners can stay or take meditation instruction. There are also numerous vendors outside the temple proper selling flowers, fruit, and incense for donation.

At Mahayana temples you may also see vendors selling birds, and temples often have ponds with turtles and fish in them; it is a common practice in Mahayana Buddhism to release birds or fish on holidays as an act of compassion. In North America, Buddhist groups may buy a fisherman's catch at the dock and release it. Recently some people have been re-evaluating these practices. Often birds are caught specifically to be sold for release, and sometimes when released the disoriented birds fly into cars or are seized by predators. Some temples have signs forbidding people to release fish or turtles in the ponds without permission.

When Buddhism began to spread to Europe and the Americas, many people rejected the notion of merit-making as superstitious. Over time, however, they began to realize that giving is both necessary to cover costs (teaching may be free but lighting, heat, and space are not) and a form of spiritual training, developing the perfection of generosity. The most common gifts are flowers and fruit. Of course the highest gift is

Mudras: hand gestures made while meditating in Tibetan Buddhism, often using a bell and sceptre.

the gift of self, or becoming a member of the sangha. Traditionally parents would dedicate one of their children to the sangha.

In Tibetan Buddhism, Buddha figures often have their hands in specific poses called **mudras**. These hand gestures symbolize a variety of things such as protection or compassion. One will see a monk meditating with a bell in one hand and a sceptre in the other, moving them rhythmically through a series of these gestures. Tibetan Buddhism is also known for its prayer flags and prayer wheels. People turn prayer wheels inscribed with a Tibetan mantra in marketplaces as well as temples, sending compassionate wishes to all living beings.

Pilgrimage is another body-oriented religious practice. People often go singly or in groups to sacred places. These can be mountains, stupas (relic monuments), temples, specific monasteries, or sometimes people. Pilgrims often go to the various sites important in the life of the Buddha.

The Zen tradition in both China and Japan uses art forms as a means of expressing enlightenment. An insight into one's own nature might be signified by a

Bell and sceptre used in Tibetan Buddhist meditation. The sceptre represents compassion and the bell represents wisdom. While meditating they are moved according to a set pattern of ritual hand gestures called mudras, increasing the efficacy of the meditation.

Source: Mavis L. Fenn

work of calligraphy or poetry; Zen masters frequently wrote death poems. The "way of tea" also became closely identified with Zen. It was the tea master Rikkyu who identified its essence in the way that we refer to the preparation of tea and tea rituals as being "in the moment." One is taking the time together with a group of people, sharing tea mindfully made. That moment will never occur again. One is refreshed by more than the tea.

Tibetan Buddhism is famous for its impressive mandalas, maps of the enlightened mind and visualizations of buddhas in their palaces with their retinues. These are crafted into large wall hangings or created as intricate designs in sand that are then destroyed as a symbol of the impermanence of all things.

Modern Buddhist practice in Asia and the West is often referred to as Engaged Buddhism. The term was coined by Thich Nhat Hahn and refers to engagement in social issues from a Buddhist perspective. It requires both grounding within oneself and outreach into the community or world. Examples of engaged Buddhism are the Buddhist Peace Fellowship and the Zen Peacemakers sangha in New York, which helps street people learn trades.

Practices of Speech

We automatically think of chanting when we think of religious practices that use speech. There are different types of chanting. In Theravada, the Three Refuges are chanted in Pali, as are chants honouring the Buddha. Another is the *nembutsu*, the recitation honouring Amitabha Buddha chanted in the Pure Land Buddhist tradition, as is the daimoku, the recitation honouring the Lotus Sutra. In Tibetan Buddhism the mantra (sacred verse) is *Om mani padme hum*, "O, the jewel in the lotus." People often wear beads on their wrists or around their neck, similar to a rosary, to keep track of their repetitions. Chanting focuses the mind and quiets the body; it can be done internally or voiced. It can be carried out individually or as part of a large group. Chanting tends to forge a sense of community among those chanting. Tibetan monks have developed extra nodes on their vocal cords so that each monk can chant a whole chord by himself. All Buddhist traditions also use protective chants meant to protect against violence, untimely death or disease, famine, or other natural disasters.

Because many people in the West associate the heart of Buddhism with individual meditation, chanting in traditions such as Pure Land Buddhism and Nichiren Buddhism has frequently been dismissed as magic practice or simply an Asian cultural practice easily dispensed with. However, scientific studies are emerging that note the benefits of chanting for promoting feelings of peace and well-being, and more people are beginning to recognize its value.

Practices of the Mind

Meditation is often thought of as *the* practice of the mind, but meditation includes a broad spectrum of mental attitudes. For example, a layperson who goes on a pilgrimage to a site containing a relic of a Buddhist sage may spend his or her travel time thinking about the life of the sage, his virtues and deeds. Such "calling to mind" is an important mental practice in Buddhism. Meditation also involves the body, as a focus on posture is important; if the body is not placed correctly, it can become a distraction. Zen Master Dogen was known for being very insistent on proper posture for his method of "just sitting" in awareness.

The basic form of mental practice is mindfulness, beginning with mindfulness of breathing. When one breathes in, one notes this; when one breathes out, one notes this. Or breaths are sometimes counted up to ten. Whenever the mind gets distracted (as it will), effort is made to bring it back into focus. This is a basic mode of thoughtful awareness that anyone can utilize in daily life. For example, you may be feeling angry, but turn your thoughts instead to how that anger may have arisen. What might release it? By paying attention to your body, mind, and emotion, you become better equipped to also know yourself better.

Through the development of this type of mindfulness, one can learn to hold one's focus longer, eventually moving to deeper, stabilizing meditations. These meditations usually involve the use of an object, physical or mental. Finally, when certain levels of stability and depth have been attained in meditation, the mind can turn to an analysis of the heart of the matter, the Four Noble Truths. This type of analytic meditation, called vipassana, was Buddhism's contribution to wider Indian meditative practices.

As well as meditations to develop insight, there are meditations to develop compassion and manage one's

> **Wesak:** the yearly commemoration of the Buddha's birthday, enlightenment, and death, held at various times in the spring (April or May).

emotional life. One begins with oneself and a quality such as loving kindness or sympathetic joy, and then radiates this progressively to family, to friends, to people one might feel animosity toward, and finally, to all living beings. The successful accomplishment of each stage brings a benefit, the final benefit being equanimity, that is, the ability to deal with both the ups and downs in life in the same way.

Zen meditation provides meditation through focus on a koan (Rinzai) or just sitting (Soto). One can also do visualizations of the Pure Land, or Tibetan Buddhists may visualize a Vajrayana deity or one's teacher as a deity.

Holy Days and Festivals

Buddhist holy days and festivals work on a lunar calendar (based on the cycles of the moon), so exact dates for festivals will vary. Each month there are two holy days: the new moon and the full moon. Time is set aside for laypeople to make donations and to hear a sermon. There is a rains retreat of about three months for the monks, which in India was tied to the monsoon. During this time, monks and nuns focus on personal meditation or study. Near the end of their retreat, the nuns and monks conduct a service of confession and chant the major rules together. The rains retreat concludes with a ritual in which the laity donates new robes to the sangha.

All Buddhist traditions celebrate **Wesak**, a commemoration of the Buddha's birthday, enlightenment, and death. Although the exact date varies among the different traditions, this usually occurs in April or May. New Year's is also an important festival for many Buddhist traditions, although again the exact date varies among traditions and from that in the West. Many festivals are cultural ones shared with non-Buddhists as well; this is particularly true for festivals honouring the ancestors in China and Japan.

Rites of Passage

In Thailand and other countries of Southeast Asia it is common for young men to temporarily enter the monastic life. The period may be as long as three months but may also be shorter. This gives the young men an opportunity to learn more about Buddhism and its central doctrines and ethics. It is also believed to make them more suitable as husbands.

There is no wedding ceremony in Buddhism. Monks may be invited to the house, however, where they are given gifts and blessings are bestowed. In Japan, Buddhists has been largely responsible for taking care of death rituals, as Shinto is focused on purity and impurity, and death is understood as polluting. Some Buddhist temples also provide services for individuals or couples who have experienced an abortion (LaFleur 1994). Birth control pills were legalized in Japan only in 1999, so abortion had been the primary form of birth control for many years. As Buddhism sees life as beginning with consciousness, many feel a need to apologize to the aborted fetus and to relieve their feelings of guilt and prevent retaliation from the fetus. There is controversy about this ritual, of course. Some see it as positive, in that the participants can give recognition to the lost potential and come to terms with the consequences of their decision. Others criticize the temples for making money on such a service when it results from breaking the First Precept, against the taking of life (Hardacre 1999).

AUTHORITATIVE STRUCTURES

Although the Buddha left no successor and thus there is no one authoritative head of Buddhism, there are structures of authority. At the lowest level, seniority is the guideline. In the monastery there is an abbot, and if the monastery is large there will be several senior monks in charge of various aspects of life such as the kitchen, accommodations, and teaching. The traditional way of standardizing doctrine and practice was through councils of elders. Each tradition within Buddhism has some kind of governing council for its particular group; for example, the Soto school in Japan has its own administrative structure and the Rinzai has another. Because Buddhist traditions have been isolated geographically—Theravada in Sri Lanka and Vajrayana in Tibet—there has never been a cross-traditional Buddhist organization, although Buddhist representatives are active in local interdenominational activities with other Buddhist traditions and other religions.

Women are becoming more influential within contemporary Buddhism. Some Taiwanese masters are simply ignoring the traditional eight rules for nuns. The nuns of Fo Guang Shan, for example, head temples, teach, and engage in a wide variety of outreach and administrative activities. Another major Taiwanese influence is Dharma Master Cheng Yen, founder of the Buddhist Compassion Relief Tzu Chi Foundation, or simply Tzu Chi. She is a powerful female leader of an organization run by lay volunteers, mostly women. Venerable Bhikkhuni Dhammananda, the Thai nun formerly known as Dr. Chatsumarn Kabilsingh, was one of the founders of Sakyadhita in 1987. She is the author of *Thai Women in Buddhism* (1991), among other books and articles. She organized the first international conference on Buddhist women in Thailand in 1991. In the Theravada tradition, Venerable Bhikkhuni Kusuma, who was one of the early advocates for re-establishing the nuns' order in Sri Lanka, runs the Ayya Khema International Meditation Centre. Several nuns within the Tibetan tradition have become respected public figures, such as British-born Tenzin Palmo, who spent twelve years meditating in a cave high in the Himalayas, and Karma Lekshe Tsomo, an American Buddhist scholar. Both are well known in their own right and as advocates for nuns in their tradition. One of the most prominent teachers in the West is Pema Chodron, also from a Tibetan tradition.

The teacher is an important authority figure, and lineage (the succession of teachers) is important in all traditions. The teacher or master is seen as the example of what one wishes to achieve, and one has faith that the teacher can guide one in the right direction. Narratives within the Zen and Tibetan traditions often paint fascinating pictures of teachers who make strange demands of their students or set them impossible tasks. Students are encouraged to choose their teacher carefully, as the relationship is understood as being closer than that of a mother and her child. So, too, lineage provides legitimacy for a teacher and a window into the likely content of his or her teaching.

In Asia the relationship between student and teacher is a formal one. The focus is on the instruction and practice a student needs to proceed on the path. There may be great respect for the teacher and genuine affection, but there is also distance. Students in the West tend to expect a more informal relationship with their teacher and for the teacher to function more like a therapist or to provide life coaching. This has caused some problems, and many Buddhist organizations have established rules regarding student–teacher interaction. In the West many teachers are laypeople. There are a variety of reasons for this, including the fact that the West, especially North America, does not have a strong tradition of monasticism, but also because many Westerners do not believe that celibacy is necessary for the Buddhist religious path.

RELIGIOUS IDENTITY

The notion of identity is more complex than it appears. To say that one is Buddhist presumes that one is not Daoist. But in Chinese religion, elements of Buddhism and Daoism are mixed with folk religion and Confucianism. The same problem occurs in the modern West, where many people may be Christian but read books on Buddhism, meditate, and attend retreats with a dharma teacher. Many people also adopt different features from all three Buddhist traditions. Finally, in countries where one religion may be the sole or dominant religious expression, one does not think in terms of identity; one simply practices. Some immigrants from countries where Buddhism is the dominant tradition have commented that moving to Canada has made them "more Buddhist." What they mean is that because Buddhism in Canada is a minority religious tradition (about 3 per cent of the population), they have had to think about their Buddhist practice and how it differs from that of others. Being consciously Buddhist becomes a more important element of their identity. But clearly identity is flexible and varies with the roles played in life and its various stages.

Generally speaking, a Buddhist is one who has taken the Three Refuges—Buddha, Dharma, and Sangha— and the Five Precepts. This is frequently done with a teacher or in a group, but that is not necessary. Many people who call themselves Buddhist have never been to a dharma centre or a temple. Those who decide to become monks or nuns take the Ten Precepts, then go through a one- or two-year novitiate in which they learn the monastic rules of their school and study its teachings and philosophy. In many countries secular education is combined with Buddhist study. While one "takes the robes" presumably for a lifetime, there is no shame in disrobing if one wishes to take up lay life again.

RELIGIOUS DIVERSITY

The three major streams of Buddhism—Theravada, Mahayana, and Vajrayana—have already been discussed. Within each of these streams there is some diversity. The least diversity appears to be within the Theravada tradition, but the question of female ordination is challenging its general unity. In September 2009 a Theravada monk in Australia ordained some nuns. When an accommodation with the main temple in Thailand proved impossible, the Australian temple was excommunicated. The Thai Buddhist hierarchy also disapproves of recent ordinations in Sri Lanka and shows no sign of relenting on female ordination. It would appear that in this regard, two distinct forms of Theravada Buddhism are emerging.

Mahayana Buddhism has the greatest diversity. Zen, Pure Land, and Nichiren, among others, are all forms of Mahayana, and their teachings and practices tend to be quite different in emphasis. Vajrayana Buddhism reached Tibet, China, and Japan but evolved differently in Japanese Shingon, which has ritual and mental practices but no sexual imagery.

THE CANADIAN CONTEXT

Buddhism has been in Canada since the middle of the nineteenth century, although it was relatively unknown until the late 1960s. Chinese migrants came to Canada to build the Canadian Pacific Railway and to work in gold mines in British Columbia. Chinese religious practice is syncretic, including Buddhist elements. Asian religious practices, when considered at all by Canadians, were thought to be superstitious and barbaric. The first specifically Buddhist temple was built in Vancouver in 1905 by Japanese Pure Land Buddhists, who also built temples in Alberta, Ontario, Manitoba, and Quebec. Early twentieth-century Canada was marked by institutional racism and immigration laws designed to keep Asian immigration to a minimum. During the Second World War, Japanese Buddhists saw their assets seized and they were forcibly interned in camps. It is no coincidence that just after the war the term *church* replaced *temple* for Pure Land Buddhists.

In the late 1960s both Canada and the United States changed their immigration laws from a race-based system to a points system. That is, people were given points for education, training, background, and skills and were allowed to immigrate based upon those characteristics rather than the government's simply allowing a set percentage of non-white people into the country each year. The second major change in Canada was the adoption of a policy of multiculturalism.

Applying the term *multicultural* to the official policy of a nation-state such as Canada has a far deeper significance than simply describing a country composed of various groups of people from diverse cultural and religious backgrounds who share the same geographic boundaries. It implies a national identity, a decision-making process that is rooted in difference, and a commitment to establishing a common good. Multiculturalism in Canada encompasses every aspect of Canadian life: political, economic, linguistic, and educational as well as religious and cultural. This means that every group within Canada has an obligation to share with others its culture, religion, language, and skills and ideas. From this highly varied raw material a "Canadian identity" is crafted.

A number of Buddhist women have commented that they see their active participation in interreligious and cultural activities as part of their contribution to Canada. Just outside Winnipeg, Manitoba, you will find a stupa constructed by the entire Buddhist community of the area—Theravada, Mahayana, Tibetan, lay, ordained, Asian, and non-Asian. This same community holds a combined Wesak ceremony every spring and invites the local community to celebrate with them. And one Theravada group in Toronto explicitly refers to its commitment to childhood education as fostering both good Buddhists and good Canadians (Fenn, 2008, 2009a, 2009b).

As well as the increased number of immigrants who were Buddhist and the adoption of a policy that encouraged them to share their traditions with others, there was a desire among many non-Buddhists in the late 1960s and 1970s to experiment with new things: new ways of organizing society, new ways of relating to each other as men and women, and resistance to traditional values and structures that a new generation felt had encouraged war. People who had become alienated from traditional Western religions such as Christianity and Judaism turned eastward, exploring Hinduism, Buddhism, and Daoism as well as Native spirituality.

This stupa, on the outskirts of Winnipeg, Manitoba, was built through the combined efforts of the entire local Buddhist community under the supervision of a Burmese monk. It provides a focal point for communal celebrations such as Wesak, the celebration of the Buddha's birth, enlightenment, and death.

Source: Mavis L. Fenn

The number of Buddhists in Canada is small—less than half a million people—and most of these Buddhists have family roots in Asia. The largest group is Chinese, not just from China but also from Taiwan and Vietnam (Beyer 2010). The predominant tradition is Mahayana. Fo Guang Shan has a large network of temples and lay associations, including a large temple in Missassauga, Ontario, and a teahouse in Waterloo, Ontario. The small community of Lindsay, Ontario, was the first community to welcome Tibetan Buddhists, in 1961. Halifax is the headquarters for Shambala (formerly Vajradhatu), a Tibetan Buddhist lineage established by Chogyam Trungpa Rinpoche in order to bring the insights of Tibetan Buddhism to the West. Shambala also has a monastery on Cape Breton Island called Gampo Abbey (Fenn and Koppedrayer 2008).

Immigrant Buddhists face a number of challenges in their practice. In Asia, many temples hold rituals or teachings daily. In Canada many of these activities have to be moved to a weekend in order to accommodate work schedules. There are also the challenges posed by the second generation, who frequently want to leave their traditions behind or who do not speak the language of their parents, also the language of the temple (Boisvert 2005). Studies of Christian religious participation show that many young people return to church once they begin to have families of their own; it is too soon to say whether this pattern will hold for Buddhism.

Canadians from non-Buddhist backgrounds are increasingly influenced by Buddhism as it makes its way into mainstream culture. Many have taken up meditation, read books on Buddhism, and go on retreats. Most do not frequent a temple, although some do. A nun in London, Ontario, conducts services in Vietnamese on Saturday and in English on Sunday. Fo Guang Shan provides meditation and dharma classes in both Chinese and English on separate nights and provides a translator when necessary. Occasionally a Chinese speaker will sit beside an English speaker and summarize the dharma talk. Most English- or French-speaking Buddhists practice at a dharma centre. Dharma centres usually have a teacher and offer various programs such as retreats, meditation, visiting teachers, or a library.

Practice is most often a combination of various Buddhist traditions rather than being limited to Theravada or Mahayana or Vajrayana. One of the oldest retreat centres in North America was established at Kinmount, Ontario, in 1966 and it is still in existence. The teacher, Nyangmal Rinpoche, was non-Asian but had trained in both the Theravada and Tibetan traditions, had spent considerable time in Asia, and had established centres internationally. Dharma centres often adapt Western traditions to a Buddhist context; for example, the Blue Heron Zen Centre in Hamilton, Ontario, has developed services for Mother's Day.

The Western sangha also faces challenges. As noted earlier, financial difficulties can arise in Western Buddhism; as a minority tradition it does not have a large lay community to provide financial support. Further, few can afford a resident teacher, so access to advanced teachings may be difficult, and senior teachers often travel widely, giving teachings across several continents. One thing both Asian and Western nuns share is a lack of educational and financial support: they receive no money from their monastic unit. But financial security is essential in order to spend extensive periods of time in meditation and study; visiting one's teacher in Asia, perhaps, every second year for advanced teaching also takes money. Monastics are divided as to whether or not having a job or career violates the monastic code. Some simply accept it as a necessary adaptation to both Western life and the modern world. This in turn raises the question of whether or not monks and nuns should wear their robes at all times. If so, that might inhibit their ability to perform some jobs or invite discrimination in other cases.

Research in Canada generally shows good relations between Asian-roots Buddhists and other Buddhists. There is not a lot of interaction between them, for a variety of reasons accepted by both groups. The first is that both accept that different cultures express Buddhism differently. When asked if her group did much outreach outside the Chinese community, one young Chinese Buddhist woman responded with puzzlement. Why, she wondered, would non-Chinese want to practice Chinese Buddhism? Culturally different practices are accepted within the same Buddhist framework. This is not to say, however, that there are no tensions within transplanted cultures or between cultures regarding what is and is not proper Buddhist practice in a modern Western context.

Below you will find reference to a website that lists a wide variety of Buddhist groups in Canada. You will be amazed at the number of groups and the wide representation of Buddhism we have in Canada. Traditions previously separated by geography are now found just streets apart in many large cities. What unites them is the common elements of Buddhism discussed above and the common rituals that flow from them. What separates them is language. As time goes on, that will change. For now, bilingual men and women help to bridge the gap.

BUDDHISM AND THE INTERNET

The Internet has a wide variety of Buddhist sites, lists, blogs, and social network sites. Some are geared toward scholars, some are designed to provide information about Buddhism to those outside the tradition, and others are for particular groups of Buddhists. Some sites combine elements of scholarship and a practitioner's focus. Some are very good; others are not. When you visit a Buddhist site, how do you know whether the information you are receiving is accurate? There are a few things to consider, such as the difference between history and sacred history. If the site does not make those distinctions, it is going to provide material from that tradition's perspective, what we would call an insider's perspective. Such a site might be very valuable for finding out how believers understand certain historical details or symbolic artifacts but not so much for writing a paper on the historical development of Buddhism. A scholarly site might provide a student with information about a particular aspect of the tradition— meditation, for example—but there will likely be little or no information on how one experiences that meditation. It is not a question of one site's being right and another being wrong. It is a question of what one is investigating.

Some websites are geared toward the members of a specific temple or dharma centre. They keep members informed about group activities, social occasions, visiting teachers, and activities within their tradition in other centres across the country or around the world. Others are more elaborate, providing details about Buddhism, their tradition, and teachers and providing online resources for learning more. Often these sites are bi- or even trilingual in nature. They provide for members of a community a shared sense of identity, especially in regions where there may be few Buddhists, and they provide a safe way for non-Buddhists to find out about Buddhism, specific traditions, teachers, and practices.

Within the Western context, discussion lists, news groups, and subscription lists are generally limited to English-language sources. This means, of course, that one receives a fairly narrow insight into the questions that may be discussed online. Clearly, however, these websites offer good insight into the issues that concern adoptive Buddhists. There are two basic types of groups: discussion boards and subscription lists. The discussion boards are forums where a topic is listed and people will comment under that heading, perhaps building a dialogue between commentators. The other type is a subscription list, where people join a particular group and comments are limited to members of that group. The list itself may be moderated or not. If it is moderated, comments go first to the moderator, who screens them and then sends them to the list members. If it is not moderated, comments go directly to list members.

According to scholar Richard Hayes, who founded a subscription list called Buddha-l in the mid-1990s, the most common topics on the list involve questions of authority, doctrine, practice, and the role of cultural identity (Hayes 1999). Discussions, particularly between scholars and practitioners, can become quite heated. At times, sectarian arguments—between people who argue about which tradition or teacher has the best approach to practice or interpretation of doctrine—take place on these online forums. Sites get set up by former members of a group to air their complaints about the original group. There are sites devoted to internal disagreement within a tradition; the divisive and sometimes violent disagreements about Dorje Shugden in Tibetan Buddhism come to mind. And clearly the People's Republic of China and the Tibetan government in exile disagree about the territory of Tibet and how to settle that disagreement.

How does one decide whom to believe? Who really speaks for a community? The Internet provides a wide variety of information, some of which is conflicting. Part of what students do in university is learn how to sort out the issues, weigh the evidence, examine possibilities, and, if possible, make an educated decision. This chapter set out to give basic information about lineages, the role of the teacher, and central tenets of the traditions. Additional research will help in understanding the complexities of a particular issue being examined, allowing students to exercise their critical faculties, ask questions, and hopefully come to a conclusion about specific issues. Listed at the end of the chapter are some scholarly sites on Buddhism as well as a number of sites devoted to Western Buddhist magazines.

CONCLUSION

In this chapter you learned about a young prince whose wealth and comfortable life could not protect him from fear of old age, disease, and death. His quest for a solution to the problem of suffering led to the creation of a major religious tradition, Buddhism. You learned about the insights he had as summarized in the central concepts of Buddhism. You learned about Buddhism's doctrinal development into Theravada, Mahayana, and Vajrayana traditions and the important role played by Emperor Asoka in making Buddhism a major force in India and other parts of Asia. You learned how Buddhism adapted to the needs of many people through time and across cultures, including Canada. You learned about Buddhist practices that encompass body, speech, and mind and some of the issues that have arisen within Buddhism concerning doctrine and practice. You should now have a good grasp of the basics of Buddhism and be able to explain them to others. You should be able to explain to others how Buddhism sees the human condition and what it suggests as a way to live a contented life in the face of that condition.

KEY TERMS

Arhat, p. 161
Bodhisattva, p. 160
Buddha, p. 157
Buddha nature, p. 179
Daimoku, p. 189
Dependent origination, p. 165
Dharma, p. 157
Dukkha, p. 165
Four Requisites, p. 169
Humanistic Buddhism, p. 186
Jataka Tales, p. 160
Karma, p. 161
Kensho, p. 188
Mandala, p. 177
Mantra, p. 157
Mudras, p. 194

Nien-fo, p. 185
Nirvana, p. 167
No soul, p. 164
Pali canon, p. 172
Prajnaparamita, p. 162
Sakyadhita, p. 181
Samsara, p. 166
Sangha, p. 169
Skill-in-means, p. 175
Sramana, p. 161
Stupa, p. 157
Tantra, p. 177
Three Poisons, p. 167
Three Refuges/Jewels, p. 172
Vinaya, p. 170
Vipassana, p. 182
Wesak, p. 195

CRITICAL THINKING QUESTIONS

1. What is enlightenment? We often talk about people being enlightened or having put an end to suffering. But in practical terms, what does it mean? Does an enlightened person feel pain, for example?

2. What sorts of ethical problems can the idea of skill-in-means present? Can you see ways in which this notion can be abused?

3. The Tibetan Buddhist tradition stresses the importance of the teacher and the authority of the teacher. How is this problematic? How should one examine this question?

4. How do you think physical practices and mental practices work? Does faith play any role in this?

RECOMMENDED READING

Bartholemeusz, Tessa. *Women Under the Bo Tree*. Cambridge: Cambridge University Press, 1994.

Cabezon, Jose Ignacio, ed. *Buddhism, Sexuality and Gender*. New York: State University of New York Press, 1992.

Dialogues of the Buddha. 3 vols. London: Pali Text Society.

Findly, Ellison Banks, ed. *Women's Buddhism, Buddhism's Women*. New York: Wisdom, 2000.

Grant, Beata. *Eminent Nuns: Women Chan Masters of Seventeenth Century China*. Honolulu: University of Hawaii Press, 2009.

Harding, John S., Victor Sogen Hori, and Alexander Soucy, eds. *Wild Geese: Buddhism in Canada*. Montreal and Kingston: McGill-Queen's University Press, 2010.

Kraft, Kenneth, ed. *Zen: Tradition and Transition*. New York: Grove Press, 1988.

LaFleur, William R. *Liquid Life: Abortion and Buddhism in Japan*. Princeton, NJ: Princeton University Press, 1994.

Lopez, Donald. *Buddhism in Practice*. Princeton, NJ: Princeton University Press, 1995.

Matthews, Bruce, ed. *Buddhism in Canada*. London: Routledge, 2006.

McLellan, Janet. *Many Petals of the Lotus: Five Asian Buddhist Communities in Toronto*. Toronto: University of Toronto Press, 1999.

Mitchell, Donald William. *Buddhism: Introducing the Buddhist Experience,* 2nd ed. Oxford: Oxford University Press, 2008.

Powers, John. *Introduction to Tibetan Buddhism*, rev. ed. Ithaca, NY: Snow Lion Publications, 2007.

Prebish, Charles S., and Damien Keown, eds. *Encyclopedia of Buddhism.* Abingdon, UK: Routledge, 2007.

Queen, Christopher S., ed. *Engaged Buddhism in the West*. Somerville, MA: Wisdom Publishing, 2000.

Queen, Christopher S., and Sallie B. King, eds. *Engaged Buddhism: Buddhist Liberation Movements in Asia*. New York: State University of New York Press, 1996.

RECOMMENDED VIEWING

Kundun. Dir. Martin Scorcese, 1997. The life of the Dalai Lama.

Ten Questions for the Dalai Lama. Dir. Rick Ray, n.d.

The Life of the Buddha. Dir. Michael Wood. PBS, 2010.

The Reincarnation of Khensur Rinpoche. Dir. Ritu Sarin and Tenzing Sonan, 1992. The search for a reincarnate teacher.

The Little Buddha. Dir. Bernardo Bertolucci, 1993. This has a good story of life of the Buddha in the middle.

The Cup. Dir. Kyentse Norbu, 1999. A wonderful story of young Tibetan monks and the football World Cup.

Words of My Perfect Teacher. Dir. Leslie Ann Patten, 2003. Follows Kyentse Norbu and some of his Western students.

Principles and Practices of Zen. NHK (Japanese National Broadcasting System), 1988. The first section is on monastery training; the second section, on art, is flawed.

USEFUL WEBSITES

Access to Insight
Information related to the practice and study of Theravada Buddhism.

Dharmanet
A non-sectarian resource for education and information about Buddhism.

Sakyadhita
The International Association of Buddhist Women.

The Buddhist Channel
News and audio/video from around the world of interest to Buddhists.

Sumeru Books
Includes a listing of various Buddhist groups across Canada.

Journal of Buddhist Ethics
The first online scholarly journal.

Journal of Global Buddhism
A scholarly journal more geared toward a social scientific approach.

Tricycle
An e-zine of Buddhism, geared to modern North American audience.

Shambala Sun
An e-zine of Buddhism.

Buddhanet
A non-sectarian resource for education and information about Buddhism.

REFERENCES

Arai, Paula. 1999. "Japanese Buddhist Nuns: Innovators for the Sake of Tradition." In *Buddhist Women Across Cultures*, ed. Karma Lekshe Tsomo. New York: State University of New York Press.

Bartholemeusz, Tessa. 1994. *Women Under the Bo Tree.* Cambridge: Cambridge University Press.

Boisvert, Mathieu. 2005. "Buddhists in Canada: Impermanence in a Land of Change." In *Religion and Ethnicity in Canada*, ed. Paul Bramadat and David Seljak. Toronto: Pearson Education.

Cousins, L. S. 1996. "The Dating of the Historical Buddha: A Review Article." *Journal of the Royal Asiatic Society*, ser. 3, 6, no. 1: 57–63. http://indology.info/papers/cousins/.

Beyer, Peter. 2010. "Buddhism in Canada: A Statistical Overview from Canadian Censuses, 1981–2001." In *Wild Geese: Buddhism in Canada*, ed. John S. Harding, Victor Sogen Hori, and Alexander Soucy. Montreal and Kingston: McGill-Queen's University Press.

Falk, Nancy. 1989. "The Case of the Vanishing Nuns: The Fruits of Ambivalence in Ancient Indian Buddhism." In *Unspoken Words: Women's Religious Lives in Non-western Cultures*, ed. Nancy Auer Falk and Rita M. Gross. Belmont, CA: Wadsworth.

Fenn, Mavis. 2008. "Canadian Buddhist Women and Multiculturalism." Paper presented at the Tenth International Association of Buddhist Women, Mongolia.

———. 2009a. "Canadian Buddhism and Multiculturalism." Paper presented at the American Academy of Religion Annual Meeting, Montreal.

———. 2009b. "Canadian Buddhist Interaction—or Not?" Paper presented at the Eleventh International Association of Buddhist Women, Vietnam.

Fenn, Mavis, and Kay Koppedrayer. 2008. "Sakyadhita: A Transnational Gathering Place for Buddhist Women." *Journal of Global Buddhism* 9. http://www.globalbuddhism.org/toc.html.

Hammond, Phillip, and David Machacek. 1999. *Soka Gakkai in America: Accommodation and Conversion.* Oxford: Oxford University Press.

Hardacre, Helen. 1999. *Marketing the Menacing Fetus in Japan.* Berkeley, CA: University of California Press.

Harvey, Peter. 1999. *An Introduction to Buddhism: Teaching, History and Practice.* Cambridge: Cambridge University Press.

Hayes, Richard P. 1999. *Land of No Buddha: Reflections of a Skeptical Buddhist.* Newtown, NSW, Australia: Windhorse.

Koppedrayer, Kay, and Mavis Fenn. 2006. "Sakyadhita: Buddhist Women in a Transnational Forum." *Canadian Journal of Buddhist Studies* 2.

———. 2006. " Buddhist Diversity in Ontario." In *Buddhism in Canada*, ed. Bruce Matthews. New York: Routledge.

LaFleur, William R. 1994. *Liquid Life: Abortion and Buddhism in Japan.* Princeton, NJ: Princeton University Press.

MacQueen, Graeme. 1981. "Inspired Speech in Mahayana Buddhism." *Religion* 11: 303–19.

———. 1982. "Inspired Speech in Mahayana Buddhism." *Religion* 12: 49–65.

McRae, John. 2003. *Seeing Through Zen: Encounter, Transformation, and Genealogy in Chinese Chan Buddhism.* Berkeley: University of California Press.

Powers, John. 1995. *Introduction to Tibetan Buddhism.* New York: Snow Lion.

Robinson, Richard H., and Willard L. Johnson. 1997. *The Buddhist Religion: A Historical Introduction.* 3rd–5th eds. Belmont, CA: Wadsworth.

Robinson, Richard, Willard Johnson, and Thanissaro Bhikkhu. 2005. *Buddhist Religions: An Historical Introduction*, 5th ed. Belmont, CA: Thomson-Wadsworth.

Samuel, Geoffrey. 1993. *Civilized Shamans: Buddhism in Tibetan Societies.* Washington, DC: Smithsonian.

Schopen, Gregory. 2004. *Buddhist Monks and Business Matters: Still More Papers on Monastic Buddhism.* Honolulu: University of Hawaii Press.

Sharf, Robert H. 1993. "The Zen of Japanese Nationalism." *History of Religions* 33, no. 1 (August): 1–43.

Shaw, Miranda. 1994. *Passionate Enlightenment: Women in Tantric Buddhism.* Princeton, NJ: Princeton University Press.

Williams, Paul. 1989. *Mahayana Buddhism: The Doctrinal Foundations.* London: Routledge.

Timeline

- **c. 10,000–2100 B.C.E.** Neolithic period: legendary Three Sovereigns: Yellow Emperor (Huangdi), Shennong (The Divine Farmer), Fuxi (the Ox Tamer).

- **c. 2100–1600 B.C.E.** Xia dynasty: first historical dynasty; time of sage-kings and King Yu.

- **c. 1600–1050 B.C.E.** Shang dynasty: divination by oracle bone; Yi Oracle; King Tang.

- **c. 1046–256 B.C.E.** Zhou dynasty.

- **c. 475–221 B.C.E.** Warring States period.

- **6th century B.C.E.** "Laozi" (Lao Dan) born (traditional date).

- **c. 551–479 B.C.E.** Confucius (Kongzi).

- **c. 430 B.C.E.** "Mozi" (Mo Di).

- **4th century B.C.E.** "Mengzi" (Mencius).

- **350–270 B.C.E.** Zou Yan and the Five Elements.

- **3rd century B.C.E.** Guodian version of The Way and Its Power (Daodejing).

- **221–206 B.C.E.** Qin dynasty and first emperor of China (259–210 B.C.E.).

- **213 B.C.E.** Burning of books.

- **c. 195 B.C.E.** Mawangdui version of The Way and Its Power.

- **206 B.C.E.–220 C.E.** Han dynasty: Emperor Han Wudi (141 – 86 B.C.E.).
Confucianism favoured.
Daoist institutionalized religion begins.
Buddhism comes to China.

- **220–589 C.E.** Six dynasties period: instability; Chinese settlement in the south.
Growth of Buddhist and Daoist institutions and production of texts.
Neo-Daoism; Seven Sages of the Bamboo Grove.

- **581–618** Sui dynasty.
Block printing developed (c. 600); books become more accessible.

- **618–906** Tang dynasty.
High point of Buddhism.
Confucian "Return to Antiquity" movement.

- **960–1279** Song dynasty.
Daoist canon printed (1019).
Confucian revival.
Zhu Xi (1130–1200).

- **1279–1368** Yuan dynasty: Mongolian rule and patronage of Buddhism.

- **1368–1644** Ming dynasty.
Wang Yangming (1472–1529).

- **1644–1911** Qing dynasty: Manchurian rule.
Taiping Rebellion (1850–1864); Boxer Rebellion (1900); Wuchang uprising (1910).

- **1911–1949** Republican period.
Sun Yatsen (1866–1925) becomes first provisional president of new republic; known as "the father of modern China."

- **1919** May Fourth movement.

- **1937–1945** Second Sino-Japanese War.

- **1949–present** Communists win civil war and Nationalists retreat to Taiwan.
People's Republic of China established.

- **1966–1976** Cultural Revolution.

- **1973–1974** Anti-Confucius campaign.

- **1976** Mao Zedong (1893–1976) dies.

- **1978–1994** Deng Xiaoping (1904–97) era.
New religious freedom in 1982 and recognition of five religions: Buddhism, Catholicism, Daoism, Islam, and Protestantism.

- **1989** Tiananmen Square incident: military suppression and deaths of protestors.

- **2008** Olympic Summer Games held in Beijing.

- **2010** Release of film Confucius 2010.

- **2011** Statue of Confucius erected and then removed from Tiananmen Square.

CHAPTER 6

Daoism and Confucianism

Alison R. Marshall

INTRODUCTION

Walk along Cormorant, Pandora, or Fisgard Street in Victoria, British Columbia, and you will encounter the world of a Canadian Chinatown in the 1870s, as well as many traditional patterns and ideas that stem from Daoism and Confucianism, two major religions of China. On Fisgard Street you will see the **Chinese Benevolent Association** Building, festooned with auspicious red lanterns. Built in 1885, it housed a school that provided traditional Confucian education for the children of Chinatown residents. The building also contained the Palace of Sages, a hall where early Chinese migrants could make offerings of incense and spirit money and pray to Daoist deities such as the god of wealth, Guangong or Guandi, and the Empress of Heaven (Tianhou or Mazu). Four years after the offering hall was built, **Confucius** and Hua Tuo, a noteworthy Han dynasty physician, were also added to the altar.

Chinese Consolidated Benevolent Association Building

Source: © Chris Cheadle/All Canada Photos/Corbis

Chinese Benevolent Association: also known as the Chinese Consolidated Benevolent Association, founded in Victoria, B.C., in 1884 to provide new Chinese immigrants with legal, social, and cultural services.

Confucius: the Latinized name for Kong Qiu (*chee-o*), or "Kong of the Mound" (traditional dates 551–479 B.C.E.), whose conversations are contained in the Analects.

Community celebrations during important festivals throughout the year or in celebration of a deity's birthday would include songs, chants, prayers, and offerings of incense, spirit money, and wine, tea, crispy pork, vegetarian dishes, and other food items that are later eaten at a banquet (Lai 2010; Marshall 2009, 2011). Traditional forms of Confucianism and Daoism may also be found in other parts of the Chinese cultural sphere. In Taiwan, for example, Confucius's birthday is celebrated annually on September 28. In this celebration, which is based on material in the Analects, sixty-four boys clad in Ming dynasty red and yellow costumes and black hats hold long pheasant feathers. A dance formation traditionally patterned to venerate an emperor, with eight rows of eight dancers (*bayi*), is adapted here to recognize the enormous importance of Confucius as a teacher. Following the ceremony, those who have hosted and organized the event distribute "wisdom cakes" to the guests.

In this chapter we examine both traditional and modern religious dimensions of Confucianism and Daoism, as well as the different ways that each religion is practised within the Chinese cultural sphere. We also examine the many ways in which Chinese Confucianism, Daoism, and everyday practices (social acts that extend beyond the traditional category of religion) are difficult to define as religion. The term *religion* (in Latin, *religio*; in Chinese, *zongjiao*) is not native to China; it was imported from Japan in the late 1800s. Although there is no equivalent term for *religion* in Chinese, this does not mean that Chinese people do not behave religiously. In daily life and during festivals they create and maintain a bond between themselves and divine beings who hold the highest and revered positions. But the way that the bond is established is different and more ambiguous than the way the bond is established in Abrahamic religious traditions. Gods do not have all the power, and nothing is absolutely right or wrong, good or bad. Religion and religiosity are determined by tradition. Behaviours that function in religious ways for Chinese people (for instance, relationships) may seem less religious to others.

What constitutes Chinese religiosity is constantly in flux as people adapt some beliefs and practices for modern life and erase others. There is an acceptance that deities and rituals are dynamic and layered. Chinese religious identity and behaviour are also ambiguous and overlapping. People may go to both Daoist and Confucian temples, perform rituals in either tradition, and be familiar with both Daoist and Confucian texts. Daoism and Confucianism are complex and are best expressed by the

Bayi dance to celebrate Confucius's Birthday, Tainan, Taiwan, September 28, 1997

Source: Alison R. Marshall

term **ling**, sometimes defined as "efficacy" or "practical power." Sincere performance of rituals and maintenance of traditions (that is, ling) are at the core of Chinese religion. Ling has been referred to as a magical power created by both worshippers and deities that materializes because of human efforts and out of human needs. Through ling and rituals sincerely performed, the realms of heaven, earth, and human beings are harmonized. What looks political, social, or secular to an outsider has religious dimensions for an insider! One example of this is the practice of offering special meals to **ancestors** (relatives who have died). Food is an essential part of Chinese religiosity, and food rituals and customs are a constant theme in this chapter. Offerings are presented to a god/goddess/ancestor for him/her to take a share, and then the participants take theirs. Or food can be eaten at a banquet with family or close friends where no overtly religious ceremonies are involved, but there are still religious dimensions because many have worked together to produce and share the food (Marshall 2011; Chau 2012).

We will also be looking at both traditional and modern aspects of Chinese religiosity. Unlike most of the other chapters in this textbook, Chinese religion is shaped by a character-driven language. Chinese characters are seen to be patterns of culture transmitted from the **sages** and written in more or less the same way and with the same codified meanings since early history. In this chapter we use the pinyin system of romanization that is currently used to spell the sounds of Chinese characters. For instance, **Dao** is both the English word and the pinyin spelling for that particular Chinese character. History and language are thus key components in the discussion of Chinese religion.

Chinese civilization (and especially Confucianism) has always been associated with education, literacy, and familiarity, at least in elite circles, with what are called classical texts. When one refers to Confucianism or Daoism, one must first refer to the chief text of that tradition and historical period. As with other chapters in this textbook, while giving textual context to both Confucianism and Daoism we will also learn about religious practices associated with these traditions. This chapter will also examine historical gender roles in Confucianism and Daoism (Marshall 2011). Women who played important political and religious roles have been highlighted throughout, as have specific texts and rituals pertaining to women. You will also learn how gender roles changed over time, particularly as Chinese immigrants came to Canada.

Ling: Daoism and Confucianism's core idea, sometimes defined as magical power or efficacy and referring to the sincere performance of rituals and maintenance of traditions; also conveys the idea that power is held by both worshippers and deities and materializes because of human efforts and out of human needs.

Ancestor: deceased parents, grandparents, and other kin to whom food and other offerings are made on the ancestor's birthday, at Chinese New Year, during the mid-autumn, and at other annual festivals.

Sage: a ruler or person who is wise; traditionally believed to hear what was communicated by the Divine and transmit that to the people, thereby uniting the three realms of heaven, earth, and humanity.

Dao: nature, Daoism's main idea.

Mandate of Heaven: *tianming*, a traditional Chinese concept that emerged in the Zhou dynasty to establish the Zhou rulers as part of an all-male line of rulers extending back to the Three Sovereigns of the legendary period. Rulers are seen to have a mandate to rule from the Divine when there is peace and no drought, for instance.

CONFUCIANISM

Confucianism is broadly defined by traditional and modern Chinese thought and culture; it takes it name from the teacher Confucius (551–479 B.C.E.). In the words of Julia Ching, Confucianism offers a kind of "moral humanism" (1993). China's Three Sovereigns of the prehistoric period—Fuxi ("the Ox Tamer"), Shennong ("the Divine Farmer"), and the Yellow Emperor—became moral examples and transmitters (as opposed to creators) of early Chinese culture and patterns. Although the school takes its name from Confucius, it actually refers to older ideas that were associated with a group called the "emerging scholars," or Ruists. Emerging scholars were experts in the early arts of rites, music, history, archery, and numbers associated with the Classic of Changes.

While the Shang dynasty was the first historical period in Chinese history, it was during the following Zhou dynasty that Confucius, along with other early thinkers and important concepts such as the **Mandate of Heaven**, emerged. The Zhou dynasty god was called Tian ("Heaven") and resided

Li: propriety, or rites relating to social conduct, outlined in the Classic of Ritual; the *li* character depicts a person bending over a sacrificial vessel filled with soybeans.

in the celestial realm. In addition to other heavenly gods there were earthly ones as well. Each god had a position within the religious hierarchy and a specific role to play in Chinese civilization.

During the last few hundred years of the Zhou dynasty, known as the Warring States period, new thinkers and philosophers emerged. Overwhelmed by near constant warfare, the Zhou were in decline, and initially as many as 120 states were fighting for power. By the time of Confucius's death, many were still fighting. Philosophers and teachers known later as part of the Hundred Schools of Thought travelled about lecturing nobles and rulers who, though at war, were known for their privilege, greed, and extravagant wardrobes and lifestyles. According to legendary accounts, these philosophers spread ideas about **li**, or ritual propriety, and how to treat others humanely and create social harmony during this period of intense conflict.

Confucius (traditional dates 551–479 B.C.E.) is known today by the Latinized name given to him by seventeenth-century Catholic missionaries. Confucius (Kong Qiu, or "Kong of the Mound") was born and buried in Qufu, China. The rest of what we know about him, as well as about many other early Chinese figures, comes from Sima Qian's *Records of the Grand Historian*. It is unknown how Confucius came to acquire such erudition in music and rituals. The Analects contains a passage about his life indicating that he started learning when he was fifteen years old. Sima Qian's account tells of his high noble lineage in the state of Song and says that he was an orphan by the age of seventeen. Three years after that, Confucius became a low-ranking official. When he was fifty years old, Confucius became a minister under Duke Ding of Lu but was exiled after some wrongdoing until 484, when he returned to Lu and became the teacher he is known as today. Confucius's conversations, compiled by direct and indirect disciples, became known as the Analects (Lunyu); they outline the ways in which rituals and virtue create harmony among heaven, earth, and man (Riegel 2006).

Confucianism since the time of Confucius has continued to expand, change, and adapt. It includes the writings of a later disciple and Confucian innovator named Mencius (372–289 B.C.E.). Mencius is the only other Chinese figure to be known exclusively in the West by his Latinized name, also given by Catholic missionaries. The Mencius (Mengzi), a collection of his teachings, is attributed to his disciples. Like the Analects, it contains

Words

From the Analects

Confucius said: Personal cultivation begins with poetry (the Classic of Poetry), is made firm by *li* (the Classic of Ritual), and is perfected by music (the Classic of Music). (8:8)

    Lin Fang asked about the fundamental principle of rites. Confucius replied: You are asking an important question! In rites at large, it is always better to be too simple rather than too lavish. In funeral rites, it is more important to have the real sentiment of sorrow than minute attention to observances. (3:4)

    At fifteen I set my heart on learning
    At thirty I became firm
    At forty I had no more doubts
    At fifty I understood Heaven's will
    At sixty my ears were attuned to this will
    At seventy I could follow my heart's
desires, without overstepping the line [virtues]
    (15:20)

The Master said, "In strolling in the company of just two other persons, I am bound to find a teacher. Identifying their strengths, I follow them, and identifying their weaknesses, I reform myself accordingly." (7.22)

When you meet persons of exceptional character think to stand shoulder to shoulder with them; meeting persons of little character, look inward and examine yourself. (4.17)

… Authoritative persons [ren persons] establish others in seeking to establish themselves and promote others in seeking to get there themselves. Correlating one's conduct with those near at hand can be said to be the method of becoming an authoritative person [ren person]. (6.30)

The Master said: "Governing with excellence (*de*) can be compared to being the North Star: the North Star dwells in its place, and the multitude of stars pay it tribute." (2.1)

The Master said, "Lead the people with administrative injunctions and keep them orderly with penal law, and they will avoid punishments but will be without a sense of shame. Lead them with excellence (*de*) and keep them orderly through observing ritual propriety (*li*) and they will develop a sense of shame, and moreover, will order themselves." (2.3)

The Master said, "Learn broadly of culture (*wen*), discipline this learning through observing ritual propriety (*li*), and moreover, in so doing, remain on course without straying from it." (12.15)

Ji Kangzi asked Confucius about governing effectively (*zheng*), and Confucius replied to him, "Governing effectively is doing what is proper (*zheng*). If you, sir, lead by doing what is proper, who would dare do otherwise?" (12.17)

Source: *Confucius: The Analects*, trans. D. C. Lau. (New York: Penguin Books, 1979).

conversations with rulers and others during what was known as the Warring States period of the Zhou dynasty. The Mencius develops many of Confucius's earlier ideas about humanity and personal cultivation, but Mencius's teachings are most famous for saying that human nature is innately good. He does not deny that some people are bad but states that good nature needs to be cultivated. This inborn good nature is recognizable by a natural inclination toward compassion, which is understood as one of the four dimensions of human nature. According to Mencius, everyone is capable of being a sage, which was an important development in Confucianism.

Words

From the Mencius (Mengzi)

Mengzi said, "Humans all have hearts that will not bear [the suffering of] others. The former Kings had hearts that would not bear [the

suffering of] others, so they had governments that would not bear [the suffering of] others. If one puts into practice a government that will not bear [the suffering of] others by means

(continued)

of a heart that will not bear [the suffering of] others, bringing order to the whole world is in the palm of your hand.

"The reason why I say that humans all have hearts that will not bear [the suffering of] others is this. Suppose someone suddenly saw a child about to fall into a well: everyone [in such a situation] would have a feeling of alarm and compassion—not because one sought to get in good with the child's parents, not because one wanted fame among their neighbors and friends, and not because one would dislike the sound of [the child's] cries.

"From this we can see that if one is without the heart of compassion, one is not a human. If one is without the heart of disdain, one is not a human. If one is without the heart of deference, one is not a human. If one is without the heart of approval and disapproval, one is not a human. The heart of compassion is the sprout of benevolence. The heart

of disdain is the sprout of righteousness. The heart of deference is the sprout of ritual propriety. The heart of approval and disapproval is the sprout of wisdom.

"People having these four sprouts is like their having four limbs. To have these four sprouts but to say of oneself that one is unable [to be virtuous] is to steal from oneself. To say that one's lord is unable [to be virtuous] is to steal from one's lord. In general, having these four sprouts within oneself, if one knows to fill them all out, it will be like a fire starting up, a spring breaking through! If one can merely fill them out, they will be sufficient to care for [all within] the Four Seas. If one only fails to fill them out, they will be insufficient to serve one's parents."

Five Relationships: defined in the Doctrine of the Mean (Zhongyong), a text ascribed to Confucius's grandson Zisi. The five relationships are between subject and ruler, father and children, husband and wife, siblings, and friends.

Xunzi (fl. 298–238 B.C.E.) disagreed that human nature was by nature good. He was an official and teacher who came from the state of Zhao. Xunzi was known for saying that goodness was cultivated, not inborn. He distinguished human nature, or what comes naturally, and what is socially appropriate behaviour. Human beings, he said, would behave badly without rules that order and limit human greed, selfishness, and emotions.

Xunzi's philosophical discussion of human nature leads to another important thinker with an odd name, Mozi (or Mo Di; fl. 479–438 B.C.E.), which means "ink." Mozi founded a school of skeptics called Mohism that presented different ideas about how to make society peaceful and orderly. His text *Mozi*

influenced the development of later Chinese literature and fiction, but mostly it was famous for advocating utility and frugality. Mohism was most commonly known for its doctrine of universal love, which criticized the way that the **Five Relationships** determine how we should treat others according to whether they are mother, daughter, or friend. While Mozi was originally a disciple of Confucianism, he also came to be associated with Daoism, which will be examined later.

By the time of the Han dynasty (206 B.C.E.–220 C.E.) the term *Confucianism* had evolved to encompass all aspects of traditional Chinese culture associated with northern China and the elite Han ethnic group. During this time the term also came to be associated with Confucian classics, state doctrine, and rationalization. New Confucian writers emerged at this time who combined Daoist and Confucian ideas.

Han Wudi (ruled 141–87 B.C.E.) was emperor from the age of fifteen. Limiting the control of princes and lords, he emphasized instead the importance of the master–retainer relationship. In this relationship, masters were expected to treat with respect those who were inferior to them, thus ensuring the loyalty of their retainers. Wudi also strengthened the military, trade relations, and the tribute system. There were many important religious innovations during the Han dynasty as well. In 124 B.C.E. Han Wudi established an examination system at the Imperial Academy to inculcate an understanding of the Confucian classics in scholar officials and students. Although it was suspended during periods of unrest or foreign rule, this examination system remained in place throughout Chinese history, until the end of the Qing dynasty, and was used to both train scholar officials and maintain Confucianism as the orthodox Chinese teaching.

The scholars studied and became familiar with five of the six early Confucian classics: the Classic of Changes, the Classic of Poetry, the Book of Documents, the Record of Rites, and the Spring and Autumn annals. The sixth text, the Classic of Music, had been lost by that time. The Imperial Academy served to impart to state officials a thorough understanding of the five classics, particularly the virtuous behaviours and ritual practices contained within them. This period also witnessed the beginning of scholarly commentaries on the texts.

The Han dynasty also saw a flourishing of literature and the development of a literati class with works such as Sima Qian's *Records of the Grand Historian*—130 chapters containing events, accounts, and biographies of Confucius, Mencius, Xunzi, Zhuangzi, **Laozi**, and many others. Ban Gu produced *History of the Han*; Liu Xiang (202–9 C.E.) wrote *Biographies of Virtuous Women*, which defined feminine morality; and Ban Zhao (45–116 C.E.) wrote *Admonitions for Women*, which instructed women on proper behaviour in the inner (domestic) quarters as daughters, mothers, and wives. This text continued to guide normative understandings of feminine domestic roles and attitudes to women up until 1950, and in some places even later.

During the various dynasties following the Han, Confucianism developed an increasingly privileged concept of male social and family roles. At this time marriages were arranged; these clan unions were seen to perpetuate the pure and elite Han race. During the Tang dynasty (618–907) polygamous marriages and divorces rose and widows remarried more frequently. With the exception of temple visits, women (at least those in elite circles) seldom left the home, where they resided in a domestic sphere along with concubines, dancers,

Laozi: Lao Dan, one of the earliest and the most famous of the Li/Lee family, who was a court archivist during the sixth century B.C.E. and lectured about Confucian ritual; once thought to be author of *The Way and Its Power*.

Yin and yang: a binary term first occurring in a Zhou dynasty poem from the Classic of Poetry, which refers to oscillation from a yang state of light and movement to a yin state of darkness and stillness; during the Han dynasty came to be associated with femininity and weakness (yin) and masculinity and strength (yang).

musicians, and servants. The height of empowerment and virtue for a woman came when she bore her first son. At this point in Chinese civilization many of the formative ideas related to social construction of gender and the low status of women in religion and society coalesced. Society was organized by a patriline (descent through the male line from a founding male ancestor) and women were ideally assigned to the inner sphere—associated with **yin**—and inferior roles in contrast to their **yang** superior male counterparts. Women could become powerful only through male progeny and were protected by chastity and loyalty to their husbands. Men, in contrast, derived their power from neither chastity nor spousal loyalty, but rather through the intellect and their privileged connection to ancestors. Nonetheless, the Tang dynasty produced some women who managed to achieve power in unconventional ways.

Wu Zetian (625–705) was a concubine of Emperor Taizong, and upon his death she became a concubine of one of his sons, the new emperor Gaozong (ruled 650–83). She bore Gaozong several male heirs, surpassing others in the harem and becoming head concubine, in which role she was allowed to perform the important imperial sacrifices. When Gaozong suffered a stroke, she engineered her further ascent, proclaiming herself the new (female!) emperor upon his death. Emperor Wu Zetian was also known for patronizing Buddhism, which flourished under her rule. She was eventually deposed in 705 at the age of eighty. Wu Zetian became a powerful woman because she did not conduct herself according to Confucian virtues and, to some extent, because she was interested in heterodox arts associated with those on the periphery of life and culture. She became virtuous not just because of her beauty but also because she managed to attain status

Qi: energy or life force, a key idea in Daoist and Neo-Confucian texts; the *qi* character shows vapour or energy rising from rice being cooked.

Three Obediences: *sancong*, a requirement of women that emphasized their comparatively inferior social and familial status, that they obey their fathers when they are daughters, their husbands when they are wives, and their sons when they are mothers.

within political hierarchies that were not available to those of her gender.

Yang Guifei (719–56) also flouted Confucian rules about propriety and relationships to her own advantage. Originally the wife of a prince, she left her husband, became a Daoist priestess, and took up residence with the other women in the palace's inner quarters. There she managed to beguile the elderly emperor Xuanzong (ruled 712–56) with her beauty and dancing, and he gave her the title "Precious Consort." She convinced Xuanzong to pass on key administrative positions to her kin; in the process, an adopted foreign son known to be a villain orchestrated a rebellion and eventually seized the capital. Xuanzong had Yang Guifei executed. The story of Yang Guifei and Emperor Xuanzong was embellished by poetry to memorialize their relationship as an iconic model of feminine and masculine love and loyalty.

The Song dynasty (960–1260) brought forth a vision of meritocracy and social mobility for men in which a new class of gentry elite was determined by merit and civil service exam results, not by birthright. Eventually this overemphasis on meritocracy and the civil service weakened the military, and that eventually led to the dynasty's downfall. Importantly, during the Song dynasty the accessibility of books increased with the beginning of printing with wooden blocks. The most significant religious change was the emergence of a Confucian school of thought called Neo-Confucianism.

Neo-Confucianism—known as *lixue*—was a study of *li*, or principle (not to be confused with the *li* meaning rites). *Principle* is a concept used to describe that which gives all things their forms and patterns; as a passive entity, it works alongside the dynamic **qi**, or energy. Neo-Confucianism evolved from the writings of numerous scholars including Zhu Xi (1130–1200), who created a new canon known as the Four Books, comprising the Analects, the Great Learning, the Doctrine of the Mean, and the Mencius. It is not uncommon for Chinese

Canadians to own a copy of the Four Books today. This new canon articulated the predominant characteristics of Confucian philosophy and included important spiritual ideas from early Confucian philosophy (both Confucius and Mencius) as well as Daoist and Buddhist concepts and ideas related to mediumship (the process by which a person becomes possessed by a deity). The new canon continued to uphold Confucianism's relevance, dominance, and position as state doctrine. Further, a new category of Confucian classics and scripture came to be developed, called the Thirteen Classics, which included many of the earlier classics as well as a dictionary and a new classic about how to be loyal and respectful to parents (filial devotion).

Neo-Confucianism relied increasingly on the ideas put forward by Mencius and Confucius and less on the practice of religion through performance of rituals and sacrifices. Song dynasty scholars mined Han dynasty and other texts to determine what was to be emphasized in major life-cycle rituals. For instance, marriage rituals focused on the need for brides to be obedient and on containment of the two genders within what were understood as the inner (female) and outer (male) spheres. Family values were strengthened and women's rights eroded. Women finding themselves widowed could generally either marry their deceased husband's older brother or take a lifelong vow of chastity. If they remarried they faced severe property restrictions.

The Song dynasty defined many of the ways in which women and Chinese religion are perceived today, particularly by Westerners. Men were either brave, strong heroes or talented, civil, and cultured scholars. In the Song, the talented scholar exemplified the favoured kind of masculinity. Women, in contrast, generally had subordinate roles, and power only when they were delicate and abided by the **Three Obediences** as chaste and loyal daughters, wives, and mothers within the family hierarchy. The practice of foot-binding, which made women even more dependent and physically restricted, though it predated the Song, was indicative of attitudes that curtailed women's movements and subordinated them.

The Song dynasty was followed by the Mongolian rule of the Yuan (1279–1368) and their ensuing patronage of Buddhism. The Yuan dynasty was followed by the Ming dynasty (1368–1644), which was notable for many things, including being the last native Chinese dynasty. It is during the Ming that the Chinese capital returned to the north, to the city known today as Beijing. The Confucian exam system, which had been disbanded during the Yuan, was reinstated, and the core curriculum became Zhu Xi's Four Books.

The Ming has been criticized as a time when China was asleep, lacking in experimentation and innovation, xenophobic, and tending to reject foreign ideas, especially those of missionaries such as the Italian Matteo Ricci (1552–1610). But it was also a period of Confucian strength. Wang Yangming (1472–1529) is known for his doctrine of unity of thought and action and for proposing a kind of Neo-Confucianism that was very close to Ch'an (Chinese Zen) Buddhism. While Zhu Xi's Neo-Confucianism privileged principle or li, Wang Yangming's privileged the mind/heart, based on the notion that the mind/heart and the universe were one. Drawing on Buddhism, Daoism, and the Mencius, Wang posited that the mind as true self made life meaningful. The goal was to ensure that one cultivated oneself enough to be able to reveal that true self during an experience of unity—akin to the Buddhist notion of enlightenment. This came to be expressed by the phrase "unity of thought and action." Wang Yangming's efforts represented another attempt to adapt Neo-Confucianism to the needs of contemporary life.

In 1644 the Manchurians were asked to help the Ming defeat rebels, but instead they took over the northern capital. This was the beginning of the Qing dynasty (1644–1911). The Manchurians required all men to wear the queue (a long pigtail that also required shaving the sides of the head daily) in a show of deference to the new emperors. This period was characterized by territorial expansion into Taiwan, Tibet, and Mongolia, as well as intellectual endeavours such as production of authoritative sets of classical texts, called the Complete Library of the Four Branches of Literature, as well as a set of Tang poetry.

It was a period in which missionary and Christian influence grew in China, creating conditions ripe for uprisings such as the Taiping Rebellion (1850–64) and the Boxer (anti-Christian) uprising of 1900. During the Taiping peasant rebellion, a Hakka (southern Chinese) who had been unsuccessful in the civil service examinations became a messiah figure to many poor peasants in the south. He proclaimed himself the brother of Jesus and drew heavily on Christian doctrine, rejecting many Manchurian customs such as the queue and Confucian teachings such as ancestor worship. The Boxer Rebellion

refers to a period that began during the summer of 1900. Members of a secret society skilled in martial arts, in response to an increasing foreign and missionary presence, began killing Europeans and Americans and destroying foreign-owned buildings; they believed their boxing skills would make them insusceptible to bullets. The rebellion failed but substantially weakened Manchurian China. Roughly 250 foreigners were killed in the rebellion, including the German envoy to China.

Although the Qing was a period of Manchurian and foreign rule, many Confucian customs and rites to acknowledge the imperial ancestors and other Chinese gods continued. The civil service examination system also continued, but the highest-ranked places were reserved for those of Manchurian descent. The Five Relationships were also emphasized during the Qing as a way to ensure that rulers could demand loyalty of the men who served them.

The 1911 Wuchang Rebellion led to the fall of the Qing and brought abrupt political, social, cultural, and other changes that affected the formal practice of Confucianism and Daoism. But even in the following Republican era, Confucian ideals continued to inform government leaders. Yuan Shikai, president of the republic from 1912 to 1916, was well-versed in Confucian thought and culture. During the constitutional conference of January 26, 1914, Yuan drew on his understanding of classical texts to make the role of president equivalent to that of an emperor and reinstated some of the formerly disallowed Confucian rites.

The military general Chiang Kai-shek (1887–1975), leader of the Chinese Nationalist Party or Kuomintang (KMT) after Sun Yatsen's death, was an admirer of Neo-Confucian thinkers such as Wang Yangming. He established the Christian- and Confucian-influenced New Life Movement in 1934, designed to further the goals of a new, modern China and seeking to instil Confucian values such as frugality and honesty and virtues such as propriety and righteousness. The New Life Movement was set up to inspire and cultivate patriotism and courage among Nationalist soldiers and supporters and overseas Chinese (Taylor 2009, 108–9).

In 1949 the People's Republic of China was founded and various campaigns were initiated by Mao Zedong (1893–1976), leader of the Chinese Communist Party (CCP) since 1935, to reform traditional Chinese thought and culture. Since 1949 Communist leaders have consistently drawn on Confucian ideas to motivate

Chinese support for the People's Republic. New, simplified forms of Chinese characters were introduced in 1956, and by 1957 Feng Youlan (a Chinese philosopher) had initiated a campaign to reinvigorate certain ideas in traditional Chinese culture. The land reform movement of the 1950s placed restrictions on temple activities and practices, but it was not until 1963 and the Socialist Education Campaign—also known as the Four Cleanups—that more uniform banning of temple festivals and the manufacture and sale of incense and spirit money took place all over China.

In 1966 the universities were closed (some had reopened by 1969), signalling the beginning of the proletarian revolution and a backlash against intellectuals and other vestiges of traditional China. The famous "Criticize Li Biao and Confucius" campaign in 1974 revealed the authority of anti-traditionalism. But just two years later Mao died, and 1978 began the Deng Xiaoping era, in which the government began to reassess past CCP public policies and restrictions on religious freedom. In 1982 the Chinese Communist Party issued Document 19, which protected certain rights related to religious freedom in Buddhism, Catholicism, Daoism, Islam, and Protestantism (in 1987 Taiwan's almost four decades of martial law and restrictions on religious practice also ended). After many years of economic, social, cultural, and political reform, China was experiencing a move toward democracy that culminated in the Tiananmen Square incident of June 4, 1989. During the military crackdown on this widespread popular democracy movement, many were killed and worldwide condemnation of China began.

There have been profound economic, social, cultural, and religious changes in China in the decades following the Tiananmen incident. The first McDonald's opened in Beijing in 1991, Hong Kong and Macau reverted to Chinese control in 1997 and 1999 respectively, and China joined the World Trade Organization in 2001. Today people speak openly and positively about the similarities between Communism and Confucianism, such as their emphasis on the collective as opposed to the individual, and meritocracy versus aristocracy. Confucianism was a strong theme at the opening ceremonies of the 2008 Beijing Olympics, which included passages from the Analects. The film *Confucius 2010* was produced in China and, though not a blockbuster, received Chinese Communist Party approval. Moreover, the Chinese government continues to promote and craft new policies based on Confucian virtues related to governance, democracy, learning, and harmony. In January 2011 a huge bronze statue of Confucius was erected in front of Beijing's National Museum, overlooking the eastern quadrant of Tiananmen Square, but by April of that year it had been removed. China has been busily promoting the teaching and study of traditional Chinese thought and culture through more than three hundred Confucius Institutes set up in universities around the world. And it is not unusual for Chinese leaders today to quote from the Analects and other Confucian thinkers (Bell 2008).

DAOISM

Daoism is seen to be China's second native religion. Both Daoism and Confucianism share the Dao, or way, as a core value. For Confucians the Dao relates to personal and moral self-cultivation. For Daoists the Dao is a less personal, more spiritual entity and natural way of being. Decades ago it was commonly taught that Daoism was a term that defined what was not Confucian, but this is no longer the approach taken by academics. Daoists and Confucians present many of the same ideas in Chinese religion, and any discussion of Daoism must attend to its diverse social and religious history. Decades ago it was also commonly taught that Daoism was either philosophical or religious. This binary approach enabled scholars and students of Daoism to divide the tradition into neat historical and conceptual bundles. The first of these bundles contained the earlier forms of Daoist texts such as Laozi, Zhuangzi, and Huainanzi. This so-called school was distinguished from the later, institutionalized and religious forms of Daoism (and their texts, deities, and practices) that developed following the Han dynasty (206–21 C.E.).

Perhaps the most important aspect of the study of Daoism is that the student must understand that this so-called school was never a school per se: the tidy ordering of early Chinese history is owed to Han dynasty writers and editors. None of the texts that we will be examining in this section—Laozi's The Way and Its Power (Daodejing) and the Zhuangzi and the Huainanzi—were written by one author. Moreover, traditional ideas about Chinese thought and culture have dictated what and how much we know about them. Sima Qian (145–86), the Grand

Historian of the Han dynasty, in his *Records of the Grand Historian* included biographical information about Laozi (whom he recognized as Lao Dan) that stated he was the earliest Daoist and a mentor to Confucius. This is no longer accepted as factual.

Laozi has been an inspiring, though legendary, figure to writers of history before and after 1900, when the modern Chinese period began. Emperor Huan of the Han dynasty built a shrine to pay homage to him, foreshadowing Laozi's ascent in later Daoist religious schools to be their chief deity. Chinese clans trace their lineage back to famous historical figures with the same family name. The Li/Lee clan traces its ancestry back to Laozi, who is thought of as one of the earliest and the most famous of all Lis in history. Following Sima Qian, he is presented as a court archivist during the sixth century B.C.E. who lectured about Confucian ritual, but there is scant evidence today that the sixth-century B.C.E.

Lao Dan was the author of the Way and Its Power (Daodejing; also referred to as just the Laozi). There are many debates about the text's authorship. Some propose that it was a third-century B.C.E. product that was not written down at the time, while others suggest it is a composite work by several authors.

The Way and Its Power has been widely read, commented on, translated, and appreciated by both Chinese and non-Chinese audiences. It is a very short book, consisting of approximately five thousand characters, that some say was meant to be memorized. While the book is short and the chapters are brief, the pithy and often rhyming style of writing make interpretation of the meaning a challenge. With themes ranging from emptiness, spontaneity, creation, and governance to returning to a purer and more virtuous state of existence, to personal cultivation, gender, yoga, and beyond, this book has had a huge impact on modern Western society.

Words

From The Way and Its Power

1 The way that can be spoken of
   Is not the constant way;
   The name that can be named
   Is not the constant name.
   The nameless was the beginning of heaven and earth;
   The named was the mother of the myriad creatures.
   Hence always rid yourself of desires in order to observe its secrets;
   But always allow yourself to have desires in order to observe its manifestations.
   These two are the same
   But diverge in name as they issue forth.
   Being the same they are called mysteries,
   Mystery upon mystery—
   The gateway of the manifold secrets.

3 Not to honor men of worth will keep the people from contention;
   not to value goods which are hard to come by will keep them from theft;
   not to display what is desirable will keep them from being unsettled of mind.
   Therefore in governing the people, the sage empties their minds but fills their bellies, weakens their wills but strengthens their bones.
   He always keeps them innocent of knowledge and free from desire, and ensures that the clever never dare to act.
   Do that which consists in taking no action, and order will prevail.

4 The way is empty, yet use will not drain it.
   Deep, it is like the ancestor of the myriad creatures.

(continued)

Blunt the sharpness;
Untangle the knots;
Soften the glare;
Let your wheels move only along old ruts.
Darkly visible, it only seems as if it were there.
I know not whose son it is.
It images the forefather of God.

6   The spirit of the valley never dies.
This is called the mysterious female.
The gateway of the mysterious female
Is called the root of heaven and earth.
Dimly visible, it seems as if it were there,
Yet use will never drain it.

28 Know the male
But keep to the role of the female
And be a ravine to the empire.
If you are a ravine to the empire,
Then the constant virtue will not desert you
And you will again return to being a babe.
Know the white
But keep to the role of the sullied
And be a model to the empire.
If you are a model to the empire,
Then the constant virtue will not be wanting
And you will return to the infinite.
Know honour
But keep to the role of the disgraced
And be a valley to the empire.
If you are a valley to the empire,

Then the constant virtue will be sufficient
And you will return to being the uncarved block.
When the uncarved block shatters it becomes vessels.
The sage makes use of these and becomes the lord over the officials.
Hence the greatest cutting does not sever.

32 The way is forever nameless.
Though the uncarved block is small
No one in the world dare claim its allegiance.
Should lords and princes be able to hold fast to it
The myriad creatures will submit of their own accord,
Heaven and earth will unite and sweet dew will fall,
And the people will be equitable, though no one so decrees.
Only when it is cut are there names.
As soon as there are names
One ought to know that it is time to stop.
Knowing when to stop one can be free from danger.
The way is to the world as the River and the Sea are to rivulets and streams

Source: *Tao Te Ching*, trans. D. C. Lau. (UK: Penguin Books, Penguin Classics, 1964).

Another important text, the Zhuangzi, consists of thirty-three chapters in its current version; it is attributed to Zhuang Zhou, of the third century C.E., though he likely wrote only the first seven chapters. The Zhuangzi is a popular and humorous text that contains stories debating the difference between waking and dream states, the meanings of life and death and usefulness and uselessness, problems with judging others based on appearance, the limits of the rational mind and consumerism, human potential, and the benefits of self-awareness. While Confucian tradition emphasizes human beings, proper behaviour, and the importance of order, stability, and virtues, this text emphasizes a more natural vision for establishing a link between heaven and humans. As well, it emphasizes the importance of change, transformation, and self-awareness and criticizes what are considered to be artificial virtues inculcated through texts and the deeds of sages from the past. Buddhist ideas and the importance of meditation are foreshadowed in the story of a man sitting in a trance and thinking about emptiness, nothingness, being and non-being, and existence. In the story describing the death of Zhuang Zhou's wife in the chapter called Perfect Happiness that follows, these ideas are repeated.

From *The Complete Works of Chuang Tzu*

Perfect Happiness

Is there such a thing as perfect happiness in the world or isn't there? Is there some way to keep yourself alive or isn't there? What to do, what to rely on, what to avoid, what to stick by, what to follow, what to leave alone, what to find happiness in, what to hate?

This is what the world honors: wealth, eminence, long life, a good name. This is what the world finds happiness in: a life of ease, rich food, fine clothes, beautiful sights, sweet sounds. This is what it looks down on: poverty, meanness, early death, a bad name. This is what it finds bitter: a life that knows no rest, a mouth that gets no rich food, no fine clothes for the body, no beautiful sights for the eye, no sweet sounds for the ear.

People who can't get these things fret a great deal and are afraid—this is a stupid way to treat the body. People who are rich wear themselves out rushing around on business, piling up more wealth than they could ever use—this is a superficial way to treat the body. People who are eminent spend night and day scheming and wondering if they are doing right—this is a shoddy way to treat the body. Man lives his life in company with worry, and if he lives a long while, till he's dull and doddering, then he has spent that much time worrying instead of dying, a bitter lot indeed! This is a callous way to treat the body.

Men of ardor are regarded by the world as good, but their goodness doesn't succeed in keeping them alive. So I don't know whether their goodness is really good or not. Perhaps I think it's good—but not good enough to save their lives. Perhaps I think it's no good—but still good enough to save the lives of others. So I say, if your loyal advice isn't heeded, give way and do not wrangle. Tzu-hsu wrangled and lost his body. But if he hadn't wrangled, he wouldn't have made a name. Is there really such a thing as goodness or isn't there?

What ordinary people do and what they find happiness in—I don't know whether such happiness is in the end really happiness or not. I look at what ordinary people find happiness in, what they all make a mad dash for, racing around as though they couldn't stop—they all say they're happy with it. I'm not happy with it and I'm not unhappy with it. In the end is there really happiness or isn't there?

I take inaction to be true happiness, but ordinary people think it is a bitter thing. I say: perfect happiness knows no happiness, perfect praise knows no praise. The world can't decide what is right and what is wrong. And yet inaction can decide this. Perfect happiness, keeping alive—only inaction gets you close to this!

Let me try putting it this way. The inaction of Heaven is its purity, the inaction of earth is its peace. So the two inactions combine and all things are transformed and brought to birth. Wonderfully, mysteriously, there is no place they come out of. Mysteriously, wonderfully, they have no sign. Each thing minds its business and all grow up out of inaction. So I say, Heaven and earth do nothing and there is nothing that is not done. Among men, who can get hold of this inaction?

Chuang Tzu's wife died. When Hui Tzu went to convey his condolences, he found Chuang Tzu sitting with his legs sprawled out, pounding on a tub and singing. "You lived with her, she brought up your children and grew old," said Hui Tzu. "It should be enough simply not to weep at her death. But pounding on a tub and singing—this is going too far, isn't it?"

Chuang Tzu said, "You're wrong. When she first died, do you think I didn't grieve like anyone else? But I looked back to her beginning and

(continued)

the time before she was born. Not only the time before she was born, but the time before she had a body. Not only the time before she had a body, but the time before she had a spirit. In the midst of the jumble of wonder and mystery a change took place and she had a spirit. Another change and she had a body. Another change and she was born. Now there's been another change and she's dead. It's just like the progression of the four seasons, spring, summer, fall, winter.

"Now she's going to lie down peacefully in a vast room. If I were to follow after her bawling and sobbing, it would show that I don't understand anything about fate. So I stopped."

Source: *The Complete Works of Chuang Tsu*, trans. Burton Watson, section 18 (New York: Columbia University Press, 1968).

The Guanzi dates to the third century B.C.E. and is one of the oldest and largest Daoist texts. Its authorship has traditionally been attributed to an official named Guan Zhong (645 B.C.E.) though it was likely written by several people. The focus of the Guanzi is a loyal minister's efforts to advise a duke, and thus it deals with political, economic, and social issues. The Neiye ("Inward Training"), comprising three chapters of the Guanzi, contains 1,600 characters written in verse form like the Way and Its Power. It is also recognized as a central Daoist work. Inward Training is a collection of Daoist poetic writings about yin-yang, the Five Elements, self-cultivation, meditation, health, diet, and other early Chinese beliefs. It influenced the development of ideas in Confucianism, later Daoism, Legalism, Buddhism, and Neo-Confucianism during the Song and later dynasties (Rickett 1985; Ames 1994).

The text known as the Huainanzi is attributed to a prince (sometimes referred to as a king) of Huainan named Liu An (179–122 B.C.E.). Liu sponsored a literary think-tank for scholars and Daoist adepts, and the Huainanzi represents a collection of writings from his court. It includes essays written on a wide range of subjects from myth to governance, philosophy, and personal cultivation. Like many other Chinese works, the Huainanzi seeks to discover and communicate the characteristics of the ideal or true person (usually not seen to be a woman) who will be able to order the realms of heaven, earth, and man. It also contains patterns for harmony. Parts of the text are humorous too: In one particular passage there is an account of a man who has been defeated in battle and a robber who has stolen his bell. The robber, fearing that people will hear the bell clanging as he runs away with it, covers his ears but does not bother to muffle the sound of the bell (Kirkland 2004; Roth 1999; Ames 1994).

The authorship, origin, and dating of the Classic of Mountains and Waters are unknown. It was thought that Yu, the legendary sage-king and founder of the Xia dynasty, had authored the text. Interpretations of the Classic of Mountains and Waters have focused on the geographical content of the text as a possible reason to explain why it was written and what it means. The Classic contains 144 hybrid creatures, including a variety of strange beings that are either chiefly animal or chiefly human, feminine or masculine, and that have too many or too few limbs, tails, eyes, horns, ears, faces, or wings. The feminine hybrids are often fierce and powerful. The strange beings inhabiting the landscape of the Classic of Mountains and Waters have often been associated with foreign tribes and with cultures beyond the pale of Chinese civilization. Historically, scholars have been unable to discern its origin or the category to which the text belongs; they instead tend to use the text to describe the "otherness" of marginal people. Han and later scholars emphasize the idea that the text was either written by foreigners or described their appearance.

While Han dynasty scholars, biographers, and writers had an enormous impact on the development of Confucianism and the unification of Chinese thought and culture, they also made a similar mark on Daoism. Daoism absorbed different religious strands from Confucianism, Buddhism, and mediumship (possession by a divinity) that stemmed from southern Chinese cultures. Huang-Lao Daoism was the predominant form of Daoism during the Han. It is named after one of the legendary Three Sovereigns, Huangdi (the Yellow Emperor), and Laozi.

Two revolutionary uprisings occurred during the late Han. One in the east, called the Great Peace (184 C.E.), was led by the Yellow Turbans, revolutionaries who fastened yellow cloth around their heads and called themselves the leaders of a new era of great peace. The rebellion in the west was known as the Celestial Masters movement, led by Zhang Daoling (180 C.E.). The Han dynasty eventually fell as rebellions continued on the margins of the empire, eroding the centralized power. The Six Dynasties period (220–589) following the Han was characterized by instability and uprooting of Chinese thought and culture as people moved into the warmer southern regions, while the north was ruled by the Tagbach people and other foreign invaders. This was also a period of religious innovation that saw Buddhism and Daoism develop temples, monasteries, and Daoist gods.

Both the Great Peace and Celestial Masters movements elevated Laozi to the status of a deity. New Daoist rites were created to remove individual sin. The Yellow Turbans vanished, but the Celestial Masters' beliefs and practices continue today as the Orthodox Unity (Zhengyi). It traces its lineage back to Zhang Daoling, who is said to have had a vision of Laozi during which he was presented with a "covenant" that set out the structure of the Daoist pantheon and the status and duties of various deities within it. Zhengyi remains the primary orthodox Daoist group today (Kohn 2000; Kirkland 2004).

Another key development within Daoism was the emergence in the fourth to fifth centuries of the Highest Clarity school (Shangqing, sometimes referred to as Maoshan or Grass Mountain). The school developed out of scriptures, biographies of perfected persons, and oral instructions and was founded by a woman named Wei Huacun (251–334) who had visions of immortals. This was the most popular Daoist school between the sixth and tenth centuries. The goal of Highest Clarity practice was to become a perfected person and enter a realm that had the same name, Highest Clarity. Perfected persons, according to this school, lived in the highest part of the heavens as well as in underground caves and within parts of human beings (Kohn 2000; Kirkland 2004).

There were many ways to become a perfected person in Highest Clarity, including meditation, visualization, fasting, exercises, sexual practices, textual studies, ingesting elixirs (for senior practitioners under supervision), living like a hermit, using charms, taking spirit journeys, and, most dramatically, committing suicide. Highest Clarity beliefs were an amalgamation of ideas stemming from Daoism, Buddhism, and Confucianism. Among the beliefs was the Daoist notion of human power (*de*) and perfection of that power through a combination of opposites, such as the sun and the moon, and becoming one with ancestors, spirits, and immortals. Buddhist ideas of rebirth, celibacy, individual pursuit, salvation, and luminosity of the adept's body were also found within Highest Clarity doctrine. Some of the beliefs were millenarian, proclaiming that the world would end and those who had prepared themselves would be saved by a messiah-like sage (this belief in a messiah died out early in the history of the school). Potential perfected immortals (perfect men) practised and read texts in order to harmonize with and be transformed and saved by the Dao. Texts also describe the importance of individual moral purity, an idea that was influenced by both Buddhism and Confucianism (Kohn 2000; Kirkland 2004).

Lingbao ("Spiritual Treasures") was a southern school of Daoism that developed out of early texts (390 C.E.) attributed to Ge Chaofu (fl. 402). The term *lingbao* originates in the Anthology of Chu, where *ling* means "spirit" and *bao* refers to the treasures received from that spirit. Lingbao texts combined ideas from the Highest Clarity and Celestial Masters traditions. The goal of followers of this Daoist school was in some ways similar to that of the Buddhist bodhisattva—to relieve the suffering of all beings, have a good rebirth, and finally enter the Dao. The methods to achieve this goal were less individualistic than in Highest Clarity and included meditation, self-cultivation through specific precepts, textual study, exercises, charms, ingesting elixirs, breath control, and sexual practices. This school of Daoism had the strongest Buddhist influence, including selflessness and the impermanence of the body. Similarly to Buddhism it also contained many categories of threes: three types of clergy, three kinds of scripture (*tripitaka*), and three forms of ritual—ordinations, fasts for the dead, and offerings. Its major contributions to Daoist religion include the three forms of ritual, a celestial bureaucracy, and salvation.

During the Six Dynasties period women's religious roles were increasingly related to spirit mediumship, healing, and black magic. Aside from these minor and marginal roles, women existed for the most part in the inner quarters of high society as mothers, daughters, and wives, following the Three Obediences. Elite Chinese society was dominated by men educated in the classics. But as Chinese civilization moved southward and China came to be ruled by a series of southern dynasties, educated men found themselves out of work because there were fewer positions for officials. Instead they filled their time by reading and commenting on the Confucian and Daoist texts. One early group that emerged during the last years of the Han was called the Seven Geniuses of the Jianan Period and was associated with the reinvention of Confucian ideas.

A subsequent group was the Seven Sages of the Bamboo Grove. Known as Neo-Daoists, these male elite writers, poets, politicians, and musicians gathered to read the Zhuangzi, the Laozi, and other texts, play music, philosophize, drink, and experiment with and abuse drugs that were believed to confer immortality (for example, five-stone powder). One of the seven, Liu Ling, was famous for his love of drinking, for taking off his clothing while drunk, and for this poem in which he berates people who chastise his fondness for drinking in the nude as "meddling in (his) earthly affairs, or his pants." Despite their excesses, the group produced new kinds of Daoist-inspired discourse such as "pure talk and dark learning," based on studies of the Zhuangzi and the Way and Its Power.

During the Tang Dynasty, emperors and the elite Li clan came to see Laozi as the chief Li ancestor. Daoism came to function as an institutionalized religion with scholars contributing works on self-cultivation and meditation. In monasteries, mainly celibate males but also a few female Daoist priests were in charge of both rituals and ceremonial fasts. Many Daoist traditions and rituals emerged following the Tang dynasty, including the Clarified Tenuity (Qingwei) school, established by a young female in the late Tang. The Ming dynasty school became known for its thunder rituals, performed by young male mediums who drew on the power of thunder in order to harmonize with the Dao, heal, get rid of malevolent forces, and treat children. The Tang dynasty is known as a time when Daoism had a positive relationship with the ruling officials of the day, including the popular emperor Xuanzong (ruled 715–55) (Kirkland 2004).

Contemporary Daoism

The northern Daoist tradition known as Perfect Realization was one of the few Daoist schools to survive into the modern period. Perfect Realization was founded at the end of the Northern Song dynasty (960–1160) by a scholar named Wang Zhe (1113–70), who emphasized the merits of seclusion to cultivate one's nature and harmonize one's life or fate. "Realization" refers to the way in which the school synthesized the three traditions of Daoism, Buddhism, and Confucianism. The wisdom of a celestial worthy in Perfect Realization Daoism consisted of self-cultivation; the "original mind" being perceived as good and needing cultivation to maintain that goodness; celibacy, understood as purifying the body and mind; and finally transformation by the Dao and immortality being conferred by it through the practices of internal alchemy, fasting, chanting, and meditation. Today Perfect Realization temples have been established not only in Taiwan but also in North America. A Daoist named Ni Huajing is credited with adapting Perfect Realization teachings for North American audiences (Kohn 2000; Kirkland 2004).

Chief among the schools in the post-Tang period was the Orthodox Unity school that continued the traditions of the earlier Celestial Masters and still exists today. This school actively promoted the idea that all Daoist beliefs and practices outside its periphery were heterogeneous and dangerous. During the latter half of the Qing dynasty (1644–1911), the emperors grew tired of the school, foreshadowing its gradual decline into the modern period of the People's Republic of China. Today Orthodox Unity priests perform traditional rituals and other healing for their congregations (Kohn 2000; Kirkland 2004).

The Daoist canon was complete by 1445, during the Ming dynasty. It included all the extant Daoist works—1,120 at the time—and more than five thousand volumes pertaining to philosophy, scripture, biography, rituals, talismans, mudras (hand gestures), and other aspects believed to be important in Daoism. Until 1926 it could be found in only a few Daoist temples in China, including the famous White Cloud Temple in Beijing. Since that time it has been reproduced and is now widely available (Kirkland 2004). The Way and Its Power (Daodejing) is a widely translated and read text. Qi, the Dao, and the workings of yin and yang have modern, global, and sometimes

New Age meanings; they are also seen as part of the general fabric of Chinese thought and culture.

Buddhism, Catholicism, Daoism, Islam, and Protestantism have been officially recognized and given freedom to practise in China. Since the 1980s there has been a resurgence, revival, and reconstruction of formerly (though unevenly until 1963) banned Daoist temples, practices, and beliefs that from a Communist perspective were deemed to be superstitious. These new religious freedoms have enabled thousands of Daoists to make pilgrimages to sacred mountains such as Taishan, temples, and famous priests. Daoists throughout the Chinese cultural sphere have transformed their practice by spearheading reforestation and anti-consumption movements, ordaining trees, and protecting endangered species. The government has recently begun to use Daoism, events such as Laozi's birthday, and popular centres such as the Shaolin Temple (associated with kung fu and many films) to promote Chinese tourism.

In Taiwan, Daoism today combines rituals, divinations, beliefs, and practices from the many schools of Daoism examined in this chapter, as well as mediumship. Daoist rituals and practices have traditionally been divided into two groups, but in practice there are variations throughout the Chinese cultural sphere. This traditional division splits the practice and its practitioners into those led by the authoritative Daoist priests (*daoshi*) and those led by subordinate Daoist ritual masters (*fashi*), who are distinguished by the colour of their hats and the kind of rituals they perform. Daoist priests are literati who are ordained and sometimes inherit their positions. They wear black hats and use classical Chinese during communal rituals in which trance and exorcism usually do not play a part. Daoist ritual masters, in contrast, do not belong to the literati class and do not inherit their positions. They wear red hats and use vernacular Chinese during rituals for the local communities they serve. The ritual master provides a link between the formal aspects of Daoist religion and local traditions, often taking on the role of medium, healer, and fortuneteller.

Mediums

Mediums associated with everyday Daoist practices can be found throughout the Chinese cultural sphere and in southern China, Taiwan, and Singapore (where there are more legal restrictions on practice) and have many different names. Some have names like the *wu* of

> **Five Elements:** wood, metal, fire, water, and earth, associated with Zou Yan (350–270 B.C.E.).

Chinese antiquity, while others have names that imply childlike qualities. There are male and female mediums called diviners of the spirit, and female mediums called *hongyi*. Contemporary mediums perform many functions, sometimes alone and sometimes with the help of a Daoist ritual master. He or she is a spirit medium, exorcist, diviner of fortunes and dreams, spirit writer, healer, and ritual dancer. During important festivals and on pilgrimages, entranced male and female mediums may perform self-mortification, using one of five sharp objects (referred to as "treasures") to strike their backs and foreheads to show the power of the possessing spirit.

Key Ideas and Symbols in Confucianism and Daoism

Dragons

Within Chinese thought and culture, dragons are auspicious creatures. They were imperial symbols, used to decorate the robes of Chinese emperors and Daoist priests, temple structures, and *qipao* (Manchurian Chinese dresses) and mandarin-style jackets worn during special celebrations. Unlike their negative, violent, and fearsome counterparts in the West, the Chinese dragon is associated with the emperor, fertility, and rain. Chinese dragons who inhabit the eastern region of a mythical world are known to be blue-green (an inky colour like that of the night sky). Their nemesis is the western white tiger, which is associated with the end of life.

Taiji Tu

The *taiji tu* is both an emblem and a concept that has been influential in Daoism and Neo-Confucianism. It comprises yin ("shady" or "dark"), indicating stillness, and yang ("light" or "white"), indicating movements that are created by the Taiji, or "Supreme Ultimate." Together, yin and yang generated by the Supreme Ultimate further create the **Five Elements**—fire, wood, earth, water, and metal—and later, heaven and earth hexagrams (see below). Heaven and earth are what give birth to qi (life force) and all manifest things. In the West and more commonly today, we recognize many of these ideas in the yin-yang symbol,

The yin-yang symbol illustrates oscillation from light and movement to darkness and stillness. The yin side contains some yang, and vice versa.

Source: Sybille Yates/Shutterstock

Hexagrams: sixty-four combinations of six broken and unbroken lines that signify natural phenomena or abstract concepts.

Trigram: a divided hexagram with three lines, patterned after natural imagery.

which depicts oscillation from light and movement to darkness and stillness. It is important to note that the yin side contains some yang, and vice versa.

Qi

The character *qi* shows the vapour or energy that rises up from rice as it is being cooked. Qi, or life force, is a key idea in Daoist and Neo-Confucian texts. It is also central to the beliefs and practices of *qigong*, some new religious movements, traditional Chinese medicine (TCM), and all forms of self-cultivation. Over time qi came to have individual and otherworldly religious dimensions and associations.

Hexagrams and Trigrams

Hexagrams are patterns composed of sixty-four different combinations of broken (yin) and unbroken (yang) lines. The sixty-four hexagrams have natural meanings such as "heaven" and "earth" (the first two hexagrams) and represent concepts such as peace or enthusiasm. Each hexagram is divided into two parts, or **trigrams**,

which contain three broken and/or unbroken lines. The trigrams (of which there are eight) are patterned after natural imagery such as fire, wind, and water. The sixty-four hexagrams are transient forms that correspond to a specific time in the lunar calendar when the *yi* oracle is performed. Performing this oracle—*yijing* (known in the West as I Ching)—renders a hexagram that offers advice and solutions to problems.

The Five Elements

The Five Elements are wood, metal, fire, water, and earth. Han dynasty thinkers emphasized that the world humans inhabit is a living organism, and harmonious living depends on understanding how different elements in nature interact. In later ideas related to Chinese medicine, the human body and its organs are interpreted according to the five elements, as well as qi and yin and yang. There are also heaven, earth, and human correspondences. Seasons, colours, musical notes, tastes, dynasties, the five directions, and animals are all assigned one of the five elements. These elements become the patterns and pathways for creating harmony. To a large extent the Five Elements replaced sacrifices, mediums, and other customs that from the Han dynasty rationalist perspective now lacked efficacy, or ling.

Dao

Dao, or "way," is Daoism's main idea, referring to nature. But it is also a concept shared by Confucians, to whom it means a path and a way of doing things related to propriety and virtue. The Analects include a passage suggesting that if one hears the Dao in the morning, in the evening one can die a happy person (4:8). According to the Daodejing, the Dao couldn't be named: "The *Dao* that can be *dao'ed* is not the constant *dao*. The name that can be named is not the constant name" (Chapter 1). In the Zhuangzi we also read that the Dao is inexpressible and cannot be made clear.

Ling

Ling, or "efficacy," is defined as miraculous power and spirit. Ling emphasizes the dominance of divine power and the agency of human actions. If humans stop worshipping deities, then the deities cease to exist as important to us, and temples and practices that acknowledge their power also disappear. New ones that are seen as efficacious—for instance, Han dynasty innovations promoting use of the Five Elements and other rational correspondences between the human body and gods—are then introduced.

Self-cultivation

Self-cultivation is a concept that is common in both Confucianism and Daoism. In early Confucianism it became a pivotal idea pertaining to the cultivation or perfection of one's personal nature. Confucius noted that cultivation began with the Classic of Poetry, was made firm by propriety (the Classic of Ritual), and became perfected through music (the Classic of Music) *(Analects 8.8)*. Mencius said that human beings by nature are good but that their nature needs to be continually cultivated through study, practice, and behaving appropriately according to one's social and familial roles. Xunzi disagreed that human nature was intrinsically good. He noted that gentlemen and commoners were different and noted that goodness came only through conscious effort. Perfect Realization Daoism promoted fasting, chanting, and meditation as self-cultivation practices that would reveal the "original mind." Later Daoists focused on perfection of the original mind and original nature through a growing number of self-cultivation techniques that involved body, mind, and spirit. Despite its diversity, especially today, Daoism places even more emphasis on self-cultivation as the way to perfection and the harmonization of the realms of heaven, earth. and man.

Mandate of Heaven

The Mandate of Heaven (*tianming*) is a traditional Chinese concept that emerged in the Zhou dynasty to establish the rulers as part of an all-male line extending back to the Three Sovereigns of the legendary period. Zhou rulers wanted to be like the Three Sovereigns, who were virtuous and sages and ruled because they had the Mandate of Heaven. Droughts and floods were averted if a ruler had the Mandate of Heaven. Similarly, inability to end a drought or defeat another in battle was understood as a sign that a ruler did not have the Mandate. The Mandate of Heaven continued to be the dominant way that people judged a ruler until the modern period (beginning in 1900). Related to this idea was the notion of the ruler being the Son of Heaven.

> **Benevolence:** *ren*, or humaneness, the most important Confucian virtue; the character *ren* shows the radical for "person" and the number two, signifying human relationship.
>
> **Reciprocity:** *shu*, another important Confucian virtue; it is expressed by the characters meaning "like" above and "heart"/"mind" below, conveying the idea that reciprocity is to be of like heart or mind.

Benevolence

One of the most important Confucian virtues is **benevolence** or humaneness (*ren*). Scholar Julia Ching has noted that the character *ren* depicts two people in relationship to each other and that relationships require humanity and recognition of the other person's needs. The Analects contain many conversations between Confucius and his disciples about *ren*, which enables people to create social harmony and cultivate themselves while also attending to the needs of others.

Reciprocity

Reciprocity (*shu*) is another important Confucian virtue. The word is composed using the characters meaning "like" above and "heart"/"mind" below, conveying the idea that reciprocity is to be of like heart or mind. Often this virtue is explained to Western students as the "reverse Golden Rule": "Do not do to others what you do not want them to do to you" (Analects 15:25).

Li

Li—propriety or rites—relates to social conduct as outlined in the Classic of Ritual. The character *li* depicts a person bending over a sacrificial vessel that has been filled with soybeans. This character communicates how in daily life one should fill oneself with (or defer to) Confucian wisdom, just as the vessel is filled with beans. By becoming a vessel filled with wisdom transmitted to us from the past, we will be able to become like an honourable sage. An important aspect of propriety is the obedience or filial piety required of children toward parents. Propriety may also be explained as a code of conduct or set of polite behaviours. These codes of conduct create smooth and harmonious social relations. All the virtues may be considered as belonging to the virtue of propriety.

The Five Relationships

The five relationships are defined in the Doctrine of the Mean (Zhongyong), where relationships are ranked, and thereby articulate the manner in which family and state are joined. The five relationships were understood as ways to maintain relationships with those who are alive (family and friends) and those who are dead (ancestors). According to Chinese tradition, a person has a specific place within social, political, and economic networks that is defined by education and family. These five relationships are (1) subject to ruler; (2) father to son or daughter; (3) husband to wife; (4) son to son or siblings; and (5) friend to friend. Children should be obedient, filial, and respectful toward their fathers. Friendships are the least important and the least religious of relationships because they do not pertain to kin. Women are mentioned only as wives and daughters. A woman's comparatively inferior social and familial status was further emphasized by the Three Obediences: to her father as a daughter, to her husband as a wife, and to her son as a mother. The spheres of influence and connection in China were understood as defined by the first four of these normative relationships.

Loyalty

The Confucian virtue of loyalty reminds us of the importance of attachment to the people who are related to us in the Five Relationships. It describes being centred in one's heart and mind both in relationships with other people and in the Chinese cultural sphere.

Jing

According to traditional Chinese thinking, *jing* is the classic or foundational text and is roughly equivalent in meaning to "scripture." The classic is an important pattern of Chinese thought and culture. When a compound contains the character *jing*, this indicates that the text has authority.

Oracle Bone and Yi Oracle Divination

Scripture in Chinese religion relates to the authority of written characters, the earliest of which were believed to have been transmitted through divination from the spirit world. Surviving materials suggest that there were two kinds of divination: by oracle bone and by the Yi Oracle. Oracle bones are our sources for the beliefs and practices of early Chinese religion. They tell us that the ruler routinely consulted the Divine for wisdom on matters related to the hunt, battles, fertility, and calamities and to determine when rituals and sacrifices should be performed. At times the ruler needed advice or simply confirmation from the Divine that his chosen action was correct. The consultations used statements that allowed for a simple yes-or-no answer, such as "We will prosper from the harvest" or "It is good to proceed to the hunt."

Oracle bone divination was performed by a team of experts who saw the process through from beginning to end. Cattle scapula (shoulder blades) and turtle plastrons (shells) were carefully prepared by washing, drying, and polishing them. Then a heated instrument was applied to create a set of cracks. A diviner would then interpret the cracks and convey the Divine's response to the statement. The diviner could be very creative (and vague—so he couldn't be seen to be wrong!) in his interpretation. Divinations were perceived as occasionally unreliable, so if the king performed a divination and did not like the result, he could simply perform another one—and the ruler was rarely wrong. The oracle bone was one way in which rulers continued to control their people by showing they had the support of divine agents, or the Mandate of Heaven.

The second form of divination in early China was the Yi Oracle. This procedure used milfoil or dried yarrow stalks to interpret advice from the Divine. The Yi Oracle existed for a millennium as an oral tradition and then was recorded as the Yijing, the Classic of Changes (also known as I Ching). The Yi Oracle, like oracle bone divination, was performed by a diviner at a specific time determined by the lunar calendar (see the description of hexagrams above).

The Six Arts

Before the Six Classics (see "Words" box), scholars, officials, and warriors were expected to cultivate themselves by learning the Six Arts. These included practices that were both martial (archery and chariot riding) and scholarly or cultural (ritual, music, calligraphy, and numerology) and were associated with the practices and beliefs of the Emerging Scholars.

The Six Classics

The classics are the earliest bodies of traditional knowledge, which were first transmitted orally and eventually set down in writing. They were seen to contain the patterns for civilized behaviour and harmony in Chinese society. The most authoritative corpus is known as the Six Classics.

The Poetry Classic is a set of 305 poems (often called the Three Hundred Poems), with the earliest dating to 1500 B.C.E. While authorship of the poems was traditionally attributed to Confucius, modern scholars now recognize them as folksongs that were collected by the Zhou court and later edited and performed as ceremonial hymns. The poems offer key historical information about early Chinese society, religion, customs, politics, and relations with neighbouring people.

The Classic of Documents is the first historical piece of Chinese writing and contains twenty-eight sections. It survived what is known as the book burning of 213 B.C.E., when the first emperor of China attempted to break from the past by following the advice of Li Si (d. 208 B.C.E.), his prime minister, to destroy vast quantities of texts. It was also traditionally (and falsely) believed to have been edited by Confucius and his later disciples. It provides information about early Chinese legends and the actions and speeches of virtuous sage-kings who ruled in the pre-historical period.

The Classic of Changes was considered by Confucius to be the most important of the classics, and he was fond of reading the Yijing (pronounced *e-jing* and often spelled I Ching and mispronounced *eye-ching*) in later life. The Classic of Changes contains sixty-four possible hexagrams that can result when the Yi Oracle is performed. Each of the hexagrams is translated into a character that adds meaning, and each also contains two sets of trigrams, for which there are eight combinations. Statements or judgments were written for each hexagram as well as for arrangements of the hexagrams in a particular order. These were later followed by commentaries appended to the classic.

The Classic of Rituals contains the Record of Rites, Ceremonies and Rites, and the Rites of Zhou. This classic describes a wide range of rules about social conduct or ritual propriety (li), including behaviour and practices for specific social and religious situations, ceremonies, and other formal court behaviours. It includes descriptions of life-cycle and death rituals, proper behaviour during audiences with the ruler, and what to wear during mourning. It also provides detailed information about the types of music and dances appropriate for various occasions and the roles, gender, age, and numbers of religious functionaries who performed at court and in rituals and ceremonies that took place outside the court.

The Classic of Music was lost during the 213 B.C.E. book burning but fragments of it survive in other texts. It presented a traditional understanding of the way music was to be performed during rituals. In the Classic of Music the five musical notes were said to mirror the five political offices, stressing the importance of keeping the notes orderly and outlining the negative political consequences if they were in disarray.

The Spring and Autumn Classic, complete with commentary texts, is named for a period in Chinese history during the reign of numerous dukes from the state of Lu (720–481 B.C.E.). Since Mencius's time this classic has been attributed to Confucius and seen as Confucian wisdom and morality. Short, impersonal entries discuss diplomacy, governance, wars, natural disasters, and other events during the Spring and Autumn period.

SPIRITUAL AND RELIGIOUS PRACTICES

Confucian and Daoist Deities

Confucian Deities

When discussing deities in Confucianism and Daoism, it is important to keep in mind that Confucianism in the past was primarily associated with imperial state rule and important rites and sacrifices. It was also associated with ancestor worship (or offerings) and maintenance of the patriline. The Temple of Heaven in Beijing is an example of a traditional though elaborately designed Confucian temple built during the Ming dynasty. Emperors would make annual offerings to heaven there at the winter solstice and during other seasons and festivals. Other natural deities that received offerings were representatives of the sun, the moon, and earth.

Qufu, where Confucius was born and buried, had a temple built in 478 b.c.e. that has since been reconstructed and dedicated to Confucius. The temple houses genealogical records relating to Confucius and the Kong family. A statue of Confucius is located on an altar in the main offering hall and rituals are performed to venerate him as a sage and teacher; his image is accompanied by those of favourite disciples.

Daoist Deities

Daoist deities are ranked, with titles and distinct personalities that have been revealed by legends. There are two categories of deities: earlier-heaven deities—in existence since the beginning of time, before heaven and earth were split—and later-heaven deities—human beings, such as family members, who have been transformed into immortals. The Daoist pantheon is huge and evolving. Deities are believed to inhabit a parallel world to the one of humans and to hold ranked positions in a bureaucracy.

Yuanshitian is recognized by many to be the highest-ranked deity of the Daoist pantheon and is followed by Great Pure, Highest Pure Jade Emperor and manifestations of Laozi. The Great Emperor of the Eastern Peak oversees the realm of the dead and the souls who enter it. There are also martial and city gods or gods from a local region. Some gods are in charge of destiny, such as the stove or kitchen god. Other gods are responsible for areas related to wealth or the earth. Often the earth god is depicted as a kindly old man who helps people out of hell.

Guangong The loyal, courageous, fierce-looking general Guan Yunchang served the warlord Liu Bei during the latter part of the Han dynasty and after the dynasty fell. Most people today know about Yunchang, or Guangong, from the fictional *Romance of the Three Kingdoms*, popularized in novels and made-for-television series. Today Guangong is known by many names and is a ubiquitous figure with strong connections to Chinese revolution and Chinese migration history. Around 1762 an early Chinese brotherhood (triad) known as the Heaven and Earth Society was founded that worshipped Guangong; new members were initiated into the society by drinking blood, offering incense, and swearing allegiance to the figure they recognized as the god of righteousness. He continues to be a fearsome guardian figure even in North America, where he may be found in Chinatown police stations and in the buildings and halls of clan and friendship associations and dramatic and martial arts centres. Guangong is also a common sight in many North American Chinese restaurants. There he sometimes shares an altar and receives offerings of incense and food items alongside the friendlier-looking Buddhist Guanyin, goddess of compassion. Guangong also holds a place of honour in Daoism as the martial god Guandi or Guanyu.

General Fan and General Xie General Fan and General Xie are popular Daoist gods and good friends. Xie is often portrayed as pale-skinned, tall, and slender, with his tongue sticking out, while Fan is dark-skinned, short, and fat. They appear in most Taiwanese temple processions. Originally these two generals of justice worked as a team, but one day the rains came and Xie told Fan to wait under a bridge while he went to get something to shield them from the rain. Xie became distracted and returned much later to find his friend drowned beside the water (which is why Fan's skin is dark). Xie was so stricken by grief that he hung himself on a nearby tree, his face, pale in death, frozen in an expression of horror.

Daoist Goddesses

Daoist goddesses have relationships with higher male gods and are often their consorts. Most of them are associated with reproduction or the family. There was a strong tradition during the Tang dynasty for widowed women to become Daoist nuns, but this trend tapered off in the Song, Ming, and Qing periods. Daoist nuns lived in special quarters and were supposed to be celibate, though there is evidence that some had sex with monks and others who frequented their quarters.

Dou Mu Also known as Doulalo Yuanjun, Primordial Sovereign of the Big Dipper, or Dipper Mother, Dou Mu emerged as a Daoist goddess in the fifteenth century, during the Ming dynasty. A healer and protector of women during labour, she is associated with the northern Dipper and to a lesser extent with the sun and the moon. Dou Mu represents the light from the night sky and can control human destiny.

Linshui Furen This popular contemporary Daoist goddess, also known as Chen Jinggu, has many altars dedicated to her in southern China and Taiwan. She helps expectant mothers and babies, and for this reason she is often associated with female worshippers. Lady Linshui's personal, though likely legendary story is a powerful one that centres around her efforts to help a young pregnant girl who is in danger of losing the child. This legend conveys her agency as a goddess of childbirth who helps those who offer their prayers; anyone having trouble with pregnancy or childbirth or who wants a boy can pray to her.

Mazu Mazu, or Lin Moniang (960–87), is also known as Mother Ancestor, goddess of the South China Sea, and empress (or goddess) of heaven. Early on, Mazu

Linshui Furen has many altars dedicated to her in southern China and Taiwan. She helps expectant mothers and babies and for this reason is often associated with female worshippers.

Source: © TAO Images Limited/Alamy

was known simply as a goddess of the sea. Later she was thought to help those who were suffering, especially women who needed help with fertility (that is, producing a son) and childbirth. Named "Silent Girl" (Moniang) because she did not cry at birth, Mazu is traditionally believed to have become a Buddhist when she was ten years old. She joined the Daoist pantheon in the early fifteenth century. Legends describe how Mazu in her lifetime distinguished herself through her Buddhist, Daoist, and Confucian erudition. In addition to her breadth of knowledge, she was also known to be a talented healer and medium who could expel malevolent spirits and end drought. She died a young woman and a virgin.

The Mazu temple on the island of Meizhou, located off China's Fujian province, is recognized as the place from which she eventually ascended to heaven and gained her status as a popular goddess. Even though Mazu's origins can be traced to south-eastern China, she also has strong ties to southern Taiwan and to

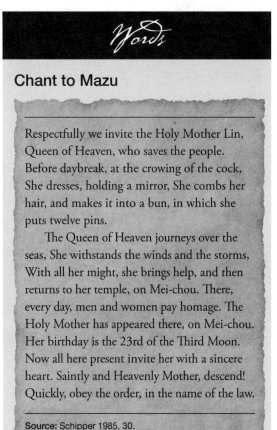

Words

Chant to Mazu

Respectfully we invite the Holy Mother Lin, Queen of Heaven, who saves the people. Before daybreak, at the crowing of the cock, She dresses, holding a mirror, She combs her hair, and makes it into a bun, in which she puts twelve pins.

The Queen of Heaven journeys over the seas, She withstands the winds and the storms, With all her might, she brings help, and then returns to her temple, on Mei-chou. There, every day, men and women pay homage. The Holy Mother has appeared there, on Mei-chou. Her birthday is the 23rd of the Third Moon. Now all here present invite her with a sincere heart. Saintly and Heavenly Mother, descend! Quickly, obey the order, in the name of the law.

Source: Schipper 1985, 30.

Taiwanese national identity. Every year, on the twenty-third day of the third lunar month (April or May), between four and five million worshippers mark her birthday by making a pilgrimage to Chaotian Temple in Beigang Township in Yunlin county, Taiwan.

Queen Mother of the West Xiwang Mu, or Queen Mother of the West, is also known as Metal Mother of the Tortoise Pond, Metal Mother of the Nine Rays of Supreme Emptiness of the Tortoise Pond, Nine-Soul Great Sublime Metal Mother of the Tortoise Mountain, Primordial Ruler, Metal Mother, Sage Mother of the Tortoise Pond, Metal Mother, or Western Queen. The Queen Mother is a very old deity in Chinese religion (from about the time of the Zhou dynasty) and is possibly linked to an even older Chinese deity who

Mazu, or Lin Moniang (960–87), also known as Tianshang Shengmu, Tianhou, or Tianfei—Mother Ancestor, goddess of the South China Sea, empress (or goddess) of heaven

Source: © Guo Jian She/Redlink/Redlink/Corbis

was not necessarily female. According to Daoist legend, the Daoist goddesses lived with the Queen Mother of the West in a walled palace on the peak of Kunlun Mountain in the land of the immortals.

While the Queen Mother was the female head of the pantheon, male deities predominated in the upper tiers of the religious hierarchy. As the personification of yin—associated with the colour white and the element metal, the west, death, and the afterlife—the Queen Mother is less important in popular forms of religion, where Mazu is the highest-ranked goddess. Legends tell that she had sex with many men so as to steal their essence in order to strengthen her own vital energy and become an immortal. As a protector of singsong girls (female entertainers), dead girls, nuns, and adepts, and generally of women outside traditional roles, as well as children, she heals and changes fate.

Qixing Niangnian Usually called Auntie of the Seven Stars, Qixing Niangniang is also known as Elder Sister or Nun of the Seven Stars, in folk stories as Girl of the Seven Stars, and in Taiwanese folklore as the Maiden of the (Double) Seven or the Weaving Maiden. This deity is called upon by women to help with fertility. She is also a protector of children and presides over ceremonies and rituals on the seventh day of the seventh month. After a child's first year of life, he or she will be brought to the temple on Double Seven (the seventh day of the seventh month of the Chinese lunar calendar) and offerings will be made so that the deity will enable the child to continue to grow.

Qixing Niangniang is also known for her role in traditional coming-of-age rituals when a child is sixteen years old. In the past this ritual was used to enable children of sixteen and older to earn a higher wage and to marry. On Double Seven, children dressed in traditional garb pray to the goddess and then crawl under a ceremonial table at temples where she has altars. With the exception of Tainan, Taiwan, this traditional ritual is seldom performed these days, and when it is, only the first-born child of the family participates.

Goddess of the Morning Clouds Like many other Daoist goddesses, Bixia Yuanjun helps women with issues related to fertility and childbirth. However, there are important differences between Daoist goddesses such as Lady Linshui and the Goddess of the Morning Clouds. Early on she enjoyed court patronage, reaching the peak of her popularity in the Ming dynasty. By the time of the Qing, however, worship of Bixia had been pushed to the periphery of court life and many literati had distanced themselves from her image. The reason for this changed attitude was that Bixia was increasingly seen as a manipulative goddess who empowered infertile daughters-in-law to get pregnant with male children to assure themselves status in family hierarchies.

CONFUCIAN AND DAOIST WORSHIP

Customs associated with the Emerging Scholars and Confucians had their origins in early Chinese civilization. One of the most well-known early civilizations was the Yangshao, or "painted pottery," culture (3000 B.C.E.), whose civilization is recognized by their pottery's painted animal and fish designs. Yangshao people were known to have practiced fertility rituals, sacrifices, and burials. The Longshan, or "black pottery," culture (2000 B.C.E.) were known for their black and unpainted pottery designs. The Yangshao fertility rituals were replaced by ancestor worship during the Longshan period. Divination using the Yi Oracle emerged as a religious practice during this period.

The Xia dynasty (China's first prehistoric dynasty) is associated with legendary rulers and the sage-kings. Religious practice during the Xia is hard to determine but included ancestor worship, divination, and sacrifice.

Shang dynasty deities existed in a ranked hierarchy, and Shang kings made offerings and performed five main rituals that included divination on specific days of a ten-day week. They also made sacrifices, offerings, and appeals. Burial records indicate that elite women had inferior status in Shang society, as evidenced by secondary burial customs in which women followed their husbands in death. Women were buried with spindle and jade pendants and men were buried with tools to indicate their roles in society. Although non-elite women laboured on farms, worked in markets, and did needlework, inside the elite circles women might only be noble consorts who were signs of a man's social status. The more consorts a man had, the more power that ensued. Divination records also give evidence of women's low status during the Shang dynasty. Having a boy child was seen as lucky or good, while having a girl was unlucky.

During the Zhou dynasty, the most important sacrifices and ceremonies continued to take place at the capital. Lesser ones could be conducted by the leaders of aristocratic families who had been granted religious and military power to rule beyond the centre. Zhou society developed through the refinement of ritual actions, which were the dominant form of social conduct and governed everything from divination and sacrifices to rulership. Ritual actions carried out appropriately maintained social harmony and status.

Different sacrifices and rituals were used to acknowledge the various gods during the Zhou. Heaven (Tian) was the realm of the heavenly gods; there were also earthly gods. Each god had a position within the religious hierarchy and a specific role to play in Chinese civilization. Sacrifices and ritual offerings maintained these distinctions. The victims of sacrifices to the heavenly gods (and those offered to the sun) were incinerated, while earthly sacrifices (and those for the moon) were buried. Blood and intestinal fat were offered to heavenly deities and raw meat was offered to ancestors; boiled meat and, later, seasoned meats were eaten by those who attended banquets after the sacrifice or ritual. For the most part, human sacrifices had ended by the late Warring States period (Boileau 1998–99, 23–24).

During the Han dynasty, emperors continued to worship, offer prayers, and make sacrifices to heaven at Taishan, as well as to a growing list of earth, rain, wind, mountain, river, crop, and other gods, in addition to their ancestors. The emperor's pilgrimages, seasonal offerings, sacrifices of sheep and pigs to ancestral and deity shrines, retinues of priests and assistants, musicians, and guards became very expensive to maintain. For this and many other reasons, the Han dynasty saw a shift in beliefs that governed imperial ritual performance.

Zhu Xi's *Family Rituals*, though written during the Song dynasty, provide a glimpse of normative ancestor veneration. The proper performance of ancestral rites maintained kinship ties and lineage boundaries. As they continue to do today, ancestral rites also provided an occasion for families to gather and have a special meal. Ancestral veneration was performed on days deemed to be auspicious in the lunar calendar. Ritual purification was gendered and divided into the outer and inner domestic spheres; three days before the rite took place, male and female kin would bathe, drink moderately, eat only lightly seasoned food, and refrain from listening to music and other activities deemed to lead to impurity. Ancestors were given separate, disconnected place settings around the room, beginning in the northwest corner. Women set the ritual tables, cleaned the vessels, and prepared the food for each ancestor. Spoons and chopsticks were placed on the table at daybreak.

After daybreak the family, led by the head male and female and in order of gender roles and age, proceeded into the outer region of the offering hall. The ancestral tablets were taken to their place settings—for the males by the head man and for the females by the head female. The head man then reported to the ancestors. The family bowed twice and the spirits were called by lighting incense as attendants filled the wine cups. Food was offered to the ancestors by the head man and male attendants, and the ancestors were encouraged to partake of it. Then the wine was sacrificed. The family bowed twice at the culmination of the event, the ancestral tablets were removed from their place settings, and the meal was consumed by the family—except for the wine, which was returned to its bottles (Ebrey 1991). Ancestral rites may be classified as Confucian and have persisted into the modern period, with many variations.

Daoist rites persist as well. Just as there are diverse forms of Daoist practice, there are also diverse deities. Each of these deities has a personality, a history (usually legendary), and sometimes a medium who becomes possessed by him or her. Many Daoist temples were destroyed during the Taiping Rebellion. Destruction of Daoist temples continued into the modern period, during the second Sino-Japanese War and especially after 1950, when Mao came to power and made the practice of religion illegal until 1979. A slow resurgence of religious freedom developed during the Deng Xiaoping era (1978–94) and today there are more than twenty thousand practising Daoists in China and thousands of temples.

CHINESE TEMPLES AND PRIVATE ALTARS

Before China's modern period (beginning around 1900), most homes would have an altar to gods such as the god of the earth, the kitchen god, or other gods such as Guanyin, Guangong, or Mazu. Private altars take on a variety of forms. An affluent district magistrate's home might be large enough to include an entire hall to hold an altar and offering table just for the ancestors, in addition to a hall dedicated to the main deities such

as Guanyin. In contrast, a farm family might have only enough room and resources to set up a simple altar or shelf for deity offerings near the entrance to the home. In all cases, however, the "worship" that takes place in front of such an altar is understood somewhat differently from other traditions because of the centrality of efficacy in the Chinese context. Deities and ancestors receive offerings and prayers from people who revere and respect them and their power, but the relationship between human beings and the Divine is seldom one-sided. The Divine needs to respond to human needs in order to maintain its position and earn that reverence, which makes the English word *worship* unable to fully explain this important aspect of Daoist and Confucian religiosity.

The majority of Daoist temples may be south-facing rectangular spaces that are diverse in appearance. They are dedicated to deities specific to the region and the lineage of families who live there. Daoist worship takes place before an altar that links the physical, this-worldly space of the temple to the sacred one where the deities reside. Once imbued with the spirits through special ritual processes, altar statues carved from wood represent the deity and the place of ling, when spirits are invoked and welcomed to a ritual in order to be venerated and communicated with in the space. Temples often consist of several buildings (each with its own offering hall and altar, for both minor and major deities) connected by courtyards.

Practices may be casual. In Tainan, Taiwan, for instance, devotees drop by a local temple dedicated to Mazu during lunch hour or after dinner, to bow and offer incense, spirit money, and prayers. More formal and traditional ritual practices also exist, some of which are associated with Daoist schools such as Complete Perfection. Daoists in monasteries and temples offer prayers and incense before public temple altars and also in front of their own private home altars at the beginning and end of each day.

Chinese temples are traditionally painted in bright colours. Predominantly red, Daoist temples are the most striking in appearance, making liberal use of accent colours such as yellow, gold, green, blue, white, and black. Red is an auspicious yang colour symbolizing the power of the sun and the element fire; yellow is an imperial colour symbolizing the element earth; and bluish green is related to longevity and the land of the immortals, symbolizing the element wood. Black is another imperial colour that only through Western influence has come to be associated with death. Black symbolizes the element water and white represents yin and death and symbolizes the element metal. Intricate winged and brightly tiled temple roofs are decorated with auspicious animal figures such as dragons, snakes, phoenixes, and tigers. Images of famous Daoist and Confucian historical and legendary figures, as well as the four plants associated with Chinese virtue (plum, orchid, bamboo, and chrysanthemum) and animals with positive associations are carved into temple beams, posts, and trusses.

Temple interiors are similarly filled with paintings of animals, plants, and figures representing the importance of longevity, wisdom, prosperity, and health in Daoism and Confucianism. Throughout the temples, on ceilings, screens, walls, vases, wall hangings, paintings, and sculptures, Daoist symbols such as the eight trigrams, *taiji tu* (yin-yang symbols), the "eight immortals," and deities associated with the Chinese hells are displayed. Floors are most often plain. Windows can be circular or square and symbolize yang and yin as well as heavenly and earthly correspondences and meanings. Temples are fronted by a pair of male and female guardians, most often open-mouthed lions, who scare away the malevolent spirits believed to always be lurking outside the temple. The male has one paw on a ball, while the female may have a cub beneath her.

FESTIVALS AND CELEBRATIONS

There are many Daoist and Confucian festivals and celebrations throughout the year. Daoist temples hold birthday celebrations for deities (each deity has its own story and its birthday is known by followers) and organize pilgrimages. The Daoist festivals are too numerous to detail here, but below I summarize the important Chinese festivals.

New Year

New Year is the most important Chinese celebration and has both Confucian and Daoist religious dimensions. Chinese New Year usually falls between January 19 and February 23, as determined by the lunar calendar. Years can be either yang or yin and have other characteristics and associations such as colour (white, black, green, red or

brown) links to the Five Elements, and one of the twelve signs of the Chinese zodiac.

According to legend, the kitchen god travels to see the Jade Emperor (one of the highest-ranking deities) around this time of year. The New Year is perceived to be a time of new beginnings. People visit with family and friends, pay off debts that may have accumulated during the past year, and make amends with people with whom they have had a falling out. Mothers customarily place sweet candies in the mouths of their children as soon as they wake up in the morning. This ensures that the new year will begin with all things associated with sweetness: prosperity, happiness, and health.

Mid-autumn (Moon) Festival

The mid-autumn festival is a time of the Chinese lunar calendar in which family and friends gather to eat and observe the brightness of the full moon. Practices vary throughout the world. The traditional purpose of the festival is to celebrate the harvest and to honour "grandfather moon" and the ancestors. Special foods eaten during this Chinese festival often have a circular round shape—representing heaven—such as moon cakes, chicken dumplings, snails, pomelos, coconuts, and peanuts. Food is also offered to the ancestors during this holiday. In more traditional households a special altar is set up near a window where the family (and ancestors) can view the full moon. Moon cakes are offered there, as well as whisky, wine, or tea, incense, candles, spirit money, and a full banquet of the ancestor's and family's favourite foods.

RITES OF PASSAGE
Full Month

When a baby is born, mother and child enter into a full month of seclusion where they remain in one room that in the times before hospitals would have been where the labour took place. This seclusion cements the bond between them, protects them both from illness, and preserves the energy of the mother, who in the period following childbirth is very yin and prone to anemia and dizzy spells. The mother needs rest in order to recover from the experience of childbirth and to regain her yin-yang balance. Today, however, this custom has been adapted and women simply remain indoors with their newborns.

At the end of the Full Month, the mother has a ritual bath, cleansing herself of the birth experience. The infant is also washed, given a haircut, and presented to her or his maternal grandmother. Offerings of incense and food are presented by the infant (with the assistance of the maternal grandmother) at the ancestral altar, thus welcoming the infant into the patriline. Father and grandfather are next to receive the infant, who is given red money packets, sweet food, chicken or rooster meat, and items of clothing. The infant also receives her given name at that time. Many families then present the child to the community by hosting a sumptuous "red egg and ginger" banquet to which their family and closest friends are invited. After the Full Month has passed, some families will also take their child to the temple for the first time, where he or she will be introduced to the deities that are important to their family. Children should return to the temple after a full year has passed since the time of their birth (Baptandier 2008).

Capping Ceremony

According to tradition, when Chinese girls reach the age of sixteen and boys become twenty, they go through a hair-pinning (for girls) or capping (for boys) ceremony that marks the child's transition to adulthood. The young women's hair is gathered into a bun and pinned; young men have a cap placed on their heads. Now they have reached a marriageable age. In the pre-modern period, girls might also have moved out of the family home and into a residence for maidens awaiting marriage. Visits to temples may be made by families around this time and offerings are given to the deities to mark the child's passage from one stage of life to another.

Marriage

Traditionally, parents hired a matchmaker when their children were young to help them find a suitable spouse for them. Matchmakers determined the suitability of a pair based on Chinese astrological wisdom. They judged the compatibility of the animal signs associated with the birth year and hour, as well as the element of the birth year—metal, wind, water, fire, or earth. Chinese

at home and abroad continued this custom into the modern period. As early as 1900, young women who had received a Christian missionary education or who had attended Anglican schools in Hong Kong followed Western marriage customs.

Funerary Rites

Funerary rites are the final life-stage ritual. Like the other rituals discussed in this section, they follow a loosely defined pattern with strong parallels to Song dynasty and early Chinese practices but include modern adaptations and variations. Family members, led by the eldest son, are required to look after the graves of deceased blood kin and to venerate them with offerings. Traditionally, people consulted someone familiar with *fengshui*. *Fengshui* literally means "wind and water" and refers to a body of wisdom that is relied on by Chinese builders, decorators, and architects to determine the most auspicious positions for buildings, room arrangements, and gardens. *Fengshui* specialists also find auspicious positions for gravesites in a cemetery. According to these traditional beliefs, flat, swampy plots that do not have hills behind them are the least suitable.

Of course, these ideas had to change in overseas Chinese communities, where Chinese areas of Western cemeteries were often the cheapest, wettest, and least suitable for graves and where *fengshui* experts could not be found. Daoist funerals also require a Daoist priest to chant prayers that will help the deceased become saved in the other world. Daoist funerals are rare in overseas Chinese communities, where there are few Daoist priests and temples. People instead rely on Christian ministers to perform ceremonies.

The Record of Rites standardized the Confucian understanding of a funeral ceremony. When someone died, the news was circulated to outsiders by hanging white banners or blue lanterns symbolic of death. The mourning family showed their respect for the dead with a solemn attitude and by donning white clothing. It was appropriate to show grief by crying (not singing like Zhuangzi did when his wife died). The deceased was washed and dressed in the chosen funerary costume. Then offerings were presented, consisting of small paper models of all the items and foods the family believed the deceased would need to make a comfortable journey to the afterlife.

Ancestral Veneration

Ancestral veneration takes place throughout the year, and especially on the ancestor's birthday, at Chinese New Year, during the mid-autumn festival, and during any other festival observed by a family. Often ancestors are venerated and given offerings in addition to other deities who have a place on the family altar. Death marks a person's transition from father, for instance, to ancestor; as such he is believed to hold even greater power over the fate, progeny, health, and wealth of the family, who will now venerate him. This veneration involves presentation of many items at the altar of the ancestor.

The altar may be a very traditional one with a memorial tablet (blessed by a Daoist priest) or simpler vertical pieces of wood carved with the names of deceased ancestors going back four or five generations, which are placed on a specially carved wooden altar shelf. The altar might also contain just photographs of the ancestor, or even no sign of them at all. Alternatively, the altar may be a table pulled in front of a window so that the ancestors have a route through which to descend and partake of the delicious food and whisky, wine, or tea that have been left for them. Most ritual offerings begin with lighting ceremonial candles or turning on lights. The function of ancestral rituals is to please the deceased by transferring to them things they like to eat (for example, favourite pork dishes, shrimp dumplings, soups); paper models of things they need in the other world, such as a car, television set, a BlackBerry or iPad; and most important, money. The transfer of these items is effected when they are burned.

OTHER DAOIST PRACTICES

Everyday Daoist practices can take place at any time and on any day of the week when the temple is open. People are free to walk into the temple and purchase sticks of incense (often sold in multiples of three, such as six, nine, or twelve), light them, and place them in the sand of an urn before an altar.

Divining Blocks

People who visit the temple are also welcome to use a pair of red crescent-moon-shaped divining blocks that are on the table in front of the altar. Practitioners bow to the deity, identify themselves to the deity (with name and address), make a silent wish or ask a yes-or-no question, and then throw the blocks to receive an answer. A favourable response is indicated if the blocks fall with one rounded side up and the other flat side up. Temple personnel nearby encourage people to repeat the process until they receive three favourable responses in a row as confirmation of a correct answer. A small contribution to the donation box is appreciated in return. The moon-shaped divining blocks are available for purchase at any store that sells Daoist ritual instruments.

Divination Slips

Divination slips are common in Daoist and Buddhist temples. They are popular among temple-goers and often used along with the divining blocks. To use them, you either pay a small fee to an attendant or make an anonymous donation to a box, then draw a bamboo stick from the hundred or so in a tall wooden or metal vase on the floor. Each stick has a number on it that corresponds to a divination poem. The poem or fortune will vary from being very good (auspicious) to good, less good, and varying levels of bad (inauspicious).

Spirit Money

Spirit money (also known as hell bank money, ghost money, or joss paper) is an important component of everyday Daoist practice. The idea is that ancestors, deities, and ghosts inhabit a world where they need money to buy things. By providing them with money one extends them help and gratitude, accompanied by a sincere wish that they will help one in return. Many temples will offer stacks of spirit money for sale or allow vendors to sell it outside their doors. Devotees of particular gods leave spirit money on the table in front of the altar as offerings or when they have prayers that they wish to have answered. Those who seek advice from a spirit medium will leave stacks of spirit money in front of the altar to show respect and gratitude to the deity incarnate in the spirit medium whom they have just consulted.

Some modern temples now have special incinerators for burning spirit money: the money does not need to be hand-fed into the incinerator but rather a fan produces a current that draws in the money, sheet by sheet, to a chute leading to the incinerator. These new machines save busy temples time and money. Spirit money is available for purchase in overseas Chinatowns throughout the world.

Offerings on the First and Fifteenth Days

Many traditional people in the Chinese cultural sphere present offerings to deities on the first and fifteenth day of every lunar month. Businesses will have a big metal container where they burn spirit money on these days to transfer to the gods. Others will have tables outside with burning incense and food offerings of rice, poultry, fruits, and pastries. People do this in private as well before their home altars (and at ones inside the doors of Chinese restaurants), where they might pour three cups of tea, light three sticks of incense, and present fruit to show gratitude and respect to the deities.

Processions

Daoist processions to large martial temples often take place on Sundays in places such as southern Taiwan. Processions will include some kind of music, usually played by a band comprising members of the temple community playing drums, cymbals, and tambourines, as well as stringed instruments and occasionally wind instruments. Some processions also feature acrobatic performances, folk dancers, and an electric "flower car," which can be rented for the day. The flower car consists of attractive young women, wearing short dresses or sometimes string bikinis, on a decorated flatbed truck, dancing and singing karaoke to entertain the (male) gods.

Most performance troupes include a wide range of individuals. A male member of the temple community will carry a large paper lantern bearing the name of the temple and its god written in red ink. Another man will be charged with carrying a long pole from which hangs a black flag on which is written the eight trigrams from the Classic of Changes. Members of various other temples may also accompany the procession wearing visitor uniforms—ranging from baseball caps or tennis visors to shirts and pants—marked with the name of their temple.

Entranced male "spirit youth" dance along in the procession, barefoot and dressed in red bibs and black or red pants. They wear the bibs so that they can strike their bare backs with ritual instruments. It is not uncommon to see female mediums in the procession, also barefoot and in varying degrees of full to partial trance, wearing special backless blouses, bibs, and pants. Some perform exorcism dances. Like the spirit youth, other performers in the procession are also believed to perform while in various degrees of trance. These individuals are often boys from the temple community who have begun their training with a local temple master. They appear in the procession wearing traditional costumes and with their faces painted, transforming them into generals or martial deities.

The procession has a lighter side, featuring people wearing oversized cartoon-like costumes of the legendary friends and temple guardians Fan and Xie, as well as the Monkey King and the Vagabond Buddha from the popular novel *Journey to the West*. The wine-drinking Vagabond Buddha delights the crowd by stumbling along, sipping from a large gourd. Others toss candies to the children. Processions may also include a troupe of acrobatic dancers, both young girls and older ones, who perform to popular folksongs. There will be other troupes of dancers as well, also performing to popular folksongs, with girls of different ages wearing Aboriginal, traditional, or Western dress. Sometimes transvestites, fully made up, with hair pinned and in traditional *qipao*, will play the role of lead dancer in these troupes, flirting with the men in attendance.

Pudu

Pudu, or the Rite for Universal Salvation, is generally observed by people within the Chinese cultural sphere. It takes place on the fifteenth day of the seventh month, during the period known as "ghost month." In Chinese religion there is a long tradition of recognizing kin who have died, and ghost month provides another opportunity for Chinese people to acknowledge and help kin or ghosts who inhabit a cold place in hell or in the Lake of Blood where mothers who die in childbirth reside. The desire is to appease and free the ghosts, who will eventually become ancestors. During ghost month, hungry ghosts or people who have died and lost their way are recognized and fed. Business owners leave food on small tables outside their shops and temples set up tables along the street. Ghosts are also sent letters, which are burned, and offered incense and spirit money.

Practices

New Religious Movements

Falun Gong

Perhaps the best known Chinese new religious movement is the group known as Falun Gong, or the Practice of the Wheel of the Dharma. Founded in 1992 by Li Hongzhi (b. 1952), the practice is known in the West as a human rights movement. There is a long history of challenges to the state by sectarian groups thought to be perpetuating heterodox or threatening ideas in China. Falun Gong has between two million members, according to Li Hongzhi, and a hundred million, according to the People's Republic of China. The actual size of the group is likely somewhere between these two claims, and most members are over the age of fifty.

Fa means "law" or "Dharma" (of the three principles) and *lun* means "wheel." *Gong* refers to the practice of personal cultivation that is encouraged by the group. Many Chinese teachers throughout history have promoted personal cultivation and the creation of social harmony through meditation, exercise, diet, chanting, and reading texts. Falun Dafa practice is derived from earlier *qigong* movements in China; there are five main sets of exercises designed to lead followers to higher cultivation levels. The two core texts of the group, both authored by Li Hongzhi, are *Revolving the Law Wheel* and *China Falun Gong*. These texts outline key ideas and practices and thus are required reading for new members.

The Practice of the Wheel of the Dharma is a loosely organized group with branches in different places throughout the Chinese cultural sphere. They do not congregate at a particular temple but rather meet in places such as parks or university campuses to perform the five sets of exercises. They also distribute literature about the group as a human rights organization. Shenyun (Divine Performers), the New York–based performance wing of the group, established in 2006, was created to raise awareness about the torture and imprisonment of Falun Gong members by the Chinese government, which outlawed the movement in 1999. Shenyun's performances, seen by audiences throughout the West, offer traditional Chinese dances and songs with political and religious messages.

Lingji

A loosely organized religious movement called *lingji*, or "diviners of the spirit," has emerged in Taiwan during the past sixty years. Diviners of the spirit are atypical female and male spirit mediums who become partially or fully possessed by powerful traditional gods such as Guanyin, Mazu, and the Vagabond Buddha, Western entities such as Jesus and the Virgin Mary, and Mao Zedong. Similar to other New Age movements, these beliefs and practices cannot be contained by any one religious institution, tradition, or set of practices. As well, *lingji* beliefs and practices emphasize the need for an initiatory experience in which the *lingji* departs on a journey to discover past lives and an original spirit or soul. Although diviners of the spirit are initiated through a quest for self-transformation, the core values of *lingji* practice transcend personal needs; they are ultimately directed toward creation of a more harmonious and peaceful world with less suffering.

There is a temple in southern Taiwan known for its splendid dance floor and great acoustics, a place where all are welcome to come and dance, sing, and … burp. Burping is a common phenomenon in Taiwanese religious practice. In diviner of the spirit practice, burping indicates that the spirit is beginning to move one by stirring the qi. What makes the diviner of the spirit's burping important is that as it increases in intensity and frequency it indicates that the medium is moving into the next stage of practice, such as singing and dancing. When individual performers move the spirit, they

(continued)

believe they are moving the world closer to a state of collective peace and harmony.

For four evenings a week this temple opens its doors to the mediums, who begin to arrive around seven thirty. Some may choose to visit a healing medium before they perform; many come on their own and some come with friends. When they arrive in the huge space, most of the mediums sit on meditation mats facing the altars, where there are many Chinese Daoist and Buddhist deities. They may sit there for the entire night without ever dancing, singing, or burping, or they may be moved as soon as they arrive. By nine thirty, twenty or more diviners of the spirit will be present. By ten p.m. the number may have grown to forty and sometimes even fifty. While there are *lingji* of both genders, women are the predominant performers of dances and songs during festivals, at temples (Daoist, Buddhist, or Confucian—any temple where they are welcome), and in public places such as parks or even ice-cream parlours throughout the week for their everyday practice.

Source: Marshall 2003.

AUTHORITY

Authority in Confucianism and Daoism is defined by gender, age, lineage, kinship ties, and Chinese language and texts. Characters (and talismans) are powerful and accessible emblems that may be used by people who are not religious specialists to bestow good luck, health, longevity, and wealth. They are written and hung on walls and doors, either on their own (for instance, the character for prosperity) or, as in the case of New Year, as couplets, usually comprising four characters. An absence of such signs is believed to bring bad luck, poor health, a short lifespan, and poverty. While these good-luck symbols and signs are from a modernist perspective superstitious elements, even Chinese Canadians who have converted to Christianity continue to festoon walls and doorways with golden characters and couplets written on long red sheets of paper. Others carry carefully folded talismans and other good-luck charms in their wallet or attached to suitcases to protect them "just in case."

Other forms of authority in Confucianism and Daoism are more privileged and require a high level of literacy. They come through the process of textual production and its many privileged forms: writing (sometimes deity-inspired spirit writing), debating, commenting upon, editing, and actualizing rituals described by liturgical and scriptural texts such as the Daoist canon and Confucian classics. In Daoism, the secret and special wisdom is found in liturgical texts, which can be specific to a temple or deity and are guarded by temple committees and passed down through lineages. Liturgical texts contain entire scriptures or chapters from them; they may also contain other material such as the schedule and details surrounding performance of rituals, magical formulas and instructions, excerpts from other texts, chants, and talismans.

These valuable liturgical texts are uttered by and confer authority upon ordained Daoist priests (and Confucian ritual masters), who have apprenticed with a master and joined a lineage. Wearing a ceremonial black robe, a crowned hat, and embroidered shoes, the priest, using his religious name, presents memorials to the deities he serves within the Daoist pantheon. He is also vested with the authority to organize others who may be part of the ritual, such as the Red Hats (ritual masters), mediums, the musicians, and the ladies who prepare and serve food several times a day to those who take part in the ritual.

Authority within Confucianism and Daoism is also held by temple associations, guilds, and male community elders. These groups and individuals provide for the needs of the priests, worshippers, deities, and sometimes mediums who are served by or serve in the temple. They fundraise; organize temple banquets, birthday festivals, celebrations, pilgrimages, processions, offerings, and rituals; and maintain traditions and connections between smaller and larger temples. They also manage temple finances, deal with

community and association conflicts, adapt and inno-
vate rituals based on the wishes of the congregants, and
consult with deities and the mediums incarnated by
them to decide when new temples should be built and/
or texts should be produced.

RELIGIOUS IDENTITY

In this chapter, when we talk about Confucian or Daoist
religion, religiosity, and everyday practices, we are
referring to the religious dimensions of these two native
religions and their beliefs and practices. Throughout
the chapter we have come to see that it is common
for Chinese people to have overlapping religious
identities as Christians, Buddhists, Confucians, and
Daoists. Moreover, in some situations it is impossible
to separate Confucianism and Daoism. Christianity is
listed first among these overlapping identities because
it is associated in Asian nations with desirable Western
civilization and values. It is also growing as a religious
identity and practice in China and overseas Chinese
communities. In early overseas communities, Chinese
people often became nominal Christians or self-
identified as Christian on tax rolls and census surveys
and in response to questions posed by non-Chinese
friends about their religious identity.

Although Confucianism moved into Japan, Korea,
Vietnam, and other places, we have examined religiosity within a Chinese cultural sphere, which includes
mainland China, Hong Kong, Macau, Taiwan, and
overseas Chinese communities in Singapore, Australia,
Europe, North America, and elsewhere. To the Chinese
diaspora, which began to leave China for global migrant
work in large numbers in the 1850s, Confucianism
still defined traditional Chinese values, culture, and
some aspects of identity. Confucianism was associated
with traditional gender roles in the family that position women in the inner quarters as mother, wife, and
daughter who does the domestic work of cooking,
cleaning, and raising children. Men, according to traditional (Confucian) gendered understandings, were to
remain in the outer quarters, working in the fields or as
scholars, professionals, or merchants. Of course, most
families were not wealthy enough to live according to
those strict gender rules, but generally ideas that privilege male intellectual pursuits and community leadership have tended to survive. In the past few decades,

scholars have also looked to Confucian ideas about virtues and rituals to create a Chinese model for human
rights, ecology, and ethics. There is no doubt that the
study of Confucianism is an important one for understanding traditional and modern China.

Clearly, the beliefs and practices of overseas Chinese
people came to be adapted for modern Western life,
but the absence of Daoist and Confucian temples has
more complex reasons. In overseas Chinese communities, Daoist and Confucian practices and beliefs are
usually combined with normative Christian ones. Until
the end of the Second World War, self-identifying as
Christian, at least in the West, was the socially accepted
thing to do. A nominal Christian identity helped overseas Chinese to be welcomed and accepted and was
part of the "way or *dao* of the bachelor" (Marshall
2011). Still, they continued to observe customs and
festivals that had Confucian or Daoist religious
dimensions. Sun Yatsen (1866–1925), the "father of
modern China," was revered like a god at nationalist
Kuomintang Party events in overseas Chinese communities (Marshall 2009, 2011). After 1950, some also
practised Daoist self-cultivation, guided in their study
by the texts of Laozi and Zhuangzi and the practice of
tai chi and *qigong*.

But other practices changed. For many of the
Chinese diaspora, the worship of traditional deities
such as Guanyin and Mazu, the Buddhist and Daoist
goddesses associated with salvation, family, and childbirth, or Guangong (associated with war, Chinese
triads, and Daoism) came to be restricted to the few
public places that had altars. Some of these altars
were in Chinatown clan halls, while others were in
more remote places, such as Yale and Lytton, British
Columbia. There the Chinese labourers would pray to
Daoist and Buddhist goddesses for healing and salvation up until the 1920s, when nationalism (and eradi-
cation of "superstitious practice") swept through the
overseas communities.

Taking on a Daoist identity in the traditional sense
requires that a devotee pass through several stages
guided by a master until they join a lineage. At this
stage they are given a "register" of spirits that may be
envisioned, and empowering ritual devices that will
enable them to both call down and direct the deities. These include special mantras (chants), mudras
(magical hand gestures), and talismans (magical
maps). While these are some of the ideas and structural

> **Chinese Immigration Act:** a piece of legislation that initially served to impose a poll tax and later excluded persons of Chinese descent from Canada for sixty-two years, from 1885 to 1947.

characteristics of traditional Daoism, there is also a vibrant everyday practice. Today Daoists most usually engage in self-cultivation techniques, which can take many forms. Self-cultivation may involve meditation, Daoist yoga, *qigong*, chanting, singing, or internal or external alchemy—moving the qi around in their bodies or creating elixirs. Some Daoists also seek to become New Age spirit mediums who communicate with the spirits, heal, tell fortunes, exorcize malevolent forces, become possessed, and sometimes burp.

THE CANADIAN CONTEXT
General Overview and History

In contrast to Confucianism's and Daoism's resurgence in China and Taiwan, Daoist and Confucian temples have not flourished in the West. The reasons are many and complex. Daoist and Confucian temples require experienced religious functionaries to perform rituals and other services. For a religious community to flourish, it needs to have established networks, lineage, history, and its own traditions. It also needs to have women, as Stephen Warner, a noted expert in religion and migration, has noted (1998). Women create the impetus for new religious institutions to form. Chinese-Canadian communities had few women until after repeal of the **Chinese Immigration Act** in 1947. Canadian Chinese communities, having begun to form only in the 1870s, are too young and too disconnected. As well, these kinds of native temples require large congregations, and many Chinese Canadians often adapt to life in this country by becoming nominally Christian and sometimes actually converting. Westerners and Western culture emphasize normative Christian ideas as "belief" and "faith." In Daoism, self-cultivation is much more important than either of those concepts.

People who are Daoists in the West focus on self-cultivation, reading the Laozi or Zhuangzi or practising *qigong*. Some may visit a traditional medicine practitioner who uses acupuncture. Such everyday Daoist practices abound, but there is a lack of access to orthodox Daoist temples or masters who are connected to the global Daoist network. Although there are Perfect Realization temples in the West, most Daoists today would not identify as institutional practitioners of Daoism. However, there are Daoist

PEOPLE & PLACES

Fung Loy Kok Institute of Taoism

Downtown Toronto's Fung Loy Kok Institute of Taoism, the International Taoist Tai Chi Society's temple, is representative of Chinese religious practice in Canada. Founded in 1970 by Master Moy Lin-shin and Mui Ming To, the society's temple beliefs and practices derive from Confucianism, Buddhism, and Daoism. When I visited the temple in August 2009, I spoke with the non-Chinese temple manager and observed many non-Chinese and a few elderly Chinese women busy folding yellow paper into flowers for *pudu*, the Rite for Universal Salvation. When I asked about the beliefs and practices of the temple congregants, I was referred to the temple master for more information. Beliefs and practices included the need to end suffering and to cultivate the body and mind through meditation, chanting, and familiarizing oneself with the eight heavenly virtues, including propriety and filial piety. Community service is important as well, and this group's social, cultural, and political roles extend beyond conventional religion to provide resources such as food for the homeless, ESL programs for new immigrants, and help with filing tax returns and the paperwork necessary to qualify for government assistance programs.

On the main floor of the temple is a hall for congregants to gather, chant, and meditate; upstairs are two offering halls. The first is a memorial hall for the deceased, where plaques of elderly male and female Chinese donors are displayed on the wall. As well, some of the deceased (now ancestors) are represented by large photographs displayed on a wooden shelf.

In front of them are offerings of incense, fresh flowers, fruits, and seafood. Beyond the memorial hall is the main offering hall, dedicated to the Jade Emperor, Guanyin, and the Daoist immortal Lu Dongbin. When I visited, smaller deity statues of Mazu and Laozi accompanied the main altar deities. More than a dozen sticks of incense were burning in the urns before the altars when I arrived, and offerings of fresh flowers and vegetarian foods such as fruit and nuts had been placed on the table in front of each main deity.

PERSPECTIVES

Exclusion of Wives and Families

In 1885, with the main work completed on the Canadian Pacific Railway, Canada enacted its Chinese Immigration Act, designed to keep Chinese out of Canada. A new Head Tax of fifty dollars per person meant that most families could afford to send only their men to Canada. By 1903 the same tax had risen to five hundred dollars—the equivalent today of almost $13,000.

Twenty years later, a new version of the act that Chinese Canadians called the 'Exclusion Act' ended almost all Chinese immigration, and required every person of Chinese descent, even

those born here, to register with the government. It was not until 1947 that these laws were struck down. At last, family members left behind in China could come to Canada, and all Chinese Canadians were allowed to vote.

By then, Chinese Canadians had experienced over six decades of institutionalized discrimination. Canada's policies created extraordinary financial hardships for families both in Canada and China, and produced a terrain of racialized Chinese settlement.

temples in large urban Canadian Chinatowns, perhaps dedicated to the Daoist immortal Lu Dongbin. Some of these temples are staffed and operated by Chinese and/or non-Chinese priests, managers, and others who have ties to originating temples in Hong Kong, Taiwan, or China.

There are far fewer native Chinese Daoist temples beyond the Chinatown (or, in the cases of the Toronto area and Vancouver, Chinatowns) where most Chinese Canadians live. Confucian temples are even rarer sights, so Chinese family association halls or clan buildings are often the sites for traditional and institutionalized Confucianism in Canada. Such

buildings may be found in Victoria's and Vancouver's Chinatowns; they contain both Confucian and Daoist offering halls used for religious purposes. But Confucianism is seldom understood to be a religion. Rather, it is a part of everyday life that includes ancestral worship and traditional Chinese life and culture. One such building is Victoria's Lee Association Building. It too has an offering hall, this one dedicated to Laozi, who is recognized as a deity and is understood as a venerable Lee (Li) ancestor from thousands of years earlier (Crowe 2010). Many Canadian Lee Association spaces are no longer located in Chinatowns but are found instead in suburbs, where the majority of Chinese Canadians now reside. Association members may meet at these spaces or at a member's home, where a poster of Laozi will mark his special significance for members of this clan.

Other aspects of the Canadian context of Confucianism and Daoism include Chinese-Canadian New Year celebrations. Some aspects of the celebrations are traditionally religious, such as offerings to the ancestors, while other aspects seem secular, focusing on making food and socializing. Grown family members (except married daughters) return home on New Year's Eve for a large meal; married daughters are expected to mark the beginning of the New Year with their husband's family. New Year's Day begins with offerings to the ancestors, usually going back four generations.

Most food items served during Chinese celebrations are chosen because they invoke memories of the family's native region; for instance, many early Chinese Canadians stemmed from Taishan, in southern China. Grandmothers, mothers, and daughters are the custodians of the family recipes that reflect these tastes. Mostly it is the women who spend weeks in advance preparing fresh food and frozen items for the event, although the men often do the shopping and offer the food to the ancestors. Food offerings throughout the two-week New Year period have Chinese names that sound like and are believed to attract prosperity, peace, health, and longevity. The sweetness, shape, length, and sticky consistency of the foods, such as rice-flour pastries and dumplings, also convey these ideas. Because some early Chinese Canadians married Ukrainian women, families of mixed Chinese and Ukrainian heritage might add round potato pancakes and varenyky (perogies) to their list of New Year foods.

Around New Year, children and unmarried adults are given red packets which contain monetary gifts by family members and close friends. These packets are decorated with Chinese characters in gold: traditional couplets or sayings believed to confer prosperity, health, peace, and longevity for the year ahead. Some people also decorate their homes with long red pieces of paper on which are written couplets in gold paint. Many Chinese families post the character fu (meaning prosperity), written on a red and gold square piece of paper or fabric, on their front door or inside their home. Chinese-Canadian communities celebrate the New Year and other festivals with traditional lion dances and banquets.

The southern-style Lion Dance has two different religious dimensions, bringing good luck to businesses and exorcizing malevolent influences, and is an important component of Chinese-Canadian history. Most festival processions and events open with the Lion Dance being performed by martial arts groups. Traditional Chinese celebrations also feature fireworks, and a band with cymbals, gongs, drums, and horns that introduces the lion as it approaches.

Source: Godong/Getty Images

Practices

Grave Customs

Chinese families gather to maintain the graves of deceased relatives in the spring and in the fall. The spring event is called Qingming and the fall gathering is referred to as Chongyang. In some cities in Canada there is a third type of grave-sweeping ritual in which early Chinese-Canadian settlers are similarly venerated around Father's Day. Graveside customs provide opportunities to gather with family members or the larger Chinese community, clean up debris that has accumulated around the graves, make offerings, and then enjoy a meal together.

Practices throughout the Chinese cultural sphere vary greatly. In many parts of Canada, for instance, the traditional date of Qingming, which is determined by the lunar calendar, has been adjusted because of the climate, and the ritual is instead performed when the snow has melted and the ground has thawed. The same is true for Chongyang. Offerings also vary in the modern practice of this traditional custom. While some families continue to burn incense or spirit money and paper televisions and cars at the cemetery, others have abandoned this practice because of by-laws enacted to prevent forest fires. Many families may instead offer fresh and/or plastic flowers. Some offer ancestors their favourite foods in full banquets, followed by a graveside picnic.

Chinese families gather at the graves of deceased relatives during formal events in the spring and in the fall, as well as at other, informal times throughout the year. The spring event is called Qingming and the fall one is referred to as Chongyang. In some cities in Canada there is a third grave ritual in which early Chinese-Canadian settlers are venerated around Father's Day. Graveside customs provide opportunities to remember the deceased, gather with family, and share a meal.

Source: Alison R. Marshall

DAOISM AND CONFUCIANISM ON THE INTERNET

Is there a Daoist or Confucian presence on the Internet? There has been a proliferation of new religious movement temples run by Western followers that incorporate Daoist or Confucian figures, but the content of traditional Daoist or Confucian websites is, for the most part, textually based. These include online translations, descriptions of liturgy, schools, and deities, and grassroots practice.

Much of Daoist or Confucian practice has an embodied component. In other words, these practices include a physical aspect and a means of experiencing something with one's body; these may include burning incense, food offerings, martial arts practices, or the performance of grave customs. Owing to the limitations of current technology and because these are visceral experiences, such practices cannot be performed virtually. While online temples incorporating Daoist and Confucian ideas exist, they are generally not sought out for religious experience. Rather, their usually text-based content demonstrates the enduring importance of education and Chinese characters as patterns for Confucian and Daoist religiosity. They may also provide images of deities; YouTube clips of masters and ritual performances; articles on etiquette, food, history, and customs; and proverbs and poetry.

CONCLUSION

In this chapter on the diverse traditional and modern aspects of Confucianism and Daoism, both in China and in overseas Chinese communities, we have focused on key ideas relating to gender and the family, historical developments, ritual actions, and food customs. Generally both Confucianism and Daoism may be distinguished from Abrahamic religious traditions by an emphasis on practice rather than belief, their core idea of efficacy, a multitude of deities, and a tendency toward and acceptance of overlapping religious identities, as both Confucians and Daoists or, in the modern period, sometimes as Confucians and Christians.

KEY TERMS

Ancestor, p. 207
Benevolence, p. 223
Chinese Benevolent
    Association, p. 205
Chinese Immigration
    Act, p. 238
Confucius, p. 205
Dao, p. 207
Five Elements, p. 221
Five Relationships, p. 210
Hexagrams, p. 222

Laozi, p. 211
Li, p. 208
Ling, p. 207
Mandate of Heaven,
    p. 207
Qi, p. 212
Reciprocity, p. 223
Sage, p. 207
Three Obediences, p. 212
Trigram, p. 222
Yin and yang, p. 211

CRITICAL THINKING QUESTIONS

1. Explain the role of women in Confucianism and Daoism in China and outline key developments in the Han, Tang, and Song dynasties that either increased or diminished the strength of women in Chinese society.

2. Explain the influence of Chinese history, Chinese language, and texts on the production of modern and traditional Confucian and Daoist religiosity.

3. While traditional forms of Confucianism and Daoism have been modernized over time and have responded to social, cultural, and political changes,

some ideas have remained the same. Name at least three core concepts in Confucianism and Daoism.

4. Throughout this chapter we have examined various Confucian, Daoist, and everyday food customs and rituals. Explain how embodied practices involving food help us understand the religious dimensions of Chinese culture, gender, and identity.

5. Compare and contrast the roles of self-cultivation in Confucianism and Daoism. Are there specific kinds of self-cultivation for women and men? What are they?

6. In your opinion, is Confucianism a religion, a philosophy, or a way of life? Explain.

RECOMMENDED READING

Keightley, David. "At the Beginning: The Status of Women in Neolithic and Shang China," *NAN Nü* 1, no. 1 (1999): 1–63.

Loewe, Michael, ed. *Early Chinese Texts: A Bibliographical Guide*. Early China Special Monograph Series 2. Berkeley: Society for the Study of Early China and Institute of East Asian Studies, University of California, 1993.

Louie, Kam. *Theorising Chinese Masculinity: Society and Gender in China*. Cambridge: Cambridge University Press, 2002.

Manitoba Chinese Stories Collection: http://home.cc
.umanitoba.ca/~chinese/.

Marshall, Alison R. "Everyday Religion and Identity
in a Western Manitoban Chinese Community:
Christianity, the KMT, Foodways and Related
Events," *Journal of the American Academy of Religion*
77, no. 3 (September 2009): 573–608.

Miller, James, ed. *Chinese Religions in Contemporary Society*.
Santa Barbara, CA: ABC-CLIO, 2006.

Pomerantz, Kenneth. "Orthopraxy, Orthodoxy, and the
Goddess(es) of Taishan," *Modern China* 33, no. 1
(2007): 22–46.

Puett, Michael J. *To Become a God: Cosmology, Sacrifice, and
Self-Divinization in Early China*. Harvard–Yenching
Institute Monograph Series. Cambridge, MA: Harvard–
Yenching Institute, 2004.

Woon, Yuen-Fong. *The Excluded Wife*. Montreal:
McGill-Queen's University Press, 1999.

Yung, Judy. *Unbound Feet: A Social History of Chinese
Women in San Franscisco*. Los Angeles, CA:
University of California Press, 1995.

RECOMMENDED VIEWING

Fu qin [Father]. Chinese with English subtitles. Universities
Service Centre for China Studies, 2005.

Under the Willow Tree: Pioneer Chinese Women in Canada.
National Film Board of Canada, Directed by Dora
Nipp, and produced by Margaret Wong, 1997.
51 minutes.

Confucius 2010. Dir. Mei Hu. Dadi Century [Beijing] Ltd.,
2010.

*To Taste a Hundred Herbs: Gods, Ancestors and Medicine in
a Chinese Village*. Videocassette, 58 minutes. Long Bow
Series, 1986.

Moving the Mountain. Dir. Michael Apted, 1994.
Documentary about the Tiananmen Square incident.

Raise the Red Lantern. Dir. Zhang Yimou. ERA
International, 1991.

Bored in Heaven. Dir. Kenneth Dean. Documentary, 80
minutes.

Han Xin's Revenge: A Daoist Mystery. Centre National de la
Recherche Scientifique (http://videotheque.cnrs.fr),
90 minutes.

Through Chinese Women's Eyes. Dir. Mayfair Yang, 1997.
VHS/DVD, 52 minutes.

USEFUL WEBSITES

Temples in Cyberspace
Based on Dr. Alison Marshall's Social Sciences and
Humanities Research Council research on religious
experiences in cyberspace.

International Taoist Tai Chi Centre
A centre in Orangeville, Ontario, that offers Daoist
education in religion, meditation, and martial arts.

Temple of the Celestial Cloud
Dedicated to the study and dissemination of
esoteric Daoism, including medicine, magic, and
martial arts.

World Organization of Daoism
An international non-profit foundation dedicated to
training Daoist teachers and healers.

Dr. James Miller's Daoist Studies
Independent research portal for academic study
of Daoism, maintained by a professor at Queen's
University, Kingston, Ontario.

Taoism Depot
AN online community providing links and
discussions related to Daoism.

James Legge's Translation of the Daodejing
Translation of the text as provided by Project Gutenberg.

Cijian Temple (Daoist): Second Life's Virtual Presence for Daoism
http://www.freewebs.com/shufeizenith/cijiantemple
.htm

Online Yijing
Free online version of the text, available in English,
French, and the original Chinese.

Internet Guide For Chinese Studies
Chinese full-text databases with classical and other
texts.

Stanford Encyclopedia of Philosophy (Online)
Excellent summaries of key Daoist and Confucian
thinkers and concepts.

Internet Sacred Text Archive
Contains free online versions of the Confucian canon.

Confucius Institute at McMaster University
Education and resources related to Chinese history, culture, religion, and language.

Project Gutenberg
Offers free online versions of the writings of Confucius.

Confucius Online
A Beijing site on Confucianism and traditional Chinese culture more generally.

Timeline of Chinese History and Dynasties
http://afe.easia.columbia.edu/timelines/china_timeline.htm

Chinese Canadian Stories
Uncommon Histories from a Common Past http://chinesecanadian.ubc.ca/A web portal and repository for Chinese Canadian historical materials (textual, visual, and audio) from across Canada.

REFERENCES

Ames, Roger T. 1994. *The Art of Rulership: A Study of Ancient Chinese Political Thought*. Albany: State University of New York Press.

Ames, Roger T., and Henry Rosemont Jr. 1998. *The Analects of Confucius: A Philosophical Translation*. New York: Ballantine Books.

Baptandier, Brigitte. 2008. *The Lady of Linshui: A Chinese Female Cult*. Stanford, CA: Stanford University Press.

Bell, Daniel A. 2008. *China's New Confucianism: Politics and Everyday Life in a Changing Society.* Princeton, NJ: Princeton University Press.

Bell, Daniel A., and Hahm Chaibong, eds. 2003. *Confucianism for the Modern World*. London: Cambridge University Press.

Boileau, Gilles. 1998–99. "Some Ritual Elaborations on Cooking and Sacrifice in Late Zhou and Western Han Texts." *Early China.* 89–123.

Chau, Adam Yuet. 2012. "Efficacy, Not Confessionality: On Ritual Polytropy in China." In *Shared Sacra: Mixed Religious Spaces across Cultures*, ed. Glenn Bowman. Oxford: Berghahn Books.

Ching, Julia. 1993. *Chinese Religions*. Maryknoll, NY: Orbis.

Crowe, Paul. 2010. "Chinese Religions." In *Asian Religions in British Columbia*, ed. Larry DeVries, Don Baker, and Daniel L. Overmeyer. Vancouver: University of British Columbia Press, chapter 12.

Ebrey, Patricia B. 1991. *Chu Hsi's Family Rituals: A Twelfth-Century Chinese Manual for the Performance of Cappings, Weddings, Funerals, and Ancestral Rites*. Princeton, NJ: Princeton University Press.

Kirkland, Russell. 2004. *Taoism: The Enduring Tradition*. New York: Routledge.

Kohn, Livia, ed. 2000. *Daoism Handbook*. Leiden: E. J. Brill.

Lai, David Chuenyan. 2010. *Chinese Community Leadership: Case Study of Victoria in Canada*. Singapore: World Scientific.

Lao, D. C. Tzu. 1963. *Lao Tzu: Tao Te Ching*. New York: Penguin Books. http://terebess.hu/english/tao/lau.html.

Lau, D. C. 1979. *Confucius: The Analects*. New York: Penguin Books.

Marshall, Alison R. 2003. "Moving the Spirit on Taiwan: New Age Lingji Performance." *Journal of Chinese Religions* 31: 81–99.

———. (September 2009). "Everyday Religion and Identity in a Western Manitoban Chinese Community: Christianity, the KMT, Foodways and Related Events," *Journal of the American Academy of Religion* 77, no. 3: 573–608.

———. 2011. *The Way of the Bachelor: Early Chinese Settlement in Manitoba*. Vancouver: University of British Columbia Press.

Rickett, W. Allyn. 1985. *Guanzi: Political, Economic, and Philosophical Essays from Early China, a Study and Translation*. Princeton, NJ: Princeton University Press.

Riegel, J. 2006. "Confucius." In *The Stanford Encyclopedia of Philosophy*, ed. Edward N. Zalta. http://plato.stanford.edu/entries/confucius/.

Roth, Harold David. 1999. *Original Tao: Inward Training (Nei Ye) and the Foundations of Taoist Mysticism.* New York: Columbia University Press.

Schipper, Kristopher. 1985. "Vernacular and Classical Ritual in Taoism." *Journal of Asian Studies* 45, no. 1 (November): 21–57.

Taylor, Jay. 2009. *The Generalissimo: Chiang Kai-Shek and the Struggle for Modern China*. Cambridge, MA: Harvard University Press.

Van Norden, Bryan W. 2008. *Mencius: Mengzi, with Selections from Traditional Commentaries*. Indianapolis, IN: Hackett Publishing.

Warner, R. Stephen, and Judith G. Wittner. *Gatherings in Diaspora: Religious Communities and the New Immigration*. Philadelphia: Temple University Press, 1998.

Watson, Burton, trans. 1968. *The Complete Works of Chuang Tsu*. New York: Columbia University Press. http://www.terebess.hu/english/chuangtzu2.html#1.

Timeline

- **660 B.C.E.** Legendary first emperor of Japan, Jimmu, ascends the throne.

- **6th century C.E.** Concept of Shinto begins to emerge following Buddhism's arrival in Japan.

- **712** Kojiki (Records of Ancient Matters).

- **720** Nihon Shoki (Chronicles of Japan).

- **12th–13th centuries** Honji suijaku ("essence manifestation") theoretical system emerges. Ryobu (Dual) Shinto tradition emerges.

- **18th–19th centuries** Pro-Shinto National Studies movement.

- **1730–1801** Norinaga Motoori, National Studies scholar.

- **1776–1843** Atsutane Hirata, National Studies scholar.

- **1798–1887** Miki Nakayama, founder of Shinto-derived Tenrikyo new religious movement.

- **1868** "Separation" of Shinto and Buddhism.

- **1870s** State Shinto established.

- **1945** State Shinto abolished.

- **1946** Association of Shinto Shrines formed.

CHAPTER 7

Shinto

Kevin Bond

■

INTRODUCTION

If you ask Japanese people today, "What is Shinto?" you will likely get a wide variety of answers. Similarly, scholars of Japanese religion are not unanimous on how to best describe Shinto. Popular explanations have run the gamut from "Japan's traditional faith" to "the Japanese way of life" or even "the essence of Japanese culture." Perhaps the best-known definition tells us that Shinto is Japan's ancient native religion, and is thus strongly associated with the identity and worldviews of its people. In addition to these complexities, in this chapter you will learn that a central feature of Shinto is the worship of sacred spirits known as kami at thousands of shrines across Japan. You will

A picturesque torii at the entrance to Meiji Shrine, Tokyo. The torii is a dominant symbol of Shinto. Made from wood or stone, these iconic gateways are commonly located along the approaches to shrines to signify sacred Shinto space.

Source: Rumulo Rejon/Getty Images

Kami: the divine spirits of heaven and earth, which number in the thousands and are intimately connected to nature and human activity; the central objects of worship in Shinto; may appear as natural objects and phenomena, animals, and even human beings.

Amaterasu: "The One Who Illuminates the Heavens," the sun goddess and supreme kami of the Shinto pantheon.

Ise Shrine: Japan's most important national shrine and sacred residence of the imperial ancestor Amaterasu.

Norinaga Motoori: a famous National Studies scholar (1730–1801) who penned the classic definition of kami as anything possessing extraordinary powers or awe-inspiring qualities.

further learn how the history of Shinto is intimately connected with state powers and other religions such as Buddhism. Over the centuries, kami have been worshipped in combination with Buddhist deities, and Shinto shrines, myths, and rituals have played a major role in politics in both the distant and recent past. You will therefore come to appreciate how this intricate web of issues—the particular challenges of defining Shinto; the significance of shrines and kami worship; Shinto's coexistence with Buddhism and politics; and the role of Shinto mythology in Japanese culture and identity—is important in understanding the Shinto religion. These objectives will help you avoid the common simplistic and generalized definitions above that overlook how Shinto is a multifaceted religious tradition incorporating both "native" and "foreign" elements across what may be termed religious and secular boundaries.

CENTRAL BELIEFS

Shinto is a Sino-Japanese term meaning "way of the kami." However, the concept of Shinto is very complex. It lacks many features that we commonly use in the West to understand religion: there is no founder, no central orthodoxy, nor a clearly discernable religious goal. And since there is no official body of sacred scriptures, no clear record of organized teachings exists. Shinto doctrines and beliefs, therefore, are often ambiguous.

Worldview

The Shinto understanding of the world revolves around the existence of thousands of sacred objects of worship called **kami**, a complex term often translated as "gods" or "spirits." Kami are believed to have created the Japanese islands (though they did not produce existence itself) and to be the ancestors of the Japanese people. While some dwell in the heavens, many kami reside amidst the natural landscape alongside human beings. According to tradition, the supreme kami is the sun goddess **Amaterasu** ("The One Who Illuminates the Heavens"). Amaterasu is believed to be the divine ancestor of the imperial family and is worshipped at Japan's most important national shrine, at **Ise**. The Shinto worldview thus represents a closeness between kami, nature, and human beings, as well as the nation. Consequently, Japan has been called the "land of the kami."

PERSPECTIVES

What Is a Kami?

Like *Shinto*, the concept of *kami* is ambiguous in meaning and scope. The wide range of the term's possible meanings is revealed in the writings of the influential scholar **Norinaga Motoori** (1730–1801), who wrote what is now considered a classic definition:

> I do not yet understand the meaning of the term *kami*. Speaking in general, however, it may be said that *kami* signifies, in the first place, the deities of heaven and earth that appear in the ancient records and also the spirits of the shrines where they are worshipped. It is hardly necessary to say that it includes human beings. It also includes such objects as birds, beasts, trees, plants, seas, mountains and so forth. In ancient usage, anything whatsoever which was outside the ordinary, which possessed superior power, or which was awe-inspiring was called *kami*. Eminence here does not refer merely to the superiority of nobility, goodness or meritorious

deeds. Evil and mysterious things, if they are extraordinary and dreadful, are called *kami*. (Holtom 1993, 77–78)

According to Motoori, kami may be anything that evokes "wonder" or "awe," whether creative or destructive, benevolent or malevolent. This includes anthropomorphic gods and goddesses, but also impressive geographical features (rocks, trees, rivers, mountains), natural phenomena (thunder, echoes), animals, and even human beings such as emperors. Unlike Buddhist deities, kami are often invisible or unmanifest; statues and paintings of them are thus much less common. Kami also have strong human-like emotions: they enjoy offerings of food, music, and dance, and dislike impurities such as blood and feces. And since they are not necessarily omnipotent, omniscient, or even immortal, the Western concept of *god* as transcendental, all-powerful, and eternal is therefore an inadequate translation. One scholar suggests the more inclusive notion of *sacred* to more suitably describe kami (Holtom 1993, 79).

Tsumi: taboo human activity that produces defilements (*kegare*) that pollute the sanctity of kami and must be counteracted with ritual purification (harae).

Harae: ritual purification required to counteract impurities (*kegare*) that may pollute and offend a kami.

Kojiki: Records of Ancient Matters, dating from 712 C.E., one of the two classic texts of Shinto describing the mythic origins of Japan.

Nihon Shoki (Nihongi): Chronicles of Japan (720 C.E.), the second of the imperial chronicles, containing stories of the mythic origins of Japan and the early emperors.

Religious Goals

Although Shinto texts mention realms beyond earth, there remain no formal spiritual salvation or pressing afterlife concerns in Shinto. Nor is there belief in rebirth; upon death, one's spirit passes on to an eternal ancestral realm. Instead Shinto emphasizes the importance of the immediate physical world. Prayers to kami do not ask for otherworldly rewards but rather seek to ensure a healthy and prosperous life and to live in harmony with the kami. While Buddhist meditation and prayers also emphasize healing and protection in one's present lifetime, it is more the desire for heavenly rebirth or the realization of enlightenment that is traditionally directed toward the Buddhist gods. Since the teachings of Japanese Buddhist schools cater to life in the world beyond in addition to that of the here and now, some scholars have neglected Shinto, regarding it as "unsophisticated," in favour of Buddhism as a more "organized" religion with clearly defined spiritual goals.

The Human Condition

As descendants of kami, human beings are of a similar essence or substance, and therefore are inherently good. However, human transgressions (**tsumi**) such as murder and taboos such as contact with death, disease, or blood result in impurities of mind and body (*kegare*) that may offend a kami and thus upset the natural order of a community. This defilement, along with the subsequent need for ritual purification (**harae**), represent two basic concerns of the human condition in Shinto. Although both men and women are offspring of kami, the female body has been considered a particular threat to the sanctity of shrines. In premodern times, menstruating women were forbidden entrance for fear of introducing kegare and offending the kami. Mothers were even considered defiled by the blood shed during childbirth, and were excluded from the shrine blessings of their newborn children (Kasulis 2004, 48).

SOURCES OF THE TRADITION
The Myth of Creation

Unlike many religions, Shinto has no central scripture or formal collection of sacred texts. There do exist, however, various writings long considered "classics." The two most important are the **Kojiki**, or Records of Ancient Matters (712 C.E.), and **Nihon Shoki**, Chronicles of Japan (720 C.E.). Together they comprise the earliest recorded Japanese myths and legends that have shaped traditional

Izanagi and Izanami: the primordial male and female kami responsible for creation of the Japanese islands.

notions of national history and identity. The basic structure of the texts is a divine genealogy connecting Amaterasu to the imperial family, thereby providing a means to legitimize and sanctify its control over Japan. According to the accounts, the Japanese islands were formed from the waters by the divine union of two primordial (though not the first) kami who descended from the heavens, the male **Izanagi** and female **Izanami**.

Subsequent to their creation of the first island (see "Words" box), Izanagi and Izanami unite as husband

displeased, and said:—"I am a man, and by right should have spoken first. How is it that on the contrary thou, a woman, shouldst have been the first to speak? This was unlucky. Let us go round again." Upon this the two deities went back, and having met anew, this time the male deity spoke first, and said:—"How delightful! I have met a lovely maiden."

Source: Nihon Shoki, in W. G. Aston, *Nihongi: Chronicles of Japan from the Earliest Times to* A.D. *697* (London: Allen & Unwin, 1956).

The Creation of the Japanese Islands

Izanagi no Mikoto and Izanami no Mikoto stood on the floating bridge of Heaven, and held counsel together, saying:
"Is there not a country beneath?"
Thereupon they thrust down the jewel-spear of Heaven, and groping about therewith found the ocean. The brine which dripped from the point of the spear coagulated and became an island which received the name of Ono-goro-jima [the Japanese islands].
The two Deities thereupon descended and dwelt in this island. Accordingly they wished to become husband and wife together, and to produce countries.
So they made Ono-goro-jima the pillar of the centre of the land.
Now the male deity turning by the left, and the female deity by the right, they went round the pillar of the land separately. When they met together on one side, the female deity spoke first and said:—"How delightful! I have met with a lovely youth." The male deity was

Izanami and Izanagi Creating the Japanese Islands, **by Eitaku Kobayashi (1843–90)**

Source: *Izanami and Izanagi Creating the Japanese Islands,* © 2012 Museum of Fine Arts, Boston.

and wife, then produce the remaining lands of Japan and its numerous kami. In the painting reproduced on page 250, their initial act of creation occurs while standing atop the "floating bridge of Heaven." Their lofty position among the clouds reflects their eminent status as celestial progenitors, while their downward gaze toward the waters symbolizes their divine creation of and eventual descent to the lands of Japan below. The painting therefore emphasizes the intimate relationship between kami, Japan, and its people, and thus the strong connection between heaven and earth. The human-like appearance of Izanagi and Izanami further illustrates not only these relationships but that kami often act and speak like people, and are therefore subject to fallible human emotions such as anger, fear, and delight. The human qualities of the two deities, especially their courtly aristocratic attire, are also visual reminders of the mythological heritage shared by the ancient kami and imperial family. Not surprisingly, this hanging scroll was painted in the late 1800s, when such Kojiki and Nihon Shoki myths were used to promote the sanctity of the emperor and the divine origins of the Japanese nation.

The humanity of Izanagi and Izanami depicted in the painting also illustrates an important Chinese yin-yang cosmological influence: that creation is a collaborative union of divine opposites, in this case of the sexes. Izanagi, however, dominates the painting, both visually and through the phallic imagery of his spear, while Izanami looks on passively from the background. As seen in the "Words" box above, this patriarchal order is reinforced following their descent from heaven. Their earthly union fails the first time as Izanagi recognizes Izanami's attempt to initiate the creative process as improper and "unlucky." The patriarchal gender divide is widened still further when Izanami later dies and descends into the underworld. Izanagi attempts contact but is forced to withdraw and purify himself in water, since Izanami has been defiled by death. This dissolution of their marriage provided the inspiration for the Shinto practice of harae purification, as well as the origin of the myth of the impure nature of the female body.

Amaterasu and Divine Establishment of the Imperial Line

When Izanagi has purified his body, a series of kami appear. The most important are the impetuous Susanoo and his sibling Amaterasu, to whom Izanagi grants rule

Kagura: literally, "to please the kami"; a sacred ceremonial ritual of dance, music, and offerings to entertain and venerate kami.

Jimmu: the mythological first emperor of Japan, who ascended the throne in 660 B.C.E.

of the High Plain of Heaven. Offended by her wild, jealous brother, who defiles her palace with *kegare*, the frightened Amaterasu retreats into a cave, punishing the world with darkness. A woodblock print titled *Origins of the Rock-Cave Kagura* (see page 252) celebrates the famous myth of Amaterasu's radiant return, in which she is enticed out of hiding by Japan's kami, using a ritual mirror (visible on the left) and sacred ceremonial song and dance called **kagura**. The kagura scene imparts an essential Shinto lesson: as kami are prone to human emotions, a frightened or offended kami such as Amaterasu may become malevolent and cause illness or natural disaster in the world. The solution is therefore mythic establishment of the first kagura, a ritual ceremony designed to pacify the goddess and restore natural order. As suggested by the scene's revelry, *kagura*, which literally means "to please the kami," entertains a kami with dance, song, and other offerings they enjoy, such as food and alcohol.

The print depicts Amaterasu emerging from the cave following the successful kagura. Her divine radiance illuminates the entire image, symbolizing her cosmic supremacy over the lands and kami of Japan. It is also a strong reminder that Amaterasu was an important ancient solar deity, worshipped for plentiful harvests by early Japanese communities. Her connections to agricultural production and nurture reflect her status as the divine matriarch who gave birth to the imperial house of Japan. But Amaterasu's celestial prominence depicted in the print also carries political meaning, as it symbolizes an important connection between Shinto and government. It reinforces the divine heritage of the imperial family by establishing the magnificence of Amaterasu at the apex of a divine political hierarchy. The veneration of Amaterasu by other kami offers a clear warning: all must submit to the authority of the imperial court or risk darkness and chaos.

The myths of Amaterasu conclude with her sending descendants to rule Japan on her behalf. One of these descendants, **Jimmu**, became Japan's first emperor and

***Origins of the Rock-Cave Kagura*, by Kunisada Utagawa (1786–1865).** Amaterasu emerges from the cave while being venerated by other kami.

Source: Eric Lessing/Art Resource, NY

Imperial Regalia: the three legendary sacred treasures—a sword, a mirror, and a jewel—bestowed by Amaterasu, guaranteeing the Japanese emperors divine right to rule.

founder of the imperial house in 660 B.C.E. Jimmu and successive emperors were provided with three sacred objects to guarantee their divine authority: a sword, a jewel, and the mirror of the rock-cave myth. Together these treasures form the famous **Imperial Regalia** of Japan. For centuries the sacred mirror has been enshrined at Ise, where it is worshipped as the embodiment of the sun goddess. It is for this reason that the Grand Shrine of Ise is revered as Japan's most sacred national shrine.

HISTORY AND DEVELOPMENT
The Emergence of Shinto

It is not clear when Shinto first appeared in Japan. Its general roots can be traced to ancient times, when evidence suggests that the early Japanese worshipped kami in the forms of local animistic nature spirits. However, it was not until the arrival of Confucianism, Daoism, and (especially) Buddhism from China and Korea in the sixth to eighth centuries that Shinto began to take a distinct form. The very term *shinto*—"way of the kami"—was conceptualized to distinguish existing beliefs and practices from the newly arrived "way of the buddhas," that is, Buddhism. The imperial court then organized Shinto rituals and prayers to support its rule. Many scholars today suggest that it was at this time, through the influence of Buddhism and politics, that we can first identify a Shinto that even remotely resembles the modern tradition.

Shinto-Buddhist Amalgamation

As Buddhism increasingly spread throughout Japan, the blending of Shinto and Buddhist practices became more formalized from the eighth century onward. One of the most significant results was a uniquely Japanese form of religious expression: the redefinition of kami as incarnations of Buddhist deities. This system of thought was called **honji suijaku** ("essence manifestation"), in which kami were worshipped as manifestations of the "essence" of Buddhist gods. In other words, the heavenly buddhas and bodhisattvas had compassionately appeared in Japan as kami (in addition to their Buddhist forms) for the salvation of people, much as in the Hindu avatar system.

A prime example of this Shinto-Buddhist syncretism is **Ryobu Shinto**, which emerged around the thirteenth century. *Ryobu* means "dual" or "twofold," and refers to the teachings of Shingon Buddhism, which understood the universe in terms of two interconnected cosmological worlds. The Buddhist gods populating these two worlds became identified as the essences of many manifested kami in Japan. For example, Amaterasu became worshipped as a manifestation of the popular sun buddha Dainichi. Such teachings provided a logical explanation for how the different types of gods could harmoniously co-exist in Japan. The worship of Shinto and Buddhist deities in combination became a unique trademark of Japanese religion, and can still be found throughout the country today. Thus, while Norinaga Motoori's classic definition of kami is very useful, it neglects this essential detail: that the mutual worship of kami and Buddhist deities became a constant in Japanese religion.

Shinto Revival: Japan as the Land of Kami

Efforts to resist Shinto-Buddhist amalgamation and emphasize the special connection between Japan and kami grew over the centuries, culminating in the 1700s and 1800s with a pro-Shinto movement known as **National Studies** (Kokugaku). National Studies thinkers such as Norinaga Motoori returned to Japanese classics such as the Kojiki in order to champion Shinto as Japan's "native" tradition while downplaying Buddhism as foreign. Another prominent National Studies scholar, **Atsutane Hirata** (1776–1843), used Shinto myths to aggressively claim Japan as a divine nation and the cultural superiority of its people:

> People all over the world refer to Japan as the Land of the Gods and call us the descendants

---

> **Honji suijaku:** "essence manifestation," a combinatory system of thought in which kami ("manifestations") are understood as incarnations of Buddhist deities ("essences").
>
> **Ryobu (Dual) Shinto:** a highly syncretic amalgamation of Shinto and Buddhism that developed around the thirteenth century.
>
> **National Studies (Kokugaku):** a pro-Shinto revival of the 1700s and 1800s that promoted Shinto as Japan's "native" and national religion.
>
> **Atsutane Hirata:** a National Studies scholar (1776–1843) who promoted Japan as the "land of the kami" in order to claim Japan as a divine and thus culturally superior nation.
>
> **State Shinto:** a "nonreligious" national creed promoted by the empire of Japan to support patriotism and emperor worship.

---

of the gods. Indeed, it is exactly as they say: as a special mark of favor from the heavenly gods, they gave birth to our country, and thus there is so immense a difference between Japan and all the other countries of the world as to defy comparison. Ours is a splendid and blessed country, the Land of the Gods beyond any doubt, and we, down to the most humble man and woman, are the descend[a]nts of the gods. (de Bary et al. 2005, 512)

State and Emperor

In the past 150 years, Shinto has undergone two major revolutions. The first occurred with the birth of the modern empire of Japan in the Meiji period (1868–1912). With the deepening of ties between the emperor, kami, and nationalism advanced by the earlier National Studies movement, the government "separated" Shinto from Buddhism by dissociating Shinto shrines, rituals, and kami from Buddhism. These were then reconfigured into **State Shinto**, a "nonreligious" national creed officially segregated from religious forms, or "Sect Shinto."

Together with Confucian concepts of loyalty, State Shinto provided a national support system for emperor worship and a rationalization of military aggression

Miki Nakayama: the celebrated founder of Tenrikyo (1798–1887), one of Japan's oldest and largest new religious movements.

against East Asia and Southeast Asia during the 1930s and 1940s. The Ministry of Education promoted the myth of the emperor's divine descent from Amaterasu in schools to rally patriotism and loyalty to the throne. Many scholars today argue that the idea of Shinto as Japan's native national religion, distinct from Buddhism, became popular only during the era of State Shinto and does not reflect the syncretic nature of Shinto in the pre-modern era.

State Shinto in the Schools

To illustrate how State Shinto used Japan's myths to encourage patriotic loyalty to the throne, here is an excerpt from a 1930s primary school textbook on ethics:

> In ancient times Amaterasu-Omikami sent down her grandson, Ninigi-no-Mikoto, and caused him to rule over this country. The great grandchild of this prince was Jimmu Tenno. Since that time the descendants of this Emperor have succeeded to the Imperial Throne without interruption. ... The successive generations of Emperors have loved their subjects as children, and we subjects, beginning with our ancestors, have reverently obeyed the Emperors and have fulfilled the principles of loyalty and patriotism. ... We who are born in such a precious country, who have over us such an august Imperial Family, and who, again, are the descendants of subjects who have bequeathed such beautiful customs, must become splendid Japanese and do our utmost for our empire.

Source: Reader 1993, 172.

Shinto Today

The second major change followed the formal surrender of the Japanese empire in 1945, at the end of the Second World War. Allied occupational forces legally abolished State Shinto and forced the emperor to renounce his divinity. A new constitution was put into effect in 1947 that guaranteed individual freedom of religion and separation of religion and state. Shinto shrines, like Buddhist temples, are today private religious bodies no longer supported by the government. Participation in shrine rites is now a matter of personal choice, not a patriotic requirement.

The changes of the past 150 years have produced many new religious movements that have reinterpreted traditional Shinto beliefs and practices, such as monotheistic worship of kami. One of the first, Tenrikyo ("Teachings of Heavenly Wisdom"), was founded by a laywoman, **Miki Nakayama** (1798–1887), after receiving a revelation from the kami Tenri O no Mikoto. A distinctive feature of new religious movements such as Tenrikyo is their comparably high proportion of female founders, leaders, and members. Charismatic founders such as Nakayama represent premodern attitudes of women as capable of divine revelation and communicating new religious teachings, and thus empowerment of female spiritual leadership as opposed to a traditionally male-dominated Shinto (and Buddhist) priesthood. The strong female orientation of these movements has produced new religious spaces and discourses that better address women's concerns, devalued as they are by a discriminatory patriarchal society. Not surprisingly, many of these new religions have become prominent cultural forces in Japan. Some, like Tenrikyo, have even expanded internationally.

Despite Shinto's traumatic changes over the past 150 years, it, like Buddhism, nonetheless remains a driving cultural force in contemporary Japanese society. Shinto continues to influence many aspects of Japanese life, from architecture, storytelling, and folk beliefs to music, dance, and theatre. Shrines remain a central focus of family and community life while Shinto's rich mythology and host of vibrant kami are inspiring new generations of artists and writers beyond the immediate confines of shrine precincts. In particular, Shinto is taking on new life in popular artistic media such as manga and anime. The animated films of Hayao Miyazaki—for example, *Princess Mononoke* (1997) and *Spirited Away*

(2001)—address themes of urbanization, environmentalism, and cultural identity by exploring the damaged relationships between nature, kami, and human beings. Miyazaki's multi-award-winning anime, which have taken on the status of a national cinema, have also become celebrated internationally, and are introducing aspects of Shinto culture to Western audiences.

RELIGIOUS PRACTICES
Ritual Types

Shinto is a religion of shrines (**jinja**), sanctuaries for the worship of kami that are found in their thousands across Japan. For centuries shrines have represented a central focus for individual and communal prayers, festivals, and national celebrations. These ritual activities can be categorized into three main groups (Breen and Teeuwen 2010, 3–4). First are the annual state ceremonies, which are derived from Shinto's ancient connection with the imperial court and symbolize the intimacy between kami and nation. The autumn harvest thanksgiving festival, for example, is celebrated on

> **Jinja:** shrines; sacred religious sanctuaries constructed to enshrine and protect kami, generally distinguished from Buddhist temples by such features as torii gateways and their orange colour.
>
> **Matsuri:** shrine festivals numbering in the hundreds and held on various dates throughout the year.

November 23, when the emperor gives thanks to the kami for the year's harvest with food offerings.

More popular is the second category of ritual activities: **matsuri**, or shrine festivals. Matsuri are light-hearted celebratory events on both the national and local level that number in the hundreds. The Japanese yearly cycle is punctuated by these festivals, some of which are national holidays, such as the first shrine visit during New Year. Another popular matsuri takes place on March 3, when families with daughters celebrate Girls' Day or the Dolls Festival with displays of dolls and food offerings to promote the happiness and well-being of young girls. Larger matsuri may last several days, with local kami being paraded through the streets in portable shrines to be worshipped by

The worship hall at Kyoto's Yasaka Shrine
Source: Kevin Bond

Tenjin: the kami of scholarship and learning, popularly worshipped by students during examination periods at shrines throughout Japan.

Inari: the kami of rice and business, who often appears in the form of a fox.

Torii: iconic arched gateways commonly placed at shrine entrances, signifying the residence of a kami.

Ema: wooden prayer tablets at shrines on which to write prayer requests to the kami, often involving this-worldly concerns about health, healing, and protection.

the community. Drinking, dancing, and singing are common sights, and rowdy behaviour and public drunkenness are not uncommon. Matsuri provide an essential safety valve and a form of social cohesion for communities; they are not considered a degradation of religion. If we recall the mythic kagura of Amaterasu,

celebration, dance, song, and community spirit in fact service the worship of kami.

The third category of rituals is common prayers for the benefit of oneself or the family household. These prayers, like matsuri, petition kami for real-world material concerns such as protection and worldly success. For example, during the exams period, students visit shrines dedicated to **Tenjin**, the kami of scholarship and learning. Companies such as Mitsubishi venerate **Inari**, the kami of business. Prayers are also often tied to the human life cycle. Parents commonly present their newborns before kami to seek protection and blessings for the child. Another popular rite of passage is Seven-Five-Three (*shichigosan*), held in mid-November, when children aged seven, five, and three visit shrines to be blessed by kami for their continued health and happiness. Shrines are also the traditional setting for marriage. Shinto funerals, however, although they exist, are rare; instead, the vast majority of Japanese funerary rites are performed by Buddhist clergy.

Practices

What to Do at a Shinto Shrine

If you visit enough Shinto shrines, you will find that they come in all forms and sizes, from a single altar-sized structure in a small village to a vast precinct of several buildings. Many are painted bright orange, in contrast to most Buddhist temples. Despite their architectural variety, kami worship generally follows the same pattern. Prayers are offered in front of the worship hall located near the precinct's centre. Upon entering a shrine, you will first pass through a **torii**, an arch-like gateway representing the sacred residence of a kami and a prominent symbol of Shinto (see page 247). Near the torii entrance you find a water basin with which to purify yourself (harae) by rinsing the hands and mouth. You are then able to approach the kami, located within the main hall or sanctuary at the rear of the precinct, far opposite the entrance.

Since the main hall is the sacred abode of the kami, you cannot enter and view the kami directly. You instead approach the worship hall

and pray to the kami at a distance. At the worship hall of the famous Yasaka Shrine in Kyoto (see page 255), visitors follow the traditional custom of kami worship. First they toss coins over the railing into an offering box, ring a bell to attract the kami's attention, and bow twice. They then clap their hands twice in prayer and bow one final time. Shrines are open year-round and there are no sacred congregational days such as a sabbath. As you can see in the photograph, worship does not require people to enter a special building, allowing visitors to pray freely on their own, generally without the need for an attending priest.

In addition to prayers at the worship hall, you may also entreat a kami by purchasing special wooden prayer tablets called **ema** on which to write requests (these are also common at Buddhist temples). These tablets, adorned with a picture representing the shrine or the kami, are then hung within the precinct as prayer offerings. Shinto's this-worldly focus means that many ema specialize in benefits concerning the self and body. The ema pictured, for example, are from a small shrine in Nara dedicated to a kami that protects the female organs. Women can purchase two sorts of ema here: one for healing illnesses of the breasts (on the right) and another for gynecological issues (on the left). Like the death and blood taboos, these ema reflect Shinto's intimate connection with human affairs and life cycles, fertility, reproduction, and health. This is important to understanding the motivations for shrine visits.

You might seek the kami of matchmaking in hopes of finding a good partner, or pray at fertility shrines to conceive a child. Pregnant women and their families also venerate the kami of childbirth for a safe and easy delivery. It is common at shrines to purchase talismans or amulets (o-mamori) imbued with these divine powers to wear for ongoing protection and wish fulfilment. We should note that Japanese people do not forsake modern medicine in favour of such prayers; rather, these practices may be understood as outward manifestations of one's hopes and needs.

Ema (prayer tablets) at a local Nara shrine
Source: Kevin Bond

AUTHORITY

Until the modern period, shrines were commonly under the administrative authority of state powers or Buddhist temples. The Department of Kami Affairs (Jingikan) was established by the court at the time of the Kojiki and Nihon Shoki to administer kami prayers among a national network of shrines. Since Amaterasu was the divine ancestor of the imperial family, these prayers were closely tied to Ise Shrine and the emperor. As this system eventually weakened and Buddhist influence increased, many shrines also came under the control of Buddhist temples. This system ended with the separation of Shinto and Buddhism in the Meiji period, when the unity of kami worship and government was renewed in support of State Shinto. When

Miko: literally, "child of kami," Shinto assistant priestesses who perform a variety of religious functions at shrines.

State Shinto ended, state supervision of shrines was replaced in 1946 by the Association of Shinto Shrines (Jinja Honcho), a private organization that today oversees 80 per cent of Japan's 100,000 now legally private shrines (Breen and Teeuwen 2010, 5). Since the association considers Amaterasu the supreme kami, shrines such as Kyoto's famous Fushimi Inari Shrine have refused to join, preferring to govern their own national network of shrines that worship the popular kami Inari (Breen and Teeuwen 2010, 213).

Despite the importance of many female kami such as Amaterasu, Shinto leadership is today dominated by men. Of the approximately twenty thousand current shrine clergy, only a fraction are female. In 1993 it was reported that only one thousand priestesses existed in Japan (Okano 1993, 29). Women are instead primarily relegated to being assistants known as **miko**. Miko provide priests with ritual support and perform clerical duties such as selling talismans.

In pre-modern times, miko played a much more prominent role at shrines before being gradually being deprived of their authority. The word *miko*, meaning "child of kami," reflected their status as powerful shamans who acted as mediators between humans and kami and were accordingly ranked alongside male priests. Even women of the nobility served important shrine functions. Virgin princesses officiated at the main rites of Ise Shrine and offered prayers to the sun goddess. These historical roles became a stimulus for new religious movements founded by women in the modern period. For example, Miki Nakayama, the founder of Tenrikyo, is said to have been a miko who communicated with kami.

The religious authority of miko waned over time because of such influences as Buddhism, which reinforced the idea of the impure nature of the female body (Okano 1993, 28–29). In the Meiji period women were banned outright from the Shinto clergy. Although they were readmitted in the postwar period, women priests are still generally seen not as equals but rather as substitutes for men. This has effectively obscured traditional "female" sources of women's religious power within Shinto tradition (Okano 1993, 29).

However, despite their marginalized status, miko are still visible at many of the larger shrines across Japan, such as at Ise, especially during matsuri festivals. They are easily recognizable by their iconic traditional dress, consisting of a short white kimono over red *hakama* robes. Miko are generally adult women, but they can also include younger volunteers. Beyond their administrative duties, miko are featured most prominently today as sacred dancers who wield bells, swords, sacred tree branches, and other symbolic instruments while

A lone miko walks past worshippers at Kyoto's Fushimi Inari Shrine.

Source: © Miguel Angel Muñoz Pellicer/Alamy

dancing to the accompaniment of bamboo flutes and *taiko* drums. These ceremonial dances, like the kagura, are often performed on elevated stages; they serve not only as prayers for kami but also as entertaining performances that attract crowds of spectators.

RELIGIOUS IDENTITY AND DIVERSITY

Officially, Shinto is Japan's largest religion. But if you ask Japanese people, you will find that very few consider themselves "Shintoists," despite the common practice of visiting shrines (Breen and Teeuwen 2010, 1). This hesitancy to regard themselves as "religious" reflects the Japanese tendency to identify religion more in terms of practice than personal belief or doctrine (Swyngedouw 1993, 52). Moreover, Japanese people are often said to be "born Shinto and die Buddhist." That is, while Shinto shrines are associated with birth and life, Buddhist temples provide the necessary funerary rites for the deceased. This complementary division of labour reflects how Japanese religions rarely demand exclusive devotion. People today pray freely at both temples and shrines, often with little distinction. In fact, many do not clearly distinguish between kami and buddhas, and some even consider them one and the same (Reader 1991, 2), a result of the high degree of Shinto–Buddhist syncretism over the centuries. Since kami and buddhas are commonly worshipped together and for similar goals such as healing and protection, there is little pressing need to identify oneself exclusively as either a Buddhist or a Shintoist.

This ambiguity is facilitated by Shinto's natural diversity. The past 150 years have witnessed the birth of a variety of Shinto-derived new religious movements, and no institutional centre or head shrine exists in Japan. Though most shrines are today under the general administration of the Association of Shinto Shrines, the organization does not represent a central orthodoxy or formalized Shinto creed. Each shrine is legally independent, free to preserve its own local history, customs, and particular forms of kami worship. And although the association promotes the spiritual leadership of Amaterasu and Ise Shrine, one may pray to any and all kami as one wishes. Two popular examples (mentioned above) are Inari, the kami of rice and business, and Tenjin, the kami of learning.

The fact that no single homogeneous Shinto tradition can be identified is evidenced by the various terms used to categorize the tradition. The common daily activities associated with visiting shrines are today classified as *Shrine Shinto*. *Sect Shinto*, conversely, refers to specific traditions such as Shinto-related new religious movements that have emerged in the modern period. *Imperial Shinto* refers to Shinto practices related to the emperor and the imperial house. Yet a fourth category, *Folk Shinto*, represents unsystematized folk beliefs and practices found in rural Japan.

THE CANADIAN CONTEXT

Shinto is not found beyond Japan in any comparable institutional form, and few Shinto shrines have ever existed outside the country. While Canada has for decades been home to several Japanese Buddhist temples, there has been negligible interest in construction of formal shrines and the establishment of Shinto clergy in Canada. However, with the growing population of Japanese Canadians in major urban centres such as Toronto and Vancouver, many Japanese customs such as New Year are today celebrated on Canadian soil. Japanese fairs, festivals, and clubs are likewise growing in number; they host events that are common to shrine culture, such as cherry blossom viewing. A highlight of Vancouver's Powell Street Festival, the largest Japanese-Canadian festival in the country, is a matsuri parade of a *mikoshi* (portable shrine) to spread good fortune.

With the contemporary Western fascination with Japanese culture, artistic forms such as flower arranging, meditation gardens, and the tea ceremony are drawing attention to the aesthetics of Japanese religion, such as the bonds between people, nature, and the gods. Even sumo wrestling—a practice long associated with Shinto mythology and purification and performed in shrines as matsuri entertainment for the kami—is now practised in Canada and the United States, and thus represents yet another vehicle of Shinto culture.

While in the modern period a small number of formal Shinto shrines have been established in Hawaii, only very recently have they spread to the mainland United States and Canada. In 1986 the first formal Shinto shrine in North America, Tsubaki Grand Shrine of America, was established. Now located in Washington State, Tsubaki Grand Shrine has introduced a number of formal Shinto rituals and ceremonial items generally unknown to the average Westerner, such as matsuri, ema tablets, talismans, and traditional prayer services.

Not too far to the north, near Vancouver, Kinomori Shrine, possibly the first Shinto shrine in Canada, was established in 1999. It is an international branch of a prominent Japanese shrine that enshrines three male and female kami. It conducts a variety of traditional matsuri and rites for purification and protection under the direction of a Canadian Shinto priestess, in stark contrast to the marginal presence of priestesses in Japan. One of the shrine's publications represents the first instruction manual for English speakers wishing to practise Shinto on their own without an instructor (Spaid Ishida 2008, 17–18). The shrine distributes traditional Shinto materials and ritual paraphernalia such as talismans, and its website and literature reflect an interest in personal spirituality and meditation, aspects that are not as common among traditional Japanese shrines. Like Tsubaki Grand Shrine of America, Kinomori Shrine reflects the very young but nonetheless growing interest in Shinto culture and practice in North America.

SHINTO AND THE INTERNET

The advent of the Internet has significantly changed the academic and religious spheres of Shinto. In the past two decades it has become commonplace for shrines to maintain home pages to keep pace with Japan's rapidly changing technological society. In order to remain connected to patrons, these web pages publish information about shrine histories, events, prayer services, and even merchandise, thus serving as both proselytizing tools and advertisements. Since the late 1990s even a number of "virtual shrines" have appeared online. Tokyo's Sakura Shrine, for instance, hosts a virtual shrine allowing

online access to the shrine's kami, wherein you can emulate prayer rituals by clicking on-screen icons; you can even submit ema prayers electronically. The convenience of digital access to physical shrines reflects the realities of today's hectic lifestyles.

The Internet has likewise facilitated open access to Shinto for the non-specialist. YouTube broadcasts the sights and sounds of shrine festivals that are otherwise inaccessible outside of Japan, and there are now a number of popular online Shinto groups that fill the void left by the general lack of Shinto literature available in public bookstores. The Shinto Online Network Association manages an online community and a Yahoo! Groups discussion forum for anyone with a general interest in Shinto. These Internet-based communities often forego the technical precision of academic study in favour of exploring diverse tastes: many are interested in alternative forms of faith, mythology, and popular Japanese culture. The study of Shinto is no longer the territorial domain of scholars that it once was.

But the Internet is changing the face of Shinto scholarship too. Japanese universities and libraries are a leading force in the digitization of texts and images to preserve the country's cultural heritage and facilitate academic study. Numerous online digital museums and databases today allow scholars greater access to rare and unpublished Shinto materials. Kokugakuin University's Shinto research centre has led to numerous digital projects such as the *Encyclopedia of Shinto*, a premier reference for Shinto studies. This online accessibility is accelerating the comparatively young academic study of Shinto, which has received far less attention than the study of Japanese Buddhism.

CONCLUSION

Questions regarding Shinto are much easier to come up with than summative statements. Shinto's dramatic changes over the centuries and inseparable ties to mythology, politics, and Buddhism make it very difficult to determine where the tradition begins and ends. Is Shinto a unique religion independent of Buddhism or part of a larger, indivisible religious landscape? Does Shinto truly preserve an ancient native tradition or is it more the product of modernity? With its strong historical associations with national identity, some have even described Shinto as the essential Japanese "way of life," transcending religion. Regardless of these taxonomic

challenges, there is no doubt that what we call "Shinto" remains today very much alive and active. The rhythms of the yearly calendar and daily life in Japan continue to be shaped by important festivals, rituals, and visits to shrines. This pervasiveness makes Shinto essential to appreciating Japanese culture, both past and present.

KEY TERMS

Amaterasu, p. 248
Ema, p. 256
Harae, p. 249
Hirata, Atsutane, p. 253
Honji suijaku, p. 253
Imperial Regalia, p. 252
Inari, p. 256
Ise Shrine, p. 248
Izanagi and Izanami, p. 250
Jimmu, p. 251
Jinja, p. 255
Kagura, p. 251
Kami, p. 248
Kojiki, p. 249

Matsuri, p. 255
Miko, p. 258
Motoori, Norinaga, p. 248
Nakayama, Miki, p. 254
National Studies (Kokugaku), p. 253
Nihon Shoki (Nihongi), p. 249
Ryobu (Dual) Shinto, p. 253
State Shinto, p. 253
Tenjin, p. 256
Torii, p. 256
Tsumi, p. 249

CRITICAL THINKING QUESTIONS

1. Why is the popular understanding of Shinto as "Japan's ancient, native, or traditional religion" problematic?

2. What are the value and also the limitations of Norinaga Motoori's definition of kami?

3. How have the Kojiki and Nihon Shoki functioned mythologically and politically in Japanese history and culture?

4. Identify the key features of Shinto–Buddhist amalgamation. How does this blending complicate the understanding of Shinto?

5. How has Shinto changed in the past 150 years? How are these changes significant to contemporary Japanese religion?

RECOMMENDED READING

Aston, W. G. *Nihongi: Chronicles of Japan from the Earliest Times to A.D. 697*. London: Allen & Unwin, 1956.

Bocking, Brian. *A Popular Dictionary of Shinto*. Richmond, UK: Routledge, 1995.

Breen, John, and Mark Teeuwen. *A New History of Shinto*. Malden, MA: Wiley-Blackwell, 2010.

———, eds. *Shinto in History: Ways of the Kami*. Honolulu: University of Hawaii Press, 2000.

de Bary, William Theodore, et al., eds. *Sources of Japanese Tradition*, 2 vols. New York: Columbia University Press, 2001–05.

Hardacre, Helen. *Shinto and the State, 1868–1988*. Princeton, NJ: Princeton University Press, 1989.

Kasulis, Thomas P. *Shinto: The Way Home*. Honolulu: University of Hawaii Press, 2004.

Mullins, Mark R., Shimazono Susumu, and Paul L. Swanson, eds. *Religion and Society in Modern Japan: Selected Readings*. Berkeley, CA: Asian Humanities Press, 1993.

Philippi, Donald L. *Kojiki*. Tokyo: University of Tokyo Press, 1968.

Picken, Stuart D. B. *Essentials of Shinto: An Analytical Guide to Principal Teachings*. Westport, CT: Greenwood, 1994.

Reader, Ian. *Religion in Contemporary Japan*. Honolulu: University of Hawaii Press, 1991.

RECOMMENDED VIEWING

Buddha in the Land of the Kami (7th–12th Centuries). Dir. Jean Antoine. DVD. Princeton, NJ: Films for the Humanities, 1989.

Princess Mononoke. Dir. Hayao Miyazaki, 1997. Buena Vista Home Entertainment, 2000.

Spirited Away. Dir. Hayao Miyazaki, 2001. Walt Disney Home Video, 2003.

USEFUL WEBSITES

Encyclopedia of Shinto
Online English translation of the classic *Shinto Jiten* ("Encyclopedia of Shinto"), with additional audio-visual materials.

Glossary of Shinto Names and Terms
A comprehensive online English–Japanese glossary, including links to further information on given topics.

Images of Shinto: A Beginner's Pictorial Guide
Interactive illustrations used to explain aspects of Shinto religion and culture.

International Shinto Foundation (ISF)
Organization dedicated to promoting awareness and academic study of Shinto and dispel misinterpretations of the religion and Japanese culture generally.

Ise Shrine Home Page
The home page of Japan's most important national shrine, with additional resources on Shinto mythology and ritual.

Bright Woods Spiritual Centre
Home of Kinomori Shrine, one of Canada's very few formal Shinto sites of kami worship, offering instruction in Shinto beliefs, worship, and meditation.

Shinto Online Network Association
An independent, non-profit volunteer organization "with the objective of publicising Japanese tradition and a correct understanding of the Shinto religion."

Association of Shinto Shrines (Jinja Honcho)
Private organization that today oversees 80 per cent of Japan's shrines and promotes the spiritual leadership of Amaterasu and Ise Shrine, with additional details on Shinto shrines, beliefs, and rituals.

Tenrikyo Home Page
The online presence of Tenrikyo, one of Japan's oldest and largest new religious movements.

Tsubaki Grand Shrine of America
Web page for the oldest Shinto shrine in North America, now located in Washington State.

REFERENCES

Aston, W. G. 1956. *Nihongi: Chronicles of Japan from the Earliest Times to A.D. 697*. London: Allen & Unwin.

Breen, John, and Mark Teeuwen. 2010. *A New History of Shinto*. Malden, MA: Wiley-Blackwell.

de Bary, William Theodore, et al., eds. 2005. *Sources of Japanese Tradition: 1600–2000*. New York: Columbia University Press.

Holtom, Daniel. 1993. "The Meaning of Kami." In *Japanese Religions: Past and Present*, ed. Ian Reader, Esben Andreasen, and Finn Stefánsson, 77–78. Honolulu: University of Hawaii Press.

Kasulis, Thomas P. 2004. *Shinto: The Way Home*. Honolulu: University of Hawaii Press.

Okano, Haruko. 1993. "Women and Sexism in Shinto." *Japan Christian Review* 59: 27–31.

Reader, Ian. 1991. *Religion in Contemporary Japan*. Honolulu: University of Hawaii Press.

———. 1993. "Religion and Politics in Japan." In *Japanese Religions: Past and Present*, ed. Ian Reader, Esben Andreasen, and Finn Stefánsson, 172. Honolulu: University of Hawaii Press.

Spaid Ishida, Sarah. 2008. "The Making of an American Shinto Community." MA thesis, University of Florida.

Swyngedouw, Jan. 1993. "Religion in Contemporary Japanese Society." In *Religion and Society in Modern Japan: Selected Readings*, ed. Mark R. Mullins, Shimazono Susumu, and Paul L. Swanson, 49–72. Berkeley, CA: Asian Humanities Press.

INDEX